D1398401

Changing Values, Persisting Cultures

# European Values Studies

The *European Values Studies* is a series based on a large-scale, cross-national and longitudal research program. The program was initiated by the European Value Systems Study Group (EVSSG) in the late 1970s, at that time an informal grouping of academics. Now, it is carried on in the setting of a foundation, using the (abbreviated) name of the group (EVS). The Study group surveyed basic social, cultural, political, moral, and religious values held by the populations of ten Western European countries, getting their work into the field by 1981. Researchers from other countries joined the project, which resulted in a 26-nations data set. In 1990 and 1999/2000, the study was replicated and extended to other countries. By now, all European countries are involved in one or more waves of the study, including those in Central and Eastern Europe. This series is based on the survey data collected in this project. For more information see: www.europeanvalues.nl.

VOLUME 12

# Changing Values, Persisting Cultures

## Case Studies in Value Change

*Edited by*

Thorleif Pettersson and Yilmaz Esmer

BRILL

LEIDEN · BOSTON
2008

This book is printed on acid-free paper.

**Library of Congress Cataloging-in-Publication Data**

A C.I.P. record for this book is available from the Library of Congress

ISSN 1568-5926
ISBN 978 90 04 16234 1

Copyright 2008 by Koninklijke Brill NV, Leiden, The Netherlands.
Koninklijke Brill NV incorporates the imprints Brill, Hotei Publishing,
IDC Publishers, Martinus Nijhoff Publishers and VSP.

PRINTED IN THE NETHERLANDS

# CONTENTS

PART ONE

PART TWO: THE AMERICAS

## A. NORTH AMERICA

## B. LATIN AMERICA

PART THREE: EUROPE

## A. NORTHERN EUROPE

## B. CENTRAL EUROPE

## C. THE MEDITERRANEAN

PART FOUR: ASIA

PART FIVE: AFRICA

# LIST OF TABLES

# LIST OF FIGURES

# SERIES EDITORS' PREFACE

This is the twelfth volume in the series on European Values published by Brill Academic Publishers. The books in this series focus on human values, attitudes, beliefs and ideas in contemporary society and are based on the survey data collected within the framework of the *European Values Study*, a large-scale cross-national and longitudinal research project on fundamental values in Western societies. The project started at the end of the 1970s, aiming at empirically investigating the main fundamental value patterns of Europeans and exploring the changes in these value orientations. Since then, the project has expanded worldwide and has developed into a project in which the *European Values Study* (EVS) and the *World Values Surveys* (WVS) try to conduct surveys in as many countries all over the world. EVS focuses on Europe, while WVS aims at conducting surveys also in countries outside Europe. For more information about the start of the *European Values Study* and recent developments, see the EVS website: www.europeanvalues.nl. For information on the *World Values Survey*, we refer to their website: www.worldvaluessurvey.org.

This book is, as said, the twelfth volume in this series. Volumes one to five in this series are based on data from the 1990 and/or 1981 survey waves, and are published by Tilburg University Press. The first volume is *The Individualizing Society* (1993; revised edition 1994), edited by Peter Ester, Loek Halman and Ruud de Moor. The second book *Values in Western Societies* (1995) is edited by Ruud de Moor, and the third book *Political Value Change in Western Democracies* (1996) is edited by Loek Halman and Neil Nevitte. The fourth volume *From Cold War to Cold Peace* (1997) is a comparison of Russian and European values. The authors are Peter Ester, Loek Halman and Vladimir Rukavishnikov. This book was also published in Russian in 1998. In 1999, a fifth volume was released on *Religion in Secularizing Society*, edited by Loek Halman and Ole Riis. A second printing of this book appeared in 2003 in the re-established series on the European Values now at Brill Academic Publishers. In the sixth volume, edited by Wil Arts, Jacques Hagenaars and Loek Halman, *The Cultural Diversity of European Unity* (2003), Europe's values are examined from economic, political, social, and religious-moral points of view. The seventh volume, *European Values at the Turn of the Millennium* (2004) is edited by Wil Arts and Loek Halman. It contains chapters in which authors from all quarters of Europe try to identify, explain and interpret patterns in the basic values and attitudes of Europeans in and around the year 2000. The emphasis in this volume is on phenomena connected with civil society and citizenship, family and work, and religion and morality. In 2005, an *Atlas of European Values* was produced as the eighth volume in this series. This publication differs from the existing books in the series in the sense that it presents the ideas, values, and beliefs of Europeans in more accessible forms for a general readership, using graphs, charts, and maps in place of advanced statistical analyses. The authors are Loek Halman, Ruud Luijkx and Marga van Zundert (see also: www.atlasofeuropeanvalues.com). The *Atlas of European Values* was selected as Outstanding Academic Title 20005 by Choice Magazine. Tony Fahey, Bernadette C. Hayes and Richard Sinnott have written the ninth volume in the series. Their study on *Conflict and Consensus*, presents a detailed comparison of cultural values and attitudes in the Republic of Ireland and Northern Ireland. It is based on survey data covering the period from the 1970s to 2003, but focuses especially on the *European Values Study* as fielded in the two parts of Ireland in 1999–2000. The tenth volume in this series, edited by Peter Ester, Michael Braun and Peter Mohler, titled *Globalization, Value Change, and Generations*, addresses a number of very interesting comparative themes: whether value convergence or divergence has occurred; whether traditional values are indeed on the decline as predicted in so many theories of modernization; and whether younger generations play the proverbial vanguard role in culture shifts.

The eleventh book in the series is *Changing Values and Beliefs*. Like the *Atlas of European Values*, this volume is quite different from the other books in this series. Authored by Loek Halman, Ronald Inglehart, Jaime Díez-Medrano, Ruud Luijkx, Alejandro Moreno and Miguel Basáñez, it contains mainly tables providing insights into the trends in the basic values and attitudes of the peoples of more than 80 countries around the world from 1981 to 2004. In collaboration, EVS and WVS have produced an integrated data file containing all available data of all the countries in which the values surveys have been conducted through the years. This post hoc harmonization of all Values Surveys data since 1981 was realized by ASEP/JDS in Madrid and EVS-Tilburg, and the result is a huge dataset of almost 269,000 cases in 85 countries from all over the world. The data can be downloaded free of charge, from both the EVS and WVS websites (www.europeanvalues.nl; www.worldvalussurvey.org) or from ASEP /JDS (www.jdsurvey.net). The original data from the

European Values Study surveys in 1981, 1990 and 1999, as well as the integrated dataset of the three waves, are available from Zentralarchiv in Cologne (http://zacat.gesis.org/webview/index.jsp).

The *European Values Study*, together with the *World Values Surveys* have been the most successful global social science enterprise ever. Numerous books and countless articles, all around the globe and in many different languages, have been published based on the data collected in the surveys of these projects. Nevertheless, a publication that brings together the contributions of as many of the key researchers and principal investigators in these projects as possible and practical has so far been lacking. We, the series editors, were, therefore, very pleased when Yilmaz Esmer and Thorleif Pettersson took the initiative for this volume that is organized geographically presenting region and country level comparative analyses, describing and analyzing changes and stability in cultural values in various parts of the globe. The authors address the issue of stability and change focusing on topics that they consider important for their particular country or region. Most of the contributions deal with themes which seem to have global significance, such as political values and especially democratic values, religious and moral values and secularization, individualization vs. collective/community values, values related to family, the role of women and gender equity, materialism/postmaterialism and basic value dimensions. We are grateful to the editors for taking the initiative for this book and their efforts to bring these contributions together.

Tilburg & Leuven, June 2007

Koen van Eijck
Paul de Graaf
Loek Halman

PART ONE

INTRODUCTION

# INTRODUCTION

YILMAZ ESMER AND THORLEIF PETTERSSON

Social change was a central question for all classical founders of sociology whose theories of change are as controversial today as they were at the time of their first publication. In actual fact, the issues of change and stability occupied the minds of great social thinkers from much earlier on. Inkeles (1997:219) wrote that it would not be a great exaggeration to say that "in two thousand years of studying politics we had made no advance whatsoever beyond Plato and Aristotle. At least so it seems when we recognize that the genius of political analysis has gone mainly into the invention of new terms for old ideas..." Indeed, political science and sociology can claim very few ideas or concepts whose origins cannot be traced to ancient Greece. Most assuredly, change and stability are not exceptions to this rule.

Heraclitus is the earliest and the best known of ancient Greek thinkers who emphasized the primacy of change. He asserted that everything is in a state of change and coined the still famous phrase that one cannot step into the same river twice. "Perpetual change was what Heraclitus believed in." (Russell 1979:63) So it seemed to Heraclitus. But the question of whether change or permanence is the central feature of human social existence is still unresolved. To cite an example, again from ancient Greek thought, Parmenides was of the opinion that change was a false impression. "His doctrine in brief is to the effect that Being, the One, *is*, and that Becoming, change is illusion. For if anything comes to be, then it comes either out of being or out of not-being. If the former, then it already is—in which case it does not come to be; if the latter, then it is nothing, since out of nothing comes nothing. Becoming is, then, illusion." (Copleston 1993: 48) Thus, the polarities of the debate on change and permanence were established around 5th century B.C.

The issue is not only academic but has profound practical consequences as well. From the French Revolution to Mao's Cultural Revolution, all great upheavals and radical social change projects had their valiant proponents and opponents in both philosophical and political worlds. In this book, we are mainly concerned with value change. But if we may propose a possible definition of culture, among literally hundreds offered in anthropological and sociological literature, we would suggest that *culture is a specific configuration of values and norms*.[1] Thus, this book is also about cultural change.

How do cultures change? Put differently, what are the mechanisms of cultural change? Once again referring to the founders of modern sociology, the major difference between the Marxian and the Weberian traditions is treating culture as the dependent or the independent variable in the analysis of change. Whether it was the transition to the capitalistic mode of production that gave rise to values that are consistent with capitalism or whether it was the Protestant ethic that opened the way to capitalistic accumulation, one point is clear: cultural change is a very slow process. There is more or less unanimity on this conclusion. Making a distinction between material and, what he has called, adaptive cultures (i.e. traditions, values, norms, attitudes and social institutions) Ogburn formulated his theory of "cultural lag" which predicts that "When the material conditions change, changes are occasioned in the adaptive culture. But these changes in the adaptive culture do not synchronize exactly with the change in the material culture. There is a lag which may last for varying lengths of time, sometimes indeed, for many years." (Ogburn 1973:478) It would not be inaccurate to change the unit of time in this statement from years to decades.

Cultural patterns are change resistant but, as Inglehart (1999:26) has put it, they are "not immutable;" hence the title of this book. Certain values may and in fact do change, albeit slowly, in time. However, configurations of values or value patterns are much more persistent. We argue that cultural change refers to change in patterns or specific configurations of and relationships among values more than change in given values. Therefore we make the distinction between value change and cultural change. For instance, values related to gender and sexuality can change and indeed have changed in many societies over the past few decades. However, a given society's position on, for example, the Inglehart and Welzel cultural map (Inglehart and Welzel 2005) displays a

---

[1] This definition is very close to the one by given by Inglehart (1990:18): "Culture is a system of attitudes, values and knowledge that is widely shared within a society and transmitted from generation to generation."

very high degree of stability despite changes in specific values. In other words, values can change but cultures are much more resistant.

European and World Values Survey is by far the most comprehensive and enduring social science project for the systematic and empirical study of cultural values and value change. It started in 1981 with surveys conducted in some 20 plus societies and has grown into a project that now samples no less than about 90 percent of the world's population. The project has produced thousands of articles and hundreds of books on all aspects of study of values. In addition, for the first time in the history of social sciences, it has made available time series data on cultural values for the study of change in all inhabited continents. The present book is based on data collected by the European and World Values Surveys. However, it is unique in the sense that it is the first collection of case studies analyzing change and stability of values in a wide range of countries. All authors are members of the EVS/WVS research network and are natives of the countries that they have written about. Thus they combine their expertise and their social science perspectives with genuine and profound knowledge of the given society. All chapters in this volume are based on time series data covering the decade of the 1990s and in some cases the 1980s as well.

The countries included in the volume provide the widest possible range of cultures within the limits of data availability. All major religions are represented. Also, some of the most secular and most religious societies are analyzed. We have included some of the wealthiest countries as well as countries with per capita incomes of less than 4,000 U.S. Dollars. Some of our chapters deal with countries with the highest levels of interpersonal trust in the world (e.g. Sweden), while examples of extremely low trust cultures (e.g. Turkey) are also included. Thus, we believe the present book will be a useful reference for those who are interested in the study of values in general as well as those who would like to look at cultural change and stability in specific countries.

## References

Copleston, Frederick. 1993. *A History of Philosophy*, vol. 1. New York: Doubleday Books.
Inglehart, Ronald. 1990. *Culture Shift in Advanced Industrial Society*. Princeton: Princeton University Press.

Inglehart, Ronald and Christian Welzel. 2005. *Modernization, Cultural Change and Democracy: The human development sequence*. Cambridge: Cambridge University Press.

Inkeles, Alex. 1997. *National Character: A psycho-social perspective*. New Brunswick and London: Transaction Publishers.

Ogburn, William F. 1973. "The Hypothesis of Cultural Lag" in Etzioni-Halevy, Eva and A. Etzioni, eds., *Social Change: Sources, Patterns, and Consequences*. New York: Basic Books, 477–480.

Russell, Bertrand. 1979. *History of Western Philosophy*. London: Unwin Paperbacks.

PART TWO

THE AMERICAS

# A. NORTH AMERICA

CHAPTER ONE

## AMERICA THE TRADITIONAL

WAYNE E. BAKER

Observers of America since Alexis de Tocqueville have noted that America is unusual, deviant, exceptional, and qualitatively different from other societies (Tocqueville 1988). Kingdon (1999), for example, calls the nation "America the unusual," due to an uncommon and abiding preference for limited government. Lipset (1996) emphasizes the unique values expressed in the American Creed: "liberty, egalitarianism, individualism, populism, and laissez-faire" (p. 19). This chapter contributes to the theme of American exceptionalism by examining America's moral values.[1] First, I examine the "moral visions" of Americans. Moral visions are worldviews about the location of moral authority—in the self or in God (e.g., Jaspers 1953; Orrù 1987; Eisenstadt 1982). These moral visions are known colloquially as relativism and absolutism. Second, I examine values along two dimensions—traditional versus secular-rational values, and survival versus self-expression values (e.g., Inglehart and Baker 2000). Third, I consider the relationship of moral visions and these two dimensions to attitudes about the separation of church and state. I conclude with a discussion of the implications of the findings for the American "culture war" thesis and the widespread perception of a crisis of values in America.

The approach presented here permits America's value system to be compared directly with the value systems of many other societies. Because *specific* values (such as certain religious or cultural beliefs) may vary from society to society, valid cross-cultural comparisons can be difficult to make. However, moral visions and the two cultural dimensions capture value orientations in a way that permits valid comparisons of diverse cultures. With this approach, America is exceptional to the extent that its views of moral authority are unique or unusual, and its locations

---

[1] This is an abridged version of analyses and arguments in *America's Crisis of Values: Reality and Perception* (Baker 2004).

on the two dimensions (traditional/secular-rational; survival/self-expression) are unique or unusual. As I demonstrate, America is one of the most absolutist nations in the world, and has become increasingly so over time. Moreover, it is one of the most traditional societies in the world. Thus, America's moral visions and location on the traditional/ secular-rational values dimension are quite unusual, compared to the value systems of most economically advanced democracies. However, America is also self-expression oriented, and it has moved rapidly in this direction along the survival/self-expression dimension. In this respect, it is similar to other economically advanced democracies.

Therefore, I make the case that American exceptionalism occurs in two ways. First, America's value system is exceptionally absolutist and traditional (hence the chapter's title). Second, the nation's value system is also exceptional because it combines traditional *and* self-expression values. Among most post-industrial societies, secular values and self-expression values go hand in hand; correspondingly, among poor nations, traditional values and survival values go together (e.g., Inglehart and Baker 2000; Inglehart and Norris 2003). As I discuss in the conclusion, this mix of absolutist and traditional values with self-expression values presents contradictory guides to action, and these, in turn, contribute to the widespread perception of a crisis of values in America. These contradictory guides also produce cognitive dissonance in Americans who internalize them—a personal experience of crisis induced by conflicting principles. For some, this dissonance is resolved by using it to stimulate thinking about the purpose and meaning of life

## The Moral Visions of Americans

Moral visions are fundamental beliefs about the location of moral authority (e.g., Jaspers 1953; Sorokin 1957; Eisenstadt 1982; Orrù 1987). For absolutists, the source of moral values and moral judgment is located outside the individual in the "transcendental sphere"—usually considered to be God, but it could be society itself (Durkhiem) or even abstract ideas (Plato). Absolutists believe in a universal moral code that is independent and separate from the individuals it governs. Fletcher (1966) called this a "legalistic" approach because it applies the same rules to all people at all times in all situations.

Relativists locate the source of moral authority in the individual living in this world, the "mundane sphere." For them, moral authority resides in the self and local situation, making the individual "the final arbiter of truth" (Shanahan 1992:20). According to relativists, moral codes can—and should—vary from person to person, from time to time, and from situation to situation as people struggle with the practical challenges and problems of everyday life. Fletcher's aptly named *Situation Ethics* (1966) is one of the best known treatments of this moral vision. Relativism is often mistaken for *antinomianism*, literally, *against* laws or norms (Fletcher 1966:22). (Antinomianism is different from anomie, *without* laws or norms.) The antinomian is an anarchist who "enters into the decision-making situation armed with no principles or maxims whatsoever, to say nothing of *rules*. In every 'existential moment' or 'unique' situation," Fletcher (1966:22) notes, "…one must rely upon the situation itself, *there and then*, to provide its ethical solution."

Absolutism and relativism are a duality, two parts of one conceptual system. Rather than different ways of thinking, they make up "a *single* way of thinking which is subject to an internal tension regarding the location of reality" (Orrù 1987:5). This dual conceptual system is an example of a universal human phenomenon documented by anthropologists, historians, and sociologists—the organization of social thought (and often social institutions) in patterns of opposites (Maybury-Lewis and Almagor 1989). "This [pattern] is reported from so many different parts of the world that it is clearly a kind of system that human beings keep inventing and living by, independently of each other" (Maybury-Lewis 1989:1). As Bell (1978:155) puts it, "only man has created dualities: of spirit and matter, nature and history, the sacred [transcendental sphere] and the profane [mundane sphere]."

The roots of the dual conceptual system of moral visions run deep. Jaspers (1953) argues that the origin of absolutism and relativism and their inherent tension is the "axis of history" over 2,500 years ago (see also Orrù 1987; Seligman 1989). "It is there that we meet with the most deep cut dividing line in history," and the creation of "the fundamental categories within which we still think today" ( Jaspers 1953:1–2). A contemporary expression of this dual conceptual system is the "culture war" in America. The ultimate source of this culture war, some say, is the irreconcilable conflict between absolutism and relativism (e.g., Hunter 1991, 1994). Strong advocates of the culture war thesis argue that, over time, America has become a house divided, increasingly polarized, into two opposed moral camps: absolutists versus relativists. The stakes are high: nothing less than the future of the American way of life. In this culture war, Hunter (1991:42) argues, only one side can win, resulting in the "domination of one cultural and moral ethos over all others." Many social scientists doubt the validity of the culture war argument, but they note that culture war rhetoric is commonplace: "Images of U.S. society as polarized into warring moral camps are increasingly evoked by political leaders, media pundits, and scholars alike" (Davis and Robinson, 1996:756). Between 1993 and 1996, for example, over 1,500 articles referring to the American culture war appeared in the media (Mouw and Sobel 2001:914).

The World Values Surveys provide a direct measure of moral visions, allowing the moral visions of American to be compared with those of the peoples of many other societies. This measure also offers an empirical test of the culture war claim of polarized moral visions. Absolutism and relativism are indicated by responses to this survey item: "Here are two statements which people sometimes make when discussing good and evil. Which one comes closest to your own point of view? Statement A—There are absolutely clear guidelines about what is good and evil. These always apply to everyone, whatever the circumstances. Statement B—There can never be absolutely clear guidelines about what is good and evil. What is good and evil depends entirely upon the circumstances at the time." Each respondent was presented with the two statements and asked to choose. A respondent could disagree with both statements, but this response had to be volunteered. Those who select Statement A are the absolutists; those who select B are the relativists.

This measure of moral visions is a single dichotomous survey item, and so it is subject to potential concerns about reliability and validity. Usually, the problem of measurement reliability is addressed by creating a scale from multiple items. I would prefer, of course, to have a battery of items about moral visions, but these are unavailable in the World Values Surveys. There are multiple items about religion, which could be combined with the single item on moral visions. However, doing so would confound the distinction between moral visions and religion. Moral visions are not religious beliefs. Moral absolutists may tend to hold strong religions beliefs, but they do not have to. For example, atheists can believe in a transcendental source of moral authority, such as society itself or abstract ideas (Orrù 1987). Thus, a single survey item is better than a scale that conflates religion and moral visions. An alternative way to assess measurement reliability is to use the multiple wave design of the World Values Surveys to measure stability over time (a variant of "test-retest" reliability). This survey items exhibits high test-retest reliability (for details, see Baker 2004).

Another potential criticism of this survey item is that a dichotomous question can create a false appearance of polarization. Demerath and Yang (1997:20) criticize the use of any dichotomous measure because "it is virtually guaranteed to generate polarization when the respondents are asked to identify with one of two opposing ideological positions." Polarization would be indicated by a more or less even split: 50% absolutists, and 50% relativists. This pattern rarely emerges in the four waves of the World Values Surveys. In the 1981–1982 wave, for example, only one society (Northern Ireland) came close to the 50–50 split. In the 1995–1998 wave, only 10 of 65 societies exhibited a polarized pattern. (155) Thus, polarization is not "virtually guaranteed" by this dichotomous item.

Finally, this measure of moral visions has solid content validity. It clearly distinguishes between the two views of moral authority; it does not explicitly link moral authority to a *specific* source (such as God, society, or the self), and it does not mix religious beliefs (or social attitudes) with moral visions. The most important justification for this measure is theoretical. It was designed *purposely* to tap the dual model of thinking about moral authority. Indeed, a theologian on the original World Values Surveys design team proposed this dichotomous item to capture the dual conceptual system of absolutism and relativism (Inglehart, personal communication).

The moral visions of Americans in 2000 are almost equally divided between absolutism and relativism. As shown in Table 1, 49.2% of Americans agreed that "there are absolutely clear guidelines about what is good and evil. These always apply to everyone, whatever the circumstances." About 46.6% said that "there can never be absolutely clear guidelines about what is good and evil. What is good and evil depends entirely upon the circumstances at the time." Only 4.2% volunteered that neither statement was true.

Figure 1 displays the distribution of moral visions among Americans in each wave of the World Values Surveys. It shows that Americans were divided into approximately equal numbers of absolutists and relativists in 1995 and 1990. In 1981, however, the distribution was quite different: Americans' views of moral authority were more relativistic than absolutistic, 60% versus 37%. Thus, a shift in moral visions occurred between 1981 and 1990. Absolutism increased during the decade while relativism declined. (This change is statistically significant at p < .001). This change was not confined to specific groups or categories of Americans. A rising tide of absolutism swept over all social classes,

Table 1.1. Moral Visions by Nation, World Values Surveys.

| Society | Absolutists | Neither | Relativists | Society | Absolutists | Neither | Relativists |
|---|---|---|---|---|---|---|---|
| Morocco | 78.0 | 3.3 | 18.7 | Portugal | 39.0 | 3.7 | 57.3 |
| Ghana | 69.6 | 6.5 | 23.9 | Ireland | 38.8 | 9.3 | 51.9 |
| Tanzania | 68.7 | 4.2 | 27.1 | E. Germany | 38.8 | 15.4 | 45.8 |
| S. Africa | 62.8 | 3.3 | 33.9 | Russia | 38.6 | 3.5 | 57.9 |
| Uganda | 58.9 | 3.9 | 37.2 | Argentina | 38.6 | 4.0 | 57.4 |
| Georgia | 58.9 | 3.2 | 37.9 | Colombia | 38.0 | 2.9 | 59.1 |
| Vietnam | 58.4 | 6.3 | 35.3 | S. Korea | 37.0 | 0.0 | 63.0 |
| Zimbabwe | 57.3 | 3.5 | 39.2 | Slovakia | 36.4 | 9.4 | 54.1 |
| Azerbaijan | 56.7 | 6.1 | 37.3 | Italy | 36.4 | 13.2 | 50.5 |
| Philippines | 55.2 | 0.9 | 43.9 | China | 36.2 | 9.1 | 54.4 |
| Macedonia | 55.1 | 6.7 | 38.2 | Domn. Rep | 35.8 | 7.9 | 56.3 |
| Bosnia | 53.7 | 7.3 | 39.0 | Lithuania | 34.9 | 5.5 | 59.6 |
| Chile | 53.0 | 3.4 | 43.6 | Uruguay | 33.9 | 5.9 | 60.2 |
| Peru | 52.8 | 4.1 | 43.1 | W. Germany | 33.9 | 4.4 | 61.7 |
| Tambov | 51.5 | 3.8 | 44.7 | Bulgaria | 33.3 | 6.8 | 60.0 |
| Poland | 50.8 | 3.6 | 45.6 | Croatia | 32.2 | 4.5 | 63.4 |
| Brazil | 49.2 | 0.1 | 50.8 | Belgium | 30.7 | 6.2 | 63.1 |
| U.S. | 49.2 | 4.2 | 46.6 | India | 30.0 | 8.2 | 61.8 |
| Albania | 49.1 | 12.1 | 38.9 | Estonia | 29.9 | 8.2 | 61.9 |
| Montenegro | 48.9 | 10.9 | 40.1 | Finland | 29.3 | 4.7 | 66.0 |
| El Salvador | 48.8 | 6.2 | 45.0 | Norway | 29.1 | 3.6 | 67.3 |
| Malta | 48.7 | 3.1 | 48.3 | Switzerland | 28.4 | 8.6 | 63.0 |
| Bangladesh | 47.7 | 1.7 | 50.6 | Taiwan | 28.0 | 4.7 | 67.3 |
| N. Ireland | 46.9 | 5.1 | 48.1 | Valencia | 27.8 | 2.8 | 69.4 |
| Serbia | 46.5 | 8.5 | 45.0 | Netherlands | 26.9 | 4.1 | 69.0 |
| Andalusia | 45.2 | 4.3 | 50.5 | Galicia | 26.2 | 3.7 | 70.1 |
| Singapore | 45.2 | 1.4 | 53.4 | France | 24.9 | 7.5 | 67.6 |
| Puerto Rico | 44.9 | 3.0 | 52.2 | Belarus | 24.8 | 5.3 | 69.9 |
| Spain | 43.7 | 5.9 | 50.4 | Czech rep | 23.5 | 6.3 | 70.2 |
| Ukraine | 42.9 | 3.1 | 54.1 | Luxembourg | 23.3 | 7.7 | 69.0 |
| Canada | 42.4 | 2.4 | 55.2 | Greece | 22.6 | 7.0 | 70.5 |
| New Zealand | 42.4 | 12.1 | 45.5 | Basque | 22.4 | 7.0 | 70.6 |
| Australia | 41.7 | 2.5 | 55.7 | Slovenia | 21.9 | 13.0 | 65.1 |
| Britain | 41.5 | 4.8 | 53.8 | Austria | 20.3 | 6.4 | 73.3 |
| Armenia | 41.0 | 6.3 | 52.7 | Japan | 19.2 | 11.5 | 69.3 |
| Latvia | 41.0 | 4.9 | 54.1 | Sweden | 15.8 | 3.2 | 81.0 |
| Mexico | 40.9 | 5.7 | 53.4 | Hungary | 15.4 | 9.1 | 75.5 |
| Venezuela | 40.9 | 9.4 | 49.7 | Denmark | 10.4 | 4.3 | 85.3 |
| Moldova | 39.7 | 5.2 | 55.1 | Iceland | 9.0 | 2.8 | 88.2 |
| Romania | 39.5 | 5.7 | 54.8 | | | | |

Figure 1.1. Distribution of the Moral Visions of Americans, by Year.

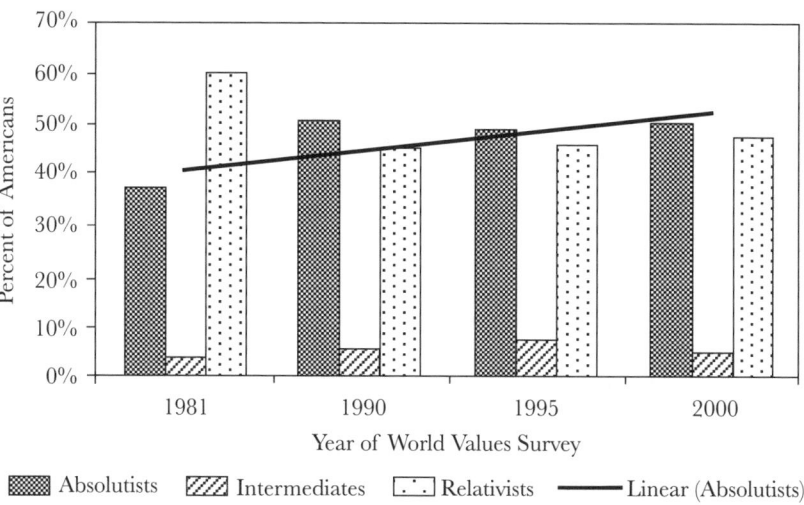

Year of World Values Survey

▓ Absolutists    ▨ Intermediates    ⊡ Relativists    ——Linear (Absolutists)

*Source*: Figure 3.5 in Wayne E. Baker, *America's Crisis of Values* (Princeton University Press 2004). Based on data from the World Values Surveys 1981, 1990, 1995, and 2000.

age cohorts, men and women, whites and nonwhites, married and not married (for details, see Baker 2004).

These findings from the World Values Surveys are consistent with other sources of data. For example, Wolfe (1998:46–47) reports a similar 50:50 split in his Middle Class Morality Project, based on in-depth interviews and a follow-up survey of a sample of 200 Americans. Similarly, in my 2003 Detroit Area Study, a representative survey of the four million residents of Wayne, Oakland, and Macomb Counties (the greater Detroit metropolitan region), I find a similar pattern: 51.3% agree with Statement A (absolutists) and 45.3% agree with Statement B (relativists). Only 3.3% disagree with both statements.

Comparing the U.S. with other nations underscores the theme of American exceptionalism (see Table 1). America is one of the absolutist nations in the world. Only 17 of 79 nations have a higher proportion of absolutists, and all of these are low-income and developing societies such as Morocco, Ghana, Tanzania, Uganda, Vietnam, Zimbabwe, Chile, and Peru. Moreover, America has the highest proportion of absolutists of *any* economically advanced democracy, and it is different from the nations with which it shares a cultural heritage, such as the historically Protestant nations and English speaking nations. Northern Ireland is the closest to the United States (46.9% absolutists versus 49.2% absolutists, respectively), but most historically Protestant nations have many more relativists than absolutists (for example, over 80% of the citizens of Sweden, Denmark, and Iceland are relativists). Thus, the moral visions of Americans are dramatically unusual, and, as we see next, this moral absolutism is consistent with the location of America on the traditional/secular-rational values dimension.

### America on Two Dimensions of Cultural Variation

Prior research with data from the World Values Surveys has identified distinctive value orientations within and across societies (e.g., Inglehart 1997; Inglehart and Baker 2000; Inglehart and Norris 2003). Two principal dimensions have emerged from this research: traditional versus secular-rational values, and survival versus self-expression values. These dimensions are based on factor analysis of the various items shown in Table 2 (Inglehart and Baker 2000). In addition to the specific items in these two scales, a wide range of values, beliefs, and meanings are associated with each dimension (see, e.g., Tables 2 and 3 in Inglehart and Baker 2000). These two cultural dimensions have been replicated with each new wave of the World Values Surveys (e.g., Inglehart and Norris, 2003), and they appear to be quite robust.

Religion is a prominent feature of the traditional/secular-rational values dimension. Traditional values include strong beliefs in the importance of religion and the importance of God in one's life. Traditionalists attend church regularly, have a great deal of confidence in the country's churches, get comfort and strength from religion, and describe themselves as religious people. God, country, and family are tightly connected. Patriotism is a traditional value. What some call "family values" are a major theme; for example, traditionalists are "pro-life" (against abortion), they believe that children should learn obedience and respect, and that a main goal in life is to make one's parents proud. Moral absolutists tend to have traditional values. Secular-rational values emphasize the opposite positions on all these topics.

The survival/self-expression dimension taps a fundamentally different value orientation (Table 2). Generally, this orientation includes differences in trust, tolerance of others, subjective well-being, political activism, and self-expression. These self-expression values appear to

Table 1.2. Two Dimensions of Cross-Cultural Variation: Nation-level analysis.

| | Factor loadings |
|---|---|
| *Traditional vs. Secular-Rational Values** | |
| TRADITIONAL VALUES EMPHASIZE THE FOLLOWING: | |
| God is very important in respondent's life | .91 |
| It is more important for a child to learn obedience and religious faith than independence and determination [Autonomy index] | .89 |
| Abortion is never justifiable | .82 |
| Respondent has strong sense of national pride | .82 |
| Respondent favors more respect for authority | .72 |
| (SECULAR-RATIONAL VALUES EMPHASIZE THE OPPOSITE) | |
| | |
| *Survival vs. Self-Expression Values*** | |
| SURVIVAL VALUES EMPHASIZE THE FOLLOWING: | |
| Respondent gives priority to economic and physical security over self expression and quality of life [4-item Materialist/Post-materialist Values Index] | .86 |
| Respondent describes self as not very happy | .81 |
| Homosexuality is never justifiable | .80 |
| Respondent has not and would not sign a petition | .78 |
| You have to be very careful about trusting people | .56 |
| (SELF-EXPRESSION VALUES EMPHASIZE THE OPPOSITE) | |

Note: The original polarities vary. The above statements show how each item relates to a given dimension, based on factor analysis with varimax rotation.

Source: From 65 societies surveyed in the 1990–1991 and 1995–1998 World Values Surveys. This table is based on Table 1 in Ronald Inglehart and Wayne E. Baker, "Modernization, Cultural Change, and the Persistence of Traditional Values." American Sociological Review 65:19–51 (2000).

* Explains 44 percent of the cross-national variation.

emerge in post-industrial societies with high levels of existential security, safety, and the satisfaction of material needs (Inglehart and Baker 2000). Fogel's (2000) concepts of "spiritual" or "immaterial" needs, and the "spiritual capital" required for a journey of self-realization, refer to the same value orientation. Once material needs are satisfied and taken for granted, he says, concerns turn to "the struggle for self-realization, the desire to find a deeper meaning in life than the endless accumulation of consumer durables and the pursuit of pleasure, access to the miracles of modern medicine, education not only for careers but for spiritual values, methods of financing an early, fruitful, and long-lasting retirement, and increasing the amount of quality time available for family activities" (Fogel 2000:176–177). At the other end of this value orientation, people whose lives are characterized by uncertainty, insecurity, political and economic turmoil, and low levels of well-being emphasize survival values, such as economic and physical security above all other goals. They feel threatened by foreigners, out-groups, and diversity; they are distrustful and resist cultural change.

These two dimensions can be used to produce a global cultural map (e.g., Inglehart and Baker 2000:29, 35). The most recent map available, which includes the latest survey results for all nations included in the four waves of the World Values Surveys, is shown in Figure 2 (Inglehart and Norris 2003:155). This map shows that America is the most traditional nation among all the historically Protestant nations, and the most traditional of all the English-speaking nations except Ireland. Thirty-one nations on this map are more traditional than the U.S. but all of these are low-income or developing societies from Africa, South Asia, and Latin America. At the same time, the U.S. is one of the most self-expression oriented nations in the world. In fact, only seven nations are more self-expression oriented: Sweden, the Netherlands, Australia, Denmark, New Zealand, Canada, and Iceland. America is an exceptional mix of traditional values and self-expression values. Its position on this map is unique; there is no nation that is more traditional *and* more self-expression oriented at the same time. The space on this map to the right of the U.S. and below it is empty.

America's value system has exhibited both stability and change over time. Since the first wave of the World Values Surveys (1981), the traditional values of Americans have shown remarkable durability. As Figure 3 demonstrates, the U.S. in 1995 (third wave) is in the same position on the traditional/secular-rational values dimension as it was in 1981. The nation's position on this dimension in 2000 (fourth wave) is almost the

Figure 1.2. Cultural Map of the World.

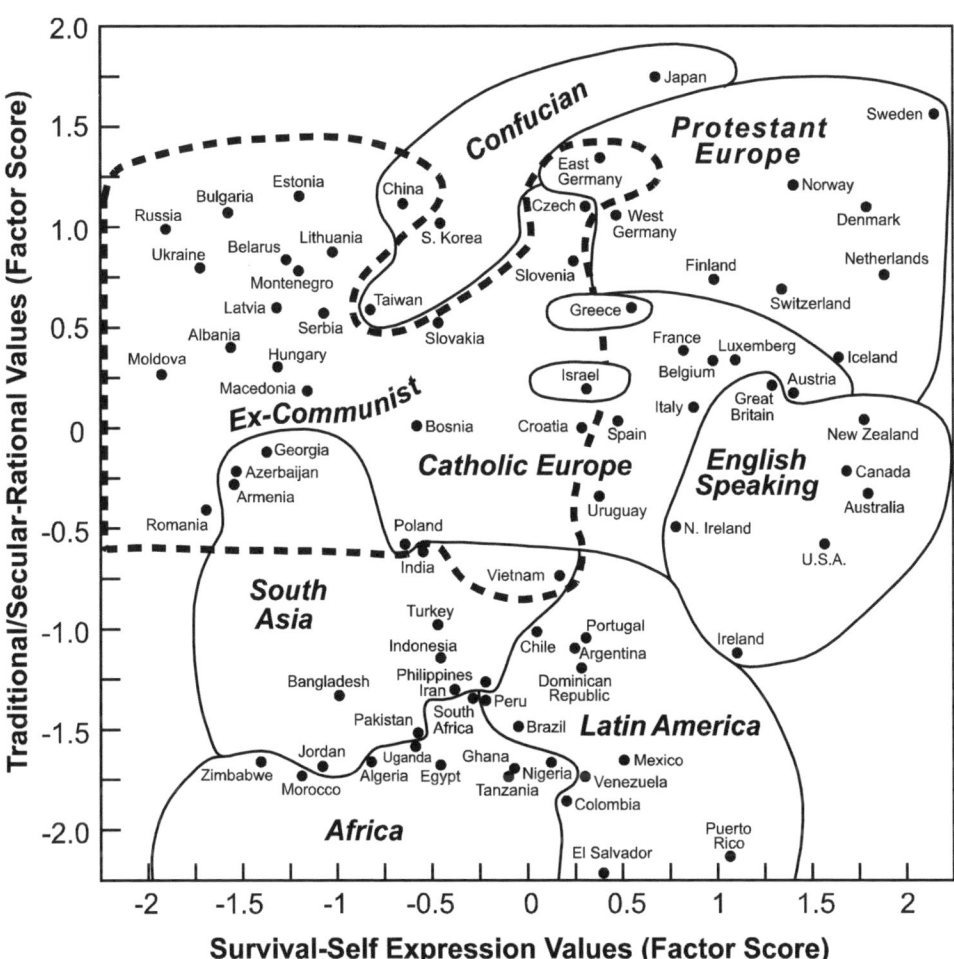

*Source*: Figure 7.1 in Ronald Inglehart and Pippa Norris, *Rising Tide: Gender Equality and Cultural Change Around the World*. Cambridge University Press (2003).

Figure 1.3. Change Over Time in Location on Two Dimensions of Cross Cultural Variation for 38 Societies.

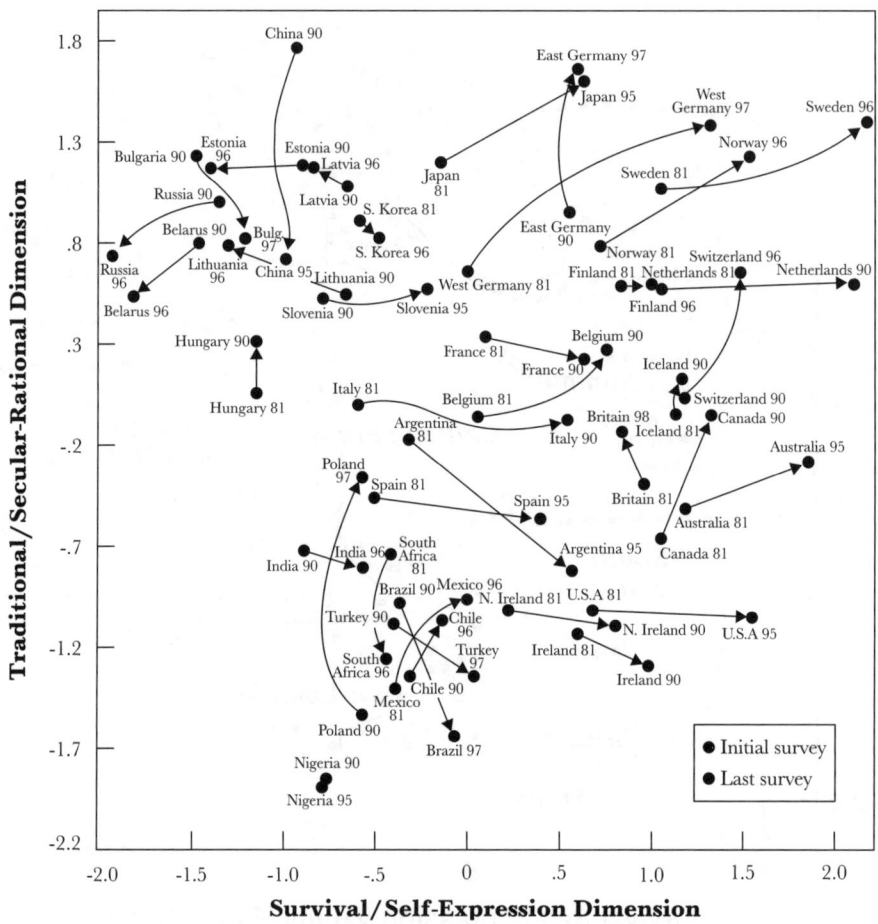

*Source*: Figure 6 in Ronald Inglehart and Wayne E. Baker, "Modernization, Cultural Change, and the Persistence of Traditional Values." *American Sociological Review* 65:19–51 (2000).

same, even though many other nations—mostly poor countries—have been added to the coverage of the World Values Surveys (Figure 2). America was one of the most traditional nations in 1981, and remains one of the most traditional almost 20 years later. In contrast to the stability of America's traditional values, the nation exhibits continuous movement along the survival/self-expression dimension. Since 1981, Americans have become increasingly self-expression oriented. There appears to be an almost perfect linear trend toward self-expression values from 1981 to 2000 (for details, see Baker 2004).

The years from the first World Values Surveys to the latest are a relatively short time span to conclusively evaluate trends, but the lack of movement along the traditional/secular-rational dimension is remarkable, especially since all of America's peers have lost or are losing their traditional values. In the 1981 surveys, all historically Protestant nations (such as Britain, Canada, Australia, Sweden, Norway, Denmark, Switzerland, Iceland, and the Netherlands) were less traditional than the United States. Since then, all of these cultural peers have shifted even further away from traditional values (Figure 3). The only exception is the Netherlands, but its values were already considerably less traditional than America's in 1981 (Figure 3). Like most of its peers, however, America has become more and more self-expression oriented over the last 20 years. Along the survival/self-expression dimension, America is similar to other historically Protestant nations.

The 2003 Detroit Area Study offers new data on these cultural dimensions, albeit only in a Midwestern region of the United States. In the Detroit Area Study, I replicated the items used to construct the two values scales (Table 2). The data from this survey and the World Values Surveys were combined, weighted so that each nation/region had equal weight, and factor analysis was used to re-compute the values for the two dimensions. The distributions of traditional/secular-rational values and survival/self-expression values for the Detroit region in 2003 and the U.S. in 2000 are quite similar. If the greater Detroit region were plotted on the cultural map (Figure 2), it would be in the same position as the nation at large.

As shown in Figure 4, the nation as a whole and the Detroit region tend to be traditional (the histograms "lean" to the left). Both the nation and the region are almost one standard deviation below the average for all societies included in the World Values Surveys. In contrast, both the nation and the region tend to be more self-expression oriented than survival oriented. Thus, the results from the Detroit Area Study lend

Figure 1.4. Percentage Distributions of Traditional/Secular-Rational Values and Survival/Self-Expression Values for the United States (2000 World Values Surveys) and the Greater Detroit Region (2003 Detroit Area Study).

United States (2000)

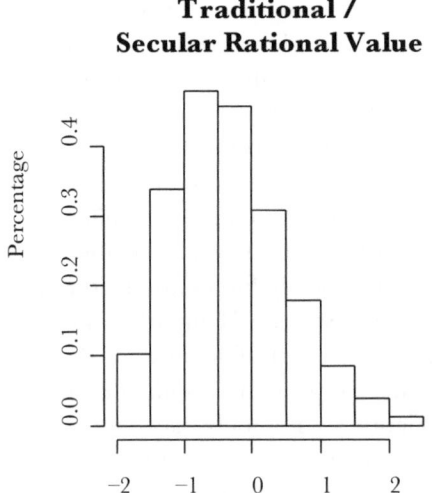

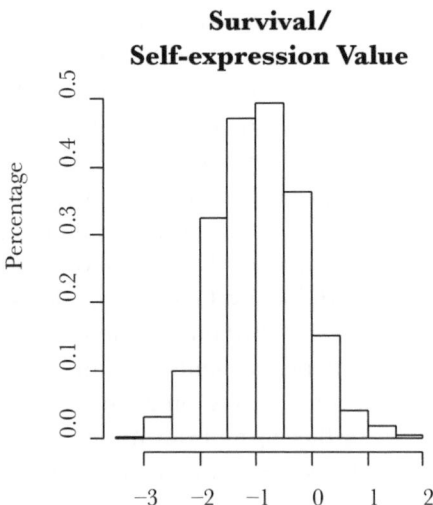

Detroit Region (2003)

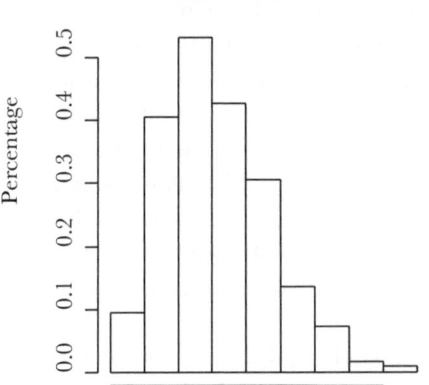

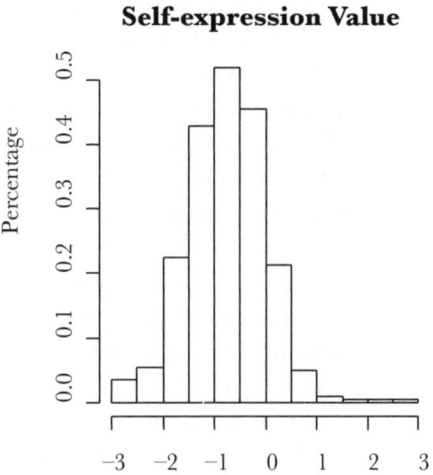

support to the national results from the 2000 World Values Survey. These histograms also show, however, that there is variation among Americans along these dimensions. In the next section, I explore how this variation relates to attitudes about the separation of church and state.

America has retained its traditional values over time, while it has shifted toward self-expression values. Why have some values changed and others stayed the same? Here, I summarize an answer that I provide in greater detail in Baker (2004). America's position on the global cultural map is often considered to be anomalous—a society that does not conform to the general tendency for economically advanced societies with a Protestant cultural heritage to be secular-rational and self-expression oriented. I argue, however, that the reason for the nation's stability on the traditional/secular-rational dimension is that same reason for the rapid shift on the survival/self-expression dimension: America's cultural heritage. America's cultural heritage counteracts the usual secularizing effect of economic development, retarding a shift toward secular-rational values. At the same time, this cultural heritage accelerates the nation's self-expression values, boosting the usual effect of economic development on this dimension.

Intergenerational replacement is a key mechanism of value change, as over 30 years of Eurobarometer data demonstrate (Inglehart 1997). Members of a generation tend to create a common outlook, collective identity, and similar basic values in their formative years—adolescence and early adulthood—which remain fairly stable throughout the life course (Mannheim 1952; Ortega y Gasset 1961; Schuman and Scott 1989; Inglehart1997). When the formative experiences of newer generations are significantly different from those of older generations, members of the younger cohorts develop values different from those of the older cohorts. Therefore, as the newer cohorts replace the older, the distribution of values in a society shifts over time. Large intergenerational value differences have been documented in, for example, the advanced industrial democracies (Inglehart and Baker 2000), where the younger generations are much more secular-rational and self-expression oriented than the older ones (Inglehart and Baker, 2000). America is different. The formative experiences of American cohorts are dramatically different (imagine the vastly different experiences of those who grew up in the Great Depression versus those who came of age in the 1960s). But Americans of all ages tend to have traditional values *and* to be self-expression oriented (for details, see Baker 2004). The theory of intergenerational replacement explains value stability and change in many societies, but not in the United States.

There are three reasons why Americans have retained their traditional values as they have become increasingly self-expression oriented. As I elaborate next, these are, 1) the establishment of a radically different culture in the early formative years of the country; 2) the recreation and reproduction of this culture over the years in social, political and economic institutions; and, (3) the critical link between traditional values and the need to preserve the American ideology. Americans have retained their traditional values, I shall argue, because traditional values are congruent with, and reinforce, the nation's core ideology. Secular-rational values are incongruent with and even threaten the definition of what it means to be American. Self-expression values, however, are congruent and compatible with the nation's culture and institutions, and so a shift from survival to self-expression values is not only possible, but probable.

Americans, says Kingdon (1996:23), "*think* differently." Thinking differently includes a preference for limited government, a distinctive distrust of authority, and strong religious beliefs. The origins of these values are the first immigrants who dominated early American culture and institutions. "American values," argues Kingdon (1999:58), "are connected to the kinds of people who came here. But the key point is that many of the people who traveled to these shores were systematically and fundamentally different from those who stayed behind in the old countries. They therefore brought ideas about government and politics with them that were systematically different from the ideas of the people who remained" (see, also, Lipset 1996; Fogel 2000).

The first immigrants were religious exiles (e.g., the Puritans and the Pilgrims). They escaped religious and political persecution in Europe, bringing with them a radical spirit of independence, self-reliance, a deep distrust of church hierarchies and state-controlled or state-sponsored religion, and a firm belief in the importance of God. The Protestants who left Europe were fundamentally different from those who remained, and these early travelers to the New World established dramatically different institutions (Lipset 1996:19–21). For example, the Puritans sought to found a new society, one that would "cleanse the churches of Christ throughout the world by restoring them to the purity and simplicity they had known in the days of the Apostles" (Erikson 1966:v). In contrast to European Protestants, American Protestants established local congregational sects; they became church members by acts of choice, not by birthright. American Protestants sought a direct personal relationship with God, not one mediated by the clergy. American congregations also paid their own clergy and self-funded their schools, unlike European Protestant churches where the clergy and schools were paid by the state and subsidized by taxes. American and European Protestants also had different views of human nature. European Protestants saw human beings as innately sinful and weak, and thus were less moralistic, less judgmental, and more forgiving about lapses in conduct. American Protestants, however, were quick to judge misconduct: "The American sects assume the perfectibility of human nature and have produced a moralistic people" (Lipset 1996:20).

The early religious exiles were joined by those who had left the Old World for better economic opportunities (Kingdon 1999:60–61), and who tended to push the center of American values and politics "in a more individualistic and antigovernment direction" (Kingdon 1999:61). Generally, these immigrants were more entrepreneurial, more independent, and bigger risk takers than those who stayed behind. Many economic immigrants shared and reinforced the core values of the religious groups that preceded them, but for different reasons. Together, they contributed to the unique constellation of American values—the American ideology or creed. "Born out of revolution," writes Lipset (1996:31), "the United States is a country organized around an *ideology* which includes a set of dogmas about the nature of a good society. Americanism, as different people have pointed out, is an 'ism' or ideology in the same way that communism or fascism or liberalism are isms. As G. K. Chesterton put it: 'America is the only nation in the world that is founded on a creed. That creed is set forth with dogmatic and even theological lucidity in the Declaration of Independence.'"

How do values originating centuries ago exert influence today? Path dependence is one answer (e.g., Kingdon 1996; Lipset 1996; Inglehart and Baker 2000). This theory says that starting conditions and initial choices send a system down a path of development that is not easily reversed. Kingdon (1996:80) explains: "America started down the path of limited government very early. We started with a distinctive distrust of authority, including governmental authority, that sprang from both the values of the immigrants and the pervasive localism of America. Faithful to and believing in that orientation, the founders deliberately built the country's fragmented governmental institutions (separation of powers, checks and balances, bicameralism, federalism) so as to limit government. Their design also contained specified limits on government action, as in the Bill of Rights, to be enforced by independent courts. Now that we have gone down the path of limited government for two centuries, we are extremely unlikely to design a wholly different set of institutions from scratch.... Some Americans think that the genius of the founders is their lasting legacy to all of us; others think that we're all stuck with these unwieldy institutions. Either way, there's no turning back."

Path dependence theory helps to explain the durability of America's traditional values. Traditional values were embodied in the nation's early social, economic, and political institutions, and then reinforced and reproduced over time. For example, "cross-cultural differences linked with religion [such as America's early Protestantism] have become part of a national culture that is transmitted by the educational institutions and the mass media of given societies to the people of that nation" (Inglehart and Baker 2000:37). The nation-state is "a key unit of shared experience and its educational and cultural institutions shape the values of almost everyone in that society" (Inglehart and Baker, 2000:37). Socialization into a national culture has a homogenizing effect on the people of a given society, regardless of their religious preferences. Indeed, Etzioni (2001) calls America the "monochrome" society because its diverse peoples share the same American values and aspirations. For example, the values of Protestants and Catholics in America today are quite similar, but quite different from the values of Protestants and Catholics in other nations (see, e.g., Figure 5 in Inglehart and Baker 2000:37).[2]

Contemporary expressions of a durable American ideology and its traditional values are clear. Bellah (2000) argues that Protestantism is still the "deep structure" of American culture.[3] The institutionalization of early Protestant values has produced and continues to reproduce a national culture that is so strong and monolithic that Bellah (2000)

---

[2] Similarly, Hindus in India have more values in common with Muslims in the same nation than they do with Muslims in Nigeria, and Christians and Muslims in Nigeria have more in common with one another than they do with their religious counterparts elsewhere (Inglehart and Baker, 2000). There are built-in limits to the global convergence of national cultures and economies (Guillén, 2001).

[3] Numerically, Protestants are still the largest religious group in America. According to a 2003 Gallup poll, 49.4% of Americans say that "Protestant" is their religious preference. The next largest group, Roman Catholics, is 23.7%. The same poll shows that more Protestants (60%) than Catholics (55%) say that religion is "very important in your own life." Protestants also attend church more frequently than Catholics, though this difference is not big.

brands it a "monoculture." America remains one of the most religious nations on earth, with only 19 of 75 nations rating higher than the United States on Inglehart and Norris's (2003:53–55) religiosity scale,[4] all of which are poor or developing countries, such as Uganda, El Salvador, Iran, South Africa, Peru, and Turkey. The U.S. is considerably more religious than all the historically Protestant nations, and more religious than all the English-speaking nations with the exception of Ireland (which is only slightly more religious). The Survey of American Political Culture reports "remarkably high levels of support for the 'American creed'" (Hunter and Bowman, 1996). Ninety-two percent of respondents "agree that children should be taught that 'Our founders limited the power of government, so government would not intrude too much into the lives of its citizens," eighty percent "expressed a high degree of 'support for our system of government'," and 96% agree with "the principle that 'with hard work and perseverance, anyone can succeed in America' should be taught to children." The National Opinion Research Center's study of patriotism in 22 nations finds that Americans are the most patriotic people (Smith and Jarkko 1998).

Symbols of the close connection between God and country abound in American society. "In God We Trust" appears on U.S. currency, and the U.S. Supreme Court's opening invocation includes "God save the United States and this honorable court," and millions of children in public schools across the country daily pledge allegiance to "the flag of the United States of America and to the republic for which it stands, one nation, under God, indivisible, with liberty and justice for all."[5]

Path dependence helps to explain the durability of America's traditional values but it is not the whole story. Another reason, I argue, is that America's traditional values play a vital role in the preservation of America's "imagined community." Every nation-state is an "imagined

---

[4] This religiosity scale comes from a factor analysis of the proportion of people in each nation "(1) who say that religion is 'very important' in their lives, (2) who find comfort in religion, (3) who believe in God, (4) who identify as religious, (5) who believe in life after death, and (6) who attend religious services regularly" (Inglehart and Norris, 2003:54–55).

[5] The U.S. Congress inserted the phrase "under God" in 1952 to distinguish America's religious values and religious heritage from "Godless communism." In March 2004, the U.S. Supreme Court heard a case brought by an American atheist who argued that the phrase "under God" was unconstitutional because it violated the separation of church and state. Eighty-seven percent of adult Americans favor keeping the phrase "under God" in the Pledge, according to an Associated Press-Ipsos poll taken a few days before the U.S Supreme Court heard the case.

community" (Anderson 1991), or what Habermas (1998) calls the popular self-consciousness of belonging to a people. This self-consciousness
forms "a relation of solidarity between persons who had previously
been strangers to one another" (Habermas 1998:111). The solidarity
of a nation-state is based on a common heritage (common ancestry,
language, religion, history, customs, traditions, and territory), which,
says Habermas (1998:113) produces "the consciousness of belonging to
'the same' people, and makes subjects into citizens of a single political
community—into members who can feel responsible *for one another*. The
nation of the *Volksgeist*, the unique spirit of the people—the first truly
*modern* form of collective identity—provided the cultural basis for the
constitutional state."

But America does not have common ancestry, language, religion,
history, customs, traditions, and territory (Habermas 1998). It is not,
as Lipset (1996) calls it, a "birthright" community, and so the popular
self-consciousness of belonging to a people must stand on another base.
For Americans, this foundation is a shared set of ideas and values: an
ideology. The relation of solidarity in America is its "civil religion"
(Habermas 1998), or what Ralph Waldo Emerson and Abraham Lincoln
called America's "political religion" (Lipset 1996:18). Americans imagine
they belong to the "same people" because they believe Americans share
the same values. This imagined community overcomes differences in
ancestry and ethnic origin, differences in religion, differences in customs,
and even differences in language. Being an American "is an ideological
commitment. It is not a matter of birth. Those who reject American
values are un-American" (Lipset 1996:31).

Because the foundation of America's imagined community is a set of
ideas and values, its preservation is paramount. Firm beliefs in religion
and God, family values, absolute moral authority, national pride, and
so on are fundamental to America's collective identity, to what it means
to be American, and the loss of traditional values is a threat to the
nation's imagined community, a direct assault on the nation's ideological core. The Swedes or the Germans or the Swiss or any birthright
nation can lose traditional values and still retain their collective identity
because the popular self-consciousness of "a people" does not stand
on a base of ideas and values. National identity is not an ideological
commitment. With or without traditional values, birthright nations still
have their common ancestry, history, religion, language, and customs.
America would not be America, however, if its people lost their traditional values, and the nation does not have another foundation to fall

back on. Therefore, Americans have retained their traditional values over time, successfully resisting the secularizing forces of affluence and economic development.

Why has the nation shifted toward self-expression values? Value shifts that are *congruent* with the social structure and culture of a nation are more likely to occur than changes that are not. For example, incongruence is one reason why socialism and unionism never caught on in America as they did in Europe. "The American social structure and values foster the free market and competitive individualism, an orientation which is not congruent with class-consciousness, support for socialist or social democratic parties, or a strong trade union movement" (Lipset 1996:108). Self-expression values are congruent with America's cultural heritage, and so the potential exists for change along the survival/self-expression dimension. But this is just a potential; it is a necessary, but not sufficient cause for value shift. This potential was realized through economic development. As I outline below, culture and economics combined to produce the shift toward self-expression values (for details, see Baker 2004).

Self-expression, or what is also called self-realization, is "a particularized creative process of individual growth" (Shusterman 1994:396–387). This value orientation is consistent, compatible, and congruent with American culture. For example, individualism, a core American ideal (Lipset, 1996), supports the pursuit of self-realization. Beliefs about human nature encourage self-realization. The Puritans believed that human nature was evil but perfectible and made self-perfection a moral project.[6] Over time, Americans increasingly adopted the belief that human nature is inherently good, but still in need of perfection, and, like their Puritan ancestors, Americans today believe in the importance of pursuing self-development and individual growth. For example, Wuthnow (1998) argues that more and more Americans are engaged in a "spirituality of seeking"—a personal quest for sacred moments and the exploration of new spiritual avenues. Data from the World Values Surveys and Detroit Area Study support his argument. In 1981, and again in 1990, 48% of Americans said they often think about the meaning and purpose of life. In 1995, the figure dropped by

---

[6] Every society develops a conception of human nature, with inherently good at one pole and inherently evil at the other. Evil but perfectible falls somewhere in the middle of this continuum (Kluckhohn and Strodtbeck, 1961).

two percentage points, but then rose dramatically by 2000 to 59%—a twenty year high. In the 2003 Detroit Area Study, 64% of Americans say that they often think about the meaning and purpose of life.

Gallup reports even higher numbers for a similar survey item: "How often have you thought about the basic meaning and value of your life during the past two years—a lot, a fair amount, or only a little?" 69% of Americans said "a lot" in 1998 (Gallup, Jr. and Lindsay, 1999). The proportion of Americans who often think about the meaning and purpose of life is higher than the global average, and higher than the proportion in almost all economically advanced democracies, in each wave of the World Values Surveys (see, e.g., Inglehart and Baker 2000:48). Generally, only poor and developing nations report percentages that are similar to the U.S. (Inglehart and Baker, 2000:48).

God is very important in the lives of Americans. For example, in 2000, 58% of Americans rated the importance of God in their lives as "10" on a 10-point scale, a 20-year high, up from 50% in 1981, 48% in 1990, and 50% in 1995 (Inglehart and Baker, 2000:47). Sixty-three percent of respondents in the 2003 Detroit Area Study rated the importance of God in their lives as "10." The majority of Americans attend religious services at least once a month. In 2000, for example, 60% of Americans said they attended religious services at least once a month, the same percentage as in 1981. Forty-seven percent of Detroit region residents attend religious services at least once a month. This figure is surprising, given how important God is in their lives. Overall, the strength of religious beliefs (importance of God in one's life) and religious practices (attending religious services) are marks of American exceptionalism. All nations with a Protestant heritage, and almost all economically advanced democracies, report much lower figures. Generally, only low-income and developing nations report higher figures than the U.S. (e.g., Inglehart and Baker 2000:46–47).

America's culture heritage is fertile ground for a shift toward self-expression values. Culture provides the potential, economic development supplies the means. Like the peoples of most societies who have come to experience and enjoy existential security, material affluence, peace, and safety, Americans have become focused increasingly on self-expression.[7] Because the same cultural heritage is inhospitable

---

[7] The terrorist attacks on September 11, 2001 jolted Americans' sense of safety and security, but does not seem to have had a lasting impact on America's values. Many

to secular-rational values, and the preservation of traditional values is essential for sustaining America's imagined community, Americans have resisted the usual secularizing effects of economic development. Therefore, America's position on the global cultural map—like the position of each country—is influenced by culture *and* economics (Figure 2). America's position on the survival/self-expression dimension is a result of America's culture and economic development working together and pushing in the same direction. The nation's position on the traditional/self-expression dimension is a result of the two forces pushing in opposite directions, with culture suppressing the secularizing effects of economic development.

*Moral Visions, Cultural Values, and Socio-Political*
*Attitudes among Americans*

Moral visions, cultural values, and attitudes are related in what I call a "hierarchy of beliefs." This three-level hierarchy is illustrated in Figure 5. Moral visions are an overarching framework, and religious-cultural values are the middle tier, residing under the moral visions. As Geertz (1973:126) argues, religion "objectivizes moral and aesthetic preferences." Religious-cultural values, in turn, are the framework for social and political attitudes since, "[religious] orthodoxy provides an overarching moral framework from which individuals may derive positions on specific policy-related issues" (Davis and Robinson 1996:769).

    This hierarchy suggests that moral visions have both direct and indirect effects on attitudes. Elsewhere, I analyze both direct and indirect effects (Baker 2004). Here, I focus on the total effects of both moral visions and the two cultural dimensions on socio-political attitudes, specifically attitudes about the separation of church and state.[8] Opinions about the separation of church and state are interesting to consider because they are subject to an internal tension. On the one hand, the separation of church and state is so important that it is enshrined in the

---

Americans have reported that their sense of personal safety and security have been shaken (Traugott, Groves, and Kennedy, 2002), and a Pew survey right after the attacks showed dramatically higher levels of religious belief and national pride. Six months later, however, Pew reports that religious belief and national pride had returned to their pre-9/11 levels (Religion and Public Life Survey, 2002).

    [8] For analyses of the effects of moral visions and the two dimensions on other attitudes, such as "economic ethics" and "family values," see Baker (2004).

Figure 1.5. The Hierarchy of Beliefs.

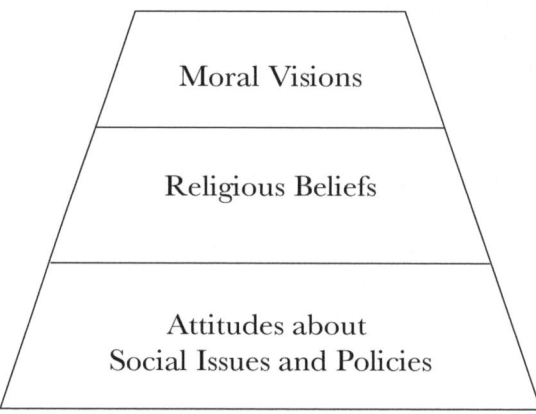

*Source*: Figure 3.2 in Wayne Baker, *America's Crisis of Values* (Princeton University Press, 2004).

U.S. Constitution.[9] On the other hand, the connection between God and country is exceptionally strong in American culture. This tension produces continual debates about the proper role of government in legislating religion, and continual testing of the limits placed on the government by the Constitution (such as the case brought before the U.S. Supreme Court in March 2004 to ban the phrase "under God" from the Pledge of Allegiance).

The 2000 World Values Surveys contain four items about the relationship between government and religion (these items were not included in the three prior waves): (1) "It would be better for [America] if more people with strong religious beliefs held public office." (2) "Politicians who do not believe in God are unfit for public office." (3) "Religious leaders should not influence how people vote in elections." (4) "Religious leaders should not influence government decisions." Moral visions and the two cultural dimensions are significantly related with each of these attitudes, after controlling for a variety of socio-demographic variables (Table 3). Moral absolutists favor less separation, believing it would be better for the America if more people with strong religious

---

[9] The First Amendment reads, "Congress shall make no law respecting an establishment of religion, or prohibiting the free exercise thereof; or abridging the freedom of speech, or of the press; or the right the people peaceably to assemble, and to petition the government for a redress of grievances."

Table 1.3. OLS Coefficients from Regression of Attitudes about Church-State Separation on Moral Visions and Two Dimensions of Cultural Variation, Controlling for Socio-demographic Variables, United States, World Values Surveys, 2000.

| Independent Variables | Politicians who do not believe in God are unfit for public office. | Religious leaders should not influence how people vote in elections. | It would be better for America if more people with strong religious beliefs held public office. | Religious leaders should not influence government decisions. |
|---|---|---|---|---|
| *Moral Visions* | | | | |
| Absolutism | −.220*** | .243*** | −.326*** | .238*** |
| *Cultural Indices* | | | | |
| Traditional/Secular-Rational Values | .465*** | -.310*** | .555*** | −.366*** |
| Survival/Self-Expression Values | .321*** | −.007 | .287*** | −.199*** |
| *Sociodemographics* | | | | |
| Age | .001 | −.007*** | .004* | −.007** |
| Race | .192** | .266*** | .001 | .178* |
| Gender | .237*** | −.004 | .122* | −.136* |
| Marital status | .002 | .006 | −.002 | −.001 |
| Social class | .008* | −.007 | .006 | −.005* |
| Education | .001 | .007*** | −.001 | .008*** |
| Protestant | −.157 | .006 | −.255*** | .122 |
| Other religion | −.146 | −.006 | −.001 | −.008 |
| *Constant* | 2.375*** | 1.147** | 2.652*** | 1.296** |
| Adjusted R sq. | .21 | .10 | .32 | .14 |
| N of observations | 1198 | 1200 | 1198 | 1195 |

Notes:
See Appendix for definitions of all variables.
Coefficients reported are unstandardized OLS regression estimates.
Omitted category is unmarried, nonwhite, female, and Catholic.
* p < .05, ** p < .01, *** p < .001 (one-tailed test for moral visions).

*Source*: Table 3.7 in Wayne Baker, *America's Crisis of Values* (Princeton University Press, 2004).

beliefs held public office, and that politicians who are atheists are unfit for public office. Moral relativists take the opposite position on each of these expressions of church-state separation. Relativists believe that religious leaders should not influence how people vote in elections, and that religious leaders should not influence government decisions. Absolutists take opposite positions.

Given the religious content of traditional values (Table 2), Americans with traditional values should favor less separation of church and state. The results show that they do (Table 3). Traditionalists believe that atheists are unfit for office, and that it would be better for America if religious people held office. Secular-rationalists take opposite positions, believing that religious leaders should not influence how people vote or influence government decisions. Americans who are survival oriented favor less church-separation; those who are self-expression oriented favor more. The reasons may be that Americans who are survival oriented interpreted less separation to mean greater economic and physical security, while those who are self-expression oriented interpret more separation as less restraint on freedom of expression.

Moral visions exert their force on attitudes directly and indirectly. Table 3 reports the direct effect of moral visions on each of the four opinions about church-state separation, controlling for the two cultural dimensions and various socio-demographics. But moral visions are also significantly associated with each of the two dimensions (as well as with other indictors of religious values and practices[10]). Absolutists tend to hold traditional values and to be survival oriented, controlling for various socio-demographics. Conversely, relativists tend to hold secular-rational values and to be self-expression oriented, controlling for the same socio-demographics (for details, see Baker, 2004). Thus, moral visions influence attitudes through three paths: 1) a direct path (absolutists favor closer ties between religion and politics, compared with relativists); 2) an indirect path via the traditional/secular-rational dimension (absolutists hold traditional values, and traditionalists favor closer ties, compared with secular-rationalists); and 3) an indirect path via the survival/self-expression dimension (absolutists tend to be survival-oriented, and those with this orientation favor closer ties between church and state, compared with relativists).[11]

These findings demonstrate that the three levels of the hierarchy of beliefs (Figure 5) are interlinked. Moral visions form a canopy over

---

[10] Other analyses show that moral visions and religious values and practices are closely connected. For example, absolutists are significantly more likely than relativists to believe in God, the soul, Heaven, Hell, and life after death (see Table 3.2, in Baker, 2004).

[11] The indirect effect of moral visions on attitudes is stronger through the traditional/secular-rational dimension than it is through the survival/self-expression dimension, but both indirect paths are significant (see Table 3.13, in Baker, 2004).

religious-cultural values and attitudes. The dual conceptual system of absolutism and relativism has direct effects on religious-cultural values, and both direct and indirect effects on attitudes. Religious-cultural values have direct effects on attitudes. Together, differences in beliefs about moral authority and differences in value orientations help to explain variation among Americans in their attitudes about a defining principle of American society: the separation of church and state.

## *Cultural Contradictions and the Search for Meaning*

The analyses and arguments above make the case that American exceptionalism occurs in two ways. First, America's value system is unusually absolutist and traditional, more so than virtually all economically advanced democracies, and even more so than the majority of nations in the world. Second, America's value system is unusual because it combines traditional *and* self-expression values; it is a mixed system. A mixed system contains cultural contradictions with prevailing principles that provide contrary guides to conduct. For example, the "cultural contradictions of capitalism" arise from the conflict of principles in economy and culture (Bell 1978). On one side, the principle of "efficiency" in a capitalist economy demands "self-control and delayed gratification, of purposeful behavior in the pursuit of well-defined goals" (Bell 1978: xvi). On the other side, culture dictates "self-expression and self-gratification" (Bell 1978: xvi). The principles of efficiency and self-expression, Bell (1978: xvii) argues, "now lead people in contrary directions." Similarly, I argue that America's mixed value system—traditional values and self-expression values—contains cultural contradictions and contrary guides to conduct. Obedience to an absolute, external, transcendental authority (God and country) is the principle behind traditional values. Obedience to a mundane source of moral authority (the self) is the principle behind self-expression values. These two principles lead Americans in contrary directions.

Americans who internalize the cultural contradictions of traditional and self-expression values and their contrary guides to conduct experience cognitive dissonance. Cognitive dissonance is a feeling of psychological distress. It can be caused by a discrepancy between two beliefs, or between behavior and belief. According to dissonance theory, a person who experiences cognitive dissonance is motivated to reduce it by changing beliefs, behaviors, or both. For example, one could reduce the cognitive dissonance caused by the contradictions of traditional and self-expression values by abandoning religious values (change in beliefs), or by attending religious services less often (change in behavior). These dissonance-reduction strategies may be difficult to implement. For example, social sanctions and networks can effectively prevent one from going to religious services less frequently. It is possible, I suggest, that the cognitive dissonance caused by America's mixed value system could be managed in a different way, that is, by thinking often about the meaning and purpose of life.

To test this possibility, I created a measure of "value incongruence" that compares a person's location on the traditional/secular-rational values dimension with the person's location on the survival/self-expression values dimension (see Baker, 2004, for details). Value incongruence is the extent to which a person holds contradictory values, such as traditional values coupled with self-expression values, or secular-rational values coupled with survival values. Value congruence is the extent to which a person holds compatible values, such as traditional values with survival values, or secular-rational values with self-expression values. American society, on average, exhibits value incongruence (traditional and self-expression values), and so the "mainstream" form of value incongruence for individuals is the same. However, some Americans experience the other form of value incongruence (secular-rational and survival values), while still others experience the two forms of value congruence. The measure of value incongruence is a continuous variable, where 0 indicates complete value congruence, negative scores indicate the mainstream form of value incongruence (traditional and self-expression values), and positive scores indicate the other form of value incongruence (secular-rational and survival values). The magnitude of a score, positive or negative, indicates the extent of the discrepancy between a person's locations on the two values dimensions.

Generally, Americans who have internalized the mainstream form of value incongruence are significantly more likely to think often about the meaning and purpose of life, compared to those with the alternative form of value incongruence, even when holding constant the effects of moral visions and socio-demographics (Table 4). Moral visions also have significant effects. Absolutists are more likely than relativists to think often about the meaning and purpose of life, controlling for the two value dimensions and socio-demographic variables. Why do absolutists who hold traditional and self-expression values tend to think often about the meaning and purpose of life? It may be that the struggle

Table 1.4. Binary Logit Coefficients from Regression of Thinking Often About the Meaning and Purpose of Life on Value Incongruence, Controlling for Moral Visions and Sociodemographic Variables, United States, World Values Surveys, 2000.

| Independent Variables | Often think about meaning and purpose of life (Excluding value incongruence) | Often think about meaning and purpose of life (For value incongruence, left of zero vs. right of zero) | Often think about meaning and purpose of life (For value incongruence, left tail vs. right tail) |
|---|---|---|---|
| *Value Incongruence* | | | |
| Traditional and self-expression values† | — | .224 | .437*** |
| *Moral Visions* | | | |
| Absolutism | .585*** | .603*** | .335* |
| *Sociodemographics* | | | |
| Age | .128** | .109** | .050 |
| Race | −.971*** | −1.060*** | −.927*** |
| Gender | −.345** | −.316** | −.342* |
| Marital status | −.257* | −.324** | −.192 |
| Social class | −.063 | .065 | .105 |
| Education | .072* | .041 | −.025 |
| Protestant | .080 | .022 | −.179 |
| Other religion | .020 | −.038 | −.182 |
| *Constant* | −.943 | .446 | 1.004 |
| Nagelkerke pseudo R sq. | .09 | .11 | .09 |
| N of observations | 1011 | 958 | 478 |

Notes:
See Appendix for definition of all variables.
† Value incongruence = 1 if a person tends to have traditional and self-expression values. For the first column, this is left of 0 in the distribution in Figure 4.7. For the second column, this is the 25 percentile.
Omitted category is unmarried, nonwhite, female, and Catholic.
* p < .05, ** p < .01, *** p < .001.

*Source*: Table 5.8 in Wayne Baker, *America's Crisis of Values* (Princeton University Press, 2004).

to reconcile conflicting guides to conduct—obedience to a transcendental moral authority which comes with absolutism and traditional values versus obedience to the self which comes with self-expression values—stimulates such thinking. In contrast, a survival orientation, coupled with the principle of obedience to oneself that comes with secular-rational values and relativism, may foster a focus on the here-and-now of everyday life in the mundane world.

The gap between America's locations on the two value dimensions has been widening over time as the nation retains its traditional values but continues to move toward self-expression values. If this trend continues, the cultural contradictions in American life will become greater, and more and more Americans hold a mix of traditional and self-expression values. If so, then the proportion of Americans who often think about the meaning and purpose of life will rise over time as well.

*Conclusion*

This chapter contributes to the theme of American exceptionalism by examining America's moral visions, value orientations, and socio-political attitudes. Moral visions are worldviews about the location of moral authority. Absolutists locate the source in the transcendental sphere (God or society); relativists locate it in the mundane sphere (the self). Americans are exceptionally absolutist. Comparing the proportions of absolutists and relativists in the United States with a large number of societies demonstrates that America is one of the most absolutist nations on earth. Examining the United States over time shows that the proportion of Americans who are absolutists has been increasing. Only one of three Americans was absolutist in 1981, but in 2000 it is one of two. The high proportion of absolutists in the United States ranks it alongside poor and developing countries.

America's locations on two value dimensions—traditional versus secular-rational values and survival versus self-expression values—is also unusual. The nation is exceptionally traditional. It is more traditional than other economically advanced democracies (with the exception of Ireland), more traditional than all nations with a Protestant heritage, and more traditional than the majority of nations in the world. Only poor and developing nations have more traditional values. Like most economically advanced democracies, however, the United States has become increasingly self-expression oriented over time. America is exceptional in two ways: its stable traditional values are exceptional, and it is has become an exceptional mix of traditional and self-expression values.

The reasons why Americans have retained their traditional values but have become increasingly self-expression oriented are, 1) the establishment of a radically different culture in the early formative years of the country; 2) the recreation and reproduction of this culture over the years in social, political and economic institutions; and, 3) the critical link between traditional values and preservation of the ideological foundation of America's imagined community. Self-expression values are consistent, compatible, and congruent with America's culture and its religious-cultural heritage. Therefore, the nation could move rapidly along the survival/self-expression values dimension as the country developed economically and more and more Americans experienced existential security, material affluence, and safety. But the same culture and religious-cultural heritage are inhospitable to secular-rational values. From its beginning until now, American culture has been based on a close connection between two sources of transcendental moral authority: God and country. In America, these sources provide clear moral guidelines about what is right and wrong. These guidelines always apply to everyone, whatever the circumstances. Of course, Americans hold and apply these moral values in varying degrees, they have innumerable lapses in conduct, and the validity of the two transcendental sources are continually debated and contested. For example, Americans who are absolutist and traditional support closer ties between religion and government, while those who are relativist and secular-rational want more separation between church and state. But all of these differences take place in a cultural context that, at its core, is absolutist and traditional. Preserving this core sustains America's imagined community—its popular self-consciousness of belonging to "an American people."

Most Americans perceive a crisis of values, as I document in Baker (2004). Many believe that the nation has lost, or is losing, its traditional values, that it is in moral decline, that it has become a land of relativists, and that is it hopelessly divided. For example, in the 1993 and 1994 General Social Survey of the U.S., 62% said, "Americans are greatly divided when it comes to the most important values." About 86% of Americans agreed that, "there was a time when people in this country felt they had more in common and shared more values than Americans do today," according to a 1995 poll by Princeton Survey Associates (DiMaggio, Evans, and Bryson, 1996:63). A Pew survey, conducted in spring 2001, reports that 55% of Americans felt that religion was "losing its significance" as an influence on American life. This percentage dropped right after the September 11, 2001 terrorist attacks, but rose to 52% in March 2002 (Religion and Public Life Survey, 2002). In the same March 2002 survey, 75% of Americans said "no" to the question, "Do you think people in general today lead as good lives—honest and moral—as they used to?" In a May 2003 Gallup poll, 77% of Americans

rated the "overall state of moral values in this country today" as "only
fair" or "poor," and 67% said they "think the state of moral values in
the country" is "getting worse."

The "culture war" debates are another expression of the pervasive
perception of moral decline, discord, and dissension. As described
above, proponents of the culture war thesis says that Americans are
divided into two irreconcilably opposed moral camps—absolutists
versus relativists—and that the members of these camps hold vastly
different religious values and attitudes about social issues and policies
(e.g., Hunter 1991; Guinness 1993; Himmelfarb 2001).

There is a wide reality-perception gap in America. The findings in this
chapter and elsewhere (Baker 2004) show that America has not lost its
traditional values. America was and remains one of the most traditional
nations on earth. Religious practices and beliefs remain strong, much
stronger than they are in most economically advanced democracies.
Americans have not become relativists. On the contrary, absolutism
is on the rise; America today is one of the most absolutist nations on
earth. The 50:50 split of absolutists and relativists appears to support
the culture war claim of opposed moral camps, but this division does
not translate into two groups with widely different religious values and
social attitudes. Instead, Americans tend to hold traditional values (e.g.,
see Figure 4). Moral visions are related to value orientations and to social
and political attitudes, but the links between levels in the hierarchy of
beliefs (Figure 5) are not strong enough to conclude that the culture
war thesis is correct. There are some differences between absolutists
and relativists, but they are not that great. Generally, Americans have a
lot in common and share many important values, beliefs, and attitudes
(see, also, DiMaggio, Evans, and Bryson, 1996).

What explains the reality-perception gap in America? Why do Americans perceive a crisis of values? In the conclusion of this chapter, I can
only sketch the answer I develop and support in detail elsewhere (Baker,
2004). First, there is evidence that most societies experience cycles of
crisis. Technological and economic transformations drive these cycles
by disrupting the preexisting social order, destabilizing culture, and
creating crises of meaning (e.g, Castells 2000; Fogel 2000). America
appears to be in the transition phase of such a cycle, driven by the
revolution in information technologies (Castells 2000) and the accelera-
tion of the "technophysio evolution of human life" brought about by
breakthroughs in several areas, including the "extension of control of

human biology, particularly in the fields of reproductive technology and organ transplantation" (Fogel 2000:44). Crisis is the personal experience of many who are witnessing, participating in, and sometimes suffering from this transition. This personal experience may be labeled a "crisis of values" even when traditional values have not been lost, and most Americans continue to share important values and beliefs.

Second, some values have changed though traditional values have not: Americans have become increasingly self-expression oriented. Stable traditional values coupled with continuous movement toward self-expression values produces a widening gap between locations on the two dimensions. This widening gap represents increasing cultural contradictions and contradictory guides to action. Though Americans have retained their traditional values and absolutist moral visions, they are pulled increasingly in different directions: obedience to a transcendental moral authority (from traditional values) and obedience to a mundane moral authority (from self-expression values). This tension appears as a crisis of values which, for some Americans, is resolved by using it to stimulate thinking about the about the purpose and meaning of life.

Finally, I believe the "crisis of values" serves a rhetorical function. Traditional values are a base of America's imagined community, and so their preservation is paramount for sustaining a sense of collective identity. Repeated warnings, public alarm, and political and intellectual debates about the loss of traditional values (or a culture war) serve to remind Americans of the values and ideals that make them who they are. A function of deviance is to maintain "a sense of mutuality among the people of a community by supplying a focus for group feeling. Like a war, a flood, or some other emergency, deviance makes people more alert to the interests they share in common and draws attention to those values which constitute the 'collective conscience' of the community" (Erikson, 1966:4; Durkeim, 1958, 1960). America's "crisis of values" affirms and reinforces the ideological core of the nation's imagined community—the values that define "who we are."

## References

Anderson, Benedict. 1991. *Imagined Communities: Reflections on the Origin and Spread of Nationalism*, revised edition. Verso Books.
Baker, Wayne E. 2004. *America's Crisis of Values: Reality and Perception*. Princeton, NJ: Princeton University Press.

Belah, Robert N. 2000. "The Protestant Structure of American Culture: Multiculture or Monoculture?" Fall lecture in Culture and Social Theory, Institute for Advanced Studies in Culture, University of Virginia.

Bell, Daniel. 1978. *The Cultural Contradictions of Capitalism*. NY: Basic.

Castells, Manuel. 2000. *The Rise of the Network Society*, second edition. Volume 1 of The Information Age: Economy, Society, and Culture. Oxford: Blackwell.

Davis, Nancy J. and Robert V. Robinson. 1996. "Are the Rumors of War Exaggerated?" *American Journal of Sociology* 102.

Demerath III, N.J. and Yonghe Yang. 1997. "What American Culture War? A View from the Trenches as Opposed to the Command Posts and the Press Corps." Pp. 17–38 in Rys H. Williams (ed.), *Cultural Wars In American Politics*. NY: Aldine de Gruyter.

DiMaggio, Paul, John Evans, and Bethany Bryson. 1996. "Have Americans' Social Attitudes Become More Polarized?" *American Journal of Sociology* 102:690–755.

Durkeim, Emile. 1960. *The Division of Labor in Society*, translated by George Simpson. Glencoe, IL: The Free Press.

———. 1958. *The Rules of Sociological Method*, translated by S.A. Solovay and J.H. Mueller. Glencoe, IL: The Free Press.

Eisenstadt, S.N. 1982. "The Axial Age." *European Journal of Sociology* 23:294–314.

Erikson, Kai T. 1966. *Wayward Puritans*. NY: John Wiley and Sons.

Etzioni, Amitai. 2001. *The Monochrome Society*. Princeton, NJ: Princeton University Press.

Fletcher, Joseph. 1966. *Situation Ethics: The New Morality*. Louisville, KT: Westminster John Know Press.

Fogel, Robert William. 2000. *The Fourth Great Awakening and the Future of Egalitarianism*. Chicago: University of Chicago Press.

Galbraith, John Kenneth. 1996. *The Good Society*. Boston, MA: Houghton Mifflin Co.

Gallup, George Jr. and D. Michael Lindsay. 1999. *Surveying the Religious Landscape: Trends in U.S. Beliefs*. Harrisburg, PA: Morehouse Publishing.

Geertz, Clifford. 1973. *The Interpretation of Cultures*. NY: Basic.

Guillén, Mauro F. 2001. *The Limits of Convergence*. Princeton, NJ: Princeton University.

Guinness, Os. 1993. *The American Hour: A Time of Reckoning and the Once and Future Role of Faith*. NY: Free Press.

Habermas, Jürgen. 1998. *The Inclusion of the Other*. Edited by Ciaran Cronin and Pablo De Grieff. Cambridge, MA: MIT Press.

Himmelfarb, Gertrude. 2001. *One Nation, Two Cultures*. NY: Alfred A. Knopf.

Hunter, James Davison and Carl Bowman. 1996. *The State of Disunion*. Ivy, VA: In Medias Res Educational Foundation.

Hunter, James Davison. 1991. *Culture Wars: The Struggle to Define America*. NY: Basic.

———. 1994. *Before the Shooting Begins: Searching for Democracy in America's Culture War*. NY: Free Press.

Inglehart, Ronald and Pippa Norris. 2004. *Rising Tide: Gender Equality and Cultural Change around the World*. Cambridge University Press.

Inglehart, Ronald and Wayne E. Baker. 2000. "Modernization, Cultural Change, and the Persistence of Traditional Values." *American Sociological Review* 65:19–51.

Inglehart, Ronald. 1997. *Modernization and Postmodernization: Cultural, Economic and Political Change in 43 Societies*. Princeton: Princeton University Press.

Jaspers, Karl. 1953. *The Origin and Goal of History*. Translated by Michael Bullock. London: Routledge & Kegan Paul.

Kluckholn, Florence Rockwood and Fred L. Strodtbeck. 1961. *Variations in Value Orientations*. Evanston, IL: Row, Peterson and Co.

Kingdon, John W. 1999. *America the Unusual*. NY: St. Martin's/ Worth.

Lipset, Seymour Martin. 1996. *American Exceptionalism*. NY: W.W. Norton.

Mannheim, Karl. [1928] 1952. "The Problem of Generations." Pp. 276–332 in *Essays on the Sociology of Knowledge*. Edited by P. Kecskemeti. London, England: Routledge and Kegan Paul.

Maybury-Lewis, David. 1989. "The Quest for Harmony," pp. 1–17 in David Maybury-Lewis and Uri Almagor (eds.), *The Attraction of Opposites: Thought and Society in the Dualistic Mode*. Ann Arbor, MI: The University of Michigan Press.

Maybury-Lewis, David and Uri Almagor (eds.). 1989. *The Attraction of Opposites: Thought and Society in the Dualistic Mode*. Ann Arbor, MI: The University of Michigan Press.

Mouw, Ted and Michael W. Sobel. 2001. "Culture Wars and Opinion Polarization: The Case of Abortion." *American Journal of Sociology* 106: 913–943.

Orrù, Marco. 1987. *Anomie: History and Meanings*. Boston: Allen & Unwin.

Ortega y Gasset, José. 1961. "The Concept of the Generation." *The Modern Theme*. NY, 1961.

Religion and Public Life Survey. 2002. Pew Research Center for the People & the Press and Pew Forum on Religion and Public Life. Survey conducted by Princeton Survey Research Associates. Available at http://www. people-press.org/.

Shusterman, R. 1994. "Pragmatism and Liberalism between Dewey and Rorty." *Political Theory* 22:391–413.

Schuman, Howard and Jacqueline Scott. 1989. "Generations and Collective Memories," *American Sociological Review* 54:3590–381.

Seligman, Adam B. 1989. "The Comparative Study of Utopias." Pp. 1–12 in Adam B. Seligman (ed.), *Order and Transcendence: The Role of Utopias and the Dynamics of Civilizations*. Leiden: E.J. Brill.

Smith, Tom W. and Lars Jarrko. 1998. "National Pride: A Cross-national Analysis." National Opinion Research Center/University of Chicago. General Social Survey Cross-national report No. 19.

Shanahan, Daniel. 1992. *Toward a Genealogy of Individualism*. Amherst, MA: University of Massachusetts Press.

Sorokin, Pitirim. 1957. *Social and Cultural Dynamics*. Boston: Porter Sargent Publisher, 1957.

Tocqueville, Alexis. 1988. *Democracy in America*, translated by George Lawrence, edited by J.P. Mayer. NY: HarperCollins.

Traugott, Michael W., Robert M. Groves, and Courtney Kennedy. 2002. "How American Responded: Public Opinion after 9/11/01." Paper presented at the 57th Annual AAPOR Conference, St. Pete Beach, FL, May 17.

Wolfe, Alan. 1998. *One Nation, After All*. NY: Viking.

Wuthnow, Robert. 1998. *After Heaven: Spirituality in America Since the 1950s*. Berkeley, CA: University of California Press.

# CHAPTER TWO

# CLEAVAGES, VALUE GAPS AND REGIME SUPPORT: EVIDENCE FROM CANADA AND 26 OTHER SOCIETIES

Neil Nevitte & Mebs Kanji

## Introduction

Canada, along with such countries as the Netherlands, Belgium, Austria and Switzerland, is usually identified as being among that small cluster of states that qualify as "deeply divided" societies. Thirty-five years ago, Seymour Martin Lipset and Stein Rokkan (1967) developed a comprehensive account of how deep and reinforcing social cleavages presented states with the challenges of integration and political support. Their pioneering account focused primarily on how party systems mediated societal cleavages based on religion, class, language and region.

Contemporary evidence suggests, however, that the "old" cleavages, which Lipset and Rokkan claimed decisively shaped states during the industrializing period, may be less prominent now than they once were. Some argue, for example, that class has become a progressively weaker predictor of voting behavior (Franklin, 1985; Franklin *et al.* 1992), and that the influence of organized religion seems to have waned as publics in most advanced industrial states have become more secular (Halman and Riis, 1999). Others contend that the shift towards post-industrialism has been accompanied by the emergence of "new" salient cleavages (Dalton, 2002). This exploration examines the impact of social differentiation and diversity from the vantage point of new cleavages.

We begin with an aggregate perspective of value change and stability in Canada over the last two decades. Our focus then shifts to consider the dynamics and potential implications of value differences across three "new" cleavages: those based on gender, generation, and differences between immigrants and native born Canadians. Two questions structure the investigation. First, to what extent has there been stability or change in the fundamental values of Canadians on different sides of these respective cleavages? Have the number of significant value gaps across such "new" cleavages increased, decreased or remained stable? Second, does the presence or absence of value differences across these societal cleavages have any systematic consequences for regime support? Our general hypothesis is that societies with larger value differences across these cleavages are likely to have lower levels of regime support. The concluding section of the analysis expands the scope of the investigation to incorporate data from 26 other societies in order to test the generalizability of this proposition.

*Cleavages*

The place to start is with a clearer specification of the cleavages that are to be examined, and the determination of which fundamental values are under consideration. The gender cleavage, of course, is not a "new" cleavage in any literal sense; it has become more salient during the course of the last two decades or so in part because of the dynamics associated with post-industrialism. Norris and colleagues (Norris and Inglehart, 2003a; also see Inglehart, Norris and Welzel, 2003) make a strong case indicating that societal modernization and human development (see Welzel, Inglehart and Klingemann, 2003; Welzel and Inglehart, 2001) bring with them a rising tide of gender equality in post-industrial societies. They argue that,

> throughout history, women in virtually all societies have had their life options restricted to the roles of wife and mother. Increasingly today, in postindustrial societies, almost any career and almost any lifestyle is opening up to them. These cultural changes have been important for men, but the transformation in the lives of women is far more dramatic, moving them from narrow subordination toward full equality. A radical change is altering women's education, career opportunities, sexual behavior, and worldviews. With this in mind, it is not surprising to find that gender issues constitute such a central component—arguably, *the* most central component—of value change in postindustrial societies. (p. 159)

There is no reason to believe that Canada has escaped the effects of these same trends. Indeed, Canadian women have experienced the same structural changes that have transformed the position of women in other post-industrial states. The proportion of women enrolled in post-secondary educational institutions, for example, now outnumbers men, and women make up nearly half of the paid work force (Statistics

Canada). One consequence has been that, over the past twenty years, there has been a very substantial increase in the proportion of highly educated women in the paid workforce. Given these kinds of dramatic structural changes, it is not difficult to see why the gender gap has become more salient for Canadians today than it was in the past.

The second line of cleavage considered here concerns generational differences, the value differences between the young and the old. In the sociological sense, generations are usually defined as encompassing individuals "who belong to the same generation, who share the same year of birth, (and who are) endowed, to that extent, with a common location in the historical dimension of the social process" (Mannheim 1952:290). Inglehart's (1977, 1990, 1997) theory of postmodern value change contends that economic development has contributed to an intergenerational shift in the value priorities of mass publics in advanced industrial states. Because younger generations were socialized during a period of relative affluence, they are likely to have worldviews that are different from those of older generations socialized under conditions of substantially less physical and material security:

> During the period since World War II, advanced industrial societies have attained much higher real income levels than ever before in history. Coupled with the emergence of the welfare state, this has brought about a historically unprecedented situation: most of their population does not live under conditions of hunger and economic insecurity. This has led to a gradual shift in which needs for belonging, self-expression and a partici-pant role in society became more prominent. (Inglehart, 1997:132)

This transformation, Inglehart argues, is just one part of a much broader shift in the values of younger generations which includes changing value orientations towards a variety of domains including "politics, work, family life, religion and sexual behavior." There is clear evidence that intergenerational value change has been taking place in the Canadian setting. Furthermore, it is similar in direction and scope to intergenerational value changes found in other advanced industrial states (Nevitte 1996). Thus, the dynamics of population replacement in Canada suggest that, as elsewhere, the generational cleavage has the potential to demarcate a significant line of value differences within the Canadian population.

The third cleavage centers on value differences between immigrants and native-born Canadians. This cleavage is of increased concern to a growing number of states that seek to bolster sagging population levels through immigration, but it is of particular relevance to the Canadian

setting for a combination of reasons (Beaujot, 2003). First, more than
virtually any other advanced industrial state, Canada has relied upon
immigration as a source of population replacement. According to recent
census data, immigration accounted for more than 50% of Canada's
population growth between 1996 and 2001, and a very substantial
18% of the Canadian population was not born in the country. From
the vantage point of value diversity, the implication is clear; this very
sizable proportion of the Canadian population could not, by definition, have been socialized into "mainstream" Canadian norms during
their formative years. Some of the aggregate level effects of these different socialization experiences on various political outlooks have been
documented elsewhere (Nevitte and Kanji, 2003a, 2003b; Bilodeau
and Nevitte 2003), and it is reasonable to suppose that such differences
might apply equally to a variety of social and economic outlooks. Second, since the 1960s, there has been a dramatic shift in the countries
of origin of Canadian immigrants. Until the 1960s, immigrants from
"traditional" source countries (Western Europe and the United States)
outnumbered those coming from non-traditional source countries (Asia,
Africa, Latin America and the Caribbean) by a ratio of about 9:1. By
the middle of the 1980s, that pattern had completely reversed; immigrants from non-traditional source countries outnumbered those from
traditional source countries by a ratio of about 3:1. Given that new
immigrants tend to increasingly come from environments that are more
culturally dissimilar to their new host country, there are good reasons
not only to anticipate significant value differences between immigrants
and native-born Canadians, but also to expect to find substantial value
differences between immigrants from traditional versus non-traditional
source countries.

*Value Dimensions*

The similarities and differences between men and women, the young
and the old, and immigrants and non-immigrants, might be compared
across a vast array of value outlooks. To identify, empirically, a manageable number of coherent value domains for analysis, we employed an
exploratory factor analysis of the 1981, 1990 and 2000 waves of the
WVS. The initial step in the research began by considering some 80
indicators representing a broad range of values including what people
valued in life, orientations toward family life, attitudes toward work,

.

Table 2.1. Factor Analysis—Fundamental Value Dimensions in Canada.

| Dimensions and indicators[a] | Factor loadings | Communalities |
|---|---|---|
| **1. *Subjective religiosity*** | | |
| Belief in heaven | .78 | .67 |
| Belief in God | .74 | .59 |
| Importance of God | .73 | .59 |
| Belief in life after death | .63 | .42 |
| Importance of religion | .62 | .51 |
| Belief in hell | .60 | .48 |

Eigenvalue: 4.48
% of variance: 13.17
Cronbach's Alpha: .79

| **2. *Church leadership*** | | |
|---|---|---|
| Churches give adequate answers to moral problems | .83 | .71 |
| Churches give adequate answers to family problems | .81 | .71 |
| Churches give adequate answers to social problems | .73 | .59 |
| Churches give adequate answers to spiritual needs | .71 | .54 |

Eigenvalue: 2.09
% of variance: 6.15
Cronbach's Alpha: .81

| **3. *Moral permissiveness*** | | |
|---|---|---|
| Divorce is justifiable | .76 | .59 |
| Abortion is justifiable | .76 | .62 |
| Homosexuality is justifiable | .69 | .54 |
| Euthanasia is justifiable | .63 | .45 |
| Suicide is justifiable | .55 | .36 |

Eigenvalue: 2.34
% of variance: 6.88
Cronbach's Alpha: .74

| **4. *Civil permissiveness*** | | |
|---|---|---|
| Avoiding a fare on public transports is justifiable | .75 | .57 |
| Accepting a bribe on duty is justifiable | .72 | .53 |
| Claiming government benefits that are not entitled | .72 | .53 |
| Cheating on taxes is justifiable | .71 | .53 |

Eigenvalue: 1.99
% of variance: 5.85
Cronbach's Alpha: .67

Table 2.1 (*Cont.*)

| Dimensions and indicators[a] | Factor loadings | Communalities |
|---|---|---|
| 5. *Market economics* | | |
| Competition is good vs. harmful | .77 | .63 |
| Private vs. government ownership should be increased | .74 | .58 |
| | | |
| Eigenvalue: 1.14 | | |
| % of variance: 3.35 | | |
| Cronbach's Alpha: .40 | | |
| | | |
| 6. *Technology and science* | | |
| More emphasis on the development of technology | .79 | .64 |
| Scientific advances will help (or harm) mankind | .79 | .64 |
| | | |
| Eigenvalue: 1.36 | | |
| % of variance: 4.00 | | |
| Cronbach's Alpha: .48 | | |
| | | |
| 7. *Women and work* | | |
| Both husband and wife should contribute to household income | .81 | .68 |
| A working mom can have a good relationship with her kids | .78 | .65 |
| | | |
| Eigenvalue: 1.33 | | |
| % of variance: 3.90 | | |
| Cronbach's Alpha: .45 | | |
| | | |
| 8. *Teaching children independence* | | |
| Independence is important for children to learn at home | .80 | .68 |
| Obedience is important for children to learn at home | .73 | .63 |
| | | |
| Eigenvalue: 1.13 | | |
| % of variance: 3.31 | | |
| Cronbach's Alpha: .41 | | |
| | | |
| 9. *Workplace conditions* | | |
| Good hours is an important aspect of a job | .74 | .58 |
| Good pay is an important aspect of a job | .68 | .51 |
| Generous holidays is an important aspect of a job | .68 | .59 |
| | | |
| Eigenvalue: 1.38 | | |
| % of variance: 4.07 | | |
| Cronbach's Alpha: .58 | | |

Table 2.1 (*Cont.*)

| Dimensions and indicators | Factor loadings | Communalities |
|---|---|---|
| 10. *Workplace motivations* | | |
| An opportunity to use initiative is an important aspect of a job | .68 | .50 |
| A job that meets one's abilities is important | .66 | .47 |
| A job in which you can achieve something is important | .58 | .38 |
| A responsible job is important | | |

Eigenvalue: 1.90
% of variance: 5.59
Cronbach's Alpha: .55

11. *Posmaterialism*
As measured by Inglehart's standard 4-item battery

Note: The preceding factor analysis was conducted using Principal Component Analysis, with Varimax rotation.

ᵃ For exact question wording and coding see Appendix A.

*Source*: 2000 World Values Survey.

future orientations, views about the economy; their religious outlooks, ethical outlooks, and moral priorities. After repeated iterations, ten fairly robust factors, based on 34 different indicators emerged. We note that the ten dimensions encompass a wide variety of value domains, and these same domains also emerge from exploratory factor analysis of the WVS data in other countries.[1]

The first two dimensions consider religious values. *Subjective religiosity* measures personal religious belief, while the *church leadership* factor reflects views about the adequacy of church leadership on issues of the day. The third and fourth dimensions consider orientations toward *moral* and *civil permissiveness*,[2] while the fifth and sixth dimensions consider support for free markets (*market economics*) and beliefs about the role of *technology and science* in society. Two dimensions capture different aspects of family values. The first deals with attitudes toward *women and work* (or working mothers), and the second with, *teaching children independence*

---

[1] Following each "sweep" of the data, variables with the weakest factor loadings or communalities were dropped from consideration. These same value dimensions repeatedly re-emerged across different time points, and across different countries.

[2] These dimensions have repeatedly emerged in other analyses of WVS data. Norris and Inglehart 2003; Nevitte 1996.

(or child rearing values). Two dimensions related to the workplace also emerge. The first, *workplace conditions*, is a dimension that has to do with the importance of factors such as hours of work, the level of pay, and the number of holidays, while the *workplace motivations* dimension measures support for such expressive considerations as opportunities to use one's initiative, and the desire to be personally challenged in the workplace. In addition to these ten value dimensions, our analysis also includes the now standard four-item post-materialism scale (Inglehart, 1977; Inglehart, Baganez and Moreno 1998), which is designed to tap material versus post-material outlooks. In all, the following analysis considers eleven value dimensions.

*Findings*

Table 2.2 begins by looking generally at the evolution of Canadian values on these dimensions, and the evidence indicates that there have been significant value shifts across ten of the eleven value dimensions considered. The exception to the pattern concerns value stability on the workplace conditions dimension. Moreover, in the cases for which there are data across the entire two decades, the indications are that the 1990–2000 value changes have typically continued along the trajectory evident from the trends found in the 1981–1990 period. Most striking, perhaps, are the relatively sharp increases in subjective religiosity, the increased support for women in the workplace, and the increased proportion of people who attach great importance to teaching children the value of independence. There are also some noteworthy changes in the opposite direction: significantly fewer people think that church leadership on the issues of the day is adequate, there has been a significant decline in the importance people attach to expressive workplace motivations, and support for the market economy has also declined. These aggregate changes are an important starting point. If significant value changes have taken place, it is entirely possible that there may also be significant changes in the scope and scale of the value gaps across various cleavages. However, what needs to be determined is first, whether the value gaps across cleavages have widened, remained stable, or narrowed, and, second, whether those value gaps are consequential for political support.

Table 2.2. Value Change in Canada.

| Value dimension | Year 1981 | 1990 | 2000 | Trend Trajectory |
|---|---|---|---|---|
| Subjective religiosity *(high)* | | 29% | 38%*** | Rising |
| Church leadership *(adequate)* | | 36% | 28%*** | Falling |
| Moral permissiveness *(high)* | 8% | 24% | 27%*** | Rising |
| Civil permissiveness *(low)* | 76% | 79% | 83%*** | Rising |
| Market economics *(high support)* | | 75% | 68%*** | Falling |
| Technology and science *(high support)* | 52% | 58% | 62%*** | Rising |
| Women and work *(strong support)* | | 8% | 16%*** | Rising |
| Teaching kids independence *(strong support)* | 21% | 37% | 48%*** | Rising |
| Workplace conditions *(very important)* | 21% | 20% | 20% | Stable |
| Workplace motivations *(very important)* | 32% | 30% | 21%*** | Falling |
| Postmaterialism | 15% | 24% | 28%*** | Rising |

*** significant at p < .001

*Source*: 1981, 1990 and 2000 World Values Surveys.

*The gender gap*

Table 2.3 captures the evolution of gender differences across each of the eleven value dimensions and, on balance, the indications are that there has been a widening of the average gender gap on these value dimensions. Canadian males and females both became more religious over the last decade, but the increase was steeper for women than for men, and thus there has been a slight value divergence on this dimension. Conversely, confidence in the adequacy of church leadership declined over the 1990–2000 decade, but the rate of decline was steeper for men than for women, and the gender difference on this dimension is now statistically significant.

When it comes to moral and civil permissiveness, the trends are less consistent. Although the magnitude of the gender gap on the moral permissiveness dimension has narrowed, the gender differences have

Table 2.3. The Gender Gap in Canada.

| Value dimension | 1981 Male | Female | Gap | 1990 Male | Female | Gap | 2000 Male | Female | Gap | Gap 1981–2000 |
|---|---|---|---|---|---|---|---|---|---|---|
| Subjective religiosity (high) | | | | 26% | 32% | 6%*** | 33% | 41% | 8%*** | Diverging |
| Church leadership (adequate) | | | | 34% | 37% | 3% | 24% | 31% | 7%* | Diverging |
| Moral permissiveness (high) | 6% | 11% | 5% | 22% | 26% | 4% | 25% | 28% | 3%* | Converging |
| Civil permissiveness (low) | 74% | 77% | 3% | 76% | 82% | 6%* | 79% | 85% | 6%** | Stable (1990–2000) |
| Market economics (high support) | | | | 75% | 74% | 1% | 71% | 65% | 6%* | Diverging |
| Technology and science (high support) | 55% | 49% | 6% | 62% | 54% | 8%*** | 70% | 56% | 14%*** | Diverging |
| Women and work (strong support) | | | | 7% | 10% | 3%* | 13% | 18% | 5%** | Diverging |
| Teaching kids independence (strong support) | 16% | 27% | 11%*** | 35% | 39% | 4%* | 46% | 49% | 3% | Converging |
| Workplace conditions (very important) | 23% | 18% | 5%** | 22% | 19% | 3%* | 22% | 20% | 3%** | Stable (1990–2000) |
| Workplace motivations (very important) | 33% | 31% | 2%* | 30% | 30% | 0% | 23% | 20% | 3%** | Diverging (1990–2000) |
| Postmaterialism | 16% | 13% | 3%* | 29% | 19% | 10%*** | 31% | 25% | 6% | Converging (1990–2000) |
| **Average gender gap (total gaps/total value dimensions)** | **5%** | | | **4.36%** | | | **5.73%** | | | |

* significant at p < .05; ** significant at p < .01; *** significant at p < .001.

*Source*: 1981, 1990 and 2000 World Values Surveys.

become more significant. Conversely, the difference between males and females on the issue of civil permissiveness has remained relatively stable over the last decade, and it continues to remain significant.

With respect to economic values, support for the market economy has declined among both men and women, but men are consistently more supportive of free markets than women, and the gender gap has become significant. The most striking finding of all concerns the very substantial gender gap on values related to beliefs in technology and science. This significant value gap has almost doubled in size over the course of the last twenty years, with men being more inclined to support the advancement of science and technology in spite of the sharp increases in the proportion of women with very high levels of formal education.

As far as family values are concerned, both Canadian men and women have become more supportive of working mothers, but support for working mothers has increased more sharply among women than among men. Thus, the gender gap on this dimension has not only widened, but continues to be significant. Intriguingly, however, when it comes to child rearing values, both men and women increasingly support the idea that independence is an important value to teach children. In fact, this is one of the few dimensions where the gender gap has narrowed to become insignificant.

Workplace values have also changed. Such working conditions as good hours, good pay and good holidays have gradually become more important for women, but remained more or less stable for men. Thus, on this dimension, the gender gap has narrowed slightly, but continues to be stable and significant. On the other dimension of workplace orientations, however, the evidence indicates that expressive considerations have become less important factors in motivating both men and women's employment choices, although the gender gap in this case has reemerged as being significant.

Finally, with respect to the post-materialist value dimension, the overall trend is consistent; both men and women in Canada have become increasingly post-materialist in their outlooks over the last two decades, but on this dimension the gender gap has narrowed and is no longer significant. Men are no longer significantly more post-materialist than women.

On balance, the bulk of evidence points to an increasingly significant and widening gender gap across these value domains. Of the eleven different value dimensions examined, the value differences between men and women in Canada have clearly converged and become insignificant on only two dimensions.

## The generation gap

Table 2.4 considers the very same value dimensions, and, in this case, we consider the generational divide to be defined as those born before 1945 and those born after 1960. The intriguing finding here is that the overall pattern is one of value convergence rather than divergence. Even so, there are nonetheless significant generational value gaps on seven of the eleven dimensions under consideration.

As one would expect, older Canadians tend to be more religious than their younger counterparts, but both the young and the old have become more religious since 1990. In this instance, the generation gap remains intact. Furthermore, older generations are more inclined than the young to believe that churches provide adequate leadership, although both groups have become less sanguine about the role of the church since 1990. However, even on this dimension, the generation gap remains significant.

The generation gap turns out to be widest on the two dimensions that measure different aspects of permissiveness. In both cases, younger generations tend to be significantly more permissive than older generations. The truly striking finding concerns the shifts within the moral permissiveness dimension. Here, the size of the generation gap has virtually tripled over the last two decades. With respect to the civil permissiveness dimension, there are also very substantial generational differences, but the overall pattern is one of convergence; both young and old have become less inclined to regard as justifiable violations of what might be regarded as "community standards'.

While different generations exhibit substantial differences with respect to permissiveness, differences in their orientations towards the economy, and technology and scientific advances have become insignificant. Support for the market economy has declined both among the younger and older generations, while support for technology and science has increased.

Support for women working outside the home virtually doubled between 1990 and 2000, but, not surprisingly, younger generations tend to be more inclined to support the idea than their older counterparts. On balance, the generation gap on this dimension has remained stable and significant. When it comes to child rearing values, however, the

Table 2.4. The Generation Gap in Canada.

| Value dimension | 1981 | | | 1990 | | | 2000 | | | Gap 1981–2000 |
|---|---|---|---|---|---|---|---|---|---|---|
| | Pre45 | Post60 | Gap | Pre45 | Post60 | Gap | Pre45 | Post60 | Gap | |
| Subjective religiosity (high) | | | | 34% | 25% | 9%* | 44% | 35% | 9%** | Stable |
| Church leadership (adequate) | | | | 47% | 29% | 18%*** | 36% | 23% | 13%*** | Converging |
| Moral permissiveness (very permissive) | 5% | 11% | 6%** | 17% | 25% | 8%** | 16% | 32% | 16%*** | Diverging |
| Civil permissiveness (low tolerance) | 84% | 58% | 26%*** | 87% | 69% | 18%*** | 91% | 76% | 15%*** | Converging |
| Market economics (high support) | | | | 70% | 77% | 7%* | 68% | 67% | 1% | Converging |
| Technology and science (high support) | 54% | 46% | 8%* | 60% | 56% | 4%*** | 61% | 62% | 1% | Converging |
| Women and work (strong support) | | | | 6% | 10% | 4%*** | 13% | 17% | 4%*** | Stable |
| Teaching kids independence (strong support) | 21% | 20% | 1% | 29% | 43% | 14%*** | 42% | 48% | 6% | Converging (1990–2000) |
| Workplace conditions (very important) | 21% | 20% | 1% | 22% | 18% | 4%** | 17% | 20% | 3%*** | Converging (1990–2000) |
| Workplace motivations (very important) | 30% | 31% | 1% | 30% | 30% | 0% | 21% | 21% | 0% | Stable (1990–2000) |
| Postmaterialism | 15% | 13% | 2% | 24% | 24% | 0% | 24% | 31% | 7%*** | Diverging (1990–2000) |
| **Average generation gap (total gaps / total value dimensions)** | **6.43%** | | | **7.82%** | | | **6.82%** | | | |

* significant at p < .05; ** significant at p < .01; *** significant at p < .001.

*Source:* 1981, 1990 and 2000 World Values Surveys.

generation gap has narrowed. Since 1990, the outlook of the older generation of Canadians has "caught up" with those of younger generation, to the point that the generational gap is no longer significant.

The evidence concerning workplace outlook is that there are modest but significant differences between the young and the old on working conditions; the young are somewhat more inclined than older Canadians to think that traditional job benefits are important. There is, however, no evidence of any generation gap when it comes to the importance attached to expressive benefits of the workplace. However, there have been significant shifts in the distribution of post-materialist values across the generations, and these are consistent with the direction of change predicted by the theory; younger Canadians are significantly more post-materialist than their older counterparts, and this gap has widened considerably, particularly since 1990.

On balance, the data indicate that, on these basic value dimensions, younger Canadians are more likely to disagree than to agree with their older counterparts. There is a significant generational gap on the majority of dimensions considered, even though the gap appears to be narrowing somewhat.

## The immigration gap

To what extent is there evidence of significant value divides between native born Canadians and immigrants? Table 2.5 examines the value differences between native born Canadians and immigrants from both traditional and non-traditional source countries. Overall, and for reasons already outlined (Schultz, Unipan and Gamba, 2000), the expectation is that the value orientations of immigrants from traditional source countries will be more like those of native born Canadians, and that the "value gap" will be wider between native born Canadians and those from non-traditional source countries. The data support that expectation. The values of immigrants from non-traditional source countries are diverging from those of native born Canadians on nine of the eleven dimensions considered. By comparison, there is value divergence between immigrants from traditional source countries and native born Canadians on only four dimensions. The widest and most significant gaps emerge on the following dimensions: immigrants from non-traditional source countries are more supportive of church leadership, they are less post-materialist, and they are less permissive on moral questions. By the same token, immigrants from non-traditional source

Table 2.5. The Immigration Gap in Canada.

| Value dimension | 1990 Native born | Immigrants[a] Trad. | Nontrad. | Gaps[b] 1 | 2 | 2000 Native born | Immigrants Trad. | Nontrad. | Gaps 1 | 2 | Gap 1990 2000 Native born vs. Trad. | Native born vs. nontrad. |
|---|---|---|---|---|---|---|---|---|---|---|---|---|
| Subjective religiosity (high) | 28% | 33% | 33% | 5%** | 5%* | 37% | 40% | 45% | 3%* | 8% | Converging | Diverging |
| Church leadership (adequate) | 35% | 38% | 50% | 3% | 15% | 27% | 28% | 35% | 1% | 8%** | Converging | Converging |
| Moral permissiveness (very permissive) | 24% | 25% | 18% | 1% | 6%** | 28% | 27% | 15% | 1% | 13%*** | Stable | Diverging |
| Civil permissiveness (low tolerance) | 79% | 79% | 79% | 0% | 0% | 83% | 86% | 77% | 3% | 6% | Diverging | Diverging |
| Market economics (high support) | 76% | 67% | 66% | 9%* | 10% | 68% | 76% | 61% | 8% | 7% | Converging | Converging |
| Technology and science (high support) | 57% | 58% | 60% | 1%* | 3% | 61% | 64% | 71% | 3% | 10%* | Diverging | Diverging |
| Women and work (strong support) | 9% | 6% | 11% | 3% | 2% | 17% | 12% | 13% | 5% | 4%* | Diverging | Diverging |
| Teaching kids independence (strong support) | 37% | 40% | 36% | 3% | 1% | 49% | 55% | 34% | 6% | 15%** | Diverging | Diverging |
| Workplace conditions (very important) | 21% | 18% | 22% | 3% | 1% | 20% | 22% | 24% | 2% | 4% | Converging | Diverging |
| Workplace motivations (very important) | 29% | 32% | 29% | 3% | 0% | 21% | 24% | 19% | 3% | 2% | Stable | Diverging |
| Postmaterialism | 23% | 27% | 28% | 4% | 5% | 28% | 32% | 18% | 4% | 10%* | Stable | Diverging |
| **Average immigration gap (total gaps/total value dimensions)** | | | | **3.18%** | **4.36%** | | | | **3.55%** | **7.91%** | | |

[a] The preceding results compare the immigration gap between native born Canadians and two distinct types of immigrants – those from traditional source countries (trad.) and those from nontraditional source countries (nontrad.).

[b] Gap 1 reflects differences between native born Canadians and immigrants from traditional source countries. Gap 2 reflects differences between native born Canadians and immigrants from nontraditional societies.

* significant at p < .05;  ** significant at p < .01;  *** significant at p < .001.

Source: 1990 and 2000 World Values Surveys.

countries are also more inclined than native born Canadians to express greater confidence in science and technology, they are less likely to be preoccupied with teaching their children independence, and they are less likely to support working mothers.

Overall, these data show more significant value gaps between native born Canadians and immigrants in 2000 than in 1990, and, on average, the value gaps between native born Canadians and both types of immigrants have widened.

*Value Diversity and Regime Support: Two Tests*

Evidently, there are significant value gaps across the three lines of cleavage. Moreover, the aggregate evidence indicates that there was greater value diversity in 2000 than in 1990. For all three cleavages, and across all eleven dimensions considered, the number of significant value gaps increased during the course of the decade.

One central insight provided by the Lipset and Rokkan line of theorizing was that deep value differences across cleavages signified challenges to societal integration that were consequential for regime support. In their original formulation, Lipset and Rokkan presumed, quite reasonably, that such objective differences as class, religious denomination, and cultural peripheries and centers provided reliable proxies for salient subjective value outlooks within different segments of these industrializing populations. In the post-industrial context, however, it is less clear that objective structural differences correspond as neatly as they once did to subjective value differences because of the value changes that have taken place. With the WVS data supplying directly comparable cross-time measures of the subjective values of populations, it becomes possible to provide a more direct test of the central proposition; namely, that *value diversity* across cleavages is associated systematically with variations in regime support.

A deeply divided society, one with a history of deep internal regional divisions (Simeon and Elkins, 1980), and one that evidently does have growing value gaps across significant cleavage lines, Canada serves as a useful initial test case. In this instance, the hypothesis is that, in those regions where value diversity is greatest, regime support is expected to be lowest.

By taking together the cumulative size of all of the value gaps across all three cleavages as indicating the extent of value diversity, it becomes possible to evaluate which of Canada's four main regions are relatively more, or less, diverse. By that measure, Quebec and Western Canada turn out to exhibit greater value diversity than do either Ontario or Atlantic Canada.

The data summarized in Figure 2.1 locate respondents in each of Canada's regions in a conceptual grid defined by levels of value diversity and confidence in governmental institutions. Levels of political support are measured by the extent to which respondents express higher or lower levels of confidence in the key institutions of the regime—"parliament" and "the government of Ottawa". The data indicate support for the hypothesis that support for governmental institutions is lowest in those regions where there is greater value diversity across the three cleavages (Quebec and Western Canada), and it is highest in the region (Ontario) where there is less value diversity.[3]

Demonstrating that greater value diversity is associated with variations in regime support within one country suggests only that the central hypothesis is plausible. However, a far more stringent set of tests is required for a theory to be potentially generalizable. First, the test would have to be conducted in multiple settings. Second, such a test would also have to empirically take into account other plausible explanations that might be considered as equally compelling reasons for variations in political support.

To conduct a broader test of the general hypothesis we can turn, once again, to WVS data from a variety of other countries. Figure 2.2 summarizes the general findings for the relationship between value diversity and regime support in 27 countries in 2000. In this instance, it is not possible to examine the value diversity across the immigrant versus native born populations because the country of birth variable was not included in the WVS in most countries participating in the surveys. The analysis reported in Figure 2.2, therefore, considers the same eleven value dimensions across the two cleavages (gender and generation) for which reliable data are available.

The essential finding is that there appears to be a significant cross-national pattern; the greater the value diversity within publics across the two cleavages, the lower the levels of public confidence in governmental institutions. In effect, for every one hundred point increase in

---

[3] Clearly, it is not social differentiation but value diversity that appears to be more important to regime support. In the Canadian setting, Ontario is socially more diverse than other parts of the country.

Figure 2.1. Diversity and Confidence in Government Institutions in Canada.

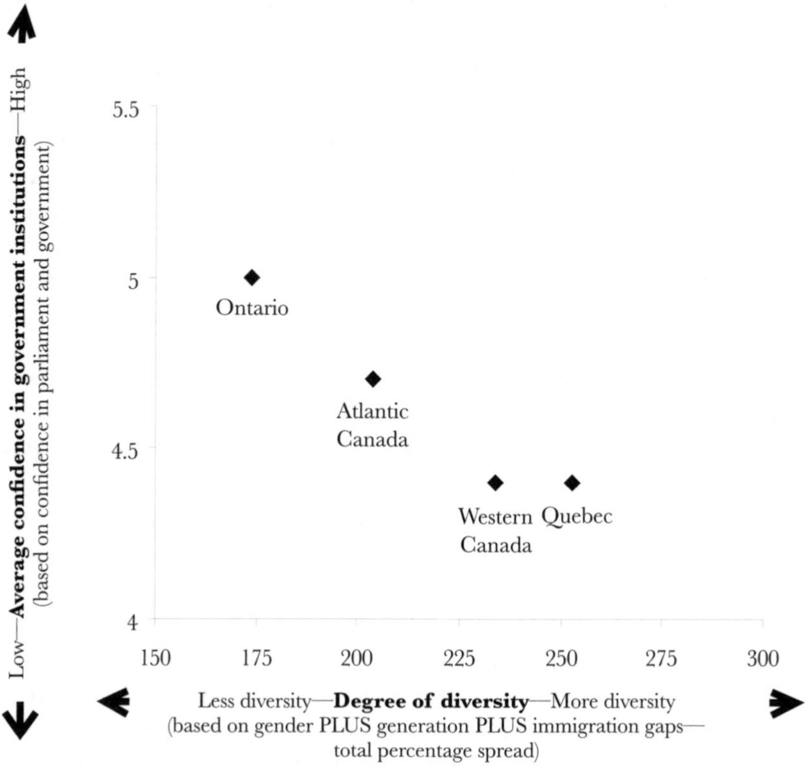

*Source*: 2000 World Values Surveys.

the value diversity index, there is a one point decline on the confidence in governmental institutions index.

There are, of course, a variety of possible reasons other than value diversity itself that might prompt publics to have greater, or lesser, support for governmental institutions (Listhaug and Wiberg, 1995; Newton and Norris, 2000). A more robust test turns on the question of whether the degree of value diversity remains a significant predictor of variations in confidence in governmental institutions once other possible sources of variation are taken into account. First, there are possible political explanations to consider. Publics who generally support democratic political systems, and who are more politically engaged, might be expected to express greater confidence in governmental institutions regardless of levels of diversity, or cohesion, in their core values. Then

Figure 2.2. Diversity and Confidence in Government Institutions in 27 Societies.

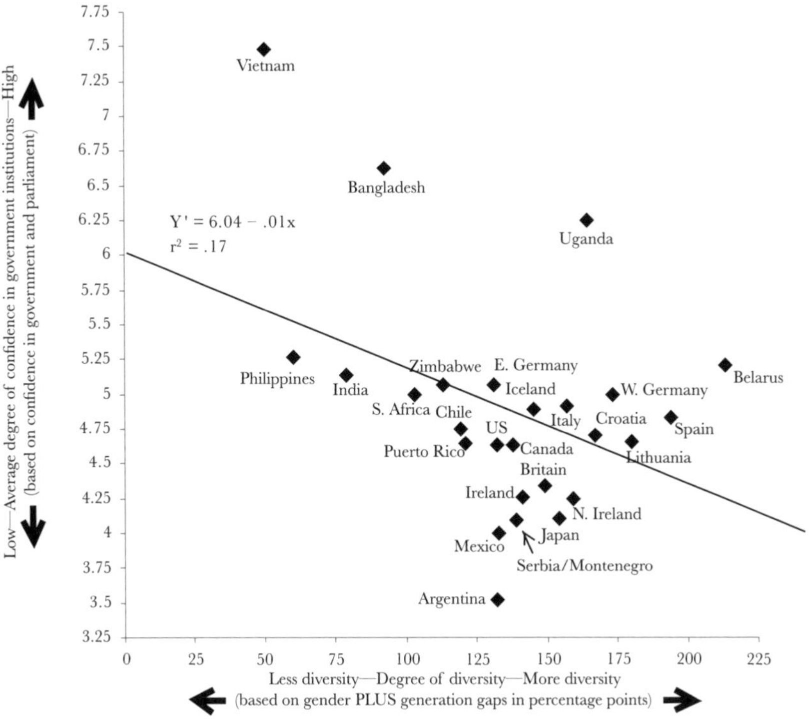

*Source*: 2000 World Values Surveys.

again, confidence in governmental institutions might well be related to such basic political outlooks as those relating to authority orientations (Eckstein 1969; Nevitte 1996).

In addition to these "political" explanations, there are also possible societal explanations to consider. For example, there are strong reasons to suppose that confidence in governmental institutions could well be attributable to levels of interpersonal trust. Both Coleman (1988) and Putnam (1993, 2000) make a persuasive case that the effective functioning of governmental and non-governmental institutions is closely related to interpersonal trust and "the norms of reciprocity". One also might suppose that publics with high levels of "life satisfaction" might be inclined to express greater "satisfaction," or confidence in governmental institutions.

Table 2.6. Regression analysis—The Determinants of Confidence in
Governmental Institutions

| Predictors | Beta |
|---|---|
| Life satisfaction<br>*(societies with high levels of life satisfaction)* | −.28** |
| Support for the democratic political system<br>*(societies where support for democracy is low)* | −.42** |
| Political engagement<br>*(societies where the frequency of political discussion is high)* | .20** |
| Willingness to challenge political authority<br>*(societies with higher protest activity/potential)* | −.17** |
| Interpersonal trust<br>*(societies with high levels of interpersonal trust)* | .01* |
| **Degree of diversity**<br>***(more diverse societies)*** | **−.35** |
| Constant | 11.19** |
| R² | .49 |

\* significant at p <. 05; \*\* significant at p <. 001.

*Source*: 2000 World Values Survey.

To explore whether value diversity is related systematically to levels of confidence in governmental institutions, we turn to a multivariate model, one that is tested using 2000 WVS data from all of the 27 countries considered in Table 2.6. Confidence in governmental institutions, our proxy for political support, is the dependent variable, and indicators for life satisfaction, support for the democratic political system, political engagement, willingness to challenge political authority and interpersonal trust, along with degree of societal value diversity, are entered as control variables.

The overall findings are clear. All of the variables exhibit statistically significant effects, and the effects operate in the direction that most of the theoretical literature would expect. Political engagement, for example, is positively and significantly related to confidence in governmental institutions, and, in those societies where protest activity and potential is higher, confidence in governmental institutions is lower. The only exception is that greater life satisfaction appears to lead to lower, and not higher, levels of confidence in governmental institutions.

The most significant findings to emerge, however, concern the relative predictive power of the independent variables which together account for a very substantial 49% of the variance in the dependant variable. It comes as little surprise to find that all of the explicitly political variables—support for the democratic system, political engagement, and willingness to challenge political authority—emerge as significant predictors. Indeed, general evaluations of the democratic political system is the single most powerful predictor of all. Two other findings are, perhaps, more surprising. First, of all of the "non-political" variables, the degree of value diversity is by far the most powerful predictor of levels of confidence in governmental institutions (−.35). The greater the level of value diversity in these societies, the lower the levels of public support for governmental institutions. The second surprising finding to emerge is that, once other factors, including value diversity, are taken into account, interpersonal trust contributes very little explanatory leverage (.01) in levels of public confidence in institutions.

*Concluding Discussion*

We began with the observation that value cleavages have long been considered to be pertinent to understanding variations in regime support. The pioneering contribution of Lipset and Rokkan serves as a foundation for interpreting how party systems mediated powerful societal cleavages during the transformations associated with the dynamics of industrialism. This analysis has attempted to advance those conceptual concerns in two directions. First, we argue that objective cleavages, by themselves, are not a significant basis from which to understand variations in regime support; rather, what is required is a more nuanced view of the interactions of cleavages and structural and value change. Second, we suggest that the scope and scale of value gaps across "new" cleavages may provide a useful vantage point from which to explore variations in regime support in post-industrial states. As societies become more diverse, and as new cleavages emerge as increasingly salient to more mobile societies, the goal of understanding the linkages between value diversity and "governability" becomes more pressing.

The Canadian case is an apt starting point for evaluating how value change and diversity might be related to regime support. It is a deeply divided advanced industrial state with atypically high levels of population mobility. Of course, one case, however illuminating, is an insufficient foundation for exploring a general hypothesis.

The analyses of cross-national evidence, however, suggests a broader application with broader implications. For reasons of practicality, this particular investigation was limited to considering two cleavages and eleven value dimensions in 27 countries. What is clearly required is a broader research agenda that includes for consideration a greater number of cleavages, in more countries, and across more time points.

*Appendix A: Operationalization and Coding*

Interpersonal trust

*Question: Generally speaking, would you say that most people can be trusted or that you need to be very careful in dealing with people?*

Most people can be trusted = 1; need to be careful = 0.

Civic engagement

*Question: Please look at the following list of voluntary organizations and activities and say which, if any, you belong to.*

Included in the 1981, 1990 and 2000 WVS were:

Social welfare services for elderly, handicapped or deprived people (belong = 1; not mentioned = 0)
Religious or church organizations (belong = 1; not mentioned = 0)
Education, arts, music or cultural activities (belong = 1; not mentioned = 0)
Labor unions (belong = 1; not mentioned = 0)
Political parties or groups (belong = 1; not mentioned = 0)
Local community action on issues like poverty, employment, housing, racial equality (belong = 1; not mentioned = 0)
Third world development or human rights (belong = 1; not mentioned = 0)
Conservation, the environment, ecology, animal rights (belong = 1; not mentioned = 0)
Professional associations (belong = 1; not mentioned = 0)
Youth work (e.g. scouts, guides, youth clubs etc.)

New organizations and activities added to the 1990 and 2000 WVS include:

Sports and recreation (belong = 1; not mentioned = 0)
Women's groups (belong = 1; not mentioned = 0)
Peace movement (belong = 1; not mentioned = 0)
Voluntary organizations concerned with health (belong = 1; not mentioned = 0)
Other groups (belong = 1; not mentioned = 0)

Religious beliefs

*Question: For each of the following, indicate how important it is in your life. Would you say it is: very important, rather important, not very important, not at all important?*

Religion (not at all important = 4; very important = 1)

*Question: Which, if any, of the following do you believe in?*

Do you believe in God? (no = 1; yes = 0)
Do you believe in life after death? (no = 1; yes = 0)
Do you believe in hell? (no = 1; yes = 0)
Do you believe in heaven? (no = 1; yes = 0)

*Question: How important is God in your life? Please use this scale to indicate: 10 means very important, and 1 means not at all important.*

(1 to 5 = 1; 6 to 10 = 0)

The "religious beliefs" index adds the preceding six indicators into a composite measure, where 0, means highly religious, and 6, means not very religious.

Role of the church

*Question: Generally speaking, do you think that the churches in your country are giving adequate answers to:*

The moral problems and needs of the individual? (no = 1; yes = 0)
The problems of family life? (no = 1; yes = 0)
People's spiritual needs? (no = 1; yes = 0)
The social problems facing our country today? (no = 1; yes = 0)

The "role of the church" index adds the preceding four indicators into a composite measure, where 0, means that the church plays an adequate role, and 4, means that the church plays a not so adequate role.

## Moral permissiveness

*Question: Please tell me for each of the following statements on this card whether you think it can always be justified, never be justified, or something in between.*

Homosexuality (6 to 10 = 1; 0 to 5 = 0)
Abortion (6 to 10 = 1; 0 to 5 = 0)
Divorce (6 to 10 = 1; 0 to 5 = 0)
Euthanasia (6 to 10 = 1; 0 to 5 = 0)
Suicide (6 to 10 = 1; 0 to 5 = 0)

The "moral permissiveness" index adds the preceding five indicators into a composite measure, where 0 means not very morally permissive, and 5 means very morally permissive.

## Civil permissiveness

*Question: Please tell me for each of the following statements on this card whether you think it can always be justified, never be justified, or something in between.*

Claiming government benefits to which you are not entitled (6 to 10 = 1; 0 to 5 = 0)
Avoiding a fare on public transport (6 to 10 = 1; 0 to 5 = 0)
Cheating on taxes if you have a chance (6 to 10 = 1; 0 to 5 = 0)
Someone accepting a bribe in the course of their duties (6 to 10 = 1; 0 to 5 = 0)

The "civil permissiveness" index adds the preceding four indicators into a composite measure, where 0 indicates a low tolerance for civil permissiveness, and 5 a high tolerance for civil permissiveness.

## Market economics

*Question: Now I'd like you to tell me your views on various issues. How would you place your views on this scale? 1 means you agree completely with the statement on the left; 10 means you agree completely with the statement on the right; and if your views fall somewhere in between, you can choose any number in between.*

Competition is good. It stimulates people to work hard and develop new ideas (statement on the left). OR Competition is harmful. It brings out the worst in people (statement on the right).

(0 to 5 = 1; 6 to 10 = 0)

Private ownership of business and industry should be increased (statement on the left). OR Government ownership of business and industry should be increased (statement on the right).

(0 to 5 = 1; 6 to 10 = 0)

The "market economics" index adds the preceding two indicators into a composite measure, where 0 indicates low support for a market-based economy, and 2 means a high level of support for a market-based economy.

Technology and science

*Question: I'm going to read out a list of various changes in our way of life that might take place in the near future. Please tell me for each one, if it were to happen, whether you think it would be a good thing, a bad thing or you don't mind.*

More emphasis on the development of technology (good = 3; don't mind = 2; bad = 1)

*Question: In the long run, do you think the scientific advances we are making will help or harm mankind?*

(help = 3; both = 2; harm = 1)

The "technology and science" index adds the preceding two indicators into a composite measure, where 2 means a low support for technology and science, and 6 means a high level of support for technology and science.

Women and work

*Question: For each of the following statements I read out, can you tell me how much you agree with each. Do you agree strongly, agree, disagree or disagree strongly?*

A working mother can establish just as warm and secure a relationship with her children as a mother who does not work (agree strongly = 4; agree = 3; disagree = 2; disagree strongly = 1)

Both husband and wife should contribute to household income (agree strongly = 4; agree = 3; disagree = 2; disagree strongly = 1)

The "woman and work" index adds the preceding two indicators into a composite measure, where 2 means low support for working mothers, and 8 means very strong support for working mothers.

## Child rearing

*Question: Here is a list of qualities that children can be encouraged to learn at home. Which, if any, do you consider to be especially important? Please choose up to five.*

Independence (important = 1; not mentioned = 0)
Obedience (not mentioned = 1; important = 0)

The "child rearing" index adds the preceding two indicators into a composite measure, where 0 indicates low support for encouraging children to learn to be independent, and 2 means a high level of support for encouraging children to learn to be independent.

## Conditional attributes of employment

*Question: Here are some more aspects of a job that people say are important. Please look at them and tell me which ones you personally think are very important?*

Good pay (mentioned = 1; not mentioned = 0)
Good hours (mentioned = 1; not mentioned = 0)
Generous holidays (mentioned = 1; not mentioned = 0)

The "conditional attributes of employment" index adds the preceding three indicators into a composite measure, where 0 means low support for the conditional attributes of employment, and 3 means a high level of support for the conditional attributes of employment.

## Intrinsic attributes of employment

*Question: Here are some more aspects of a job that people say are important. Please look at them and tell me which ones you personally think are very important?*

An opportunity to use initiative (mentioned = 1; not mentioned = 0)
A job in which you can achieve something (mentioned = 1; not mentioned = 0)
A responsible job (mentioned = 1; not mentioned = 0)
A job that meets one's abilities (mentioned = 1; not mentioned = 0)

The "intrinsic attributes of employment" index adds the preceding four indicators into a composite measure, where 0 means low support for the intrinsic attributes of employment, and 3 means a high level of support for the intrinsic attributes of employment.

## Post-materialism

This indicator is operationalized using Inglehart's standard 4–item battery.
For details, see (Inglehart, 1977; Inglehart, Basanez and Mareno, 1998)

## Degree of social cohesion

For the Canadian component of this analysis, this indicator is measured by adding the gender, generation and immigration gaps. For the cross-national component of this analysis, this indicator is measured by adding the gender and generation gaps.

(regional/societal scores = total percentage spread)

## Life satisfaction

*Question: All things considered, how satisfied are you with your life as a whole these days?*

(societal scores = average life satisfaction on a scale from 1, meaning dissatisfied, to 10, meaning satisfied)

## Support for the democratic political system

*Question: I'm going to describe various types of political systems and ask what you think about each as a way of governing this country. For each one, would you say it is a very good, fairly good, fairly bad or very bad way of governing this country?*

Having a democratic political system (societal scores = average societal ratings)

## Political engagement

*Question: When you get together with your friends, would you say you discuss political matters frequently, occasionally or never?*

(societal scores = average percentage of frequent discussion)

## Willingness to challenge political authority

*Question: Now I'd like you to look at this card. I'm going to read out some different forms of political action that people can take, and I'd like you to tell me, for each one, whether you have actually done any of these things, whether you might do it or would never, under any circumstances, do it*

Signing a petition (have done = 3; might do = 2; would never do = 1)

Joining in boycotts (have done = 3; might do = 2; would never do = 1)

Attending lawful demonstrations (have done = 3; might do = 2; would never do = 1)

Joining unofficial strikes (have done = 3; might do = 2; would never do = 1)

(societal scores = average level of willingness to challenge political authority based on an additive index constructed form the preceding four indicators)

## References

Beaujot, Roderic. 2003. "Effect of Immigration on the Canadian Population: Replacement Migration?" Paper presented at the meetings of the Canadian population Society: Halifax.

Bilodeau, A. and Neil Nevitte. 2003. *Trust, Tolerance, and Confidence in Institutions: Evidence from the Canadian World Values Surveys, 1990–2000*. Report prepared for Canadian Heritage.

Coleman, J.S. 1988. Social Capital in the Creation of Human Capital. *American Journal of Sociology*, 94 (Supplement), S95–S120.

Dalton, R. 2002. *Citizen Politics: Public Opinion and Political Parties in Advanced Industrial Democracies*. Third Edition. Seven Bridges Press, Inc.: Chatham House Publishers.

Elkins, David and Richard E.B. Simeon. 1980. *Small Worlds*: Provinces and Parties in Canadian Political Life. Toronto: Methuen.

Franklin, Mark. 1985. *The Decline of Class Voting in Britain: Changes in the Basis of Electoral Choice 1964–1983*. Oxford: Oxford University Press.

Franklin, Mark *et al.* 1992. Electoral Change: Responses to Evolving Social and Attitudinal Structures in Western Countries. Cambridge: Cambridge University Press.

Halman, Loek and Ole Riis. 1999. *European Values Studies*. ed. Tilburg: Tilburg University Press 1999.

Inglehart, Ronald. 1997. *Modernization and Postmodernization: Cultural, Economic, and Political Change in 43 Societies*. Princeton, N.J.: Princeton University Press.

——. 1990. *Cultural Shift in Advanced Industrial Society*. Princeton, N.J.: Princeton University Press.

——. 1977. *The Silent Revolution: Changing Values and Political Styles Among Western Publics*. Princeton, N.J.: Princeton University Press.

Inglehart, R., Basanez, M., and Mareno, A. (1998). *Human values and Beliefs: A Cross cultural sourcebook*. Ann Arbor: University of Michigan Press.

Inglehart, Ronald and Pippa Norris. 2003. *Gender Equality and Cultural Change*. New York and Cambridge: Cambridge University Press.

Inglehart, Ronald and Christian Welzel. 2003. Democratic Institutions and Political Culture: Misconceptions in Addressing the Ecological Fallacy. *Comparative Politics* (forthcoming).

Inglehart, Ronald, Pippa Norris and Christian Welzel. 2003. "Gender Equality and Democracy." *Comparative Sociology* 1 (3), 321–345.

Lipset, S. Martin and Stein Rokkan. 1967. "Cleavage Structures, Party Systems, and Voter Alignments: An Introduction," in *Party Systems and Voter Alignments: Cross-National Perspectives*. eds. Lipset and Rokkan. New York: Free Press.

Listhaug, O. and M. Wiberg. 1995. "Confidence in Political Institutions," in *Citizens and the State*. eds. H.D. Klingemann and D. Fuchs. Oxford: Oxford University Press.

Nevitte, Neil. 1996. *The Decline of Deference: Canadian Value Change in Cross-National Perspective*. Peterborough: Broadview Press.

Nevitte, N. and Mebs Kanji. 2003. *"Immigrant Orientations Towards Sustainability: Evidence from the Canadian World Values Surveys, 1990–2000."* Report prepared for Citizenship Canada.

———. 2003. *"Immigrants and Work: Findings from the 1990 and 2000 World Values Surveys (Canada)."* Report prepared for Citizenship Canada.

Newton, K. and P. Norris. 2000. "Confidence in Public Institutions: Faith, Culture, or Performance?" in *Disaffected Democracies: What's Troubling the Trilateral Countries?* eds. Pharr, S. and R. Putnam. Princeton, N.J.: Princeton University Press.

Norris, Pippa. 1999. "Introduction: The Growth Of Political Citizens." In *Critical Citizens: Global Support for Democratic Governance*. ed. Pippa Norris. Oxford: Oxford University Press.

Norris, Pippa and Ronald Inglehart. 2003. "Islamic Culture and Democracy: Testing the 'Clash of Civilizations' Thesis." *Comparative Sociology*, 1(3), 235–263.

Putnam, R. 2000. *Bowling Alone: The Collapse and Revival of American Community*. New York: Simon and Schuster.

———. 1993. *Making Democracy Work: Civic Traditions in Modern Italy*. Princeton: Princeton University Press.

Statistics Canada. 2003. *2001 Census Analysis Series: The Changing Profile of Canada's Labour Force*.

———. 2003. *2001 Census Analysis Series: Education in Canada: Raising the Standard*.

Schultz, P.W., J.B. Unipan and R.J. Gamba (2000). "Acculturation and Ecological Worldview Among Latino Americans." *The Journal of Environmental Education*, 31 (2), 22–27.

Welzel, C., Ronald Inglehart and Hans-Dieter Klingemann. 2003. "The Theory of Human Development: A Cross Cultural Analysis" *European Journal of Political Research*, 42 (3), 341–379.

Welzel, C. and R. Inglehart. 2001. *Human Development and the 'Explosion' of Democracy: Variations of Regime Change Across 60 Societies*," Discussion Paper for Wissenschaftszentrum Berlin für Sozialforschung (WZB). Berlin.

# B. LATIN AMERICA

CHAPTER THREE

## VALUE CHANGE IN MEXICO, 1980–2000: EVIDENCE FROM THE WORLD VALUES SURVEYS

Miguel Basáñez and Alejandro Moreno

Mexico is one of the countries that participated with national samples in each of the four waves of the World Values Surveys (WVS) conducted between 1981 and 2000, providing, along with Argentina, the only two Latin American settings with two decades of longitudinal data. The four Mexican samples measured the persistence and change of values during the last two decades of the twentieth century in a society undergoing rapid and profound change in its political system, its economic structure, and its social features. Since the first Mexican survey, conducted in 1981, polling methodologies have improved substantially, and survey research techniques have become more widely used in Mexican social and political sciences. Although all four surveys relied on national representative samples of Mexican adults, changes in sampling techniques and the availability of better sampling frames in Mexico may raise some methodological concerns. However, even with some possible methodological differences, an analysis of the four surveys tells us much about how Mexican values persist and change over time.

In this chapter, we go beyond the descriptive review of the 1990 World Values Survey (Basáñez and Moreno 1994) and analyze general patterns of value change in Mexico by examining both the distribution of responses for some theoretically relevant questions over time, and the intergenerational differences in each year the survey was conducted. Value differences among age cohorts help us understand the nature of value change in Mexico and formulate new hypotheses about how Mexican society is likely to change in the coming years.

Our basic concern is to delineate those features of the Mexican value system that showed a significant change during the 1980s and 1990s as well as those aspects that have persisted. Of the possible approaches to the question of change and persistence, we focus on three issues that we consider of greatest theoretical significance. First, we look at the possible connection between the process of democratization and political attitudes. Second, we examine some of the value-orientations linked with the process of economic transformation. Finally, we look at social attitudes regarding the old and new issues that are salient in Mexican society.

Politically, Mexico experienced a rapid increase in electoral competition during the last two decades. The political reforms that began in 1977 and which deepened in the 1990s changed Mexican politics from a one-party regime to a competitive multi-party system, first at the local, and then at the national level. The first signs of a power transition were observed in 1989 at the state governor level. Shortly thereafter, in the presidential election of 1994, the Institutional Revolutionary Party (PRI), which had dominated the political scene for over six decades, was able to keep office, but, as we will argue later, the federal government paid an enormous price for the election, both socially with the Zapatista movement, and financially with all the funds transferred from the government to the PRI (Basáñez 1996). Also, it was unable to avoid the cyclical term-end crisis anticipated well in advance (Basáñez 1993a).

In 1997, the PRI lost control of Congress for the first time since the party was founded in 1929 and, in 2000, it lost the presidential election for the first time in seven decades. The Mexican party and electoral systems are now regarded as competitive, and elections, once fraudulent, are now free and fair. Immediately after the July 2000 elections, the majority of Mexicans, regardless of their partisan identifications, considered that Mexico was a democracy (Moreno 2003). Given this development towards democratic politics, one question we ask is whether or not there is a greater sense of political confidence among Mexicans.

Mexico's economic transformation involves the adoption of free-trade policies that were initiated in the 1980s and that intensified in the early 1990s. Economic reforms included the privatization of state enterprises, deregulation, and economic integration. The North American Free Trade Agreement (NAFTA) between Mexico, Canada, and the United States went into effect on January 1, 1994 after over four years of negotiations. Ten years later, NAFTA had changed not only much of Mexico's economic dynamics, but also many of Mexicans' preferences and expectations. Mexico has entered fully into a trend of conjunction with the U. S. and Canada (Inglehart, Nevitte, Basáñez 1996). There are clear changes in patterns of consumption, but strong social inequalities remain in the country. There is no consensus about the number of poor citizens, but the most optimistic views argue that 40% of Mexicans live in poverty. Given these patterns of economic transformation, have there been any changes in Mexicans' priorities and ideological orientations?

We would expect regional economic integration and political democratization to accompany shifts in social values and priorities, as well as a redefinition of what is preferable, desirable, and acceptable in society. Religious orientations not only persist, but seem to have strengthened among all age cohorts in the last two decades. Nonetheless, Mexicans have profound generational value differences. The 2000 survey registered some generational gaps not observed 20 years earlier. As evidenced in the most recent surveys, intergenerational value change seems to be taking place in Mexico; younger Mexicans seem to be guided by a set of values different from those of their elders, and this has had a significant political impact.

A once strong democratic-authoritarian political cleavage that crystallized in the party system in the 1990s has yielded centrality to rising social and cultural issues that seem to significantly affect party support (Moreno 1999, 2003). The liberal and fundamentalist views of politics and society contrast sharply, and age is one the main determinants. Although Mexico has a comparatively low level of economic development, Materialist and Post-materialist values have a noticeably stronger generational gap now than before, with younger Mexicans being decreasingly Materialist and increasingly Post-materialist. As we shall try to show and explain below, certain other attitudes towards society have also changed dramatically.

In the following pages, we first examine the persistence in religious values as well as the changing mix of Catholics, Protestants and the non-religious. We also comment on the possible impact of this change in religious composition on economic and political variables.

Second, we examine the trends in political confidence in a society that has experienced rapid and significant political change. Despite a widespread wave of political democratization in the world, data indicate a decline in political trust in new democracies and Mexico is part of this downward trend. However, a more precise answer depends on how political trust is understood and measured. As Catterberg and Moreno (2006:31) argue, "political trust, understood as citizen's confidence in political institutions, has declined in the new democracies during the last two decades and does not seem to have increased in established ones either." A focus on institutions shows a decline in trust that also parallels a decline in political participation as a general "post-honeymoon" trend in new and emerging democracies (Catterberg and Inglehart 2002).

Third, we analyze changes in Mexicans' belief systems by looking at two of the three main dimensions of Mexican ideology: a value dimension that polarizes liberal and fundamentalist views that not only seems salient in Mexico, but in other Latin American nations as well (Moreno 1999), and an economic dimension that confronts a redistributive left versus a capitalist right. Perhaps as a response to economic integration and economic reforms, there have been important shifts in the economic dimension during the last decade, which signals one of the most significant attitudinal changes among the Mexican public. However, intergenerational differences are more noticeable along the liberal-fundamentalist dimension, based on views toward homosexuality, abortion, gender roles and national pride, which suggests that this dimension has the potential to influence the dynamics of party politics in the near future, even more so than the democratic-authoritarian axis that prevailed during the 1990s (Moreno 2003).

Fourth, although the four Mexican surveys evidence the persistence of religious values over time, it is also clear that social and political views and values have changed significantly in the last two decades. On the one hand, there has been a shift from radicalism to conservatism. Although decreasingly so, a preference for moderate reforms has been the majority view since the early 1980s: the proportion of those who supported for gradual reforms as opposed to radical change or preservation of the status quo was 68% in 1981, 60% in 1990, 52% in 1996–97, and 49% in 2000. However, preferences for radical change and for the status quo have become increasingly important and, it appears, are polarizing. Moreover, "conservative" views have become more common than radical ones in the last few years, even though radical views were dominant in the early surveys. The fact that younger generations are especially favorable to this new "conservatism" implies that the idea of "defending society against all subversive forces," as the question is worded, may evoke a different frame of reference for the younger generations. It is possible that the desire to defend the status quo in the Mexican context of the new century means defending the democratic system. The peasant rebellion and major political assassinations in the mid-1990s in Mexico could have contributed to the polarization of views toward change and continuity.

Finally, we look at the rise of a Materialist/Post-materialist value gap in Mexico evidenced in the recent surveys, and explore the possible explanations of why a society with a per capita income of slightly over USD 5,000 in the year 2000, and almost 60% of income concentrated in the highest two deciles, seems to be experiencing the rise of an intergenerational value gap. Using Inglehart's (1997) four-item values index, the proportion of Post-Materialists in Mexican society increased from 9% in 1981 to 12% in 1990, and then to 17% in 1996–97. The proportion of Post-materialists in the 2000 survey decreased slightly to 15%. Although still a minority, Post-materialists in Mexico grew 66% from 1981 to 2000. Moreover, the gap between Materialists and Post-materialists has narrowed among younger Mexicans, and it has broadened among older ones.

In sum, the Mexican WVS data provide clear evidence of *both* persisting and changing values, and how different in some regards that society is at the turn of the century from what it was only 20 years earlier.[1] We now turn our attention to some of these changes, and discuss the possible trajectories.

*Persisting Religious Values*

Norris and Inglehart (2002) remind us that religion is one of the most enduring cultural traits in society. As in most Latin American societies, Mexico has a predominantly Catholic population. According to the 2000 census, about 88% of the population aged at least five years old is of the Roman-Catholic faith, 5% belongs to a Protestant-evangelical tradition, 2% to a Biblical but non-evangelical tradition, almost 4% have no religion, and the rest belong to other religions. We believe that census data over-count Catholics and under-count non-religion respondents because of a *spiral of silence* (Noelle-Neumann 1993) effect. Nevertheless, the religious market in Mexico is still a monopolistic one dominated by the Catholic Church, just as the political market used to be dominated by the PRI. According to the 2000 Mexican WVS,

---

[1] All four waves of the WVS in Mexico are nationally representative samples of adults and interviews were conducted face to face in the respondents' homes. Samples sizes are: n = 1,837 in 1981, n = 1,531 in 1990, n = 1,511 in 1996/96, and n = 1,535 in 2000.

76% of the population over 18 years old are Catholic (12% less than the census and the 1981 WVS), and 22% have no religion (18% more than the census and the 1981 WVS). This is an important discrepancy that could reflect some serious sampling problems in the 1981 survey. In Mexico the number of Protestants of all traditions has been increasing steadily, and their values are very similar to those who have no religious affiliation. The increasing number of Protestants, plus those without a religious affiliation (26% according to survey data but significantly less according to census results), are likely to have a potentially accelerating effect on further values changes in Mexico (Basáñez 1986).

In 2000, nine out of ten respondents said that God is important in their lives, and this proportion is very similar across all age cohorts, as shown in Figure 3.1. Although the 1990 survey evidenced a decrease in the importance of God in people's lives, the importance attributed to God in 2000 is very similar to the one recorded by the 1980 survey.

Similarly, the self-conception of being a religious person and the levels of self-reported church attendance have barely changed in the last two decades. Again, the 1990 survey registered a slight decrease in both variables, but the fact is that the 1980 and 2000 surveys provide very similar figures, which indicates that religious values remained almost unchanged. Three quarters of the respondents in 1980 and 2000 (75 and 76%, respectively) said that they considered themselves a "religious person;" and slightly more than half (54 and 55%, respectively) said that they attended religious services at least once a week.

Although age is not related to the importance Mexicans attribute to God in their lives, it is clear that other religious variables behave differently depending on the age cohort in each of the survey years. The proportion of respondents that consider themselves religious decreases as we move from older to younger age cohorts, and this is the case in each of the surveys. In 2000, 85% of those born before 1940, and 71% of those born between 1970 and 1982, considered themselves religious, a gap of 14 percentage points. Twenty years earlier, the gap between oldest and youngest (1960–69) cohorts was only six percentage points. Likewise, church attendance is less likely among the youth, and the gap between the eldest and the youngest is wider, as shown in Figure 3.1. In 2000, 68% of Mexicans born before 1940 said they attended religious services at least once a week, and so did 49% of those born between 1970 and 1982, a 19 percentage point gap. Twenty years earlier, the gap in church attendance between the oldest (1900–1939) and youngest (1960–1969) cohorts was 13 points (70 and 57%, respectively).

Figure 3.1. Persistence of Religion. Importance of God, Religiosity, and Church Attendance in Mexico, 1980–2000.

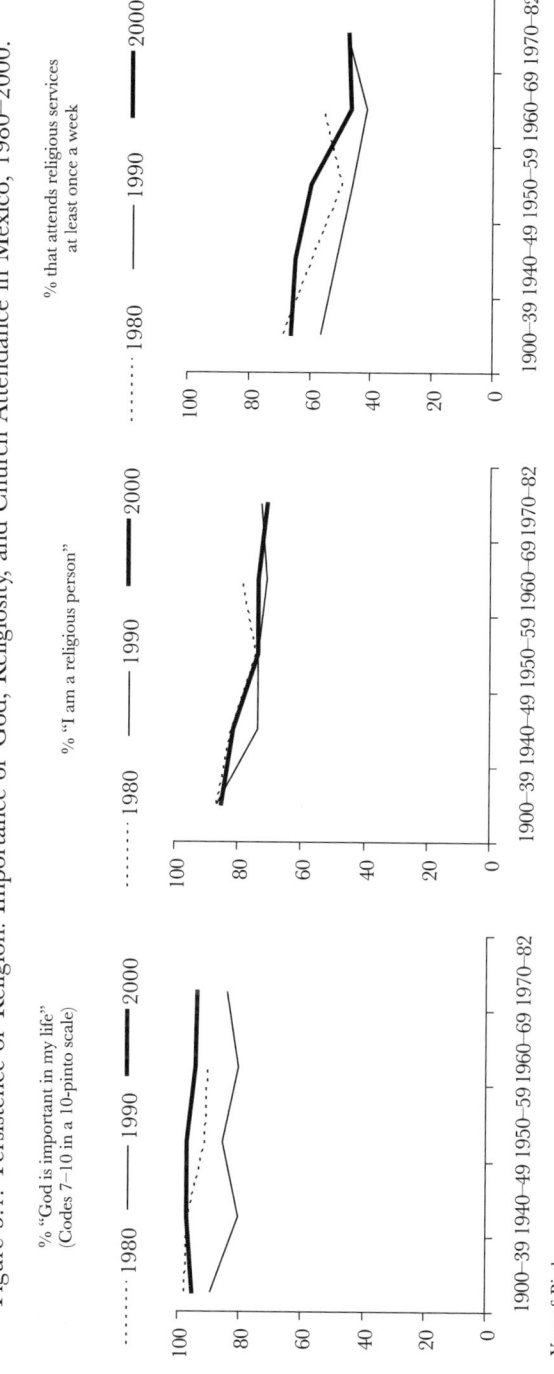

In sum, persistence rather than change is observed in the most basic religious orientations in Mexico during the last two decades. Although age seems to influence religious self-descriptions and patterns of church attendance, such influence is almost insignificant in the importance that Mexicans attribute to God in their lives. However, more and more individuals are moving away from Catholicism and embracing different value systems, although a profound political, economic, and social impact of this shift should not be expected soon. Two reasons can explain the delay. First, this is still a minority of the population. Second, and more important, the institutional environment in Mexico is Catholic.

Having noted the persistence of religious values, we now look at some of the values that indeed changed in Mexico during the last two decades of the twentieth century.

### Higher Levels of Political Trust

Based on the 1981–2000 WVS, Catterberg and Moreno (2006) found evidence of a decline in political trust in the new democracies of Latin America, Eastern Europe, and the post-Communist societies. Their dependent variable was a composite index of confidence in the legislative body and confidence in the civil service. They noted that confidence in institutions had been used as an indicator of political trust in cross-national studies, many of them using WVS data, but that the American literature, based heavily on the National Election Studies, had focused on other measures that reflect elements of ethics, honesty, and integrity of governance. Besides the typical question of confidence in institutions, the WVS questionnaire also offers a question similar to one of the items of trust in government that has been used in the American National Election Studies since 1964: "Generally speaking, would you say that this country is run by a few big interests looking out for themselves, or that it is run for the benefit of all the people?" (see Citrin and Muste 1999:483). The response that government acts for the benefit of all the people represents political trust. If this is the case, Mexicans became less distrustful over the last decade, although political distrust continued to dominate their political values (see Figure 3.2).

The proportion of Mexicans who believed that a few big interests ran their country decreased from 75 to 65% from 1990 to 2000. Despite a

Figure 3.2. Changes in Political Trust by Year of Birth.

% who said that "this country is run by a few big interests looking out for themselves" minus % who said that "this country is run for the benefit of all the people."

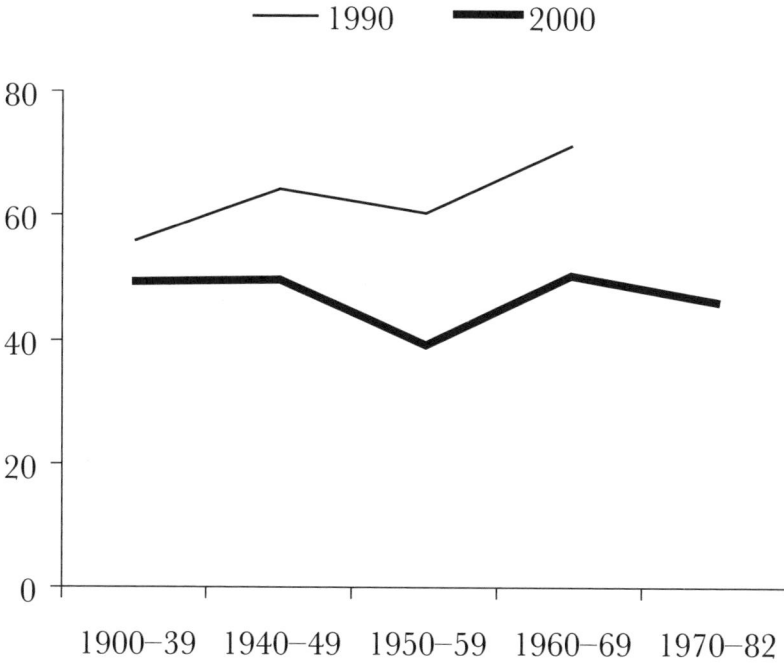

—— 1990      ━━ 2000

significant increase in political competition and more regular alternation, two-thirds still distrusted government. This may have changed after the presidential elections of July 2000, when the PRI lost the presidency to PAN candidate Vicente Fox (the values survey was conducted in February 2000, almost five months before the election). However, there is evidence that the election outcome changed many Mexican's views of their political system, not only increasing confidence in political institutions (Moreno 2002b), but also increasing the proportion of citizens that regarded Mexico as a democracy, from 37% one year before the election to 47% one month before the election, and to 66% one month after the election (Moreno 2006). The idea that Mexico is in fact a democracy almost doubled during the election year that brought political alternation in the highest-ranking office, the presidency.

Before that historical event, most Mexicans remained skeptical of government, and, in the best of cases, political distrust had only decreased slightly in the previous years. However, the proportion of respondents who said that the country is run for the benefit of all people changed from 18% in 1990 to 26% in 2000. Nevertheless, politically distrusting Mexicans still dominated.

Although there was not a monotonic relationship between political trust and age in 1990, the youngest cohorts of Mexicans were clearly more distrustful than the oldest ones that year; the net proportion of those who expressed distrust minus those who expressed trust was 71% among Mexicans born between 1960 and 1969, the youngest cohort, whereas that proportion was 56% among those born between 1900 and 1939, the oldest cohort. However, this relationship disappeared in the 2000 survey, when the net percentage of political distrust was 50 and 49 among those same-age cohorts, and 46 among the new and youngest cohort, born between 1970 and 1982.

As mentioned earlier, political trust is an ambivalent term. Broadly understood as the "faith people have in their government" (Citrin and Muste 1999:465), political trust is quite low in Mexico, but its evolution is unclear. If we look at the trends in confidence in institutions, trust has declined (Catterberg and Moreno 2006). However, if we look at the perceptions of government as working for the benefit of all people versus government run by a few big interests, the fact is that distrust has decreased. Recent changes in Mexican politics lead us to rethink the way Mexicans perceive government, and, thereby, their ability to trust government. Not long ago, government and the PRI were indistinguishable. Today, alternation at the national, state and local levels has redefined the frames of reference.

As we have seen, the value change in the last two decades in Mexican society produced the pre-conditions for a democratic transition. However, one question we posed in the introduction remains unanswered. Who drove the transition, the masses or the elites? Preliminary exploration of this question in Latin America looked into color and democracy (Basáñez 2001). We now replicate a model developed from the Afrobarometer (Mattes and Bratton, 2003) to measure democracy supply (elites) and demand (masses). We measure demand with the average score of three WVS questions: in a democracy, the economy runs badly; democracies are indecisive; democracies are not good at maintaining order. The stronger the respondent opposes those statements, the higher demand is for democracy. Supply is measured by satisfaction with democracy, satisfaction with the level of respect for

Figure 3.3. Democracy: Driven by Masses or Elites?

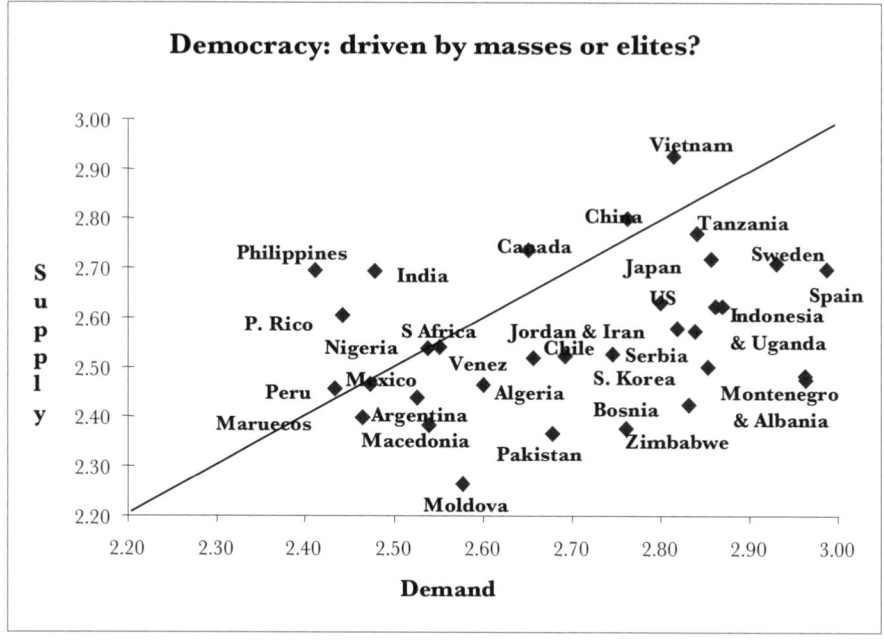

human rights, and satisfaction with government. The more satisfied people are, the higher the supply.

Figure 3.3. shows that Mexico's democracy (similar to that of South Africa, Nigeria, and Peru) is a balance of the elites' pull and the masses' push. However, that is not the case for the majority of countries plotted in the chart. Countries below the line indicate that the masses' push is stronger than the elites' push. The opposite happens for those above the line. In The Philippines, India and Vietnam, elites stand out for their high *supply* of democracy. At the other end, Moldova, Pakistan, Zimbabwe, Montenegro, and Albania societies stand out for their *demand* for democracy, as measured by these indicators.

*Shifts in Economic and Social Values*

During the 1990s, Mexicans were deeply divided along a democratic-authoritarian dimension of political conflict that had a strong influence on party competition (Moreno, 1999). Those who held authoritarian views of politics were likely to support the long-ruling PRI, and those who shared pro-democratic views were likely to support opposition parties. Political alternation may have changed this, and, in fact, the salience of the other two dimensions was already emerging in the 1996 survey and was confirmed in 2000. One of those dimensions taps liberal and fundamentalist views about society, including attitudes toward abortion and homosexuals. The other involves left and right positions on socio-economic issues, such as preferences for economic individualism versus state responsibility, and preferences for economic payoffs based on individual achievement as opposed to higher income equality.

Liberal and fundamentalist views of society are significantly influenced by age. The most fundamentalist age cohort is the one born before 1940, and fundamentalism tends to decrease in the next two younger cohorts: those born in the 1940s and 1950s, as shown in Figure 3.5. Liberalism is predominant among those born in the 1960s, and much more so among those born between 1970 and 1982 (that is, Mexicans who were 18 to 30 years old by the time of the 2000 survey). In fact, liberal views increased from 1990 to 2000 among the youngest cohort, as those born between 1973 and 1982—not interviewed in 1990 because they were not yet 18 years old—joined the adult population. Conversely, the oldest cohort became slightly less fundamentalist, not because of value change during their life cycle, but simply because the cohort born between 1900 and 1939 naturally shrank between 1990 and 2000. In the 1990 survey, 16% of respondents said they were born before 1940, whereas 10% did so in the 2000 survey. According to the 2000 census, about 8% of Mexicans were 61 years or older in 2000 (that is, they were born before 1940). The oldest cohort remained the most fundamentalist of all (that is, the group most opposed to abortion and homosexuals).

Interestingly, all three cohorts born in the 1940s, 1950s, and 1960s showed a similar pattern of change from 1990 to 2000; they became either less liberal or more fundamentalist. This suggests that, with the exception of the youngest generation (with new Mexicans brought into adulthood) and the oldest generation (naturally reduced by mortality rates), Mexican society became less liberal and more fundamentalist in the last decade of the twentieth century. The most notorious shift is observed in the cohorts born in the 1950s and 1960s. As we will show in the next section, this shift is consistent with a trend from radical to conservative views in the last two decades, and with a gradual shift to

Figure 3.4. A Ten-Year Shift in Mexicans' Belief Systems.

Average Placement of Age Cohorts on Variables from Factor Analysis.

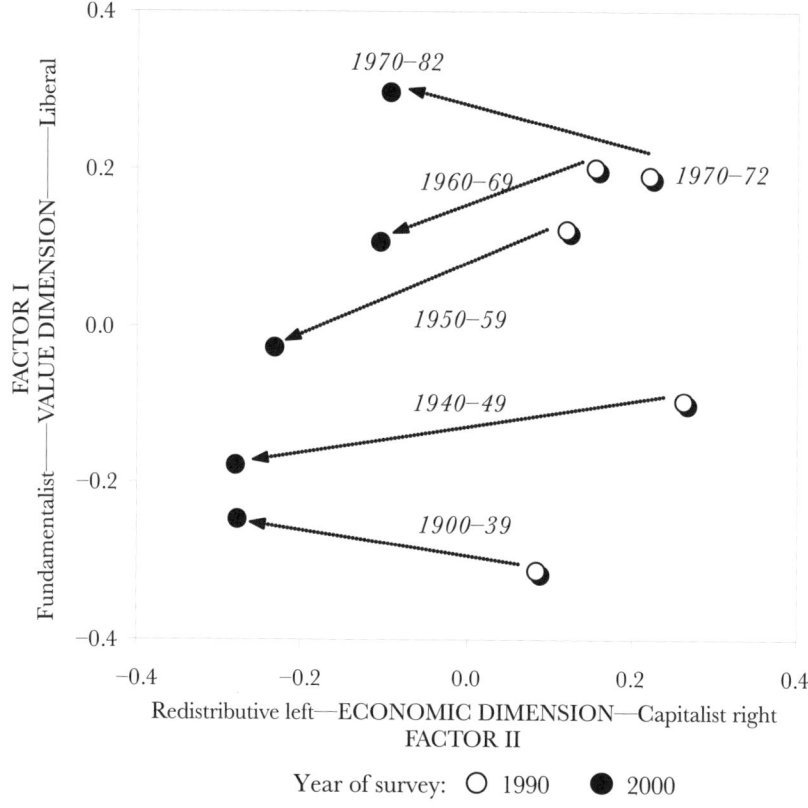

the right on a left-right scale reported elsewhere (Moreno 2003). We will return to this point later.

One of the most noticeable shifts in Mexicans' attitudes and values during the last decade is the one observed along the dimension of socio-economic issues, which shows a significant move from a capitalist, individualistic-oriented right, to a redistributive, state-interventionist left, as shown in Figure 3.4. The 1990s were a decade of privatizations and free trade policies in Mexico. Generally, Mexicans support free trade, but they are more critical of the North American Free Trade Agreement's performance (Moreno 2002a). Despite support for free trade, Mexicans turned to the left of the socio-economic spectrum during the 1990s. Perhaps the 1994 Peso Crisis explains a great deal of this shift. The Peso Crisis almost crashed the recently privatized banking system, reduced Mexico's GDP 7% in just one year, and caused a significant decrease in Mexicans' purchasing power, not to mention high rates of unemployment and a significant devaluation of the peso against the U.S. dollar. As shown in Figure 3.4, Mexicans of all ages moved significantly to the left on the socioeconomic dimension from 1990 to 2000. A more moderate version of this shift is observed in the 1996–2000 period, but mostly among particular segments of the population, especially those PRI partisans (Moreno 2003).

The shift to the left in socio-economic issues was most significant among Mexicans born in the 1940s (those between 51 and 60 years old at the time of the 2000 survey). This age cohort had lived through four serious political or economic crises: the 1968 students' massacre a week before the Olympic Games in Mexico City, the 1976 100% peso devaluation, the 1982 bank nationalization (Basáñez and Camp 1984), and the 1987 stock market crash (Basáñez 1990). Hence, by the 1994 Peso Crisis, this age cohort was well aware that the cycle was repeating for the fifth time.

In sum, Mexicans experienced a profound shift in ideological orientations that reflected the socio-economic context of the 1990s, and they are clearly divided on their views toward society depending on the age cohort to which they belong. Younger Mexicans are more liberal, and older ones are more fundamentalist.

### Radicalism and Conservatism

The WVS questionnaire has kept track of an item that reflects attitudes toward the speed at which society should be transformed, if at all. It discriminates between those who believe that "the entire way our society is organized must be radically changed by revolutionary action," and those who feel that "our present society must be valiantly defended against all subversive forces." Between the two extremes are those who think that "our society must be gradually improved by reforms." The latter view represents the largest proportion in each of the four surveys in Mexico. Nonetheless, the proportion of respondents taking that position has diminished over time, from 68% in 1980 to 49% in 2000. Consequently, there has been an increase in the other two options: radical views remained stable between 1980 and 2000, while conservative views significantly increased from 9 to 21% in that same period.

As shown in Figure 3.5, the proportion of radical views about societal change was greater than the proportion of conservative ones in the 1980 and 1990 surveys, perhaps reflecting the revolutionary discourse that permeated Latin America in the 1970s, and the wave of democratization in the 1980s. However, this was reversed in the 1990s, when the strongest expressions of radicalism were personified in the Zapatista movement, a peasant rebellion in Mexico's southernmost state of Chiapas. On January 1, 1994, the same day that NAFTA went into effect, a group of masked Indians engaged in violence and declared war on the Mexican government, demanding democracy and Indian rights, and expressing their opposition to the trade agreement. Although severe violence lasted only a few days before an armistice was called, the Zapatista spokesman, who called himself Subcomandante Marcos, maintained a high-profile movement through electronic media and frequent letters to the press.

There are two observable phenomena related to radical and conservative attitudes during the last 20 years. The first is the change from radicalism to conservatism just mentioned. The second is a change in the relationship between those attitudes and age. The 1990 survey shows a positive, yet moderate, relation between views on change and age. Both radical and conservative views increase as one moves from the youngest to the oldest age cohort. This means that the youngest cohorts were more likely to take a position in favor of gradual reforms rather than for radical change or defense of the status quo. However, in the mid-1990s and in 2000, that relationship was reversed: younger cohorts were more likely to take the radical and conservative views, which means that the last few years witnessed a certain polarization among the youth. About 88% of all respondents born after 1970 and interviewed in 2000 took either a radical position (47%) or a conservative position (41%). The sum of responses that took either of those polarized positions among the other age cohorts was less than 50%. This phenomenon had been observed since the 1996–97 survey.

In sum, Mexicans have changed the balance between radicalism and conservatism, with the latter being the predominant view in recent years. At the same time, a positive but moderate influence of age in those attitudes not only increased in significance, but also reversed in

Figure 3.5. From Radicalism to Conservatism: Attitudes towards society by year of birth, 1980–2000.

(% who agrees with each statement).

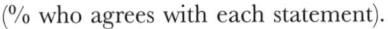

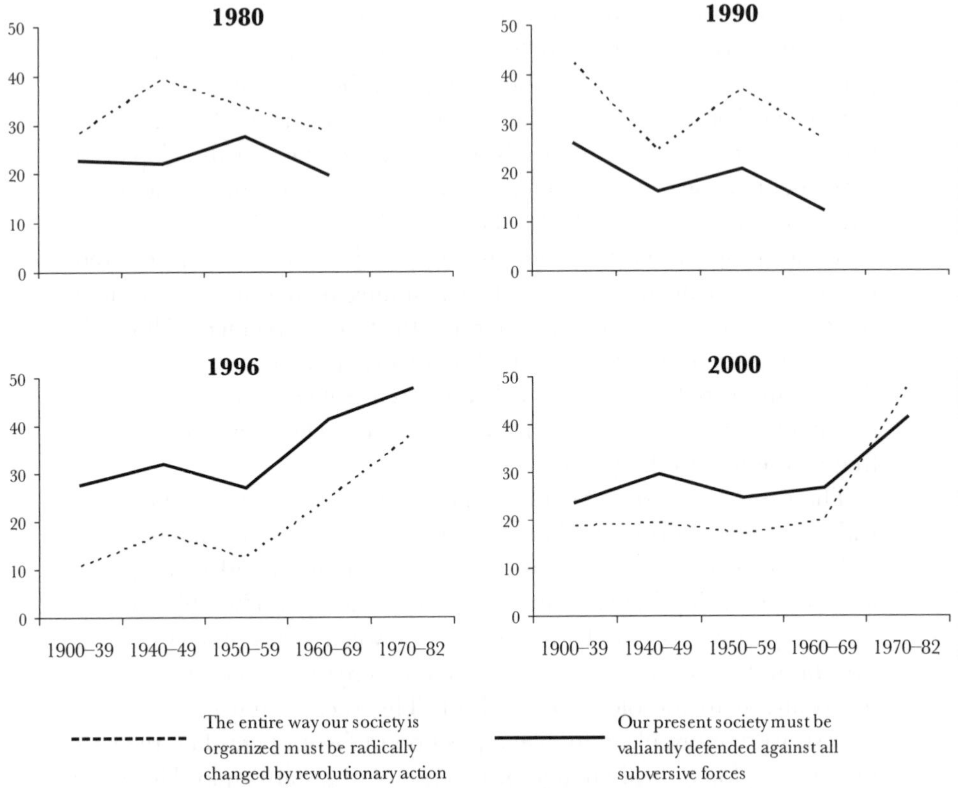

direction. From being a positive one, the relation between polarizing societal attitudes and age became negative: the lower the age cohort, the higher the percentage of individuals taking either a radical or a conservative position. The rising influence of age is also observed in a phenomenon widely studied in advanced industrial society: Materialist and Post-materialist values.

## Materialism and Post-materialism

Materialist values are broadly understood as those that emphasize economic and physical security, while Post-materialist values refer to priorities related to the quality of life and self-expression (Inglehart 1997). Evidence from the WVS depicts an interesting change in the balance of Materialist vs. Post-materialist values in Mexico. To be sure, holders of Post-materialist values represent a small proportion of the Mexican society, and the proportion has increased very little overall. However, what is striking about the last two decades is the gradual appearance of a Materialist vs. Post-materialist value gap among age cohorts (See Figure 3.6).

Almost nonexistent in 1980, the relationship between Materialist/Post-materialist values and age was statistically significant in 2000. Twenty years ago, older and younger cohorts were almost equally Materialist and Post-materialist. However, in the 2000 survey, 41% of respondents born before 1940 held Materialist values, whereas only 21% of those born between 1970 and 1982 did so. Conversely, 10% of the pre-1940 generations were Post-materialist (as well as 7% of those born in the 1940s), and 17% of the post-1970 cohort.

Mexico is far from being a predominantly Post-materialist society, but the evidence of a generational value change has been clear in the last two decades. This is leading Mexicans to a strong value gap in which older cohorts are clearly Materialist, while younger cohorts are divided in their value-orientations.

*Conclusion*

Mexican society has experienced significant changes in its value system during the last two decades, evidenced by a moderate decrease in political distrust, a shift to the left in socio-economic issues, a shift from radical to conservative views, and the rise of significant generational gaps observed in some value-dimensions of political relevance: a liberal-fundamentalist axis of conflict and the balance of Materialist and Post-materialist values. Younger Mexicans, those born during the period of political reforms and socialized under greater political and economic competition—the NAFTA generation—seem more polarized on several issues, which points to the possibility that Mexican politics will consolidate its competitiveness in the near future.

For many years, political scientists have observed decreasing support for the long-ruling PRI among younger voters, who have been more likely to support opposition parties. In 2000, in the election of change and alternation, the younger electorate voted disproportionately in favor

Figure 3.6. An Increasing Generational Value Gap in Mexico.

% of Materialists (MAT) and Post-materialists (PM) by Year of Birth.

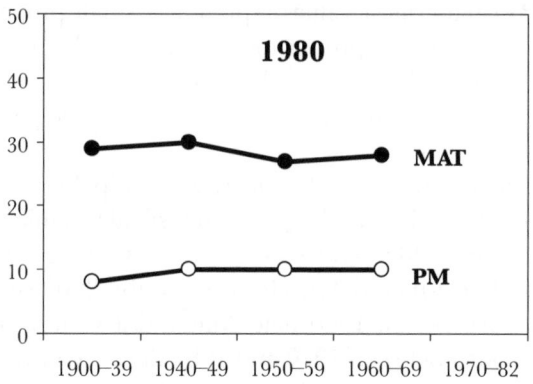

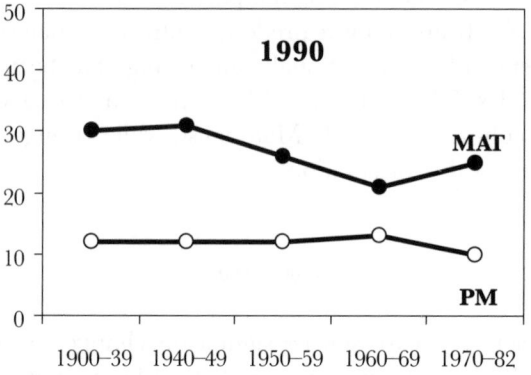

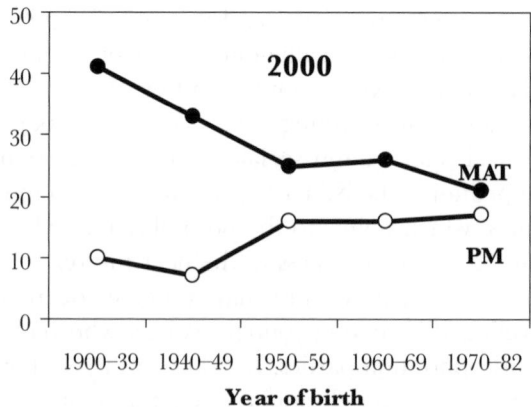

of opposition presidential candidate Vicente Fox. A national exit poll conducted by Mexican newspaper *Reforma* in 2000 showed that, among voters 18–29 years old, the vote share for Fox and Labastida, the PRI candidate, was 47% and 33%, respectively. However, exit poll data from the same source showed that the Legislative election on July 2003 diminished the age gap between the PAN and the PRI. PAN candidates obtained 35% of the vote among voters 29 years old or younger, while the PRI maintained 33% among the same segment.

Religion not only persists, but has also built up support among Mexicans. Nonetheless, there is evidence of changes in values and attitudes in social and political aspects.

## References

Basáñez, Miguel and Roderic Ai Camp. 1984. "La Nacionalización de la Banca y la Opinión Pública en México" in *Foro Internacional* 25, no 98, December, Mexico: Colegio de México.

Basáñez, Miguel. 1986. "Tradiciones Combativas y Contemplativas: México Mañana" in *Revista Mexicana de Ciencias Políticas y Sociales 32*, no. 125, September, Mexico: UNAM.

——. 1987 "Elections and Political Culture in Mexico," in Judith Gentleman (ed.), *Mexican Politics in Transition*. Boulder and London: Westview Press.

——. 1990 *El Pulso de los Sexenios: 20 Años de Crisis en México*. México: Siglo 21.

——. 1992 "Encuestas de Opinión en México," in Bazdresch, Carlos et al. (eds.), *México: Auge, Crisis y Ajuste*. México: Fondo de Cultura Económica.

——. 1993a "Is México Headed Toward its Fifth Crisis?" in Roett, Riordan (ed.), *Political & Economic Liberalization in México: At a Critical Juncture?* Boulder and London: Lynee Rienner Publishers.

——. 1993b "Protestant and Catholic Ethics: An Empirical Comparison." Paper presented at the 1993 World Values Survey Conference, El Paular, Spain, September.

—— and Alejandro Moreno. 1994 "México en la Encuesta Mundial de Valores 1981–1990" in Juan Díez Nicolás and Ronald F. Inglehart (eds.), *Tendencias Mundiales de Cambio en los Valores Sociales y Políticos*. Madrid, Spain: Fundesco.

——. 1995 "Public Opinion Research in Mexico" in Peter H. Smith (ed.), *Latin America in Comparative Perspective: New Approaches to Methods and Analysis*. Boulder, San Francisco, Boulder, Co.: Westview Press.

——. 1996 "Polling and the 1994 Election Results," in Roderic Ai Camp (ed.), *Polling for Democracy: Public Opinion and Political Liberalization in Mexico*. Washington: Scholarly Resources.

—— and Pablo Parás. 2001. "Color and Democracy in Latin America." in Roderic Ai Camp (ed.), *Citizen Views of Democracy in Latin America*. Pittsburgh: University of Pittsburgh Press.

Catterberg, Gabriela, and Alejandro Moreno. 2002. "The Individual Bases of Political Trust: Trends in Established and New Democracies." *International Journal of Public Opinion Research*, Vol. 18: 31–48.

Citrin, Jack, and Christopher Muste. 1999. "Trust in Government," in John P. Robinson, Phillip R. Shaver, and Lawrence S. Wrightsman (eds.), *Measures of Political Attitudes*. San Diego, Ca.: Academic Press.

Inglehart, Ronald, Neil Nevitte, and Miguel Basáñez. 1996. *The North American Trajectory: Cultural, Economic, and Political Ties among the United States, Canada, and Mexico*. New York: Aldine de Gruyter.

Inglehart, Ronald F. 1997. *Modernization and Postmodernization: Cultural, Economic and Political Change in 43 Societies*. Princeton: Princeton University Press.

———. 2000. "Culture and Democracy," in Lawrence E. Harrison and Samuel P. Huntington (eds.), *Culture Matters: How Values Shape Human Progress*. New York: Basic Books.

———. (ed.). 2003. *Human Values and Social Change: Findings from the Values Surveys*. Leiden, Netherlands: Brill.

———, Miguel Basáñez, y Alejandro Moreno. 1998. *Human Values and Beliefs: A Cross-Cultural Sourcebook*. Ann Arbor: University of Michigan Press.

———, and Gabriela Catterberg. 2003. "Trends in Political Action: The Developmental Trend and the Post-Honeymoon Decline." Paper presented at the Annual Meeting of the Midwest Political Science Association, Chicago, April.

Mattes, Robert and Michael Bratton. 2003. "Learning about Democracy in Africa: Performance, Awareness and History." Paper presented at the WAPOR Regional Conference, Cape Town, South Africa, May.

Moreno, Alejandro. 1999. *Political Cleavages: Issues, Parties, and the Consolidation of Democracy*. Boulder, Co.: Westview Press.

———. 2002a. "Mexican Public Opinion toward NAFTA and FTAA," in Edward J. Chambers and Peter H. Smith (eds.), *NAFTA in the New Millenium*. La Jolla: Center for U.S.-Mexican Studies, University of California, San Diego, and Edmonton: The University of Alberta Press.

———. 2002b. "La sociedad mexicana y el cambio," *Este País 134*, April.

———. 2003. *El votante mexicano: Democracia, actitudes políticas y conducta electoral*. México, D. F.: Fondo de Cultura Económica.

Moreno, Alejandro and Patricia Méndez. Forthcoming. "Attitudes toward Democracy: Mexico in Comparative Perspective," *The International Journal of Comparative Sociology*, special issue, edited by Ronald F. Inglehart.

Noelle-Neumann, Elisabeth. 1993. *The Spiral of Silence*. 2nd ed., Chicago and London: The University of Chicago Press.

Norris, Pippa, and Ronald Inglehart. 2002. "Islamic Culture and Democracy: Testing the 'Clash of Civilizations' Thesis," *Comparative Sociology* 1, nos. 3–4: 235–263.

CHAPTER FOUR

## CULTURAL TRENDS IN ARGENTINA:
### 1983–2000

MARITA CARBALLO

Data available since the early 1980s have been invaluable in assessing the cultural changes occurring in societies around the globe, and Argentina is one of the countries with uninterrupted time-series data for the last two decades. This chapter analyzes the evolution of the main cultural changes in Argentine society in the past two decades, deriving data from the four World Values Surveys conducted by Gallup, Argentina in 1984, 1991, 1995, and 1999.

In the 1980s and 1990s, the world experienced significant changes in terms of ideas, politics and technological development with profound effects on the behavior, attitudes and values of large masses. Changes, ranging from the disappearance of the hypotheses related to the world's bipolar organization and the Cold War conflicts, to developments in communication technology and the Internet, paved the way for a whole new concept of distance in terms of how people access information and interact with each other.

In addition to these exogenous factors, Argentina, as well as other Latin American countries, underwent major political changes during this period. Argentina, for example, experienced two decades of continuous democracy, something not seen since the first quarter of the twentieth century. For countries with long republican and democratic traditions, this may seem like a brief period, unlikely to have any major consequences. For Argentina, however, this represents a major institutional/legal change, with ramifications for cultural change as well. Values surveys suggest that cultural changes in Argentina extended beyond the political to many other aspects of life. Nonetheless, we start our discussion with political values.

## Argentines and Politics

Throughout the period 1916 to 1999, Argentine politics was characterized by turbulence. Three points will help summarize the institutional
setting:

1. Only five times did alternation between two democratically-elected
   presidents take place through popular vote.
2. During this period, Argentina had at least twelve *de facto* presidents
   (appointed through non-democratic means), almost as many as those
   who took office under the Constitution.
3. For 21 non-consecutive years, the Armed Forces ruled the country,
   seizing power by toppling constitutionally elected leaders.

From 1983 onwards, democratic rule has uninterruptedly prevailed
in Argentina. Although two presidents resigned before schedule, the
changes in office were conducted under the Constitution and with
the participation of Parliament. Thus, the two decades which we will
analyze happen to be the longest period of uninterrupted democracy
in Argentina since 1930. This brief historical consideration serves to
illuminate how Argentines view and perceive democracy. On the one
hand, they seem to lack the experience of living under democratic
institutions—people over 40 years old have lived half their lives under
non-democratic regimes—and, at the same time, society is convinced
that democracy is still the best system of government.

However, it is not the case that Argentines are fully satisfied with
the way democracy works in their country. In fact, 1 out of every 10
persons in 1999 were not satisfied with how their democracy worked,
and a slightly greater level of dissatisfaction was observed among those
with the lowest-income and education levels. This disapproval is basically
explained by the dissatisfaction with the performance of the institutions
linked to the political system that developed later.

Argentines' perception of democracy, then, is far from being that
of the perfect regime. They are critical of some aspects of democratic
systems and respond more favorably to others, thus giving a perspective
with varied hues. A little less than two thirds (60% to be precise) of
Argentines consider democracy to be slow in decision-making (with the
proportion varying according to socio-demographic characteristics), but
about the same proportion (59%) think it is successful in maintaining
order. Furthermore, most Argentines do not believe that the economy

would necessarily suffer under democratic regimes (upper and middle-income, and educated groups hold a more optimistic view of democracy with respect to these two aspects).

However, overall, support for democracy as a system of government among Argentines is quite high: 85% think that democracy may have its problems, but is still better than any other system (1995 and 1999). This feeling is stronger among upper income and better educated groups.

Consistent with their support for democratic systems in general, Argentines do not approve of military governments or strong leaders who do not concern themselves with Parliament or elections. Some 73% of the population considers having a military government to be undesirable. Furthermore, 51% think that having a strong leader who would ignore democratic institutions such as Parliament or elections is bad for the country, and only 36% hold the opposite view. Support for such strong leadership is higher among low and middle-income groups, those with primary education, and those aged between 25 and 34.

In order to better understand these figures, it is important to bear in mind that, even under democracy, Argentina has always placed a strong emphasis on the role of the president, and the presidencies of political parties have historically exhibited a marked personal leadership. Likewise, the absence of incentives to participate in an effective democratic life within parties could have discouraged the creation of democratic participation habits within the heart of political groupings. In addition, and considering the almost vanished prestige of parliamentarians among the Argentine people (an issue assessed later), rejection of personal leaderships gathers importance, the lesson being that Argentines are calling for institutional improvements, rather than changes of regimes entailing a lower participation through democratic institutions.

To sum up, Argentines adhere to democracy in theory and principle, but are not blind to the system's failures, which, in general, relates to their own past experiences. Criticism is higher among low education and socioeconomic levels. Currently, a critical approach has grown, a trend that intensified from 1999 to 2002, when surveys conducted by Gallup Argentina showed a marked 10 point decrease in support for democracy as the best system of government. This outcome merits two readings. The first and lineal one is concerned with democratic disapproval. The second, more optimistic, one highlights the fact that, although engulfed by a crippling economic crisis, with a 25% GDP drop in four years, and a 23% unemployment rate, confidence in democracy still prevails. In general terms, in 1999, Argentines rated their political system 4.9 (on a 1 to 10 scale), showing a higher rate in upper-income sectors (against 4.6 in 1995), but rated the military regime that ruled Argentina from 1976 to 1983 at 3.5, and believed that, by 2009, the political regime would deserve a 6.9 rating. This suggests that, although people seemed dissatisfied with their government's performance at that time (1999), they were confident that the dynamics of democracy would improve the political landscape in the following decade, and they did not long for the non-democratic systems that had prevailed until 1983.

Some explanations may be given in connection with Argentines' dissatisfaction with the government:

1. Some 69% of the population are not satisfied with the way government handles the country's affairs (similar to the 1995 figure, and could have been higher after 1999).
2. Nine out of ten Argentines believe the country is run by a few interested parties seeking to benefit their own, rather than the people's, interest.
3. Nine out of ten Argentines believe that the government does not work to reduce poverty.
4. A generalized opinion prevailed that most, or almost all, political leaders are involved in corruption cases in some way or other.

While the 1999 figures for points 1, 2 and 3 were similar to those in 1995, the issue of corruption experienced a considerable increase of 10 percentage points.

### Argentines and Daily Politics

Argentines have a rather low degree of interest in politics. As seen in Figure 1, in 1999, there was only an 18% interest in politics, against 43% in 1984, and 30% in 1991. The lack of political interest is deep in all sectors of society; in the upper classes and citizens with university degrees, two thirds claimed to have little interest, or not be interested at all, in politics; among young people aged 18 to 24, 88% declared themselves to be not interested, and in people aged 25 to 34 and 35 to 49, lack of interest exceeded 80%.

This dramatic lack of interest, along with the low levels of confidence in political institutions, does not contribute to an increase in political

Figure 4.1. Interest in Politics.

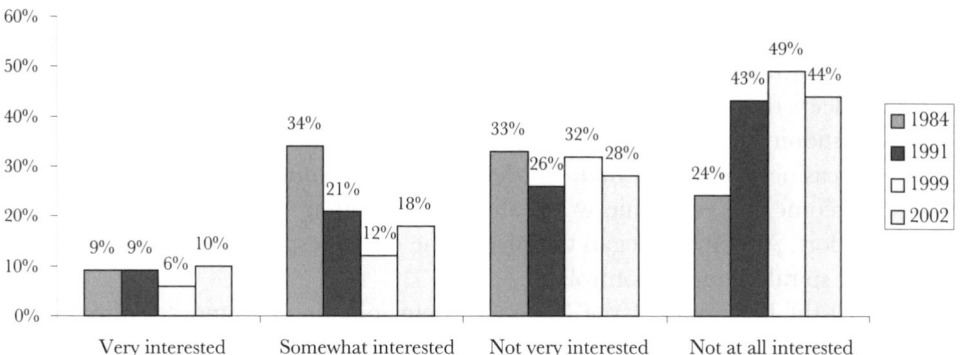

participation. This results in a reduced renewal of politicians, which makes people even less interested in politics.

Another indicator of the apathy in politics prevailing in Argentina is the percentage of people who do not talk about politics with their friends: from 21% in 1984 to 49% in 1999 (only 19% of the population often talks about politics). The sectors that talk the least about politics with their friends are young people aged 18 to 34, and the low-income, less educated class (only primary school completed).

Despite the apparently low interest in politics, 47% of the population keeps abreast of political news on television, radio or in the papers, and 24% do it at least one or twice a week. An explanation might be found in the development of the media (radio and television) in Argentina, where many general interest television programs include news briefings in between commercial spots, and there are some channels exclusively dedicated to news and information, contributing to the high follow-up of political developments.

It is important to add that, after the 2001 crisis, Argentines' interest in politics rises again by around 10 percentage points as a reaction of the people to the country's difficulties. Likewise, interest in politics brings about an increased participation of civil society in NGOs' voluntary aid tasks.

Finally, people in Argentina have not significantly changed the way they define themselves in ideological terms. If we rate an extreme left-wing position as 1, and an extreme right-wing position as 10, in 1999, Argentines rated themselves 6 on average, crowning a gradual process of shifting from left to right that started in 1984 (5.3), 1991 (5.5) and 1995 (5.7). Studies conducted in 2001 showed a 5.6 rate, reflecting the slight volatility mentioned.

These fluctuations might be associated with the government's success in carrying out public policies and tasks. In this regard, during the first years that the World Value Survey was conducted, when democracy was restored after seven years of non-democratic regime that ended in deep disgrace (economic crisis, the Malvinas War, human rights questionings), public opinion was closer to the left wing. As it became increasingly apparent that the democratic government was failing to overcome the economic woes, and was beginning to lose its popular support, Argentines began to move to the center, especially when inflation spiraled out of control.

At the beginning of the 1990s, self-determination had moved to the right within a framework of economic success, and the early economic and social reforms of the first generation. But, once reforms had been undertaken, giving way to a period of reform fatigue, criticism at how reforms had been carried out (in terms of the transparency of privatizations, the regulatory framework design, consumer protection, and so on) flourished. This phenomenon, along with the increase in unemployment and the halt in economic growth (especially in the last years of the decade), explains, from an economic viewpoint, why people started to move to the left.

As time passed, Argentines attached more importance to increased citizen participation. In fact, from 1984 to 1999, the percentage of Argentines who considered increased involvement as a priority rose from 21% to 30%, while the percentage of those who prioritized order maintenance dropped from 42% to 33%. Priority given to the protection of freedom of speech rose from 9% to 19%, while priority given to combating inflation declined from 27% to 18%.

The economic stability and democratic consolidation in the 1990s underlie this apparent change in priorities (some studies conducted after 1999 pointed to a reappraisal of the importance of stability within the framework of the economic crisis that had troubled Argentina since 1999 and the 2001–2002 turmoil). All this made Argentines become deeply aware of the need for greater citizen participation (particularly in upper-income, educated sectors) which had been limited by people's low confidence in institutions.

Lower-income classes are more worried about fighting inflation (23%) because they are most exposed to the high inflation and hyperinflation processes, while freedom of speech is the major concern for people aged 25 to 34 years old (24%).

Economic stability seems to be the priority in all sectors. However, the higher the education and socioeconomic level, the stronger the demand to move towards a less impersonal and more humane society. Interestingly, one out of four lower-middle and low class respondents considers the fight against crime as a very important priority. In this regard, not only in Argentina, but also in other Latin American countries, the feeling of insecurity has increased in past years due to the rise in the crime rate.

To sum up, in 1999, Argentine society, led by the high-income, educated sectors, seemed to be shifting its demands towards less materialistic grounds. However, conservative positions were strongly engrained, particularly among the elderly and low-income or less educated sectors of society.

The economic and political volatility recorded after 1999 slowed down this process, particularly as Argentina lost economic stability. Beyond the problems derived from growing unemployment (a cause of increased insecurity from fear of losing one's job), in the 1990s, macroeconomic stability allowed Argentines to recover the ability to foresee and plan for the future, and design a life plan protected from unexpected economic changes (for example, in simple things such as buying real estate in installments in order to leave the parental home or get married). These conditions, existent in 1999 when this study was conducted, abruptly changed in the following years, influencing Argentines' attitudes, and turning citizens to more materialistic values.

*Purpose and Shape of Changes*

In a critical context of democratic and political performance, Argentine people depict a particular attitude; they call for changes, but through gradual and peaceful means.

First of all, it is important to consider how Argentines have changed the form of their protest.

Figure 2 shows a low percentage of participation in unlawful strikes and sieges of factories. Also, the number of people involved in protests such as lawful demonstrations and signing petitions shows a decreasing trend. This last form of protest has increased in middle and high-income sectors with high educational level, and among people up to 50 years old.

Figure 4.2. Forms of Protest in Argentina.

Percentage of the people that would

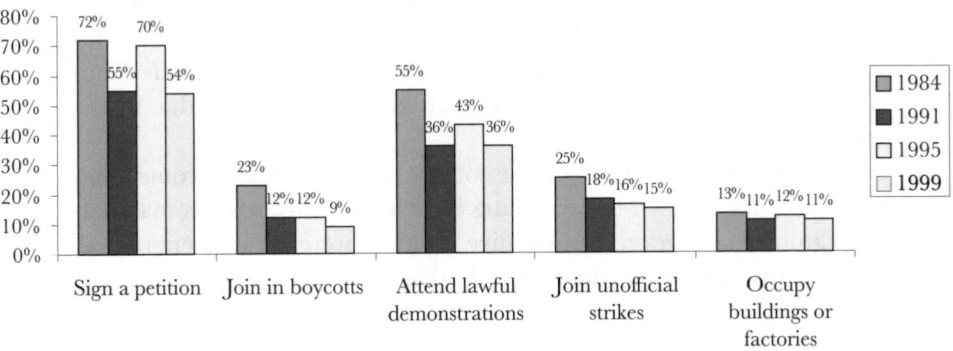

Consistently, Argentine society fully supports the idea that changes and reforms must be gradually implemented: 82% of the population agree with this view (77% in 1984 and 81% in 1991), a high stability of opinions in this regard. At the same time, opinions favoring a radical change by revolutionary means have slightly decreased from 12% in 1984, to 4% in 1999 (8% in 1991, and 5% in 1995). Disapproval of violence is high, and 86% of the population do not approve of the use of violence for political ends.

The past years have also seen the rise of new players on the social scene. In 2002, *Piqueteros* were known for blocking public roads as a way of protest, but also for running community shelters and providing aid to schools, and the government grants them official support. In the wake of the December crisis in 2001, so-called "public gatherings" began spontaneously as assemblies in the neighborhoods of Buenos Aires, and they still prevail.

A practice increasingly seen is the use of public places as the vehicle for carrying out protests by blocking city roads and streets as well as launching street marches and demonstrations. These demonstrations are carried out by organizations sometimes linked to left-leaning political parties with little electoral support but high mobilization power. People accept and tolerate these demonstrations, with mixed feelings of fear for the violence displayed by some demonstrators, annoyance at the difficulties they cause, disapproval of the ways in which protests are carried out, but with a conviction that the material needs of many demonstrators should actually be met.

Finally, it is useful to understand the purpose of the changes Argentines suggest should be undertaken in society. Although data from 1984 is not available, considering the studies made in 1991, 1995 and 1999, we conclude that more people than in 1999 welcome the participation of the State, which is consistent with the reform fatigue that public opinion seems to exhibit (and is less prone to competition than it was in 1991 for the same reason). At the same time, society holds a balanced opinion as regards hard work versus success, and the belief prevails that it is possible to be successful without detriment to other people.

In relation to point one, the choice for a more equal income distribution (value 1), or that income should derive from efforts, the average opinion stands at 4.9 (7.0 in 1991), while the greater the income and education, the higher the value grows.

As regards who is responsible for ensuring that everyone is provided for, whether it be the Government (1), or each person (10), the average is 4.4, having decreased from 6.0 in 1991, to 5.3 in 1995. The higher figures are found among youngsters and the high-income class.

Support for competition (1) has vanished due to criticism (10) in the past years. The 1999 average stood at 4.2, compared to 3.4 in 1991. Women, people under 34 years old, people with primary education, and lower-middle and low-income people are more critical of competition.

As was noted before, Argentines hold a middle stance as to whether the key to a better life lies in hard work (1) or in luck and contacts (10), for they average 4.7 (4.8 in 1991 and 5.1 in 1995). They also seem to have an intermediate position regarding the fact that ideas that have stood the test of time are the best (1), or new ideas are better than old ones (10): the average rating is 5.3, matching the 1991 figure.

Finally, the idea that wealth is enough and is slated to grow in the future (10) prevails over the opinion that individuals enrich themselves at the expense of others (1) in a sort of zero-sum game. In this case, the average rating is 6.9, also similar to the 1991 figure (7.0).

In connection with Argentines' approach to work and production, ideas on how business should be conducted reflect high stability over time, and a marked rejection of state ownership of businesses (only 6% of the population agree with this idea). Many Argentines (45% in 1999, and 43% in 1984) believe owners should appoint directors and allow for employees to participate, with a rising trend among people of up to 49 years old. By contrast, 29% approve of owners making the appointments (34% in 1984), while the ratio increases in higher socioeconomic and educational levels, and among people over 50 years old.

### Credibility in People and Institutions

Argentines showed a low level of credibility in others and institutions, creating a complex framework when it comes to seeking mechanisms to strengthen the latter.

In relation to the first aspect, in 1999, 85% of the population thought one should treat others carefully. This idea, coupled to the fact that 52% believed that people would try to take advantage of them, depicted a deep skepticism, one that reflected the above-mentioned credibility crisis hitting institutions in general. The lower the socioeconomic and/or educational level, and the younger the people, the higher this feeling of being unfairly treated. In spite of that, Argentines are tolerant and show no discrimination in terms of nationality, race and religion (although one third of the population prefers not to have heavy drinkers, drug addicts, political extremists and people with a criminal record as neighbors).

Amid the prevailing lack of credibility, Argentines take family and friends as the shelter on whom to rely, to whom they relate, and with whom they gather, as will be explained later.

With regard to the second aspect, Argentines are disappointed with the performance of institutions according to the following three indicators (Table 1):

1. General credibility in institutions is low.
2. In a few cases, Argentines' credibility in an institution is higher than the world's average.
3. Credibility in almost all institutions included in the survey has systematically decreased since 1984.

Argentines' trust is particularly low in relation to the institutions linked to the three powers of the State: the National Government (Executive Power), Parliament, and the Judiciary.

The perception of the three powers of the State shows social inefficiency (bureaucratic procedures), lack of transparency, disagreement with the Court rulings (feeling of being unprotected amid growing insecurity, slow and overdue judicial system), corruption, absence of austerity (inordinate number of offices, privileged salaries and retirement benefits), and political patronage, among others.

This lack of credibility in the Judiciary is higher in high-income and high educational sectors, and among people aged 25 to 34. By contrast, soaring mistrust in Parliament is common in all sectors of society, although slightly higher among youngsters.

Low credibility in public officials has been rising over the last decade, along with the idea that almost all of them are prone to accepting bribes.

Considering the dwindling credibility in political parties, the difficulty of them purging themselves is apparent, clearly being shown in the low electoral turnout, the high percentage of the population who implemented the so-called "punishment vote" and street demonstrations under the motto "*be gone with them all*," all of which have been increasing, especially since 1999 when the research was conducted.

Summing up, a lack of confidence in institutions related to government and public life, as seen in Table 1, is found in all strata of society, underscoring the importance attached to the credibility crisis.

Table 4.1. Credibility of Institutions.[1]

| Confidence in Institutions | | | | |
|---|---|---|---|---|
| | 1984 | 1991 | 1999 | 2001 |
| The Churches | 47% | 46% | 59% | 50% |
| The Press | 47% | 27% | 37% | 37% |
| The Armed Forces | 19% | 28% | 26% | 29% |
| The Major Companies | 36% | 24% | 24% | 19% |
| The Police | 25% | 26% | 24% | 18% |
| Justice | 59% | 24% | 20% | 12% |
| Labor Unions | 31% | 8% | 11% | 7% |
| Parliament | 73% | 16% | 11% | 7% |
| Political Parties | – | – | 7% | 7% |
| Public Officials | 50% | 7% | 7% | 5% |
| Education system | 56% | 38% | – | 43% |
| NGOs | – | – | – | 41% |

[1] Percentage of the people who trust a lot or quite a lot in each institution.

The public educational system in Argentina has historically enjoyed high credibility. This is due to its contribution to social cohesion and integration in a country with a high migration content at the time it was founded, and also to the highly qualified human resources trained in the country until the second half of the 20th century, despite its quality having worsened in recent years. Although the study conducted in 1999 did not ask people about this issue, previous and subsequent research has confirmed that Argentines hold a good opinion, in relative terms, of their educational system.

The case of the Armed Forces is interesting. In terms of institutional credibility, in the 1990s, the Armed Forces consolidated the credibility recovery from the low 1984 levels, when they carried the burden of a long-running *de facto* rule. In international terms, Argentina's credibility in the Armed Forces is half the world's average, and is demonstrably lower than most Latin American countries. However, they did not experience the credibility drop that engulfed other institutions related to the State (note that the Argentine Armed Forces are one of the most prestigious institutions worldwide). Greater confidence in the Armed Forces is found among people with primary education, in low-income sectors, and inhabitants of the interior of the country.

In international terms, trade unions rank midway in terms of credibility, and garner very little confidence in Argentina. In the 1980s, trade unions systematically confronted the democratic governments, plunging their credibility to levels from which they could not recover in the 1990s. Besides this, their image is tainted by political dealings, patronage, and lack of transparency. The higher the education and economic level, the higher the lack of credibility in trade unions.

As a counterpart, Argentines' credibility in their major businesses has also been undermined for the past two decades. Credibility fell in the 1980s, and again after 1999 within the framework of the economic crisis that forced the country to abandon the currency board. It must be noted that one of the consequences of currency board disruption was a rise in domestic prices and fears of a hyperinflationary rebound, which could have had a negative influence on public opinion. The trend matches the type of change in the course of society that public opinion would desire (greater participation of the State, a more critical approach towards competition, etc.) already addressed in this chapter. According to the 1999 survey, even in the high-income class, for every individual who trusts in large businesses, two do not, and the ratio among university students is 1 to 3. Lack of credibility is higher among women than men.

Although the media awakened more mistrust than trust (at a rate far removed from those worldwide or in Latin America), it is one of the institutions less affected by the credibility crisis tainting Argentine institutions. It emerges that Argentina is one of the Latin American countries where the population trusts the media more than the government (only 20% trusted the government in 1999), in contrast to what happens in Europe or the United States. Public opinion's reaction towards the media may be explained by the fact that Argentines blame their dissatisfaction with other political institutions on the media.

The institution that garners the highest credibility in Argentina is the Church, which has maintained a steady adherence from 45 to 50% of the population, peaking at 59% in 1999. This percentage grows in low and middle class sectors, and among people over 65, and decreases in people aged 18 to 24.

Analyzing the evolution of credibility in institutions in Argentina, and considering the historical trend and the international scenario, we may point to the existence of a general decline from 1984 to 1991 (except for the Armed Forces and the Church), a plateau in the 1990s (except for the Church and the media, which actually improved) and a steep fall in the last years, placing Argentina alongside countries with the lowest credibility in institutions.

In contrast, NGOs seem to have gained some credibility in Argentina, and participation in these organizations has increased significantly in the past years. In fact, 42% of Argentines participate in different groups, ranging from religious (16%), educational or cultural (9%), to sports or leisure (8%) organizations. Participation in the Church in particular has risen compared to 1984. The important aspect is that, through these organizations, Argentines have increased the time devoted to social and voluntary assistance. Those efforts are channeled by participating in parishes and religious centers, schools, non-profit educational institutions, *ad hoc* institutions, and so on, to such an extent that, in 2002, some 86% of Argentines were involved in those efforts (62% in 1997).

*Argentines and Family Life in Times of Uncertainty*

After an extended period of isolation, the 1990s saw Argentina introduced into the globalization process. Argentines discovered that bor-
ders could be crossed in many senses; they could travel and know the
physical world, and could have greater access to imported goods than
that they had in the 1980s when the economy was closed. In short,
they could enjoy a different quality of life. In addition, advances in
communications and the Internet opened up a gateway to the world
and knowledge.

At the same time, and despite the extended existence of the democratic regime, Argentines were forced to adapt themselves to sudden
and frequent social and economic changes. The periods of stability,
broadly speaking, had been short and brief, resulting in short horizons
for decision-making, and frequent changes in the rules of the game. In
the 1980s, inflation prompted uncertainty over the value of people's
incomes in general, and payroll wages in particular. In the 1990s, particularly in the second half of the decade, increased unemployment
put into question labor stability and working conditions, deeply fueling
people's feeling of uncertainty. In fact, lack of employment and labor
instability are considered the leading problems the country faces.

The changes mentioned above consisted in the shift from a closed
economy, with dwindling economic growth and productivity due to
the absence of external competition that ruled the 1980s, to an open
economy, with high growth and productivity rates in the 1990s. All of
that was accompanied by a drastic inflation cut, limiting companies'
ability to reduce labor costs.

Paradoxically, the new environment brought about new problems
in the way Argentines related to work. Argentina's introduction into
the world economy required adapting to the productive offer (winners
and losers) which took place simultaneously with the passage of state-
owned companies to the private sector. Both processes released a labor
force that failed to be reconverted on time, resulting in a substantial
unemployment rise, from an average 5% in the 1980s, to 15% in 1999.
This figure climbed even higher in ensuing years, when the structural
changes were also affected by economic shrinkage, and, in October
2001, although the number of urban workers was the same as three
years before, the number of unemployed (2.5 million people) had shot
up by one million, equaling 8% of the workforce.

Besides this, the quality of work deteriorated, with more workers in the informal market, bringing about greater labor uncertainty. In 1999, 49% of workers were in the informal market (37.5% and 44.7% in 1980 and 1990 respectively), totaling 80% among freelance workers. The most affected by informal work are youngsters and people over 60, and workers in the construction and trade-related fields. Interestingly, informal work is higher in low-income sectors (97% and 82% in the two lowest levels).

To this phenomenon was added a second drastic and protracted recession that gripped Argentina from 1999 to 2002. Although the country is emerging from the crisis, it is far from regaining the per capita GDP and employment rates enjoyed before the crisis.

The scenario depicts the convergence of two groups of people, whose labor stability and security have been shaken; those who were displaced by the changes in the course of the economy, and those affected by cyclical work. Of course, the socio-economic features of these groups do not necessarily coincide; hence the emergence of the "new poor", a concept referring to those people whose job and working conditions have deteriorated in the past years as a result of the first of the two above-mentioned factors. In other words, not only has the number of the unemployed and people who find it hard to join the labor market for the first time (mainly youngsters) increased, but there has also been a qualitative change in people facing those difficulties since it now also involves individuals who had never been affected by this problem.

Thus, Argentines highly value work (95% consider it important for their lives), and two out of three Argentines deem labor stability-security as the most relevant factor when choosing a job (the figure has increased since 1984, particularly in low-income sectors where cyclical work becomes a structural problem if the unemployed take a long time to re-enter the labor market).

The instability factor adds to the low credibility in institutions and the low trust in people in general (as mentioned in the first part of the chapter), resulting in a deeper attachment to family and friends (also to religion as will be explained later), and, from this reality, they define attitudes and behaviors.

Amid an atmosphere of uncertainty and concern over the low credibility in people and institutions that should protect society from crisis, Argentines keep active relations with their friends (three out of four Argentines get together with friends at least once a month), and also with the family group (98% consider it very important in their lives). It would seem that Argentines feel safer and more protected when in company of friends and family.

As in many societies, Argentina has experienced demographic, social and economic changes that have influenced the family structure. Life expectancy at birth has increased from 66 years in 1965, to 73 years in 1995, and the percentage of the elderly (over 65s) in society and families has risen, accounting for 10% in 2000. This has influenced the distribution of chores, and the make-up and economy of households (high costs for the care of the elderly considering dwindling savings in countries with weak and impoverished social security systems).

The perception that people lead their lives in a more insecure environment is related to the values that Argentines consider must be practiced when raising their children and interacting with the family. In this regard, Table 2 shows that Argentines attach great priority to good manners, sense of responsibility, tolerance and respect for work (in that order). But, taking into account the changes experienced from 1991 to 1999, greater importance was placed on the following aspects: religious faith (+16), spirit of sacrifice (+8), obedience (+5), good manners (+5). At the same time, importance in the following decreased: tolerance (−8), independence (−7), imagination (−7), perseverance (−7). In other words, a shift to a more conservative position seems to have been made as to how children are brought up for life.

Table 4.2. Children's Education: Qualities Encouraged at Home.

| Qualities encouraged at home | 1984 | 1991 | 1995 | 1999 |
|---|---|---|---|---|
| Good manners | 48% | 78% | 75% | 83% |
| Feeling of responsibility | 58% | 80% | 79% | 77% |
| Tolerance and respect for other people | 44% | 78% | 73% | 70% |
| Hard work | 50% | 53% | 55% | 57% |
| Religious faith | 19% | 28% | 36% | 44% |
| Obedience | 19% | 32% | 32% | 37% |
| Independence | 42% | 43% | 41% | 36% |
| Imagination | 22% | 31% | 25% | 24% |
| Determination, perseverance | 17% | 29% | 28% | 22% |
| Thrift, saving money and things | 16% | 15% | 16% | 15% |
| Sacrifice | 7% | 5% | 16% | 13% |

Young people seem to give more importance than the average to obedience, independence and imagination, and less importance to religious faith and hard work. Women, on the other hand, consider it more important to instill religious faith and independence (however, in both cases, there is not much difference from the average).

The second aspect influenced by the less secured environment affecting family life and the values of society concerns the relationship between parents and children.

As to whether children should always love and respect their parents, regardless of their virtues and faults, or whether parents should earn children's respect, 88% of Argentines preferred the first option. Consensus on this option has been growing over time, especially if we compare the figures in 1991 and 1984. As was expected, this preference increases in the middle and older ages (35 years onwards), and in low socio-economic and educational levels. The *quid pro quo* appears in the question of whether parents should offer their children the best, even at the expense of their own well-being, or whether they should live their own lives. A high 85% favored the first option. This percentage has not grown much since 1991, although it is higher than the 1984 figure. The lowest percentages are found among youngsters (despite the fact that they are the recipients of parent's attention), people with secondary education only, and high-income sectors.

After analyzing how parents-children relations should be, it seems clear that strong consensus exists in the Argentine society over the duties and responsibilities of parents and children, and this consensus is common to all segments of society. It could be argued that the complex economic scenario could have encouraged people to aid some members of their family and expect some help in return. This matches the growing perception that family gathers great credibility within a framework of widespread loss of confidence and offers security in the currently less safe atmosphere.

### Changes in the Role of Women

Just as happened in many other economically developed societies, Argentina has experienced a rise in the female economic activity rate (defined as the ratio of women who are part of the Economically-Active Population to the total number of women), especially from the early 1980s and the mid-1990s. It was a major change, as it pushed the labor growth rate over the population's general growth rate, and, in the particular case of Argentina, the change coincided with a boost in economic output that required a higher GDP growth rate to absorb the annual increase in the labor market.

An example of this phenomenon is the Greater Buenos Aires urban agglomerate, where the overall activity rate between 1983 and 1994 rose from 37.8% to 44.8%. However, while men's activity rate decreased to 53.4% (56.3% in 1983), the rate for women rose to 33% (24% in 1983). It must be noted that, in 1994, the activity rate for women aged from 15 to 64 years old accounted for 50.7%, and the figure rose to 60.7% for those aged 20–34 years old, and was 58.9% for women aged 35–49.

This long-term trend includes factors such as women's salaries (which represent an opportunity cost), the spouse's salary, the income of the rest of the family members, attendance at some educational institution, and so on, the influence of which can change according to the economic cycle and the situation the family undergoes. Research concludes that, in the short term, these variables strongly influence the decisions to join or withdraw from the labor market, and such decisions are made within the family framework considering family variables such as the presence of minors at home (which reduces the female share rate among married women).

Of course, this reality influences Argentines' perception of working mothers, and their relationship with the family, and this can be seen in Figure 3. As a rule, in a 3 to 1 ratio, Argentines believe that a working mother can establish just as warm and secure a relationship with her children as a non-working mother. This ratio, which has prevailed over time, is higher in women (4 to 1) than in men (2.5 to 1), and also higher among youngsters and high-income sectors. Following the same trend, more Argentines believe that both women and men must contribute to family income (91% in 1999, against 77% in 1991). While agreement with this idea is stronger among women (92%), consensus is also high among men (83%).

*New Trends in Argentines' Religiosity*

The changes observed in the attitudes of Argentines that we have referred to above relate to the changes in the levels of religiosity, and, in general terms, both faith and practice aspects of religiosity have risen.

Figure 4.3. Values Related to Gender Roles (percent who agree with the statement).

Agree with

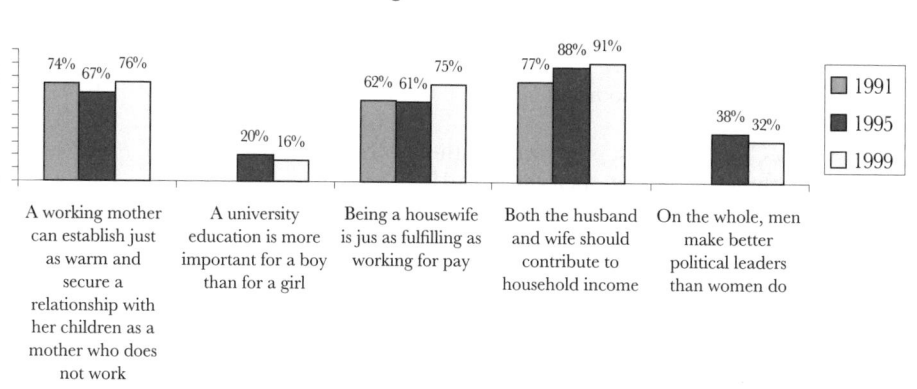

This trend, which had already been found in previous studies about the system of values, has been confirmed by the 1999 data.

Data in Table 3 are consistent with a society that faces problems of different types, where trust in people has been undermined, and where institutions fail to offer the response and solution to overcome various problems. The Church enjoys the highest approval rating within a framework of dwindling credibility.

Therefore, religious messages enable people to uphold and generate hope for a better future, and the Church conveys a reality with a protective image in times of turmoil and insecurity. In this sense, a major aspect in understanding the link between increased religiousness and Argentines' difficulties lies in the high, and growing, proportion of those seeking religion for comfort and strength (74% in 1999, against 61% in 1991).

Argentines consider themselves religious people, they pray, and think that God is important in their lives. For these three factors, the rise is significant compared to 1984 levels: an increase in 19.1% for the first, 16% for the second, and 2.9% (on a 1 to 10 scale) for the last. The percentage of Argentines for whom religion is important has considerably risen compared to the situation in the 1990s (Table 3).

It is interesting to note that the above-mentioned figures match the increase in the percentage of people who believe in some of the truths of the Catholic Church (note that 8 out of 10 Argentines claim to observe the Catholic faith): Heaven, Hell, Sin, the Devil, the Soul and God.

Table 4.3. Argentines and Religion.

|  | 1984 | 1991 | 1995 | 1999 |
|---|---|---|---|---|
| Consider themselves religious | 62% | 70% | 79% | 81% |
| Find relief in religion | 52% | 62% | 67% | 74% |
| Consider religion important | – | 64% | 66% | 93% |
| Pray or meditate | 61% | 75% | 78% | 77% |
| Go to Church at least once per month | 39% | 36% | 41% | 43% |
| Importance of God in their life (1 to 10) | 5,6 | 7,9 | 8,3 | 8,5 |
| Believe in God | 83% | 90% | 94% | 95% |
| Believe people have a soul | 62% | 75% | 82% | 81% |
| Believe in the existence of demons | 34% | 44% | 51% | 45% |
| Believe in heaven | 44% | 65% | 72% | 76% |
| Believe in hell | 32% | 38% | 44% | 40% |
| Believe in sin | 50% | 68% | 74% | 78% |

To a lesser extent, Argentines' attendance at mass has increased, especially if we compare the figures of 1999 and 1991, and this is consistent with the fact that the Church has moved closer to individuals, offering better solutions in the social field, and making people feel safer and protected. At the same time, Argentines often pray, with 6 out of 10 praying at least once a week.

Classifying the information into socio-demographic variables, we may conclude that:

• There are more religious women (85.9%) than religious men (75.2%) in Argentina.
• As age goes up, people tend to consider themselves more religious: 74% of people aged 18–24; 80% of people aged 25–34, and 86% in people over 64 years old.
• The percentage of those who consider themselves to be religious is higher among people who do not work (87%) than it is among workers (79%).
• Low education sectors are more religious.
• People living in the country's hinterland consider themselves more religious (84%).

In turn, the factors that could be labeled as alternative, such as aid from angels, telepathy, or dead relatives helping to solve the problems of the living, and the idea that the future is revealed in dreams, are beliefs showing a considerable incidence in 1999; 6 out of 10 Argentines believe in angels, and 4 out of 10 believe in the other issues.

By contrast, only 6% to 4% of the population practices such things as yoga, mental control, alternative therapy, or resort to, fortunetellers, tarotists or astrologers to learn about the future, a figure that reveals few people pursue these practices.

### The Role of the Church

The Church has been gaining credibility due to its performance in trying to solve problems, particularly in the social sphere. As a result, the latest surveys found that its approval rating has improved (Table 4). The number of people who consider this institution adjusts to the spiritual needs of its followers and their family problems has risen. Sustained growth is also found among those Argentines who think that the Church gives the right answer to the existing social and moral problems. In short, the improved approval rating of the Church involves not only the spiritual aspects, but also its efforts in the social sphere.

The positive perception of the role of the Church in society is higher among women, the elderly and people with lower educational level.

This appraisal of the Church in these issues is likely to grow in succeeding years, resulting from both the worsening of the crisis, which could have boosted the feeling of a missing horizon and the need for spiritual and material aid, and also from the fact that it embodies a reliable institution for many Argentines. Finally, because the Church channels people's efforts to help and take voluntary actions, the Church's possibilities of meeting people's needs more efficiently are enhanced, setting up a cycle: greater credibility in the Church, higher number of followers and social demands met, greater credibility.

However, this does not imply that Argentines desire the Church's greater involvement in political affairs. On the contrary, 7 out of 10 Argentines think that religious leaders should not influence people's electoral votes, and 6 out of 10 consider they should not influence government's decisions at all, thus setting the boundaries for the Church's actions.

Table 4.4. People's Perception of the Church.

|                                             | 1983 | 1991 | 1995 | 1999 |
|---------------------------------------------|------|------|------|------|
| The Moral problems and needs of the individual | 38%  | 36%  | 40%  | 49%  |
| The problems of Family life                 | 37%  | 44%  | 48%  | 54%  |
| People's Spiritual needs                    | 39%  | 50%  | 53%  | 63%  |
| Social problems present facing Argentina    | –    | 32%  | 37%  | 45%  |

*Conclusions*

• This chapter aimed to analyze the changes that occurred in the values of Argentine society for the past two decades. Empirical studies, on which the considerations herein described are based, were conducted from 1984 to 1999. That period links two important events in Argentine history: the restoration of democracy (December 1983), and the prelude of the worst crisis in Argentine history which erupted in December 2001. Three topics have been analyzed in this chapter: a) public-oriented aspects (changes in the field of political beliefs); b) private-oriented aspects (family, children and women); c) the religion-oriented sphere. Global changes coexist with local specificities in these three aspects.

• By 1999, when a public opinion poll was conducted for a study of values in Argentina, people were reaching the end of a cycle both in economic as well as political terms. On the economic front, 1998 was the last year of sustained economic expansion, since, by the middle of that year, stagnation first, then moderate recession (from mid-1998 until mid-2001), and later collapse (in the second half of 2001 and first half of 2002) gripped the country, which only began to recover in the ensuing months though maintaining deteriorated conditions that will be hard to heal.

To some extent, the reforms fatigue phenomenon appeared in connection with many economic changes introduced in the 1990s (such as privatizations). Complaints were filed against those reforms as to the way they had been implemented, the lack of transparency in control mechanisms, etc.

Public opinion had begun to shift demands, calling for a greater involvement of the State as a regulatory body than it had had in the early 1990s, guaranteeing rights, and providing aid to the excluded. In the political sphere, the government gathered little approval, and, within a general framework of support for democracy as the best system of government, Argentines criticized the way in which some problems of democracy were solved, and the extent to which it provided for particular interests.

- Against this background, new challenges appeared on the political landscape: inflation and low real wages were no longer people's major concern, giving way to unemployment, the fear of losing one's job, and worries that a close relative could be unemployed and would find it hard to join the labor market again, and so on. The size of the problem is seen in the fact that the jobless rate went from 5.5% in the 1980s, to 15% from 1995 to 1999, and exceeded 20% at the start of the new decade (2.5 million people were unemployed by October 2001, 1.0 million more than in 1998), and there was a growing informal market as well as a deterioration in working conditions.

The new negative factor that has affected the Argentine social stage for the past years and has become people's primary concern is violence. Street burglaries have changed from street pickpockets to rapid abductions (as happens in other regional countries), all within a framework of increased violence and danger. The drooping approval rating of the security forces, the lack of credibility in the Judiciary and government security officials worsens the atmosphere of helplessness.

- This situation prompted increased uncertainty and deterioration of the credibility index both in political institutions—Parliament, political parties, the judiciary—as well as in other institutions such as businesses and trade unions. That is why people have taken a more hesitant position towards their fellows, as more people consider it necessary to be careful when dealing with others and think that others could take advantage of them.

On the political front in particular, the lack of credibility in institutions reflects the growing distance citizens are taking from their leaders. While this trend is in tune with that of other societies worldwide, where strong questioning and reassessment of politics also exist, Argentina shows quite a marked case in the vanguard of skepticism. The strong shocks that have ravaged the country for the past two decades in different ways (hyperinflation, devaluation, unemployment, impoverishment, freezing of bank deposits, corruption, etc) strongly undermined credibility in leaders, politicians and many other authorities.

However, the case of Argentina also illustrates an interesting aspect. Despite the strong questioning of leadership and institutional performance, the legitimacy of the democratic system has been upheld, even in the harshest periods of the crisis (2001–2002). Between 1998 and 2002, Argentina faced a 25% fall in its GDP, and mid 2002 also witnessed a general anger towards politicians; one year later, however, Argentines were participating actively in elections even though they were choosing between already known political leaders. The normalization of Argentina (with the decrease in *piqueteros or road blockers* demonstrations, barter transactions and neighborhood board meeting) shows that democracy, understood as one of the central and undisputed values in people's lives, constitutes one of the achievements of the past century.

- As a counterpart, in view of the labor and income uncertainty and the prevailing fear for their security, Argentines seek shelter in their intimate circle, where they feel safer and can, to a certain extent, even relax. Family and friends offer a place where they find peace and quietness.

Another change, one that took place worldwide, is the growing participation of women in the labor market, which, in Argentina, translates into a greater acceptance of this new and significant change. However, such acceptance also coexists with the high appraisal of housewives (that is to say, women who are exclusively devoted to housework).

- In a different sphere, Argentines respond to difficulties by increasing their sense of religion, attaching greater importance to religion in life, praying more often, although failing to increase attendance at mass. It seems the increased religiousness results from a closer relationship with God. Although positive opinions about the way the Church responds to problems have risen—though at different levels according to the topics—the negative opinions remain higher.

In other words, religion appears as another shelter in times of uncertainty, mainly by means of each individual's interaction with God.

Despite the fact that the Church, as an institution, gathers the highest credibility rate in Argentina (50% trust a lot or quite a lot in it), the ratio is low compared to international figures.

It could be argued that, far from being ravaged by the modernization process, religions have come out stronger. This shows that a sustained process of absent credibility may give way to a new appraisal of the world against the secularization process.

- In response to a framework of low credibility in other people, Argentines get involved in the problems of society outside political parties, by participating in NGOs and voluntary assistance. These efforts, on which they increasingly spend more time and money, seems to fulfill their personal ambitions on the one hand, and offset the government's deficiencies on the other.

In other words, there is a sort of practical solidarity that goes beyond the lack of credibility in others and in institutions. To some extent, the same reason that reappraises the family as a shield and shelter in the face of the difficulties, explains this greater collaborative involvement.

- The diverse trends in Argentina described above depict how ambivalence is one of the physiognomic features of the social process of our time, and how, even amid global processes, each country will find and assimilate their own cultural and value-creating responses.

## References

Brechon, P. 2000. *Les valeurs des Francaise. Evolutions de 1980 a 2000*, Paris, Ed. Armand Colin.

Carballo, M. 1987. *Qué pensamos los argentinos? Los valores de los argentinos de nuestro tiempo*, Buenos Aires: Ed. El Cronista Comercial.

Censo Nacional de Población y Vivienda 2001, Buenos Aires, Instituto Nacional de Estadísticas y Censos.

van Deth, J. and Scarbrough, E. (ed.). 1995. *The Impact of Values*, Oxford: Oxford University Press.

Fogarty, M. et al. 1984. *Irish Values and Attitudes. The Irish Report of the European Values Systems Study*, Dublin, Dominican Publications.

Giddens, A. 1987. "Structuralism, Post-structuralism and the production of culture", in Giddens, A. Turner, J. *Social Theory Today*, California: Stanford University Press.

Inglehart, R., [DATE] *Culture Shift in Advances Industrial Society*, New Jersey, Princeton University Press.

——— (ed.). 2003. *Human Values and Social Change*, Leiden, Brill Press.

Riffault, H. 1994. *Les valeurs des francais*. Saint Germain, Presses Universitaires de France.

Soneira, A. et al. 1996. *Sociología de la religión*. Buenos Aires, Fundación Universidad a Distancia "Hernandarias": Editorial Docencia.

PART THREE

EUROPE

# A. NORTHERN EUROPE

# CHAPTER FIVE

## CHANGING SWEDISH CIVIC ORIENTATIONS: FROM SOLIDARITY TO ACTIVISM?

THORLEIF PETTERSSON

At the middle of the nineteenth century, Sweden was a poor country with one of the lowest GDPs per capita in Western Europe. At that time, it was also one of the most agrarian and least urbanized European countries. However, around the 1860s, the Swedish economy began a remarkable growth (Therborn 1988). Today, Sweden with a population around nine millions is an advanced welfare society with a solid market economy. Most ordinary indicators for standard of living rank Sweden as one of the top countries in the world, and the economic gaps between social classes are smaller than in most other countries. For many years, Sweden has also ranked high on measures of democracy and anti-corruption. For two centuries, Sweden has managed to stay outside wars and armed conflicts while remaining committed to global governance and development. Even if the Swedish welfare system has come under economic pressure, especially during the early 1990s, and some commentators have declared the so called "Swedish model" abandoned and dead, this does not alter the comparative advantages of Swedish quality of life.

In the introductory part of this chapter, the cultural background of the Swedish model of general welfare will be introduced. The second part of the chapter will investigate whether the values which are associated with this political culture have changed or not during the previous decades, and also how these changes can be accounted for.

*Swedish political culture:*
*The Balance of Top-Down and Bottom-Up Powers*

The 1930s was the decade when the Swedish parliament started to enact the social legislation that formed the basis of the Swedish model. In 1932, the Social Democrats won the general election, and in 1934 unemployment insurance was introduced, followed by a general pension reform, the first national law regulating vacation time, and the first step in providing financial assistance to families with children. Further waves of welfare legislation followed during the post-war boom years. That the Social Democrats remained in power for an unprecedented 44 years until 1976 was of great importance in solidifying the welfare reforms which were initiated during the 1930s.

But the reforms have deeper roots than so. A gradual democratization of Swedish society took place during the second half of the nineteenth century. Constitutional reforms during the 1860s abolished a parliament based on property, and restrictions on voting were removed gradually until full and equal suffrage existed as late as 1921. The social and economic conditions which prevailed during the late nineteenth century also laid ground for what later developed into the Swedish model. At that time, the social and economic structure was characterized by extreme concentration of wealth in a small group of very rich families, an unusually small middle class, and a very large class of small farmers, agricultural workers, and urban laborers. In such a relatively undifferentiated society, the burdens of poverty had to be born equally. Therefore, the role of the larger collective, rather than the individual, became crucial (Esping-Andersen 1994).

Especially two factors were instrumental in shaping the cultural basis for the Swedish model. One concerned the state, the other the peasantry. Beginning in the sixteenth century, a strong and centralized Swedish state started to develop. This development was enhanced during the seventeenth century, when Sweden was among the key players in the European wars. The development of a strong state was also strengthened by the establishment of a new administrative system and an independent and quite competent civil service, simultaneously showing fairness and professionalism in its relations to the people, and loyalty and allegiance to the legal system and state superiors (Hägg 2003: 161). The roots of the civil service date back to the seventeenth century. It is unlikely that the Swedish model of the twentieth century would have become so comparatively successful had there not been a strong and efficient bureaucracy and an independent civil service on which to build (Esping-Andersen 1993; Wetterberg 2003).

Another important part of the cultural background for the Swedish model concerned the role of the peasantry. Unlike many other European countries, land-owning peasants occupied a strong position in Sweden. At least since the sixteenth century they had been represented in the Swedish parliament through their own estate, enabling them to participate in the decision-making processes. That Sweden experienced relatively little unrest in the form of large popular uprisings, at least by comparison with much of the rest of Europe, is related to the early participation of peasants in politics. This enabled them to redress some of their grievances through participation rather than insurrection (Österberg 1998). The political participation of the peasantry could also be observed at the local levels of society. One such local arena was the parish meeting, which in the Swedish state-church context not only dealt with religious matters but over time also acquired significant control over many social, economic and political matters. The parish meeting provided a setting where different social groups could meet, discuss and interact. It also served as a nexus for contacts between the local level and the state, a connection through which the local peasantry was able to exercise influence. The local peasantry was able to influence a number of issues, and a Swedish political culture developed, characterized by relatively peaceful and consensual relations and negotiations between different groups and interests as well as participation from fairly broad strata of the population (Aronsson 1992: 337–344).

In fact, the main fault line in Swedish society was not between a poor peasantry and a rich feudal aristocracy or between the state and the burghers, but between the state and the peasantry. Various arrangements developed where these two parties could meet for deliberations and compromises, and the strong state was balanced by a people that were strong as well. "It is in this mixture, in this perpetually changing dynamic that [the] Swedish political tradition is rooted—not only in a strong, interventionist state, and, equally, not only in popular power and collectivism" (Österberg 1998: 124; cf. Österberg 1996). Thus, a major historical/cultural background to the contemporary Swedish model is the long term establishment of a working balance between the top-down authority of a strong state and the bottom-up power of a strong, active and independent people.

### Swedish Welfare as "the People's Home"

The Swedish form of general welfare has become known as the "Swedish middle way", the "Swedish third way" and the "Swedish model". The more precise meaning of this model is however disputed. According to some, the Swedish model is basically a forum for negotiations and agreements between the employer and employee organizations on the labor market. This forum is said to secure good working conditions and efficient production, and to avoid devastating strikes and conflicts. Others see the Swedish model as a kind of governance which should serve as a blueprint for social organization, especially for developing countries. In this sense, it has been seen as "a national aspiration to project globally the domestic experience of the Swedish version of the 'good society'" (Mörth and Sundelius 1995: 108). For yet others, the Swedish model refers to a specific Scandinavian social-democratic welfare regime, distinct from a liberal or conservative one. For long, Social Democratic governance has favored strong redistribution policies and established large tax-financed general welfare systems for education, health care, child and elder care, parental insurance, pensions, and so forth.

In order to understand the cultural component of the Swedish model, one should note that it is related closely to another powerful concept in Swedish twentieth century socio-political discourse, especially during the model's formative period up to the mid-1950s. This is the concept of *folkhemmet*. According to this concept, the Swedish state or rather Swedish society is *the home* (in Swedish: *hemmet*) of *the people* (in Swedish: *folk*). Among others, this concept is associated closely with the former Social Democratic Prime Minister Per Albin Hansson (1885–1946; prime minister 1932–1946). In an influential and often quoted speech, Hansson described the "people's home" in terms of solidarity and considerate equality, co-operation, democratic rule, avoidance of conflicts and abuse of power. A well-known passage of the speech said the following (translation from the Swedish original according to Tilton 1990):

> The basis of the home is togetherness and common feeling. The good home does not consider anyone as either privileged or unappreciated; it knows no special favorites and no stepchildren. There no one looks down on anyone else, there no one tries to gain advantage at another's expense, and the stronger do not plunder or suppress the weaker. In the good home, equality, consideration, co-operation, and helpfulness prevail. Applied to a home for all the citizens, this would mean the breaking down of all the social and economic barriers that now divide citizens into the privileged and the unfortunate, into rulers and subjects, into rich and poor, the glutted and the destitute, the plunderers and the plundered.

The values that were associated with the metaphor of the "people's home" came to serve as a kind of abstract hegemonic framework that influenced all political parties, not only the Social Democrats. Each party had in one way or another to relate to this powerful symbol in their programs and platforms (Fryklund et al. 1988: 638). The metaphor signaled that society can and must be deliberately improved in order to meet people's needs and preferences (Himmelstrand 1988: 19). Among others, the metaphor was intimately linked to Alva and Gunnar Myrdal, two important names in Swedish political discourse, both Nobel laureates. Their "long commitment to both research and to action towards a more egalitarian, secure and rational world has brought them eminent distinctions" (Tilton 1990: 145). Alva and Gunnar Myrdal argued that present-day social faults and injustices can be deliberately changed to the better for all with the help of welfare policies and social engineering. Rather than looking backwards to a glorious past, the metaphor of the "people's home" directed attention to a brighter future.

The metaphor of Swedish welfare as the people's home served as a kind of public myth, indispensable for any viable society (McNeill 1982). It can also be thought of as a blend of a Swedish civil religion and a secular nationalism, binding together the different sectors of the society (Gustafsson 1984). It has also been suggested that the Swedish model rested on a set of fundamental values or convictions, without which its mythical functioning would not be possible (Ingelstam 1988). One such conviction was an optimistic belief in the ever-continuing progress towards a better society which would be achieved by a combination of public policies and active and participating citizens; another was a strong and unquestioning confidence in the efficient, fair and just state, which would deliver to each and every citizen the fruits of the ever-continuing progress. In this way, the Swedish state was not seen as a threat against the individual citizen and his/her interests. In stead, a strong, protective state was seen as a necessary condition for social development and individual freedom, and not as a barrier (Ingelstam 1988). This understanding was related to the fact that the Social Democrats started to use state institutions as instruments for the implementation of their welfare policies. The citizens on their side were expected to stay within the limits of what these policies allowed, and only to demand what was legitimate and a fair share. As Prime Minister Hansson said: "In the people's home, no one tries to get advantage at another's expenses". In stead, in the good home, co-operation and helpfulness should prevail.

In summary, the value basis of the Swedish model includes confidence in state institutions, civic participation, and compliance with the rules and regulations which have been agreed upon as characteristic features of the Swedish political culture, at least until this started to change during the end of second part of the 20th century. Obviously, these three dimensions do not give the full picture of this culture, but they are nevertheless important ingredients of it. These characteristics can also be linked to the balancing top-down and bottom-up forces that came to form the Swedish political culture. The empirical analyses in the second part of this paper will therefore focus on these three dimensions.

Since the early 1980s, the previously powerful metaphor of the people's home has fallen out of fashion in Swedish socio-political discourse. One reason for this was the severe economic/fiscal problems that constrained the welfare programs during the early 1990s. But somehow, the values which were associated with the metaphor also seem to persist. In recent years, Swedish political discourse has focused heavily on the need to strengthen three of the most fundamental dimensions of Swedish welfare: medical care, public schools, and social care. Several analyses of Swedish attitudes towards welfare programs have also demonstrated that these core values have not been abandoned (see e.g. Svallfors 1999).

### Swedish Political Culture, a Special Case among Different Welfare Regimes?

Against the background of Swedish welfare policies and the high standard of living, one may ask if the Swedish political culture is specific to Sweden, or whether other developed Western societies show similar patterns. The data from the European Values Study/the World Values Survey shows Sweden and the other Nordic countries (Norway, Finland, and Denmark) to be rather exceptional on two basic value dimensions (Inglehart et al. 2004). The first dimension is the so called traditional value orientation which centers on value authorities such as "God, Fatherland, and Family". The second value orientation is the so called survival versus self-expression orientation which centers on values such as trust, tolerance, subjective well-being, and political activism. Sweden and the other Nordic countries score among the lowest on the traditional values and among the highest on the self-expression values. In fact, no other country is as far from the center of the map as Sweden. This clearly demonstrates that if any country shows deviating positions on these two basic value dimensions, it is Sweden!

Thus, there are good reasons to talk about an exceptional Swedish/ Nordic political culture, characterized by low adherence to traditional values related to religion and family life and high appreciation of self-expression values related to individual autonomy and self-expression, horizontal social trust, social activism, and tolerance for minorities. Some mixture of these values might therefore form a key cultural basis for the Swedish model of welfare. As already mentioned, this chapter will investigate whether this mixture of values have changed or not during the previous decades. In order to do so, two theoretical perspectives on value change will be introduced.

*Two Theoretical Perspectives on Value Change*

For this analysis of value change, two different theoretical perspectives will serve as analytical guidelines. According to one perspective, value change starts at the center of society and is then gradually spread to larger parts of the population (cf. Galtung 1964, 1976; cf. Diez-Nicolas 1995, 2004). As those who belong to the center have better resources, have better access to mass media, are part of more extensive and powerful social networks, are more exposed to new cultural traits, are more prestigious, hold higher social positions, they tend to be more sensitive to cultural changes and to internalize new points of view, wherever these have originated. Thus, value change would in principle start develop at the center of society, and the assumption is that *"an attitude over-represented in the center is more likely to increase whereas an attitude over-represented in the periphery is more likely to decrease"* (Galtung 1976: 14; italics in the original). Even if Galtung developed this theory with regard to how opinions on foreign policy would develop, its general scope allows that it can also be applied on attitudinal and value changes more broadly. With regard to cultural traits in a more wide-ranging sense "The center is normally the initiator, the periphery the receiver" (van der Veer 1976: 622; cf. Andersson 1998). In a way, this process parallels how one of the leading classics in sociology, Georg Simmel, analyzed the developments of fashion (Simmel 1901/1971).

The second perspective on value change assumes that this is usually driven by generational population replacements where younger birth cohorts gradually replace the older. According to Ronald Inglehart's well-known works (Inglehart 1977, 1990, 1997), value change at the societal level is expected to occur by processes of generational population replacements. Individuals are said to value most those things that are in short supply (this is the so-called scarcity hypothesis). This kind of value formation at the micro level is assumed to take place during people's formative pre-adult years. The values which are internalized during this phase are then assumed to remain (this is the so-called socialization hypothesis). For instance, the more the basic needs of successive generations have been satisfied during their formative pre-adult years, the more these generations will develop emancipative self-expression values (the scarcity hypothesis). These emancipative values are then assumed to remain more or less unchanged throughout the generation's life course (the socialization hypothesis). Value change at the societal level will then occur as a consequence of population generational replacements where the younger birth cohorts gradually replace the older ones.

It should be noted that the two perspectives on value change are not mutually excluding. Inglehart's theory on value change describes in detail how the processes of value change occur, whereas the social-position theory locates the processes of value change more firmly in different parts of society. Guided by these two theoretical perspectives on value change, the analyses reported in this paper will explore whether Swedish civic orientations have changed or not over the previous decades. Thus, the analyses will compare value profiles among the center and the periphery, and also investigate if the relations between the center and the periphery are related to subsequent value changes. The analyses will also explore how these changes are affected by generational population replacements.

## Data and Results

*Data*: Swedish political culture was characterized by confidence in state institutions, high levels of civic participation and compliance with the rules and regulations that have been agreed upon. In order to analyze these three civic orientations, the data from the Swedish EVS/WVS waves from 1981, 1990 and 1999 will be used. These data include 947, 1054 and 1015 respondents, respectively, representative for the general Swedish population aged 18–76 (see e.g. Pettersson 1988, 1992; Halman 2001). As indicators of civic participation, four indicators will be used. These concern voluntary work in social movements, horizontal social trust, participation in social protests and public self-expression values (whether one finds it important to give people more to say and to protect freedom of speech). As measures of norm compliance, four other indicators can serve. These measure dislike for cheating on taxes, claiming welfare benefits to which one is not entitled, the taking of bribes, and lying in self-interest, respectively. It should be noted that three of these indicators concern norm compliance in the economic sector and that broader indicators would be preferred. As indicators for trust in state institutions, three indicators are used. These concern confidence in the parliament, the civil service and the legal system. These cover confidence in one order institution (the legal system), one representative institution (the parliament), and one policy implementing (the civil services). Thus, the three institutions include the main kinds of state institutions. The formats of these three sets of indicators are shown by the EVS and WVS questionnaires, available at the websites for these two projects.

The findings from a confirmatory factor analysis of these eleven indicators are given in Figure 5.1. The results show that the indicators are related as expected to the three latent civic orientations. The results also demonstrate that the relations (factor loadings) between the various indicators and the latent civic orientations are the same for each of the three waves. The eleven indictors can therefore be used to measure whether the three civic orientations have changed or not between 1981 and 1999.

In order to compare the center and periphery of society, a scale for social positions that are characteristic for the center has been developed. As indicators of belonging to the center, the following have been used: Age (middle aged adults who are neither young, nor old), gender (men rather than women), education (the well-educated rather than the less educated), high income, position on the labor market (self-employed or employed in higher positions), place of living (big cities), and a cosmopolitan outlook (one identifies oneself with the international or global order rather than the national or local). For each of these criteria, the respondents received a score of one (cf. Galtung 1976; Diez-Nicolas 2004; van der Veer 1976). It should be noted that the scale for social position combines social resource features, territorial aspects, and socioeconomic categories. The inclusion of a cosmopolitan orientation as an indicator of the center should also be observed. The inclusion of this indicator mirrors that in contemporary globalized society, the definition of center and periphery should include an international component as well (cf. Pettersson and Esmer 2005). In order to distinguish those who belong to the center and the periphery, respectively, the following

Figure 5.1. Results from a explanatory factor analysis of 11 indicators for three civic orientations. Approximately 3.000 respondents, 1.000 for each year.

AGFI = ,976, RMSEA = ,040, p = ,998. Test of same factor structure and factor loadings 1981, 1990, and 1999: Chi-square/df = 2.36, p < .001, AGFI = .966, RMSEA = .023, pclose = 1.000.

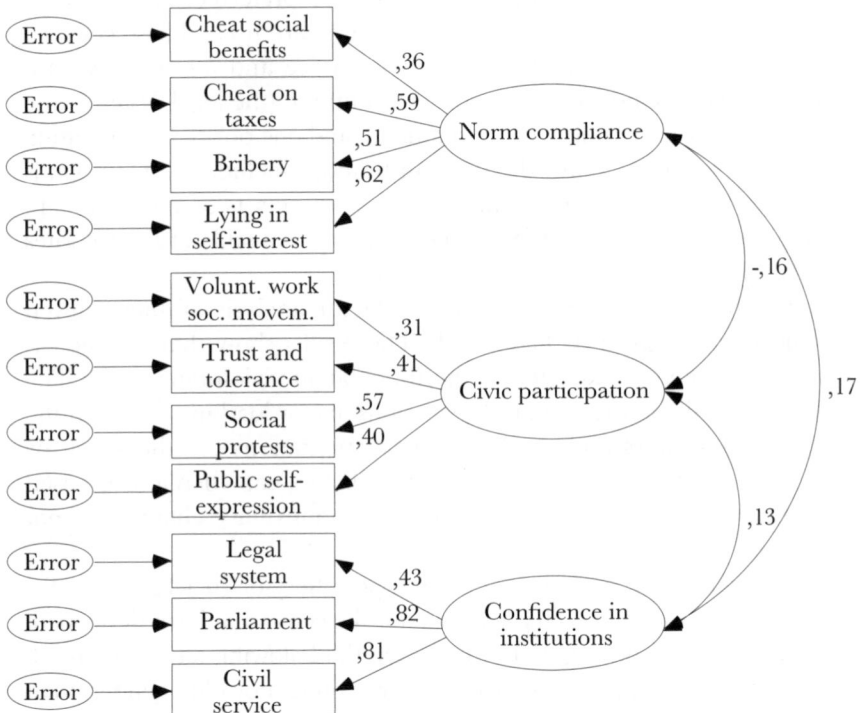

criteria were applied to the distribution for the scale of social positions: Those who belonged to the lowest annual quartile on the social position scale were defined as belonging to the periphery, while those who belonged to the highest annual quartile were defined as belonging to the center of society.

*Results*: Table 5.1 reports how the three civic orientations have changed between 1981 and 1999. The measures for each civic orientation have been standardized to have a grand mean of 100 and a standard deviation of 10 for the combined set of data from 1981, 1990 and 1999. These measures were based on factor scores from an oblique rotated principal factor analysis of the eleven indicators which were described

Table 5.1. Mean scores and variances for three civic orientations in 1981, 1990, and 1999. Results for the entire survey and the center and periphery segments from the Swedish EVS/WVS surveys.

|  |  | 1981 | 1990 | 1999 |
|---|---|---|---|---|
| **Civic participation**: |  |  |  |  |
| All | Means | 95.5 | 99.9 | 103.9 |
| All | Variances | 82.6 | 84.2 | 98.3 |
| Periphery | Means | 94.6 | 97.2 | 102.1 |
| Center | Means | 97.2 | 102.0 | 105.7 |
| **Norm compliance** |  |  |  |  |
| All | Means | 102.0 | 100.4 | 97.8 |
| All | Variances | 70.3 | 96.4 | 120.2 |
| Periphery | Means | 103.4 | 102.6 | 98.2 |
| Center | Means | 100.6 | 98.3 | 96.6 |
| **Confidence in institutions** |  |  |  |  |
| All | Means | 100.5 | 99.3 | 100.3 |
| All | Variances | 95.3 | 114.4 | 89.5 |
| Periphery | Means | 102.0 | 99.1 | 98.2 |
| Center | Means | 99.1 | 100.0 | 101.8 |

*Civic participation*:
Levels:     Increase each period (p < .001; p < .001). Increase entire period (p < .001).
Variances:  No change first period; Increase second period (p< .02); Increase entire period
Center vs. Periphery: Center > Periphery in 1981, 1990, and 1999 (p < .01)

*Norm compliance*:
Levels:     Decrease each period (p < .001; p < .001). Decrease entire period (p < .001)
Variances:  Increase first period (p < .001); Increase second period (p < .001) Increase entire period ( p < .001)
Center vs. Periphery: Periphery > Center in 1981, 1990 (p < .01). No difference in 1999.

*Confidence in institutions*:
Levels:     Decrease first period (p < .02); Increase second period (p < .05). No change entire period
Variances:  Increase first period (p < .02); Decrease second period (p < .01) No change entire period
Center vs. Periphery: Periphery > Center 1981; No difference 1990; Center > periphery 1999 (p > .001)

above. The results show that civic participation *increased* over each of
the two sub-periods, that support for norm compliance *decreased* during
each sub-period and that trust in state institutions *decreased* during the
first sub-period and *increased* during the second. As indicated in Table 1,
these changes were statistically significant.

Table 5.1 also reports mean scores for the center and periphery. The
results reveal a striking pattern. At the beginning of the two sub-periods in 1981 and 1990, the center scored higher than the periphery on
civic participation. And as expected from center-periphery theory, civic
participation increased over each of the two sub-periods. With regard
to norm compliance, the periphery scored higher than the center in
1981 and 1990. And consequently, norm compliance decreased over
each of the two sub-periods. The results for confidence in state institutions are even more surprising. At the beginning of the first sub-period
in 1981, the periphery scored higher than the center. Consequently,
confidence in institutions decreased during this period. By contrast, the
relations between the center and the periphery had changed in 1990,
and the center now scored highest. And during the subsequent sub-
period, confidence in institutions increased. Of the six predictions one
can make from center-periphery theory (two sub-periods times three
civic orientations), all are supported by the value changes that actually
took place. This is undoubtedly ample support for the center-periphery
theory as an instrument for the analysis of value change.

Table 1 also reports whether Swedes became more heterogeneous in
their civic orientations. The theoretical background for this information is that contemporary cultural changes are often assumed to drive
towards increased heterogeneity in people's values and worldviews. In
this regard, growing individualization is said to foster individual choices
for different life styles, world views, moral and religious convictions, and
so forth. When increasing numbers of individuals choose freely from
an enlarged set of options, the result will almost by statistical necessity
be increased heterogeneity (Halman and Pettersson 2003). Table 5.1
demonstrates that orientations towards civic participation and norm
compliance became more heterogeneous. Thus, both increasing and
decreasing civic orientations seem to be marked by increasing heterogeneity. In the case of confidence in institutions, the first sub-period
witnessed increased heterogeneity, while the second sub-period saw
a reversed development. Over the entire period, the net result for
institutional trust appears to have been no change in the degree of
heterogeneity.

The measures which are reported in Table 5.1 are difficult to relate to the actual response distributions for the various indicators for the three civic orientations. To illustrate the changes that took place in a more direct mode, Table 5.2 reports the response distributions for each of the individual indicators. Presented in this way, the changes that have occurred appear to be modest in size. As a rule, they hardly exceed 10–15 percent over each sub-period. It should also be noted that the individual indicators for a given civic orientation seem to follow the same trend. As an exception to this, it should however be noted that in the case of norm compliance, people's views on bribes seem to have been equally strict over the entire period. It should also be noted that the declining confidence in institutions during the first sub-period is primarily explained by decreasing values for the legal system. In contrast, confidence in the other two institutions appeared to be rather stable throughout the period. This example demonstrates that analyses of combined scores for a full set of indicators may give a simplified picture. And furthermore, should the analyses have been based on the police in stead of the legal system, confidence in institutions would have remained the same throughout the entire period. This finding suggests that that one should not put too much weight on the minor changes in institutional trust which appeared when confidence in the legal system was used as an indicator. One reason for the sudden (?) drop in 1990 in the confidence for the legal system might be that some specific negative events took place in this system at that time. Another can be that the verbal expression for the legal system which was used in the Swedish questionnaire (Swedish "rättsväsendet") is a difficult and multi-layered concept (cf. Axberger, 1996). The incidental drop in 1990 might there-fore simply be random and caused by measurement error.

Yet another analysis of the magnitude of the changes in the three civic orientations leads to a somewhat different conclusion. This analysis relates to a typology for civic virtues and good citizenship (see Table 3 below). The typology was developed in order to study Swedes' ori-entations towards two core dimensions of citizenship (Petersson et al. 1988). The first dimension concerned the civic virtue of following the top-down rules of the game, while the second concerned the virtue of bottom-up participation in the democratic establishment of rules and regulations. "Democracy, seen as autonomy, is a kind of self-regulation. Democracy does not mean the absence of rules and coercive power. On the contrary, a state and a legal system is a necessary, but not sufficient, condition for democracy. Thus, another key dimension of democracy

Table 5.2. Percentages showing civic participation, norm compliance and confidence in institutions. Results from the Swedish EVS/WVS data from 1981, 1990, and 1999.

|  |  | 1981 | 1990 | 1999 |
|---|---|---|---|---|
| **Civic participation** |  |  |  |  |
| Score high on: | Social trust and respect[1] | 40.0% | 54.4% | 59.2% |
|  | Public self-expression[2] | 43.8% | 50.2% | 51.5% |
|  | Social protests[3] | 56.6% | 72.7% | 88.7% |
|  | Voluntary work soc. movm.[4] | 13.9% | 17.8% | 26.5% |
|  | **Mean percentage** | **38.6%** | **46.3%** | **56.5%** |
| **Norm complicance** |  |  |  |  |
| Strict views on | Cheating on taxes[5] | 81.9% | 67.2% | 67.8% |
|  | Cheating on social benefits[5] | 90.0% | 84.8% | 72.2% |
|  | Taking of bribes[5] | 84.4% | 83.1% | 81.4% |
|  | Lying in self-interest[5] | 69.3% | 70.9% | 58.2% |
|  | **Mean percentage** | **81.4%** | **76.5%** | **69.9%** |
| **Confidence in institutions** |  |  |  |  |
| Confidence in | Legal system[6] | 73.2% | 55.9% | 61.1% |
|  | Parliament[6] | 46.6% | 47.1% | 51.2% |
|  | Civil service[6] | 45.7% | 43.9% | 48.7% |
|  | **Mean percentage** | **55.2%** | **48.9%** | **53.7%** |

[1] Score 2 on a 0–2 point scale; [2] Score 2–3 on a 0–3 point scale; [3] Score 1–5 on a 0–5 point scale; [4] Voluntary work in at least one movement; [5] Score 8–10 on a ten-point scale, [6] Score 3–4 on a four-point scale.

is that its coercive rules and regulations are established by the citizens themselves. Citizenship is therefore a combination of two elements: Participation in the democratic establishment of rules and regulations, and a willingness to follow the rules and regulations" (Petersson et al. 1988: 264; translated into English here). This view of democratic civic virtues, citizenship or civic culture is in accordance with a long tradition in political science (cf. Almond and Verba 1963).

Two of the civic orientations which have been discussed in this chapter have an obvious relation to these two civic virtues. Norm compliance relates to willingness to follow the rules, while civic participation relates to involvement in the creation of them. A combination of these two orientations gives the four categories which are outlined in Table 5.3.

Table 5.3. Percentages for four combinations of two civic orientations. Results for 1981 and 1999.

| Norm compliance | Civic Participation | |
| --- | --- | --- |
| | **Low** | **High** |
| **Low** | **Anti-collectivism**: | **Activism**: |
| | 1999:   23.2% | 1999:   37.6% |
| | 1981:   26.7% | 1981:   13.8% |
| **High** | **Subordination**: | **Integrative democracy**: |
| | 1999:   12.6% | 1999:   26.6% |
| | 1981:   39.5% | 1981:   20.0% |

Active civic participation in combination with a stronger emphasis on norm compliance constitutes solidarity and a kind of integrative democracy. On the other hand, active civic participation in combination with a resistance to comply with the norms can be seen as a kind of innovative democratic activism. In the religious field, this would be called prophecy. Stronger emphasis on norm compliance in combination with disregard for civic participation can be viewed as submissive conformism, whereas a negative stance on both of the two civic virtues can be interpreted as anti-collectivism (for a more nuanced and critical discussion of this, see Pettersson, 1992; Petersson et al. 1998).

This typology help illustrate the magnitude of the changes in the civic orientations which were reported in Table 5.1 and 5.2. To this end, the overall distributions for civic participation and norm compliance from the full Swedish data-set from 1981, 1990, and 1999, respectively, have been dichotomized into one low-scoring and one high-scoring category. Since this categorization is exclusively based on Swedish data, it must be noted that the categorization of a certain group of respondents as scoring low on e.g. norm compliance only refers to the Swedish situation. Should data from other countries have been included, these respondents might well have turned out to score comparatively high on norm compliance. Disregarding this, Table 5.3 reports how the relative size of the four combinations of civic participation and norm compliance changed between 1981 and 1999. The category of "Passive subordination" became reduced to one third from about 40 percent to about 13, while the "Activists" increased almost three times from about 14 percent to about 38. These developments indicate that the changing civic orientations can be epitomized as a move from subordination to activism. Described in this way, the Swedish civic orientations appear to have changed in a more substantial manner than was suggested by the analyses of the individual indicators for the three civic orientations (cf. Table 5.2). To the degree that the traditional Swedish model was marked by a combination of high levels of both civic participation and norm compliance, the differential development for these two civic virtues indicate that a substantial change has taken place towards a more activist and less orderly model.

As already noted, the changes that took place between 1981 and 1999 followed the expectations from center-periphery theory. In the theoretical discussion of value change, it was emphasized that this does not exclude that the changes might also be explained by generational population replacements. To investigate this, the developments for three birth cohorts will be investigated. The first cohort consists of those who were born between 1964 and 1973. This cohort was too young to be included in the 1981 wave. In 1990 the members of this cohort were 18–26 years of age, while in 1999 they were 27–35. The second birth cohort consists of those who were born between 1924 and 1963. This cohort participated in all three waves of the value study and it is therefore of key interest for the analysis of value stability as people get older and pass through different phases of their life cycle. In 1981, this cohort was 18–57 years old. In 1990, the cohort had become 27–66 years of age, while in 1999 the cohort was aged 36–75. The third cohort is made up of those who were born between 1914 and 1923. This cohort was too old to be included in the 1999 wave. In 1981 this cohort was 58–66, and in 1990 it was 67–75 years of age. The results for these three birth cohorts are shown in Table 4.

The results for the three birth cohorts suggest two different explanations for the changing civic orientations. In the case of norm compliance, the switch of the oldest high-scoring cohort to the youngest low-scoring cohort has contributed to the general decline. But this cohort replacement does not seem to be the only explanation for the decline. The birth cohort that was included in all three waves also showed a decline, notably during the second sub-period. Even if the decrease for this cohort was smaller than the overall decline, it nevertheless contributed to the over-all declines in norm compliance. The declining values for the middle cohort during the second sub-period are probably not related to the fact that the cohort became older between 1990 and 1999. Instead, a common period effect in this direction seems to be a more plausible explanation.

Table 5.4. Mean scores on three civic orientations for three different birth cohorts. Results from the Swedish EVS/WVS surveys in 1981, 1990, and 1999.

| | Year: | 1981 | 1990 | 1999 |
|---|---|---|---|---|
| **Civic participation:** | | | | |
| All aged 18–76 | | 95.5 | 99.5 | 103.9 |
| *Birth cohorts*: | | | | |
| Born 1964–1973 | | | 100.7 | 102.9 |
| Born 1924–1963 | | 96.3 | 100.0 | 103.9 |
| Born 1914–1923 | | 93.7 | 96.7 | |
| **Norm compliance** | | | | |
| All aged 18–76 | | 102.0 | 100.4 | 97.8 |
| *Birth cohorts* | | | | |
| Born 1964–1973 | | | 97.2 | 94.3 |
| Born 1924–1963 | | 101.2 | 101.1 | 99.3 |
| Born 1914–1923 | | 104.6 | 103.3 | |
| **Confidence in institutions** | | | | |
| All aged 18–76 | | 100.5 | 99.3 | 100.3 |
| *Birth cohorts* | | | | |
| Born 1964–1973 | | | 98.1 | 99.9 |
| Born 1924–1963 | | 100.4 | 99.5 | 100.1 |
| Born 1914–1923 | | 100.9 | 99.7 | |

The increasing levels of civic participation are to a much lesser degree explained by cohort replacements. In this case, the oldest *low*-scoring cohort was replaced by the youngest *high*-scoring cohort. However, in comparison with norm compliance, the levels of civic participation for the cohort who participated in all three waves appear to have been less stable. Instead, this cohort seems to have followed the general trend of increasing civic participation rather closely. Therefore, the overall increase in civic participation seems to be primarily affected by a general period effect, which had a similar impact on all cohorts. In addition to this effect, there was however also a rather modest effect of cohort replacements where the youngest cohort replaced the oldest.

In the case of confidence in institutions, it seems as if the minor changes that did occur were not affected by cohort replacements. The birth cohort which participated in each of the three waves showed a small decline during the first period ($p < .05$) and stable values during the second. The youngest and oldest birth cohorts did not show any significant changes for the sub-periods which they were part of. This pattern strengthens the assumption that confidence in institutions by and large remained unaffected over the entire period.

*Optimistic and pessimistic views on the political system*: It has already been mentioned that the Swedish model rested on an optimistic belief in a continuous progress towards a better society and that it tended to direct people's attention to a brighter future. Obviously, this kind of political optimism might have bearings on the increasing civic activism and the decreasing norm compliance. It has already been mentioned that Swedish welfare policies became more constrained during the 1990s. Living conditions underwent a number of changes during this period and increasing numbers of Swedes encountered various kinds of disadvantage and illfare (Palme et al. 2002: 9). The more constricted welfare policies that were a consequence of the economic crisis at the beginning of the 1990s may have caused activist efforts to restore the previous levels. It can also be assumed that disappointment with more strict welfare policies caused more lenient attitudes towards the importance of complying with the norms.

In order to investigate whether people's general optimism for the political system had any bearings on the changing civic orientations, optimism and pessimism as political attitudes needs clarification. The following conceptual model may serve to this end (cf. Pettersson 1992; Bråkenhielm 1988; Konvicka 1976; Sicinski 1976). Both optimism and pessimism implies a temporal dimension. This may concern both past, present and future situations. For instance, optimism for the political system can be based on evaluations of how this system worked some time ago, how it works today and/or how it will work in the future. But optimism and pessimism also implies some kind of change, whether things have developed or will develop to the better or the worse. These changes may have happened in the past and concern the actual developments that have taken place. But the changes can also be projected into the future and concern more imaginary or potential developments which one either tends to dislike (pessimism) or welcome (optimism). Figure 5.2 clarifies how these different components of optimism and pessimism can be combined into six different forms of pessimism and optimism.

The questionnaire for the 1995 and 1999 EVS/WVS waves contained two questions which can be used to measure the different kinds of optimism and pessimism which are outlined in Figure 5.2. The first question asked the respondents to indicate on a 10-point rating scale how the political system worked 10 years ago. The second question asked how the system worked today and the responses were given on a 10-point rating scale of the same format as the first questions. The

Figure 5.2. A conceptual scheme for optimistic and pessimistic evaluations of how the political system worked 10 years ago and how it works today (after Pettersson 1992).

| | Differences between evaluations of how the political system worked 10 years ago and how it works today: | | |
|---|---|---|---|
| Evaluation of the political system as it was 10 years ago: | No difference | Better today | Worse today |
| More negative | Persistent pessimism | Pending optimism | Absolute pessimism |
| More positive | Persistent optimism | Absolute optimism | Pending pessimism |

Table 5.5. Distributions for six kinds of optimism and pessimism in relation to the political system.

| | 1996 (n = 865) | 1999 (n = 845) |
|---|---|---|
| Absolute pessimism | 24.7% | 20.9% |
| Persistent pessimism | 17.1% | 25.4% |
| Pending pessimism | 39.0% | 20.9% |
| Pending optimism | 9.5% | 14.7% |
| Persistent optimism | 8.7% | 16.0% |
| Absolute optimism | 1.0% | 2.0% |
| Total: | 100.0% | 100.0% |
| | Chi-Square: 93.6, 5 df, $p < .001$ | |

responses to the first question can be dichotomized into two categories: More negative and more positive evaluations of how the system worked 10 years ago. The respondents' views on the changes which have taken place during the previous 10-year period can be estimated by subtracting their scores from the first question from their scores on the second. The scores which are the result from this subtraction can then be divided into three categories: Those who have indicated that the system had developed negatively, positively or had remained on the same level.

142                    THORLEIF PETTERSSON

Table 5.6. Mean scores for civic participation, norm compliance, and confidence in institutions among optimists and pessimists with regard to the political system. Results for 1996 and 1999.

|  | 1996 | | 1999 | |
|---|---|---|---|---|
| Civic orientation: | Pessimists | Optimists | Pessimists | Optimists |
| Civic participation | 99.4 | 104.5 | 101.2 | 105.7 |
| Norm compliance | 99.4 | 102.7 | 98.0 | 101.0 |
| Confidence in institutions | 97.3 | 108.1 | 97.1 | 107.3 |

In 1995 and 1999, the optimists scored higher than the pessimists on each of the civic orientations (p < .001, except for norm compliance in 1995; p < .01)

Table 5.5 reports the frequencies for the various combinations of pessimism and optimism in 1995 and 1999. The results show that both in 1996 and 1999 a majority demonstrated a pessimistic view on how the political system had developed. The results also demonstrate that pessimistic views were more frequent in 1996 than in 1999. This is also to be expected from the gradual recovery of the Swedish economy after the crisis during the first part of the 1990s. It should also be noted that very few demonstrated absolute optimism both in 1996 and 1999.

The relations between the degree of optimism for the political system and the three civic orientations are reported in Table 5.6. In order to simplify the results, the categories for pending pessimism and optimism, respectively, are not included in Table 5.6. The reason is that these two forms are somewhere in between more genuine optimism and pessimism and therefore difficult to interpret.

The results demonstrate that the optimists scored highest on each of the three civic orientations. This tendency is statistically significant. That the optimists scored highest on confidence in state institutions is almost self-evident, considering that the optimism concerned how the political system worked and that confidence in parliament was one of the indicators for institutional trust. By contrast, the results for civic participation and norm compliance are more substantial from a theoretical point of view. In the case of civic participation, the results suggest that this is more driven by optimism than by pessimism. Thus, the increasing civic participation seems to be more linked to optimistic views on the political system than pessimistic. This suggests that internal political efficacy (civic participation) and external (optimism for the political system) are related. Since one of the sub-indicators for civic participation taps voluntary work for political parties, the positive relation between civic participation and optimistic views on the political system might be spurious. However, a check on this demonstrates that the positive relation remains when the sub-indicator for political parties is removed from the analysis.

The results for norm compliance show that this is positively related to optimism for the political system. Put in other words, people's will to comply with strict norms for e.g. tax evasion and cheating on social benefits is related their evaluations of the system which have decided on these norms. The more one is optimistic about the political system, the more one is willing to comply with the rules which this system has established, while pessimistic views on the political system is associated with disregard for these rules. Thus, how people value the output from the political system and how they evaluate the system as such tend to go together. Perhaps it is more accurate to say that the evaluation of the system as such is based on the outputs from the system.

In principle, the assessment of optimism and pessimism for the political system can also be based on a future-oriented perspective. In that case, the analysis would start from people's evaluation of how the present political system works. The analysis should then consider people's expectations of the future development of this system. Since the 1996 questionnaire also included a question about how the political system would work in 10 years time, this way of conceptualizing optimism can be applied on the 1996 data. The results show similar results as when optimism and pessimism was assessed in a retrospective mode. The only exception was that the statistical significance for the difference between the optimists and the pessimists in the case of norm compliance was less definite (p < .08). Disregarding this, one can however conclude that two different methods for the assessment of optimism and pessimism have yielded similar results. Civic participation and norm compliance seems to be associated with an optimistic evaluation of the political system, disregarding whether this optimism is retrospective or prospective.

*Concluding remarks*

Sweden developed from a comparatively very poor country on the European periphery at the middle of the nineteenth century to become a rich welfare society at the end of the twentieth, being one of the top countries in the world with regard to a number of indicators for a good life. One cultural factor behind this development has been a long historical tradition of efforts to find a working balance between a top-down strong state and bottom-up popular power. During the first part of the twentieth century, Swedish welfare policies were connected to the metaphor of Swedish society as the people's home. This metaphor was associated with a set of basic socio-political convictions. One was an optimistic belief in an ever-continuing progress towards a better society, driven by social engineering and an active civic society; another a strong confidence in the efficient and fair state institutions, which would distribute the fruits of the ever-continuing progress justly to each and everyone. A third conviction emphasized the importance of complying with the norms for being a good citizen. Even if the public myth of the people's home now has been exiled to the museum for older Swedish political language, it also seems to be under some kind of repair, seeking new expressions of its core values.

Given this historical background, Swedes have come to appreciate civic participation, favor norm compliance and to have confidence in the state and its institutions. The data from 1981, 1990 and 1999 showed that civic participation had increased, that norm compliance had decreased and that confidence in state institutions saw some minor losses between 1981 and 1990 and some slight gains between 1990 and 1999. These changes had developed in accordance with center-periphery theory. Civic participation which was strongest at the center of society had grown, while norm compliance which was strongest in the periphery had declined. The differences which were found between the center and periphery in 1999 suggested that the growth of civic participation would continue and that the declines in norm compliance would persist. The discrepant developments for civic participation and norm compliance indicate a substantial change in Swedish political culture, from a high appreciation of both civic participation and norm compliance to a new pattern where civic participation has become more important and norm compliance less mandatory. The data from the upcoming fifth WVS wave will show whether this new pattern will be strengthened in accordance with the predictions from center-periphery theory. That the declining norm compliance to a certain extent could be explained by population generational replacements, where the older high-scoring birth cohorts had been replaced by the younger low scoring cohorts gives some extra support for this prediction. In contrast, the increases in civic participation seemed to be caused by some general period effect which had affected all cohorts in a similar way. It is less certain that such a period effect will continue to work.

When the levels of civic participation and norm compliance were related to optimism and pessimism for the political system, the results showed that both civic participation and norm compliance seemed to be more associated with optimism then with pessimism, even if this tendency was not particularly strong. In a way, this finding leads to a new question. If both civic participation and norm compliance are connected to optimistic attitudes towards the political system, and optimism appeared to grow during the second part of the 1990s, what is then the explanation for the differential development of the two civic orientations? One answer might be that optimism for the political system does not explain much of the variation in the two civic orientations and that therefore several other factors also have an impact on their developments. That the two civic orientations were differently related to generational population replacements supports this assumption. This assumption is also supported by the rather modest correlations between optimism and the two civic orientations. Another option might be that the relations between civic participation and norm compliance have changed over time and that they have become less associated to each other. A check of this option does however demonstrate that this has not been the case between 1996 and 1999. Both in 1996 and 1999, there was a zero correlation between civic participation and norm compliance and a slight positive correlation between confidence in institutions and each of the other two civic orientations.

It can also be argued that civic participation and norm compliance should primarily be seen as a kind of sub-dimensions of two more general and basic value orientations. In a comparative value study like the European Values Study and the World Values Survey, the so-called dimensionalist approach to the study of values dominates. To this approach, the primary aim is to find the most basic set of value axes (i.e. dimensions), which explain a broad range of "attitudes, beliefs life styles and the diversity of practices among large populations and/or organizations across societies" (Vinken et al. 2004: 11). Therefore, should the two civic orientations be parts of some more basic dimensionalist orientations which have changed over time, they would be changing as well.

In this regard, two broad dimensionalist value dimensions are of interest. These are the so-called social-liberal and the normative religious value orientations (Hagenaars et al. 2003). The first mentioned orientation is characterized by emphasis on individual freedom and personal autonomy, post-materialism and pro-democratic views. The second orientation taps strict moral standards and high evaluation of societal norms and institutions together with a strong appreciation of solidarity. It doesn't seem is especially farfetched to assume that civic participation and norm compliance would be substantially correlated to these two basic dimensionalist value orientations. Civic participation seems close to the social-liberal orientation, while norm compliance appears to be related to the normative-religious orientation. However, the overlap is not as strong as might be assumed. In the entire EVS data set from 33 countries and some 30,000 respondents, the normative-religious value dimension does not explain more than some 20 percent of the variation in norm compliance, while the social-liberal dimensions only explains about one third of the variation in civic participation. The corresponding levels for the Swedish data are slightly lower (16 and 25 percent, respectively). When the two civic orientations are compared to the more well-known self-expression and secular-rational dimensionalist value orientations (Inglehart 1997, Inglehart and Baker 2000; Inglehart and Welzel 2005), the correlations are of a similar magnitude. Therefore, it seems unwarranted to conclude that civic participation and norm compliance should first and foremost be expressions of some more basic dimensionalist value orientations and that their changes should be primarily be explained as consequences of changes in these two more basic orientations.

Nevertheless, it is well documented that expressive civic action has increased considerably in the Western world since the mid-1970s and that civil society has become both more active (see e.g. Dalton 2000) and increasingly transnational (Norris 2003). This growth of civilian power has been symbolized as a rise of a "Democratic Phoenix". It has also been shown that the rising emancipative self-expression values have tended to make people more critical of authorities (Inglehart and Welzel 2005). Even more important, it has also been demonstrated that Swedish democracy is undergoing a process of fundamental change, from a "society-based" understanding, where the individual citizen is primarily seen as a subordinated part of a sovereign and autonomous people, to an "individual-based" understanding, where the autonomous and independent citizen, responsible for his/her life course, is the acting subject (Petersson et al. 1990). Among other things, this change implies that individual allegiance is directed more towards inner convictions than towards outer authorities and rules. The increasing civic participation and the declining norm compliance can be seen as expressions of this gradual and long-term change. In this way, the empirical findings that are reported in this chapter seem to have verified these long-term changes in Swedish political culture. It should be noted that these changes have been demonstrated on a new set of empirical value data. It should also be noted that this new data set has been analyzed from both a partly new theoretical perspective and a long historical cultural background. Each of these two features adds to the significance of the findings.

*References*

Almond, G. and Verba, S., 1963, *The Civic Culture*, Boston: Little, Brown and Company.

Andersson, Å., 1998, *Framtidens arbete och liv*, Stockholm: Natur och kultur.

Aronsson, Peter, 1992, *Bönder gör politik. Det lokala självstyret som social arena i tre smolands-socknar, 1650–1850*, Lund: Lund University Press.

Axberger, H.-G., 1996, *Det allmänna rättsmedvetandet*, Stockholm: BRÅ.

Bråkenhielm, C.R., 1988, Optimism och pessimism, Mimeo, Department of Theology, University of Uppsala.

Dalton, R., 2000, "Value Change and Democracy2, S. Pharr, and R. Putnam, *Disaffected Democracies*, Princeton: Princeton University Press.

Dies-Nicolas, J., 1995, "Postmaterialism and the Social Ecosystem", Beal and Beatrix Sitter-Liver (eds.), *Culture within nature*, Basel: Wiese Publishing.

Diez-Nicolas, J., 2005, "Value systems of Elites and Publics in the Mediterranean: Convergence or Divergence", ASEP and Complutense University, Madrid.

Esping-Andersen, G., 1994, "Jämlikhet, effektivitet och makt," P. Thullberg & K. Östberg, (eds.), *Den svenska modellen*, Lund: Studentlitteratur.

Fryklund, B., Himmelstand, U. and Peterson, T., 1988, "Folklighet, klass och opinion i svensk politik under efterkrigstiden", U. Himmelstrand and G. Svensson (eds.) *Sverige—vardag och struktur*, Stockholm: Nordstedts.

Galtung, J., 1964, "Foreign Policy Opinion as a Function of Social Position". *Journal of Peace Research*, 34.

Galtung, J., 1976, "Social position and the image of the future". H. Ornauer et al. (eds.), *Images of the World in the Year 2000*, Paris: Mouton.

Gustafsson, G., 1984, "Civilreligionsbegreppet och civilreligion i dagens Sverige", *Civilreligion*, KISA-rapport 21, Uppsala: Kyrkans internationella studieavdelning.

Hagenaars, J., Halman, L. and Mors, G., 2003, "Exploring Europe's Basic Values Map", Arts, W., Hagenaars, J. and Halman, L. (eds.), The Cultural Diversity of European Unity, Leiden: Brill.

Halman, L., 2001, The European Values Study: A Third Wave, Tilburg: Tilburg University.

Halman, L. and Pettersson, T., 2003, "Differential patterns of secularization in Europe: Exploring the impact of religion on social values", L Halman and O Riis (eds.), Religion in secularizing society: Leiden: Brill.

Himmelstrand, U., 1988, "Den sociologiska analysen av Sverige", U. Himmelstrand and G. Svensson (eds.), Sverige—vardag och struktur, Stockholm: Nordstedts.

Hägg, G., 2003, Svenskhetens historia, Stockholm: Wahlström & Widstrand.

Ingelstam, L., 1988, Framtidstron och den svenska modellen, Linköpings universitet: Tema T.

Inglehart, R., 1977, *The silent revolution*, Princeton: Princeton University Press.

Inglehart, 1990, *Cultural change in advanced industrial society*, Princeton: Princeton University Press.

Inglehart, R., 1997, *Modernization and Postmodernization*, Princeton: Princeton University Press.

Inglehart, R. and Baker, W., 2000, "Modernization, Globalization, and the Persistence of Tradition: Empirical Evidence from 65 Societies", *American Sociological Review* 65.

Inglehart, R., Basanez, M., Diez-Medrano, J., Halman, L. and Luijkx, R. (eds.), *Human Beliefs and Values. A Cross-cultural Source-book on the 1999–2000 Values Surveys*,

Inglehart, R. and Welzel, C., 2005, *Modernization, Cultural Change and Democracy*, Cambridge: Cambridge university Press.

Konvicka, T., 1976, "Homology of predictions and wishes", H. Ornauer et al. (eds.), *Images of the World in the Year 2000*, Paris: Mouton.

McNeill, W., 1982, "The Care and Repair of the Public Myth", *Foreign Affairs*, Fall 1982.

Mörth, U. and Sundelius, B., 1995, "Sweden and the United Nations", K. Krause and A. Knight (eds), *State, Society and the UN System: Changing Perspectives on Mulilateralism*, Tokyo: United Nations University Press.

Norris, P., 2003, *Democratic Phoenix*, Princeton: Princeton University Press.

Palme, J. et al., 2002, *Welfare in Sweden: The Balance Sheet for the 1990s*. Reports from the government (Ds) 2002:32, Stockholm: Fritzes.

Petersson, O., Westholm, A. and Blomberg, G., 1988, *Medborgarnas makt*, Stockholm: Carlssons.

Petersson, O., Hermansson, J., Michelotti, M., Teorell, J. and Westholm, A., 1988, *Demokrati och medborgarskap. Demokratirådets rapport 1998*, Stockholm: SNS.

Pettersson, T., 1988, *Bakom dubbla lås. En studie av små oh långsamma värderingsförändringar*, Stockholm: Allmänna förlaget.

——, "Folkrörelsefolk och samhällsförändring", in S. Axelson and T. Pettersson (eds.) *Mot denna framtid*, Stockholm: Carlssons 1992.

Pettersson, T. and Esmer, Y., 2005, *Vilka är annorlunda? Om invandrares möte med den svenska kulturen*, Norrköping: Integrationsverket, In press.

Sicinski, A., 1976, "Optimism versus pessimism", H. Ornauer et al. (eds.), *Images of the World in the Year 2000*, Paris: Mouton.

Simmel, G., 1904/1972, "Fashion", D. Levine (ed.), *Georg Simmel*, Chicago: Chicago University Press.

Svallfors, S., 1999, Mellan *risk och tilltro: opinionsstödet för en kollektiv välfärdspolitik*, Umeå universitet: Umeå studies in sociology.

Therborn, G., "Hur det hela började. När och varför det moderna Sverige blev vad det blev", U. Himmelstrand and G. Svenssson (eds.) *Sverige—vardag och struktur*, Stockholm: Nordstedts, 1988.

Tilton, T., 1990, *The political theory of Swedish social democray: trough the welfare state to socialism*, London: Clarendon Press.

Van Der Veer, K., 1976, Social position, dogmatism and social participation", H. Ornauer et al. (eds.), *Images of the World in the Year 2000*, Paris: Mouton.

Vinken, H., Soeters, J. and Ester, P., 2004, "Cultures and dimensions", H. Vinken, J. Soeters and P. Ester (eds.), *Comparing cultures. Dimensions of culture in a comparative perspective*, *International studies in sociology and social anthropology*, Leiden: Brill.

Wetterberg, Gunnar, 2002, *Kanslern: Axel Oxenstierna i sin tid*, Stockholm: Atlantis.

Österberg, E., 1996, "Stark stat och starkt folk. En svensk modell med lAnga rötter," in Kjell Harstadd et al., eds., *Insikt og utsyn. Festskrift til Jørn Sandnes*, Trondheim: Historisk institutt, Norges teknisk-naturvitenskaplige universitet.

——, 1998, "State Formation and the People. The Swedish Model in Perspective," in H.R. Schmidt, A. Holenstein & A. Würgler (eds.) *Gemeinde, Reformation und Widerstand. Festschrift für Peter Blickle zum 60. Geburtstag*, Tübingen: Bibliotheca Academia Verlag.

CHAPTER SIX

DENMARK: SOLID OR FLUID?

Peter Gundelach

The European/World Values Study has been one of the most productive social science studies in the past 20 years. The possibility of making cross-national as well as longitudinal studies has made it a very fruitful means of research, and it is not surprising, therefore, that the project has resulted in an enormous number of publications both on a national and international scale. One of the theoretical problems of the project is to explain national differences. In the first volume, where the 1981 and 1990 EVS data were analyzed, Ester, Halman & de Moor (1993) concluded that there was no sign of convergence in values among the European countries. Ashford & Timms (1992: 112) have found that "national culture and opinion in Europe remain robustly diverse." Even in countries that are often considered very similar, such as the Scandinavian countries, the research conclusion is that "there is no uniform pattern of values in the Scandinavian countries" (Halman, 1992: 21).

This creates a theoretical challenge for comparative research. In this volume, where individual countries are analyzed, the problem is smaller. However, even if we abandon the ideal of uniformity among the European countries, we still need theoretical tools for the study of value change. Much of the research into values and change has been guided by two theoretical approaches: theories of modernization and theories of generations. The theories of modernization can be seen as a broad characterization of a large number of different theoretical approaches, varying from rather simple ideas of the relationship between societal wealth and values, to more complicated theories of a societal transformation from a so-called modern to a post-modern society. Such a transformation takes place in all parts of society, but the pace and scope varies in different sectors. The theory of generational change argues that some sectors are much more prone to change than others. The material conditions during childhood and adolescence influence the individual's values in a profound way, and this socialization has an impact on the individual's values for the rest of their lives. Societal changes occur during the generational change. When young generations with different values start to influence society, a general transformation of values in society will take place.

The EVS project has partly questioned and partly confirmed both theories on the general level. Ester, Halman & de Moor (1993) concluded that modernization theory did not adequately describe value changes. They identified four elements in modernization theory, but their analysis showed that the only component of modernization theory they could validate was a tendency to values fragmentation. Van den Broek's (1996) analysis of generation theory showed on the one hand that cohort replacement is instrumental in propelling political change, but, on the other hand, that the formation of generations was significantly different in the various European countries. These results indicate that value fragmentation and generational replacement of values are some of the more robust findings in the EVS-studies, and these two findings will be used as a guideline in this chapter.

As already mentioned, the results of the EVS studies indicate that it is difficult to make generalizations for a large number of countries because societal structural factors must be expected to influence values and value changes. The structure and culture in society have both an impact on values, and are influenced by values, in ways that are difficult to disentangle. This chapter presents trends in the development of Danish values, and, based on the research, we would expect that value changes in Denmark is infused with specific factors from within Danish society. A short presentation of Denmark may help to interpret the analysis that will follow.

Denmark is a small affluent society, characterized by a social-democratic welfare regime, and with a long tradition of cooperation between classes. It is traditionally a Protestant country, and the frequency of church going is very low. For a long time, Denmark was a very homogeneous country, and the number of immigrants is still low compared to many other European countries. The Danish transformation from an agrarian to an industrial society took place in the 1950s and 1960s. Women's participation in the labor market increased rapidly from the 1960s, and, today, there is no difference in job frequency between men and women. The divorce rate has increased strongly, but accurate numbers are difficult to compute because only about 75% of those who say that they live in stable relationships are married.[1]

---

[1] Computed from the 1999 values survey.

In general, values change slowly, and, based on the short characterization of Denmark, one would expect values in Denmark to have been quite stable in the last two decades. Several of the factors that may account for values change occurred before the first wave of the values survey in 1981, but the impact of increased education through generational change must have had an influence on values in Denmark as well as in most other countries.

This chapter is based on two hypotheses that proved fruitful in the previous EVS publication: value fragmentation, and generational change. We will investigate these hypotheses one at a time, but, first, we should offer a brief note on data and methods.

*Data and methods*

Denmark participated in the European Values Surveys (EVS) in 1981, 1990 and in 1999. In 1981, no professional researchers were involved in the project; the questionnaire was administered by a private data collection agency. In 1990, Peter Gundelach and Ole Riis were in change of the survey, and, in 1999, Peter Gundelach was the head of research. The data from 1981 and 1990 were analyzed in *Danskernes værdier* by Peter Gundelach and Ole Riis (1992). The 1999 data has resulted in two books: *Danskernes værdier 1981–1999* (2002, edited by Peter Gundelach) includes a number of articles on changes from 1981–1999, and this chapter is strongly inspired by this book. *Danskernes særpræg* (2004), edited by Peter Gundelach, is a comparative analysis of the 1999 data.

Random sampling was used in 1990 and 1999, but the data collection in 1981 has never been adequately described. We do know that there was an over-sampling of young persons (about 200 out of a total of about 1200). The over-sampled respondents have not been marked in the data set, so, in order to get valid frequencies of the various variables, it is necessary to use weights, and all the percentages in the present chapter are based on weighted data. In the statistical analysis, however, no weights have been used.

The chapter is based on identical questions from 1981, 1990 and 1999. The indexes in the article are taken from Halman & Vloet's documentation of the 1981 and 1990 data (see Appendix).

Data was analyzed by chain graph models for high-dimensional contingencies using strategies and techniques as described by Kreiner (1986 and 1987), integrating analyses of data with graph theoretic analyses of the so-called Markov graphs encoding properties of the statistical models. The basic idea underlying analysis by graphical models is nearly identical with Rosenberg's (1968) classic concepts of elaboration and specification in connection with analyses of conditional relationships. The statistical analysis used the DIGRAM computer program, (Kreiner 1989 and Klein et al. 1995). Partial γ coefficients were used throughout the analysis to measure association among ordinal and/or dichotomous variables. Associations involving nominal variables were investigated using $\chi^2$ tests of conditional independence. Graphical models for discrete data are log linear, but there are no statistical requirements for specific distributions of the variables apart from the assumption of log linear structure.

The generations are compared by a so-called collapse procedure. The statistical principle is to compare all generation categories in relation to a dependent variable, and then investigate whether or not there are significant differences in the distribution of the dependent variable for all categories of the generation variable. If the distribution for two variables is not significant, the two categories are collapsed and a weighted mean for the dependent variable is computed; based on the new categories the procedure starts again. The result is a categorization of the generation categories into groups where the distribution of the dependent value variable is identical within groups, but significantly different between groups. Thus, the result of the collapse procedure is the collapse of the existing categories of generation into fewer categories.

*Value fragmentation*

According to theories of late modernity, one of the elements of individualism is de-traditionalization and disembeddedness (Giddens, 1993); individuals are becoming more loosely related to traditional identity categories such as class, age or sex. Instead, values may be changing, and the individual will choose more freely among different values. In the language of survey research, this problem can be stated as a problem of correlation. Individualization means that socio-economic data are less efficient in predicting values. In other words, we should expect that the correlations between socio-economic variables and value variables will become smaller during the 20 years of study in the European Values Surveys.

Table 6.1 shows the γ-correlations between the value scales and socio-economic variables separately for 1981, 1990 and 1999. The cells in the table show the correlations. A blank cell means that the correlation is insignificant. Since employment is a nominal variable, only $\chi^2$ correlations have been computed. In this case, the plus sign in the table indicates a significant correlation.

Table 6.1. Correlations between values and socio-economic variables

| | Sex | Marriage | Employment | Generation | Education |
|---|---|---|---|---|---|
| Religiosity | | | | | |
| 1981 | .26 | −.18 | + | .40 | −.22 |
| 1990 | .35 | −.16 | + | .27 | −.12 |
| 1999 | .29 | | + | .21 | |
| | | | | | |
| Civic morality | | | | | |
| 1981 | −.23 | .32 | | −.42 | .19 |
| 1990 | −.33 | .30 | | −.38 | .12 |
| 1999 | −.22 | .19 | | −.34 | |
| | | | | | |
| Permissiveness | | | | | |
| 1981 | | | + | −.27 | .34 |
| 1990 | | .20 | + | −.21 | .41 |
| 1999 | | .08 | + | −.18 | .30 |
| | | | | | |
| Confidence in authoritarian institutions | | | | | |
| 1981 | | .23 | | −.30 | |
| 1990 | | .16 | | −.18 | .13 |
| 1999 | | | | | |
| | | | | | |
| Protest behavior | | | | | |
| 1981 | −.19 | .30 | + | −.53 | .38 |
| 1990 | −.18 | | + | −.33 | .33 |
| 1999 | | | + | −.31 | .27 |
| | | | | | |
| Traditional family values | | | | | |
| 1981 | −.42 | −.15 | + | | |
| 1990 | −.33 | −.17 | + | −.08 | |
| 1999 | −.21 | −.21 | + | | |
| | | | | | |
| Work: personal development | | | | | |
| 1981 | −.11 | .08 | + | −.22 | .27 |
| 1990 | | .08 | + | −.27 | .35 |
| 1999 | | | + | −.18 | .34 |

Note the correlations are γ's except for employment. Since employment is a nominal variable, $\chi^2$ is used. + means that the $\chi^2$ is significant (0.01 level).

The table shows that the hypothesis of diminishing γ-values can be confirmed in almost all cases. In some cases (e.g. correlations between sex and permissiveness or confidence in institutions) all the correlations are insignificant. In a few cases the correlations increase from 1981 to 1999 (sex and religiosity and civic morality; marriage and traditional family values; education and personal development in work). These are important exceptions from the general tendency, but they will not be addressed in this article. The overall picture remains that the correlations are becoming smaller. It is especially interesting that, generally, we find the highest correlations between the values and generation, and that, in all cases, there is a decrease in the γ-value. This means that, even though generation has an influence on values, it is becoming smaller. There are no cases of increase in the correlations with generation, an initial indication that generation may lose importance.

The conclusion is that the data confirm a general tendency to individualization. The relationship between values and social background is becoming of less importance.

### Generations and value changes

In Mannheim's classic formulation, people born in a certain period have "a specific range of potential experience, predisposing them for a certain characteristic mode of thought and experience" (Mannheim 1952: 291). The common experiences, especially during youth, create generational units. As Mannheim argued, belonging to such a unit may not be realized by the individual, much in the way that an individual may or may not be conscious of his or her class locations. There are, however, several important differences between class units and generational units. The material conditions that separate classes are much stronger because classes are related to work position, but more important for the purpose of this chapter is that, in contrast to class, the labeling of generations is difficult. There do not seem to be generally accepted labels of generations (perhaps with "baby boomers" as an exception). This will tend to make generations a socially less significant phenomenon, but, of course, the lack of generally accepted labels of generational units does not preclude generational units having an impact on people's values.

A core problem for generations is the identification of experiences that create generational units. It is generally accepted that such a classification must be based on people's experiences during childhood and youth. Mannheim (1952: 61) even stated more precisely that the age of 17 was possibly the time where the individual was most vulnerable to societal impact. Youth is "the impressionable years" (Alwin, Cohen & Newcomb, 1991), a period followed by successive continuance.

Inglehart's (1971) famous formulations of generation theory state that experiences of scarcity will have a major impact on people's values. In his original formulations, Inglehart argued that persons who, during childhood, had experienced scarcity before and during World War II would tend to have materialistic values, whereas persons who had not experienced such scarcity would tend to have post-materialistic values. (Scarbrough, 1995).

The Dutch sociologist Henk A. Becker is strongly influenced by Inglehart and has put forward a more elaborate theory of generations. He has outlined five generations: pre-war (1910–1930), silent (1930s), protest (1940–1955), lost (1956–1970) and the pragmatic generation (1970–). The pre-war generation experienced the economic and political crisis of the 1930s, and tends to have values that favor economic security. The silent generation is relatively similar to the pre-war generations, but an adolescence in the years after World Ward II has given them better educational and material conditions. The protesters were young during a period of high economic growth and a boom in education. Their values are less characterized by material conditions and more directed towards democracy and self-realization. The lost generation experienced the economic crisis of the mid 1970s and 1980s. This generation tends to be relatively similar to the protest generation, but it is also influenced by neo-conservatism. Finally, the pragmatic generation is numerically a relatively small generation. This will give them better opportunities on the labor market. They seem to be less influenced by traditional political and economic cleavages.

Becker's theory is based on his Dutch experience, but Danish societal development has in most ways been similar to the Netherlands, even though the stress and hardship during and after World Ward II were much heavier in the Netherlands.

If generational theories are valid, there are a number of consequences for the analysis of values. The first and most obvious hypothesis is, of course, that generations should influence values. Table 6.1 has already given evidence of such correlations, but a more careful testing of this

Figure 6.1. The statistical method.

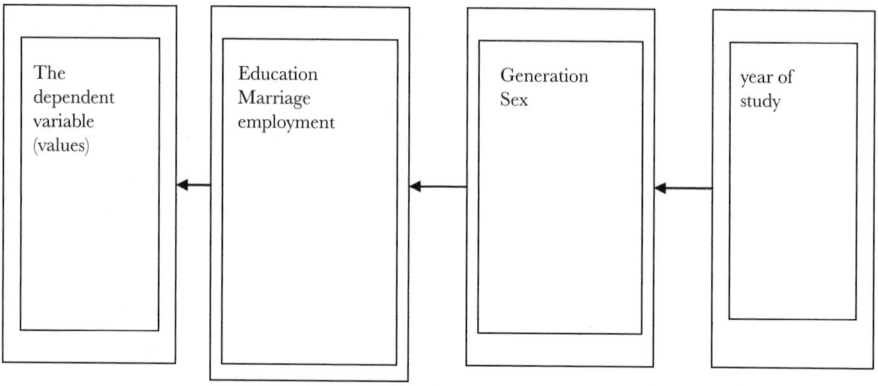

hypothesis must be based on multivariate analysis in order to rule out spurious correlations.

Second, the categories of generations should be similar for all dependent variables. The theory of generations states that societal conditions in the formative years have an impact on the individuals' lives. It is, of course, possible, that the societal impact will influence different values in different ways, but such nuances are seldom addressed in generational theory. Instead, the theory argues that the societal conditions will have a general impact on the individual and his or her values.

In this chapter, the value changes have been studied using a statistical model with a recursive structure as is shown in Figure 6.1. The dependent variables are the value indices, and the independent variables are the socio-economic variables and year of study. Table 6.2 summarizes the analysis of value changes. The first two columns in the table show the partial correlations based on the mentioned model between the dependent variables and year of study and generation. The table shows that, in all cases but one (work), there has been a change in values from 1981 to 1999. It also shows that generation has an impact on all of the dependent variables.

The test of the relationship between generation and values in the period from 1981 to 1999 has two possible results. One is that the changes are identical in all generations, and the other, of course, is that the changes are different in the various generations. The next two columns of the table show the results of such an analysis. About half of the values have changes in an identical manner for all generations, and the other half has a different development.

Table 6.2. Partial γ-correlations and categories of generations.

| | Correlation | | Categories of generations | |
| --- | --- | --- | --- | --- |
| | Year of study | Generation | Different development | Identical development |
| Religiosity | .23 | .30 | 1. −1927<br>2. 1928–1945<br>3. 1945– | |
| Permissiveness | −.06 | −.18 | 1. −1963<br>2. 1964– | |
| Civic morality | −.16 | −.32 | | 1. −1918<br>2. 1919–1936<br>3. 1937–1954<br>4. 1955– |
| Confidence in authoritarian institutions | −.21 | −.18 | | 1. −1918<br>2. 1919–1936<br>3. 1937–1963<br>4. 1964– |
| Protest behavior | .09 | −.35 | | 1. −1918<br>2. 1919–1936<br>3. 1937–1945<br>4. 1946–1954<br>5. 1955–1963<br>6. 1964–1972<br>7. 1973–1981 |
| Traditional family values | .27 | .21 | 1. −1936<br>2. 1937– | |
| Work: personal development | | −.18 | | 1. −1918<br>2. 1919–1936<br>3. 1937–1954<br>4. 1955– |

If we first look at the changes from 1981 to 1999, we find that most of the changes follow the theoretical expectations of a general moderniza- tion theory. There is a decrease in religiosity, civil morality and protest behavior, and there is an increase in permissiveness. In two cases, the changes occur in the opposite direction of that expected; there in an increase in confidence in authoritarian institutions, and in traditional family values.

The increase in confidence in authoritarian institutions may be explained by an increase in the support for law and order in society. Such an interpretation is supported by the answers to Inglehart's materialism-post-materialism index. Respondents are asked about the "aims of this country for the next ten years." One of the categories that respondents may pick is "Maintaining order in the nation." The percentage of respondents who choose this answer has increased from 40 per cent in 1981, to 59 per cent in 1999. The trend towards stronger acceptance of authoritarian institutions is probably a reflection of a general tendency in the Danish society—to a large degree pushed by the government—to stress the need to control crime and maintain law and order. Successive governments, especially in the 1990s, have repeatedly emphasized the need to fight crime—an agenda set by the mass media. The consequence has been that the population has perceived crime and crime control as important societal problems. This example shows that period effects often occur when value changes are studied. Such effects may be provoked by changes in the perception of social problems provoked by specific occurrences (such as AIDS, which has had an impact on attitudes towards homosexuality), or media agendas (as mentioned).

The second finding of this table is that generation influences values in all cases. The $\gamma$-correlations vary from 0.18 to 0.35. These must be considered strong to very strong correlations when we take into account that the presented $\gamma$'s are partial correlations. The theory of generational replacement is confirmed, but the table also shows that the relation between generations and values is very different for each dependent variable.

The overall impression from the table is that Becker's generational differentiation, or any similar categorization, gives a much simplified picture of generational changes because the generational changes are different for each of the value variables. The cut-off point between generational categories varies, and, in some cases, there is a differential development in values according to generation; in other cases, there is an identical development for all generations. This presents a major challenge for generation theory. When researchers categorize generations they expect that generations influence values in similar ways (i.e. the 1968 generation will be different from other generations in all aspects of life). The results in Table 6.2 indicate that generations are influenced in different ways depending on the type of values. If this finding can be generalized, it means that we need a more elaborate and complex theory of generational replacement. At any rate, the table shows such large differences among the value variables that we must investigate them separately.

*Religiosity*

Table 6.2 shows a positive correlation between year of study and religiosity. This may seem to be in contrast to a general modernization theory that will argue that religion plays a minor role in society. However, modernization theory is much too general to grasp the values changes within religiosity. There are at least two theories of the relation between social change and religiosity (Andersen & Riis, 2002): secularization and privatization theory. Secularization may be studied at an individual, institutional and societal level (Dobbelaere, 1981), but, for the purpose of this chapter, the individual level is more relevant. Secularization theory suggests a decrease in the individual's religious faith, activity and commitment. Privatization theory makes a distinction between religiosity in its traditional institutional forms, and a private religiosity that is more independent of the church. A private religiosity does not necessarily mean that the individual understands the church as irrelevant, but that the individual reacts against the church as a moral and religious authority; the individual samples his or her "own" religiosity from the many religious "products" that are offered in present society. Such an *a la carte* religiosity theory accepts individualization as well as religiosity. The individual's faith and religious activities are privatized in the sense that these are relatively independent of the religious institutions.

The EVS-study and index of religiosity (see Appendix) do not make it possible to test the secularization or privatization hypothesis in a very accurate way. However, the results of the analysis indicate that a privatization hypothesis is more probable than a secularization hypothesis. The increase in religiosity means that the Danes are not becoming secularized at the individual level. They may be becoming less connected to the church, but they have a more general individualized religiosity. They tend to treat religiosity in much the same way as other social phenomena, as something that you may choose from independent of authority; religion becomes a matter of negotiation and reflection.

This interpretation is supported by the generational analysis shown in Figure 6.2.

The statistical collapse analysis has divided the population into three categories: persons born before 1927, those born between 1928 and 1945, and those born after 1946. Figure 6.2 shows, as expected, that religiosity is highest in the oldest generations, but, more unexpectedly, that there has been an uneven development in religiosity within the

Figure 6.2.

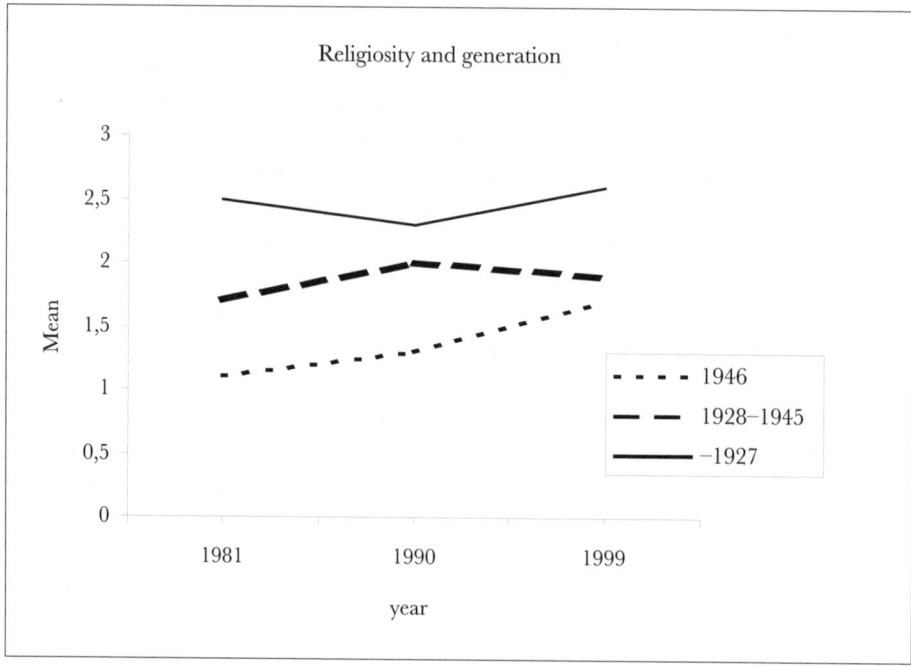

three generational categories. In the two oldest generations, there has been relatively stability in religiosity, but the generation born after World War II (Inglehart's post-materialist generation) has increased in religiosity. This must be interpreted as support for the privatization approach. Religion has gained importance because this generation has broadened the concept of religion, with the traditional Christian understanding replaced by a more general spirituality where the individual picks and chooses from existing religious elements. Some of these elements may be considered as incompatible from a theological point of view (for reincarnation and life after death), but many individuals do not care about traditional religious understandings; they construct their own religiosity.

*Permissiveness*

Permissiveness is part of the cluster of new values that are often associated with individualism. The decline of moral obligations is part of an

Figure 6.3.

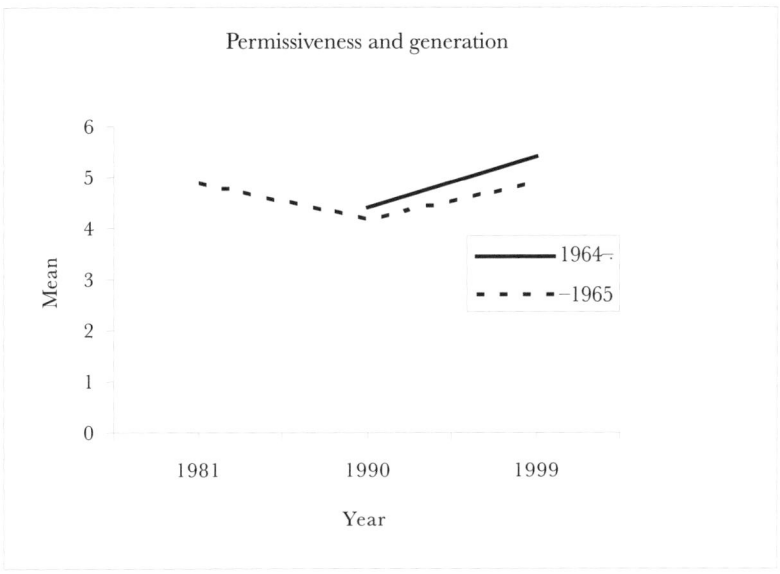

overall change in a direction where the individual puts less emphasis on authority. The post-modern individual, instead of a being morally guided by authority, will make his or her own decisions based on individual considerations. The individual's moral standards are not generalized, but may be dependent on the situation. Such a change is expected to be most prominent among the young.

Table 6.2 shows a small increase in permissiveness. The small γ is, however, misguiding. Since the γ-correlation presupposes linear relationships between variables, it will not detect changes that are curvilinear. As can be seen in Figure 3, a curvilinear relationship is exactly what is found in relation to permissiveness. The level of permissiveness is almost identical in 1981 and 1999, but permissiveness is valued to a smaller extent in 1990. A closer look at the components of the index reveals that the decrease in permissiveness is due to a lower level of acceptance of adultery and homosexuality. Based on this, the most obvious interpretation of the curvilinear shape of changes in permissiveness seems to be the fear of AIDS, which was very strong around 1990. AIDS was virtually unknown in 1981, and, at the end of the 1990s, most Danes believed that AIDS was under control, and most people did not fear the risk of being infected.

Figure 6.3 shows that there has been a slightly different tendency in two birth cohorts. Persons born after 1964 have an identical mean of permissiveness in 1981 and 1999, an average of 4.9 (this cohort did not answer the questionnaire in 1981). As one would expect, this group has a higher level of permissiveness than the oldest cohort. The youngest cohort has increased its level of permissiveness from 4.4 in 1990, to 5.4 in 1999. This is a slightly more steep increase than the older generation, and it points to an increase in generational differences in moral values. The increase is only found in the youngest cohorts. Generation theories have always argued that younger generations are more permissive than older generations, but, as can be seen in Figure 3, this is only partly correct. In these data, the cleavage between age cohorts arises in persons born after the mid 1960s. This is a much later than expected by, for instance, Becker and Inglehart. The figure shows that persons who were young during the youth rebellion in relation to permissiveness have identical values and have changed their values in a similar way to their parents. It is only the very youngest cohort that is different. In broad terms, however, and if we disregard the reactions to AIDS in the 1990 survey, the figure confirms modernization theory.

### Civic morality

When it come to the other type of morality, the picture is, perhaps, easier to understand. There is a small decrease in civil morality ($\gamma = -0.16$), but the means from 1981 to 1999 are almost identical (1.6). Compared to permissiveness, this shows that, first of all, the moral pressure of conformity is much higher in relation to civic morality than in relation to the morality that concerns the individual's private life. The Danes are very much against cheating the state and breaking public agreements. No doubt this can be explained by the character of the Danish state. This is not the place for a thorough examination of Danish history, but two remarks will perhaps suffice to illustrate important historical elements in the Danish development.

In 1864, Denmark lost a war to Germany, and even lost two provinces on the boundary between Denmark and Germany. This defeat was the last of several losses that, since the 17th century, had changed Denmark from being a European superpower to being a small and insignificant country whose existence was heavily threatened by Germany. The

Table 6.3. Civic morality and generation. Means.

|           | 1981 | 1990 | 1999 |
|-----------|------|------|------|
| 1955–     | 2.1  | 2.1  | 1.7  |
| 1937–1954 | 1.5  | 1.5  | 1.5  |
| 1919–1936 | 1.5  | 1.3  | 1.4  |
| –1918     | 1.3  | 1.2  | 1.3  |
| Total     | 1.6  | 1.7  | 1.6  |
| N         | 1121 | 1028 | 998  |

Danish government responded by putting emphasis on developing a strong national culture and what later became a welfare state. Even after World War I, when Denmark regained parts of the provinces (and especially from the 1930s and onwards), the Danish government stressed the need for a welfare state.

Danes feel that the welfare state was built from below. Cooperation between the social classes, and the special importance of the working class, turned the Danish welfare state into what Esping-Andersen (1996) has called a social-democratic type of welfare state. In Denmark, there have always been close ties between the state, voluntary associations, and the population. This has meant that Danes feel closely integrated into the state. It may be an exaggeration to say that all Danes consider the state as their friend, but surveys indicate strong support of the welfare state.

In this context it is hardly surprising that the level of civic morality is high. Generational differences are clear, but not substantial. Table 6.3 shows the means of civic morality in 1981, 1990 and 1999. The table shows that the youngest cohorts are more liberal than the oldest cohorts, but, overall, the differences are not that large.

The table shows that civic morality is fairly stable. There is a small increase in civic morality for the youngest cohort, but this is not significant. The youngest generations are less moral than the older generations, but the general level of morality is very high. A closer look at the questions in the index reveals that the question about avoiding a fare in public transportation especially shows generational differences.

## Confidence in authoritarian institutions

Theories of individualization predict that the individual will increasingly become less dependent on institutions. He or she will be less prone to accept the authority of institutions and, instead, feel the right, and even the obligation, to generate his or her own opinions and values. The relaxed attitude to authority should be seen most strongly when it comes to authoritarian institutions. Not only may they, like all institutions, be understood as a source of authority, they are also among the most suppressive of the societal institutions. As Inglehart (1998) has put it, "Postmodernization erodes respect for authority, but increases support for democracy." Based on theories of individualization, then, we should expect a strong decrease in confidence in authoritarian institutions, and the tendency may even be expected to be especially large among the youth.

As Table 6.4 shows, the individualization hypothesis does not seem to be correct. There is only a small change in the attitudes towards authoritarian institutions, and it even goes in the opposite direction than that expected; people are becoming more authoritarian. Furthermore, there are only very small generational differences. In short, when it comes to confidence in authoritarian institutions, very little has happened. This also means that there is no reason to believe in a hypothesis of neo-conservatism since, if such a theory were correct, there would be an increase in confidence in authoritarian institutions, possibly especially among the young. This is not the case. The conclusion is that the confidence in authoritarian institutions is high and stable among the Danes, possibly for the same historical reasons that civic morality is stable.

Table 6.4. Confidence in authoritarian institutions. Means.

|           | 1981 | 1990 | 1999 |
|-----------|------|------|------|
| 1964–     |      | 2.3  | 2.2  |
| 1937–1963 | 2.3  | 2.2  | 2.3  |
| 1919–1936 | 2.2  | 2.1  | 2.2  |
| –1918     | 2.1  | 2.0  | 2.1  |
| Total     | 2.3  | 2.3  | 2.2  |
| N         | 1136 | 981  | 876  |

Table 6.5. Protest behavior. Means.

|           | 1981 | 1990 | 1999 |
|-----------|------|------|------|
| 1973–1981 |      |      | 2.6  |
| 1964–1972 |      | 2.1  | 2.4  |
| 1955–1963 | 2.5  | 2.3  | 2.6  |
| 1946–1954 | 2.1  | 2.2  | 2.4  |
| 1937–1945 | 1.7  | 1.7  | 2.0  |
| 1919–1936 | 1.3  | 1.4  | 1.3  |
| –1918     | 1.0  | 1.0  | 1.0  |
| Total     | 1.6  | 1.8  | 2.2  |
| N         | 1182 | 1030 | 1023 |

*Protest behavior*

Protest behavior is another example of a surprisingly stable development. Table 6.5 shows the so-called political action battery (Barnes, Kaase *et al.* 1979) for measuring unconventional political behavior. It is often assumed that the so-called 1968 generation invented unconventional political behavior during the mobilizations of the young and student rebellion. In Denmark, the cohort of this generation may be defined as persons who were born after 1950. The cohorts born during World War II were hardly affected by the youth rebellion. Borre and Goul Andersen (1997) find a very high political stability among generations. Persons born after World War II and until about 1960 may be considered a single political generation. This generation was relatively leftwing-oriented and has maintained its political views. The followers (born after 1961) were quite similar to the 1968 generation in the beginning, but, during the 1980s, this cohort became more right-wing oriented (Borre & Goul Andersen, 1997). As Table 6.5 shows, this change in political orientations has not had impact on protest behavior.

The table shows that, for most generations, there has been a small increase in the level of protest behavior, and it has become part of the general repertory of political activity.

Since the 1980s, new areas of conflict have arisen, and the government has prioritized civic involvement in various areas and in relation to some social services (for instance in kindergartens). The political parties have stagnated, or even lost members, and there has been a general wish for opportunities for more expressive activities than in traditional political parties (Dalton, 1988). All these factors have contributed to the increased popularity of protest activity.

There are relatively large generational differences. According to the so-called collapse procedure, almost all the studied generations are different, but there seems to be a large difference between persons born before and after Word War II.

Since its mushrooming in the late 1960s and early 1970s, protest activity has become part of the everyday life of politics. The general tendency has been for citizens to involve themselves in single issues related to public services rather than large causes such as ecology and women's liberation, but the percentage of protesters has increased. Even though the political climate has changed, and the youngest cohorts have become less left wing, people continue to protest. This type of political activity is not reserved to certain cohorts; politicians and other decision-makers must always expect protest from involved citizens.

*Family values*

The traditional family model was characterized as the husbands being the breadwinner, the women working in the home, and two or three children, with marriage as a life long commitment. Even though it may be disputed whether the traditional family ever was the most frequent family type, it became a model for family life. Since the 1960s and 1970s, family life in Denmark has changed tremendously. Women's employment and the women's liberation movement have meant more equality between men and women. There are more single people in society, and, even though people today enter a relationship in the wish for a life long commitment, statistics show that a large number of persons are divorced.

The decrease of the traditional family has led some (Popenoe, 1995) to deplore this development. Poponoe asserts that divorce and one parent families creates problems for children and adults; there is a lack of security and continuity. Stacey (1996), on the other hand, contends that the ideal of the traditional nuclear family is a myth, and that there have always been many different types of families. She also argues that the present types of families are less suppressive of women and children. Stacey suggests that the most innovative types of families in the present society are single parents or homosexuals with children. Even though

Figure 6.4.

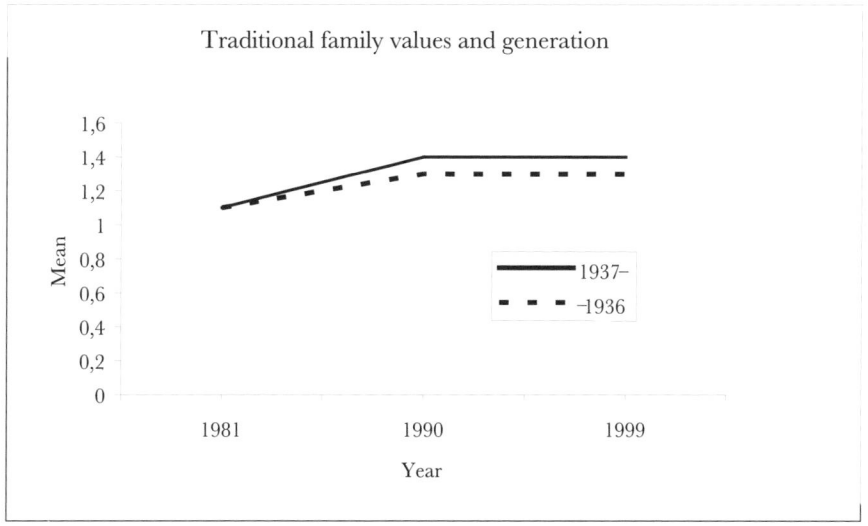

Poponoe and Stacey disagree about the ideal type of family structure, they have the same opinion about family changes and family values; both maintain that traditional family values are decreasing.

Figure 6.4 presents the Danish data on family values based on the index of traditional family values (see Appendix). The figure shows that, in contrast to what both Poponoe and Stacey believe, traditional family values are increasing and not decreasing. There is a small difference between generations, with people born after 1936 valuing the traditional "father-mother and kids family" higher than the oldest generations.

This result is very surprising. A large percentage of Danish marriages are broken, and the percentage of single people is increasing. The traditional, patriarchal family is disappearing (Castells, 1997), but the traditional family values of the nuclear family are flourishing. There may be two explanations for this paradoxical result. One is that we tend to exaggerate the changes in family structure. Most Danes still live in a family, and even divorced persons seek to establish a new family. A second type of explanation would argue that the present "post-modern" families are very different from the traditional family, but that, so far, there has not emerged a new set of family values. Even though people live in families that are different from the traditional nuclear family, basically they value a father-mother and kids family. This does not mean

Table 6.6. Personal development values at work. Means.

|          | 1981 | 1990 | 1999 |
|----------|------|------|------|
| 1955–    | 2.8  | 3.0  | 3.0  |
| 1937–1954 | 2.4  | 2.7  | 2.7  |
| 1919–1936 | 2.4  | 2.3  | 2.0  |
| –1918    | 1.8  | 2.7  | 2.0  |
| Total    | 2.3  | 2.6  | 2.7  |
| N        | 1182 | 1130 | 1122 |

that people approve of the uneven power structure or the rigid division of labor in the traditional family. It simply means that a family of two adults living with children is considered a better type of relationship.

### *Personal development and work*

Just like the family, the work place has undergone dramatic changes. The labor market has changed, and women's employment has increased dramatically since the 1960s. Many women are employed in the public sector within sectors such as care, health and education. White-collar jobs have replaced blue collar jobs, and the general level of education has increased. The hypothesis is that these structural changes will create a wish for work that is interesting, and gives the possibility of self-realization and influence. Table 6 shows that this hypothesis can be confirmed.

There is an overall increase in the wish for work that allows for personal development. This is strongest among the youngest age groups and, especially in 1999, there seems to be a relative strong cleavage between persons born before and after 1936. A closer look at the table reveals that there is a decrease in personal development values among persons born 1919–1936, and an almost stable development for people born before 1918. The different tendencies are not statistically significant, but they may be interpreted as a possible division between people in the older generations (who settle for traditional work values) and the younger generations (who claim that personal development is part of a proper job).

*Modern, post-modern values and generations*

The detailed analysis of the seven indexes of core values has shown a wide-ranging picture. In contrast to the theory of individualization, the Danish respondents value religiosity, confidence in authoritarian institutions and traditional values higher in 1999 than in 1981. There are no major changes in moral values, but protest behavior and the wish for a work characterized by personal development has increased.

This shows a diverse development, and, when we look at the Danish data in general, the result is relatively mixed. There is positive evidence for the fact that values are increasingly becoming disconnected from the individual's socioeconomic position. This must be interpreted as an element in a general tendency towards a late or post-modern situation where the individual is becoming less influenced by his or her social background. Such a tendency may be exaggerated. The analysis shows a decrease in correlations rather than that the correlations are disappearing. Socio-economic variables still play a major role for values.

It is especially noteworthy that, for all variables, generation is of importance. There are clear generational differences in all values, and the hypothesis of generational replacement is confirmed. There are many variations in the data, but the overall result is that values tend to be quite stable within a generation, and that societal changes in values occur as new generations replace older generations.

These overall conclusions challenge the fashionable theories of social change suggested by the influential social theorists of the last decades which argue that a major change in values is taking place as the old (modern) society gradually is replaced by a new (post-modern) society. There seems to be a conflict between the relatively abstract theories of societal change and the down to earth empirical analyses in the values study.

One interpretation of this difference may be due to the concepts and categories of the values surveys. In *Liquid Modernity*, Bauman (1999) studies some basic concepts around which "the orthododox narratives of the human condition tend to be wrapped" (p. 8). This endeavor also moves him to scrutinize the institutions of modern society. Borrowing a term from Ulrich Beck, Bauman argues that many of the social categories we know today are "zombie" categories. They are dead and alive at the same time. One way of interpreting the relative stability of values is that the EVS project tends to use such zombie categories. In the late 1970s, when the EVS was first imagined, the world looked different.

If we follow Bauman, it was a time of solid modernity, and the social categories were adequate frames for people's lives. The categories from previous times remain identical, but the human condition has changed. Comparisons that cover almost 20 years tend to be "conservative" and to focus on social categories that are no longer relevant, or whose contents have changed. When the respondents answer the questionnaires they talk about a world from the past so to speak.

Such an interpretation cannot be neglected, but it is questioned by theories of stability. People still live in families, go to work, and vote at elections. The idea of liquid modernity may well be an exaggeration. In a stability perspective, society changes slowly, and people's actions and values are formed by their habits. In such a Bourdieu-like perspective, it is not surprising that values hardly change, or only change through generational replacement. Societal stability varies in different parts of society and among societies. In Denmark, the most dramatic changes occurred before the first wave of the EVS studies, and, even though Denmark, as a small country, is much exposed to international influence, it seems as if Denmark's social organization and social institutions are solid rather than fluid.

It is possible that the fluidity and the stability approaches cannot be combined, but, based on traditional sociological methods such as the EVS studies, the stability approach seems to be more adequate. At any rate, theorists of liquid modernity or similar interpretations of society need to include the empirical findings of the EVS studies into their theories.

## References

Alwin, D.F., Cohen, R.L. & T.M. Newcomb, (1991) *Political Attitudes over the Lifespan. The Bennington Women after Fifty years.* Newbury Park: Sage.

Andersen, P.A. & O. Riis (2002) "Religionen bliver privat" pp. 76–98 in Gundelach, P. (edt.) *Danskernes værdier 1981–1999.* København: Hans Reitzels Forlag.

Ashford, S. & N. Timms (1992) *What Europe Thinks. A Study of Western European Values.* Aldershort: Dartmouth.

Barnes, S.H., M. Kaase et al. (1979) *Political Action: Mass Participation in Five Western Democracies.* Beverly Hills: Sage.

Bauman, Z. (1999) *Liquid Modernity.* Cambridge: Polity Press.

Borre, O. & J. Goul Andersen (1997) *Voting and Political Attitudes in Denmark.* Århus: Aarhus University Press.

Castells, M. (1997) *The Power of Identity.* Oxford: Blackwell.

Dalton, R.J. (1988) *Citizen Politics in Western Democracies: Public Opinion and Political Parties in the United States, Great Britain, West Germany and France.* Chatham: Chatham House.

Dobbelaere, K. (1981) Secularization, a multidimensional concept. *Current Sociology* 29 (2): 1–216.

Ester, P., L. Halman & R. de Moor (1993) *The Individualizing Society. Value Change in Europe and North America.* Tilburg: Tilburg University Press.

Esping-Andersen. Gøsta (1996) *Three Worlds of Welfare Capitalism.* Cambridge: Polity Press.

Giddens, A. (1993) *Modernity and Self-identity. Self and society in the late modern age.* Cambridge: Polity Press.

Gundelach, P. (edt). *Danskernes værdier 1981–1999.* København: Hans Reitzels Forlag.

———. (edt.) *Danskernes særpræg.* København: Hans Reitzels forlag.

Gundelach, P. & O. Riis (1992) *Danskernes værdier.* København: Forlaget Sociologi.

Halman, L. (1992) Scandinavian Values. How Special Are They? Institute for Social Research Tilburg University.

Inglehart, R. (1971) *The silent revolution in Europe: intergenerational change in post-industrial societies.* Indianapolis: Bobbs-Merrill.

Inglehart, R. (1998) "Postmodernism Erides Respect for Authority, but Increases Support for Democracy" in P. Norris (ed.): *Critical Citizens Global Support for Democratic Governance.* Oxford: Oxford University Press.

Klein, J., N. Keiding, and S. Kreiner, 1995. "Graphical Models for Panel Studies, Illustrated on Data." *Statistics in Medicine* 14: 1265–1290.

Kreiner, S. 1986. "Computerized exploratory Screening of large-Dimensional Contingency Tables" In Antoni, F. de, H. Lauro, and A. Rizzi (Eds.): Compstat 1986. *Proceedings in Computational Statistics.* 7th Symposium held at Rome 1986. Heidelberg, Wien: Physica Verlag: 355–359.

———. 1987. "Analysis of Multidimensional Contingency Tables by Exact Conditional Tests: Techniques and Strategies." *Scandinavian Journal of Statistics* 14: 97–112.

———. 1989. User Guide to DIGRAM. A Program for Discrete Graphical Modeling. Univ. of Copenhagen, Statistical Research Unit. Research report 89/10.

Mannheim, K. (1952) *Essays on the Sociology of Knowledge.* London: Routledge & Kegan Paul.

Poponoe, D. (1988) *Disturbing the Nest: Family Change and Decline in Modern Societies.* New York: De Gruyter

Rosenberg, M. (1968). *The Logic of Survey Analysis.* New York: Basic Books.

Scarbrough, E. (1995) Materialist-Postmaterialist Value Orientation. Pp. 123–159 in Jan W. van Deth & E. Scarbrough (eds.): *The Impact of Values.* Oxford: Oxford University Press.

Stacey, J. (1996) *In the Name of the Family: Rethinking Family Values in the Postmodern Age.* Boston: Beacon Press.

Van den Broek, A. (1996) "Cohort Replacement and Generation Formation in Western Politics" pp. 237–260 in L. Halman & N. Nevitte (eds. ) *Political Value Change in Western Democracies.* Tilburg: Tilburg University Press.

## *Appendix*

Operationalisation of variables

*Marriage* is recoded into two categories: 1) Persons who are or who have been married or lived as married, 2) Singles

*Generation* is recoded into nine age categories. Persons born before the year 1918 are coded into one category

*Employment*
1. self employed 30 hours a week or more
2. white collar 30 hours a week or more
3. blue collar 30 hours a week or more
4. unemployed, retired or employed less than 30 hours a week
In the statistical analyses, this variable is considered a nominal variable.

*Religiosity*

For each respondent, a scale of the following variables has been constructed:

Are you a religious persons. Answer yes.
(I believe that) there is a personal God
How important is God in your life. Answer 8–10 on a 10 point scale
Do you find that you get comfort and strength from religion or not? Answer yes.
Do you take some moment of prayer, meditation or contemplation or something like that. Answer yes.

*Civic morality*
The average of the following questions measured on a 10 point scale.
Justification of the following
Claiming state benefits which you are not entitled to
Avoiding a fare on public transport
Cheating on tax if you have the chance
Taking and driving a car belonging to someone else
Lying in your own interest
Someone accepting a bribe in the course of their duties
The variable is recoded into the following categories 1, 2, 3 or more

*Permissiveness*
The average of the following questions measured on a 10 point scale.
Married men/women having an affair
Homosexuality
Divorce
Euthanasia
Suicide

*Confidence in authoritative institutions*
The average of the following questions measured on a 4 point scale.
The church
The armed forces
The legal system
The Police
The Civil service
The variable is recoded into two categories 1+2 and 3+4

*Unconventional political behavior*
Number who have done or would do any of the following:
Signing a petition
Joining in boycotts
Attending lawful demonstrations
Occupying buildings or factories

*Traditional family values*
Respondents who agree that a child needs a home with both a father and a mother to grow up happily, and who disapprove of women having children as a single parent

*Work: personal development*
Number of times the following job characteristics are mentioned
An opportunity to use initiative
A job in which you feel that you can achieve something
A responsible job
A job that is interesting
A job that meets one's abilities

CHAPTER SEVEN

# WHAT HAPPENED TO DUTCH VALUES?
## INVESTIGATING GENERAL AND DIFFERENTIAL TRENDS IN VALUES IN THE NETHERLANDS

LOEK HALMAN AND RUUD LUIJKX

## 1. *Introduction*

Dutch society is amongst the most wealthy societies in the world. In the Human Development Index, the Netherlands ranks eighth, after Norway, Australia, Canada, Sweden, Belgium, United States, and Iceland (HDR, 2001:141). Until recently, the Netherlands has been one of the better performing economies in the European Union. This "Dutch miracle" must not only be attributed to the flourishing international economy (until September 2001), but also to the "polder model", the political practice of consensus: government, employers and labor unions seek consensus in "pay restraint, control of social security expenditure and an activating labor market policy" (SCP, 2001:38). The Netherlands is a classic example of consociational democracy, in which leaders of the distinct social layers cooperate to reduce or neutralize the "destabilizing effects of deep social divisions" (Andeweg, 2000:679) existing in Dutch society.

In many ways, the Netherlands is a well-developed, modern society that is, according to popular view, also famous for its tolerance, particularly with regard to drug use and sexual and ethical behavior. Indeed, Dutch legislation on drugs is (still) unique in Europe and the rest of the world, and homosexual couples can officially register their partnership and can marry in the Netherlands. Euthanasia is on the political agenda, and the law no longer prohibits medical doctors to terminate a patient's life if he or she requests so. Of course, there are strict regulations to be followed, otherwise medical doctors risk prosecution and imprisonment, but the euthanasia law was unparalleled in Europe and made the Netherlands a special case in Europe.

The Netherlands is also exceptional when it comes to the age at which women have their first child. Although the age at which women have their first child has increased all over Europe, the age at which Dutch women have their first child is among the highest. This indicates that, in the Netherlands, postponement of having children is common practice, much more than in other European countries.

For a long time, it was common practice that Dutch women, after having their first child, stopped (full-time) working, or took up a part-time job in order to be able to fulfill household obligations and duties. In this respect, Dutch society is also an outlier in Europe. For a very long time, female labor force participation has been rather limited, and, until very recently, the traditional pattern of the male as the breadwinner and the female as the housewife staying at home and taking care of the children and the household has remained popular. Female participation in the labor force has increased sharply in the last decades, but, more than elsewhere, women in the Netherlands are (still) involved in part-time jobs. Eurostat figures on employment reveal that, in the Netherlands, 68% of the employed women are in part-time jobs. In other European countries these percentages are much lower, ranging from 45% in UK, 41% in Sweden and 36% in Denmark to 11% in Greece and 14% in Italy (SCP, 2001:213).

The Netherlands is also rather special in terms of religion. In no other European country are there so many people who do not belong (anymore) to a religious denomination. On the other hand, of those who are (still) a member of a religious denomination, a large part can be characterized as core members. They are not only members, but they also attend religious services regularly and are also otherwise strongly involved in religious activities and organizations. This polar situation, with high levels of unchurched on the one hand and relatively many core members on the other, appears to be typically Dutch (Halman & de Moor, 1994).

Apart from the features already mentioned, the Netherlands seems to follow the trajectories of societal changes that other countries follow. A major characteristic of this change is individualization, the idea that individuals are increasingly willing and able to develop their own values and norms that do not necessarily correspond to the traditional, institutional (religious) ones (see also Ester, Halman & de Moor, 1994:1). More and more people turn away from traditions, the traditional institutions, and the prescribed values and norms, wanting instead to decide for themselves and determine on their own how to live their own lives. According to the Dutch Social and Cultural Planning Office, the process of individualization is "the most pertinent characterization of ongoing social dynamics" (SCP, 2001:185) in the Netherlands.

This process seems to be a universal (western) process which brings about not only more modern views, but also more diversity. Individualization is triggered and strongly pushed by the increase in the level of education of the population. More education increases people's "breath of perspective" (Gabennesch, 1972:183), and their abilities and cognitive skills, making them more critical towards the traditional suppliers of values, norms, and beliefs, more open to new ideas and arguments, other providers of meanings, values and norms, and less dependent on traditional institutions and their prescriptions and rules of behavior and conduct.

Another common development regarded as conducive to social change is the process of globalization. The contemporary world is regarded as a 'global village' in which people encounter a great variety of alternative cultural habits and a broad range of lifestyles and modes of behavior. Being free and liberated from the constraints imposed by traditional institutions (e.g., church and religion), people in a globalized society can, in theory, pick and choose what they want from an expanding global cultural marketplace. Consequently, the likelihood that they select the same options and make the same choices diminishes, and therefore the degree of diversity or pluralism in society increases.

Although surveys on cultural developments in the Netherlands seem to indicate that major changes had taken place already in the sixties and seventies before leveling off during the eighties and nineties (Nauta, 1987), the trajectory of change in the direction of individualization, secularization, and globalization seems to continue. Also Felling, Peters, and Scheepers (2000:253) concluded that the dynamics of cultural change in the Netherlands is gradual and far from severe, dramatic or radical.

In this chapter, we investigate value changes over time in the Netherlands, using the European Values Survey (EVS) data from 1981, 1990, and 1999. We focus on those areas that seem to be changing most of all, and which are the main focus of this book. We explore whether or not individualization is revealed in changing values. This will first be explored at the aggregate level: Is there a general trend in the Netherlands that indicates the ongoing process of individualization? Since it is often found that, for example, family and marital values have hardly changed over time and have remained rather traditional

(Van den Akker, Halman & de Moor, 1994; Halman, 1998; Halman & Kerkhofs, 2002; Inglehart, 1997), while in other domains values have changed, we will explore whether or not there is a general trend of individualization occurring in all value domains, the family and marital values included.

We start with some general ideas about individualization as a major source of value change, and argue that individualization not only pushes values to change in a certain direction, but also causes values to become more diverse. It will be argued that increasing diversity or pluralism is also a consequence of ongoing processes of internationalization and globalization. Next, we will describe the survey data, measures and analytical strategy. In section 4, the results of our analyses are presented and, in section 5, conclusions are drawn.

## 2. *Theoretical reflections and hypotheses*

One of the most important and far-reaching cultural changes is individualization. It is also a much debated process of change because there is little agreement on the definition and interpretation of individualization, and there are different appraisals of the implications of individualization in general, and the increase of individualism in particular. In this regard, Birnbaum and Leca have used the metaphor of a spectrum that is "haunting the West's intellectuals" (Birnbaum & Leca, 1990:1).

The current debate on the future of citizenship and civil society is strongly directed towards the negative effects of individualization. Individualization is regarded as not very beneficial to civil society and social solidarity because social responsibilities have declined, and individual citizens are less embedded in associative relations. A process of de-institutionalization has occurred, appearing as weaker social bonds and (feelings of) detachment in society. Instead, a calculative orientation among citizens prevails in the modern welfare state. It is argued that ongoing individualization will ultimately result in a society in which values, beliefs, and ideas are no longer commonly shared. Such a society is threatened by disintegration and the individual is threatened by anomie. Durkheim already recognized this problem, and, more recently, Fukuyama (2000) warned of the dangers of an individualized society. Proponents of so-called Communitarian theory also expressed their concern for the ultimate consequences of this development. They fear a trend towards radical individualism and ethical relativism because "there are social attachments which determine the self and thus individuals are constituted by the community of which they are part" (Avineri & De-Shalit, 1992:3). Beliefs and values are determined by society, and thus individuals cannot freely select their own convictions. If, as seems a characteristic of modern society, the individual withdraws from community life, "the modern self is therefore without a grounded, secure identity" (Crittenden, 1992:19). The only way to solve the problem of individualistic, modern society is, according to proponents of the communitarian theories, the re-establishment of a firm moral order in society by (re-)creating a strong "we feeling", and the (re-)establishment of a "spirit of community" (Etzioni, 1993).

However, individualization does not necessarily have to be associated with negative results. According to some opinions, new societal values will emerge, such as equality, democracy, creativity, self-expression, quality of life, and tolerance. As a result of growing individualism, people have become more interested in fulfilling needs that transcend the sheer materialistic needs, such as a concern about the environment and an interest in quality of life issues (e.g., Inglehart, 1990; 1997). So, viewed from a more positive standpoint, individualization does not necessarily lead to hedonism, egoism, and impersonal relationships, but can contribute to increasing levels of public concern. A more positive interpretation is that the process of individualization has boosted the individual's possibilities, and encourages the individual's creativity and emancipation.

The process of individualization has encouraged an unrestrained endeavor to pursue private needs and aspirations, resulting in assigning top priority to personal need fulfillment. Self-development and personal happiness have become the ultimate criteria for individual actions and attitudes. Individualization thus entails a process in which opinions, beliefs, attitudes, and values are growing to be matters of personal choice. As such, it denotes increasing levels of personal autonomy, self-reliance, responsibility, and an emphasis on individual freedom and the Self (Giddens, 1991).

Defined in a less normative way, we can describe individualization as "the social and historical process in which values, beliefs, attitudes and behavior are increasingly based on personal choice and are less dependent on tradition and social institutions" (Ester et al., 1994:7). Personal autonomy and responsibility are highly valued, and this is reflected in people's attitudes, ideas, and behaviors, which are increasingly dependent upon personal considerations and the individual's convictions, desires, and preferences, all of which are constantly open for debate, reformulation, and change. In other words, a process of privatization has occurred in the sense that "opinions and values are steadily less related to one's belonging to certain categories" (Peters, 1995:20). Views, beliefs, values, and opinions have become privatized in the sense that people's actions and behaviors are increasingly rooted in, and legitimized by, personal autonomy and preferences. Particularly with respect to sensitive issues, such as sexual and bio-ethical behavior, people are less "bound by the moral teachings imposed by religion" (Fukuyama, 2000: 48). The moral guidance of religion and the churches has come under strong pressure, and rigid moral standards, as imposed by religious leaders are no longer accepted as taken for granted. Instead, each individual seems to have become his or her own (moral) guide.

The decreasing importance of religion seems to delineate a more general process of the decline of authority and a growing anti-institutional mood. The guidelines provided by the institutions are conflicting with ideas of personal autonomy and individual desires to decide for oneself. Public confidence in institutions, particularly (but not exclusively) the traditional authoritarian ones, is on the decline because these institutions strongly limit an individual's freedom and are in conflict with ideas of personal autonomy and the emerging need for self-expression, the increased concern for freedom of speech, and self-determination. Inglehart (1990; 1997) has described this important cultural shift in terms of materialism and post-materialism. Rising levels of post-materialism indicate that self-esteem, self-expression, and personal choices are gaining in importance.

People in modern individualized society are assumed to be basically oriented towards pursuing their own happiness, self-development, and self-determination. The traditional options are less likely to be selected by more individualized persons, for they no longer take for granted the rules and prescriptions imposed by traditional institutions. This process of de-traditionalization is characterized by a decline of traditional views in a variety of life domains, e.g., male and female roles, morality, religion on the one hand, and an increase in autonomy, individual rights and personal freedom on the other. Klages (1985) uses the terminology of a decline of 'Akseptanz werte' and an increase of 'Selbstentfaltungswerte' to denote the fundamental change in values from the acceptance of traditional orientations to values emphasizing self-actualization and personal development and happiness. In other words, individualization can be regarded as a process by which the individual gradually becomes liberated from structural constraints (Beck, 1992:2).

*Hypotheses*

Following these arguments, we can formulate concrete expectations about the way individualization was and is changing Dutch society. A key notion of individualization is de-traditionalization (see also Peters, 1995; Felling, Peters & Scheepers, 2000) and it is claimed that this process has affected all domains of society and culture.

In the religious domain, the growing emphasis on autonomy, self-actualization, and self-directedness implies that "any external, superior being or principle that could impose maxims for action" (Wagner, 1994:8) is rejected by a growing number of people. Traditional religion has lost its central position in society (Berger, 1967), and has become one among many other meaning systems in society; thus, a market of "ultimate" meaning systems has developed from which the individual can choose freely (Luckmann, 1967:99). Because "individuals have liberated themselves from religious authorities and (...) their experiences are the basis of their faith" (Dobbelaere, 2002:190), we can propose the hypothesis that traditional religious beliefs are slowly fading away.

In moral issues, the guidance of the church has decreased tremendously, or has completely disappeared. Modern people act as free and independent individuals, and, in their behaviors, they are no longer willing to accept as taken for granted the judgments and the rules imposed by the church; "[t]he final authority of ethical behaviour (...) is the individual alone" (Crittenden, 1992:78). Moreover, in moral issues, the decisions people make have become dependent upon personal convictions, and thus we can expect that the traditional moral rules have diminished in favor of a personal morality of 'anything goes'.

In the political sphere, individualization and the emancipation of the individual delineates a decline of traditional authority and a growing anti-institutional mood. Institutions often restrict the freedom of the individual to behave and act as he or she prefers, and thus, in a highly individualized society, people no longer want to be ruled by such institutions. Instead people want to decide for themselves, and the guidelines and prescriptions provided by these institutions conflict with ideas of personal autonomy and individual freedom. The emancipation of the individual, the growing emphasis on personal autonomy and individual freedom, seem advantageous to "a declining acceptance of the authority of hierarchical institutions, both political and non-political" (Inglehart, 1997:15). Thus, we may expect to find a decline in levels of confidence in institutions.

Furthermore, individualization also appears in increasing levels of post-materialism. A key component of post-materialist values is personal autonomy. What Inglehart describes as the shift from materialism towards post-materialism can be easily understood in terms of increasing levels of individualization. Materialist values are held by people who give highest priority to physical sustenance and safety, to maintaining order in society, to maintaining a high rate of economic growth, and who emphasize the need for a strong army and so on. On the other hand, post-materialists emphasize self-expression, quality of life, freedom of speech, and self-determination (Inglehart 1977; 1990; 1997). It is easy to see the resemblance between post-materialist values and the key features of the consequences of individualization. Rising levels of post-materialism indicate that the key issues of individualization, such as self-esteem, self-expression, and personal choices, are gaining in importance. Therefore, we predict that levels of post-materialism should have increased in the Netherlands.

In the domain of family and marriage, the process of individualization is regarded as the engine behind fundamental changes in patterns of family life. The increased emphasis on personal autonomy makes human relations less bound to traditions, less likely to be prescribed by social norms, and less enforced by social control. Traditional institutional control has particularly weakened the control "associated with family and domestic ties and gendered expectations" (Morgan, 1996:197). The conventional, conjugal family was increasingly regarded as limiting individual freedom and impeding self-realization and confining intimacy (Elliott, 1996:9). Proponents of what is called the theory of the 'second demographic transition' have argued that the low levels of fertility in the Western world reflect behavior that is rooted in an ever-growing individualism in Western societies. In their view, the growing emphasis on the individual affects the traditional family orientation in the sense that it involves "shifts from marriage towards cohabitation, from children to the adult couple as the focus of a family, from contraception to prevent unwanted births to deliberate self-fulfilling choices whether and when to conceive a child, and from uniform to widely diversified families and households" (Van de Kaa, 1987:9). Demographic trends such as the decreasing attractiveness of marriage (which is reflected in the decline in the number of marriages and increasing levels of divorces), and the low number of children, seem to indicate fundamental shifts in values denoted in evolutionary terms "from altruism to individualism" (Van de Kaa, 1987:5; Lesthaeghe & Van de Kaa, 1986; Manting, 1994; Jansen, 2002), suggesting the incompatibility of individualization and the preservation of traditional familial solidarity. People increasingly opt for themselves and for their personal benefit, and, as a consequence, not for marriage and traditional family life. Consequently, we propose the hypothesis that traditional family and marital values have declined.

In all these domains, we thus expect that the individualization process has resulted in a decline in traditional orientations. This is what we refer to as the de-traditionalization hypothesis. Since the decline in traditional views is not expected to be restricted to only one specific life domain but will have occurred in all distinct life spheres, ranging from religion and morality, to politics and family life and marriage, we propose a generalization hypothesis: the decline in traditional views has occurred in all life domains.

Because, in an individualizing society, individual choices are increasingly based on personal convictions and preferences, the predictability of people's orientations and behavior should have decreased. It is one of the basic characteristics of postmodernity that everything is possible and unpredictable. Waters (1994:206) portrayed contemporary society as follows: "We may no longer be living under the aegis of an industrial or capitalist culture which can tell us what is true, right and beautiful, and also what our place is in the grand scheme, but under a chaotic, mass-mediated, individual-preference-based culture of postmodernity."

However, it is not only clearly defined patterns of behavior and orientations that have departed; the individual in modern or even postmodern society also faces a multitude of alternatives as a consequence of internationalization, transnationalization, and globalization. Today's world is a "global village", denoting that the world is a compressed one, and consciousness of the world as a whole has intensified tremendously (Robertson, 1992:8). The globalization of social reality is a main effect of the rapid evolution of modern communication technology. Technological developments and innovations in telecommunications, the spread and popularity of computers, the increased mobility of major companies and people, as well as the growing exposure to television, radio, video, movies and so on, have intensified worldwide social relations and flows of information. In the 'global village', people encounter a great variety of alternative cultural habits and a broad range of lifestyles and modes of conduct. Globalization makes people aware of an expanding range of beliefs and moral convictions and thus provides a plurality of choices. Because it has been argued that individualized and secularized people are liberated from the constraints imposed by traditional institutions (e.g., religion), globalization implies that people can pick and choose what they want from a global cultural marketplace. Globalization, thus, may be considered favorable to pluralism because people's choices are increasingly dependent upon personal convictions and preferences. In other words, the heterogeneity of people in their value preferences should have increased.

Therefore, we should not only expect changes in value orientations away from traditional views and in the direction of more individualistic, secular values and a decline in the acceptance of traditional authoritarian authorities, but we can also expect a growing diversity in these orientations and opinions as a result of individualization and globalization. This is denoted as the heterogenization hypothesis: "an increase in the differences in opinions between individuals" (Peters, 1995:20).

Since value changes in society are taking place gradually and, as argued by, among others, Inglehart (1977; 1990; 1997), are the result of generation replacement, we expect to find differences between age groups. Younger people are generally more sensitive to new trends and developments in society, and they usually respond more rapidly in terms of value change and value adaptations than older people. Apart from this trendsetter hypothesis, there are other reasons to assume that younger people will be more individualized than older people. The social integration theory provides some clues here: the stronger one has been exposed to social forces with traditional or conventional views and strict norms and restrictions of individual freedom, the stronger one will subscribe to the norms prevalent in the groups acting as socializing forces (Ultee, Arts & Flap, 1992:86). Older people have been raised and socialized in times when traditional norms and values were still quite dominant in society, and they have been exposed more strongly to these traditional norms, while younger people are raised and socialized in more modern, individualized, secular, more globalized and secure settings than older people. Thus, we may expect that younger people will display higher levels of modern secular and individualistic values than older people, and that the group of younger people will also be less homogeneous than the group of older people.

### 3. Data, measurements and analytical strategy

The data of the three Dutch waves of the European Values Study surveys, conducted in 1981, 1990 and 1999, will be analyzed. We investigate confidence in institutions, religiosity, moral values, orientations towards family and marriage, and post-materialism.

#### 3.1 Measures

*Trust in institutions* refers to the level of confidence in traditional institutions: the armed forces, the educational system, the press, trade unions, the police, parliament, and the civil service. This measure, like most of the following, is constructed by means of factor analysis. High factor scores indicate high levels of confidence in these institutions.

*Religiosity* is measured in terms of beliefs, and not in terms of behavior (such as church attendance) using items such as being a religious person, the importance of God, getting comfort from religion, and belief in God. High factor scores indicate high levels of religiosity.

We distinguish two moral orientations: *personal sexual morality*, and *civic morality*. The first refers to personal sexual and ethical issues and taps the acceptance of homosexuality, abortion, divorce, and euthanasia. The second refers to public issues such as the acceptance of illegally claiming state benefits, cheating on tax, joy riding, and bribery. In quite a number of studies these two dimensions have been identified by means of factor analysis. High scores on the first factor indicate high levels of personal sexual morality, while high scores on the second dimension can be interpreted as high levels of public or civic morality.

With regard to family issues, we will investigate *a traditional family pattern*, indicated by people's opinions on the need for children to have both a father and a mother in order to grow up happily, on the need for women having children in order to be fulfilled, and on the (dis)approval of women wanting to have a child outside of a stable relationship. *Parent child relationships* are indicated by the views on parents' duties towards their children, and children's duties towards their parents. High scores on this dimension reflect not only the opinion that parents have to do their utmost best for their children, even at the cost of their own well-being, but also the view that children should always love and respect their parents regardless of their parents' qualities and faults.

Finally, the dimension of *materialism vs. post-materialism* is based on the short measurement that has been used in scores of studies. Based on people's priorities for either maintaining order in the nation, giving people more say in important government decisions, fighting rising prices, and protecting freedom of speech, a distinction will be made in terms of pure materialists, mixed, and pure post-materialists.

### 3.2  *Analytical strategy*

A first indication of overall change in orientations can be obtained from a comparison of the mean scores on the dimensions distinguished. Increasing diversity (i.e., decreasing homogeneity of values) can be investigated by examining the distributions of scores indicating a person's value orientation (Halman & Pettersson, 1996a; b; Draulans & Halman, 2003). For this purpose, we make use of the standard deviations of the constructs in the three waves. The more people score differently on a given dimension, the greater the variance, and thus the less homogeneous or the more heterogeneous a population is (see also Jagodzinski & Dobbelaere, 1995:226).

### 4. *Results*

### 4.1  *De-traditionalization?*

The hypothesis on the decline of traditional values/orientations in the Netherlands in the last two decades of the 20th century is, at the aggregate level more or less substantiated (see Fig. 7.1). As expected, levels of trust in traditional institutions have declined, as well as levels of religiosity, adherence to traditional family pattern, and traditional views on parent-child relationships. Sexual permissiveness increased, and Dutch society has become more post-materialistic since 1981. Civic permissiveness, however, declined in the same period and this is the only clear exception to the trend of declining levels of traditional views and values.

Changes are generally more pronounced during the nineties than during the eighties. Religiosity, however, declined more severely in the eighties and continued to decline during the nineties, although in a less pronounced way. The same, but opposite, shift occurred with respect to sexual permissiveness. The increase in this kind of permissiveness during the eighties is larger than during the nineties, but on the whole, sexual permissiveness is steadily on the increase.

Figure 7.1. Mean scores on the 6 value dimensions in 1981, 1990, 1999.

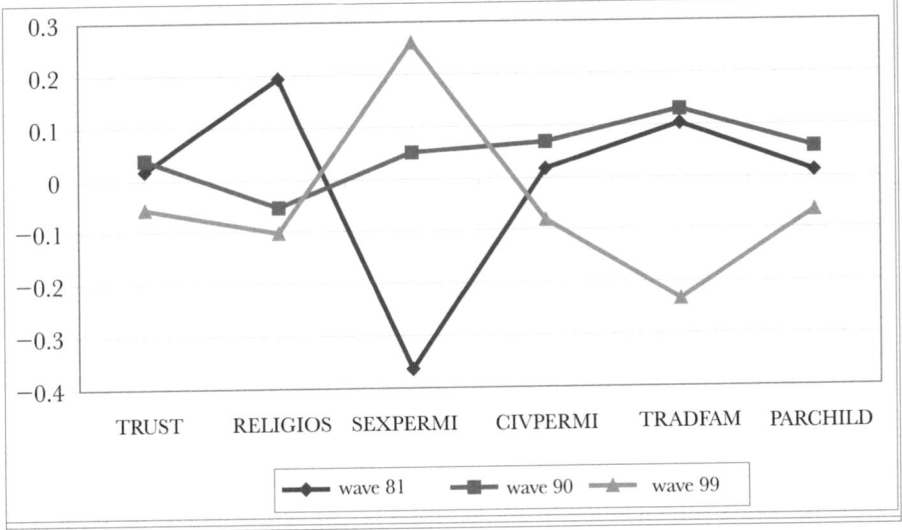

Although from 1981 to 1999 the orientations with regard to *family pattern* and *parent child relations* changed in the expected direction (that is, a decline of traditional views), the major decline took place during the nineties, while the eighties can be characterized by stability or even a slight increase in traditional views. A similar development took place with regard to civic permissiveness. From 1981 to 1990 this kind of permissiveness increased, but, from 1990 to 1999, levels of civic permissiveness declined. In addition, the trend of declining levels of *trust in institutions* was expected, but, at aggregate level, such a decline took place mainly during the nineties, not in the eighties.

Thus, as was expected, *permissiveness* with respect to *personal sexual ethical issues and behavior* increased. The idea was that an 'ideology of anything goes' or 'ethos of everything is possible' has emerged, and, indeed, permissiveness increased during the last two decades. A similar expectation was formulated with respect to deviant and indecent behavior. It is assumed that such behavior is increasingly accepted because, in an individualized society, people have to decide for themselves, which implies that they have to allow others to behave differently and even deviate from the norm. This hypothesis cannot be substantiated at the aggregate level. From 1981 to 1990, there was a small increase in this kind of permissiveness, but, from 1990 to 1999, Dutch society

Table 7.1. Percentages of Dutch respondents stating that illegally claiming state benefits, cheating on taxes, joyriding, and accepting a bribe can never or almost never be justified.

|  | 1981 | 1990 | 1999 |
|---|---|---|---|
| Illegally claiming state benefits | 94 | 92 | 94 |
| Cheat on taxes | 63 | 68 | 71 |
| Joyriding | 95 | 93 | 96 |
| Bribery | 84 | 88 | 92 |

has become stricter towards the issues and behavior incorporated in this measure of civic permissiveness. At first sight, the conclusion should be that the hypothesis is not corroborated; Dutch society has not become more lenient but instead more strict towards civic issues and behaviors. The conclusion could also be that, because the changes are not that dramatic, Dutch society remained as strict as before. Most of the behavior included is not acceptable as becomes clear in Table 7.1, which displays the percentage of respondents claiming that the behavior mentioned can never be justified (scores 1–3 on the 10 point scales ranging from 1 = never justified, to 10 = always justified) for the three waves.

The overwhelming majority does not accept these kinds of behavior, particularly the misuse of state benefits, joyriding, and bribery. Bribery appears increasingly unacceptable for Dutch people, as is the case with cheating on taxes, although Dutch people are less homogeneous with regard to this behavior.

The idea was that adherence to the *traditional family pattern* would also be on the decline. Different kinds of cohabitation are increasingly accepted and occur frequently, stimulating the assumption that the traditional forms would indeed be less favorable in Dutch society. In the period 1981 to 1990, an increase in popularity of the traditional family pattern can be observed, while the nineties seem to conform to the ideas as expressed. Indeed the traditional pattern is less favored in 1999 than in 1990 and in 1981.

We expected a decline in the traditional *parent child relationships*, but this decline only took place in the nineties, not in the eighties (where we see an increasing popularity of the traditional view on parent-child relationships).

We also hypothesized increasing levels of *post-materialism*. Inglehart's ideas about the transformation of society from materialist to post-

Figure 7.2. Mean scores on post-materialism in 1981, 1990 and 1999.

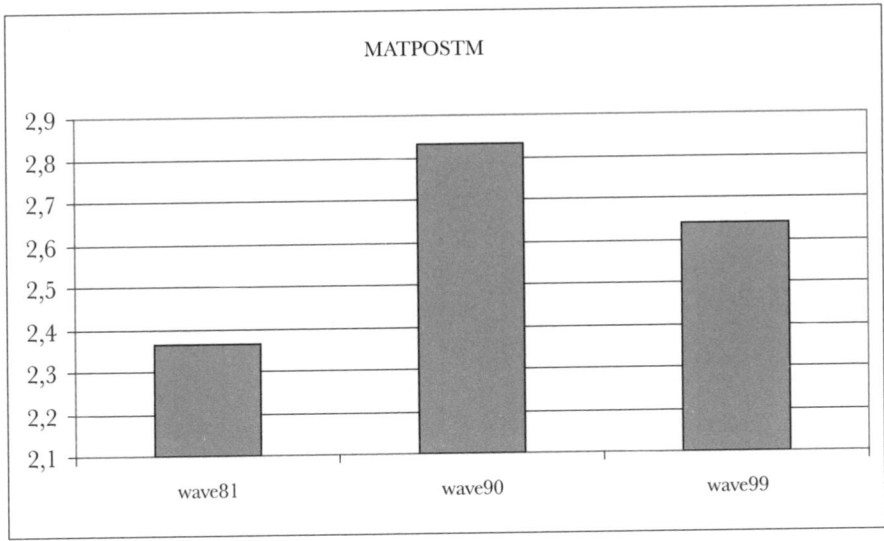

materialist can be confirmed in the Netherlands. However, this increase mainly took place in the 1981 to 1990 period. From 1990 to 1999, post-materialism was on the decline.

We do not find a steady increase in levels of post-materialism in the Netherlands. This is quite unexpected, since Dutch society experienced a prosperous era and high levels of security.

### 4.2  *Heterogenization?*

The hypothesis is that diversity has grown as a result of growing individualization and globalization. From the standard deviations displayed in Figure 7.3, we can evaluate whether this hypothesis is confirmed or not.

In three instances, heterogeneity did not increase. On the contrary, Dutch people became more homogenous with regard to their levels of trust in institutions, personal sexual ethical permissiveness, and post-materialism. This clearly refutes our expectation. This process of homogenization appears to be a steady transformation when it comes to post-materialism and sexual permissiveness, while the homogenization trend with regard to trust in institutions was stronger during the eighties, and only increased slightly during the nineties.

Figure 7.3. Standard deviations of the value orientations in 1981, 1990, and 1999.

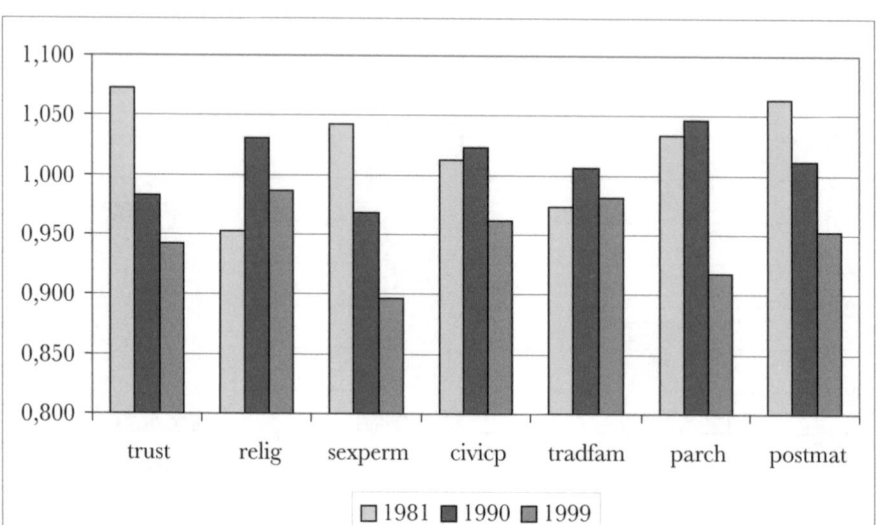

With regard to the other three orientations, the expectations cannot be corroborated either (or, if they can, it is only partly, and then only for the trend in the eighties). Heterogeneity increased from 1981 to 1990, and declined from 1990 to 1999, with regard to religiosity, civic permissiveness, and both family dimensions. Thus, a trend of hetero-genization did not continue in the nineties, but turned into growing homogeneity. In other words, the Dutch population did not become more diverse in their opinions and values, but more unanimous. The major conclusion from these analyses is that the idea that a process of growing diversity is taking place in Dutch society has to be refuted.

### 4.3   *Generalization?*

We theorized that the process of de-traditionalization was not lim-ited to one dimension only, but was a process that occurred in other dimensions as well. Furthermore, we argued that Dutch people would be increasingly diverse in their views, and, as such, increasing levels of heterogenization were expected in all dimensions identified in this chapter.

The idea that similar processes took place in all domains and all dimensions is partly answered by the previous analyses, and they demonstrate that the evidence is not very strong. It is clear that there was not a decline in all traditional values. In particular, the values in the domain of primary relations and trust remained remarkably stable in the eighties. As such, the generalization hypothesis cannot be confirmed.

In terms of an increasing heterogeneity, the hypothesis cannot be confirmed for all dimensions either. Only with regard to trust, and sexual permissiveness, did Dutch people become more diverse, but this was not the case on the other dimensions identified in this chapter. These other dimensions showed increasing levels of diversity in the eighties, and declining heterogeneity in the nineties. These figures cannot be interpreted as a falsification of the hypothesis, but the evidence is not always in line with our theoretical considerations.

## 4.4   *Trendsetters?*

The trendsetter hypothesis states that the adherence to traditional values will be less among younger than among older people. We expect that young people will be less traditional and more individualistic than older people, and further that they are more heterogeneous in their orientations than older people. In order to test this hypothesis, we regressed the various orientations on age, gender, education (measured as age, completion of education), and year of study. The results are presented in Table 7.2.

Table 7.2. Regression coefficients (B en β) for age controlling for gender, education and wave.

| Dependent variable | B | β |
|---|---|---|
| Trust in institutions | .004 | .075*** |
| Religiosity | .013 | .222*** |
| Sexual permissiveness | −.009 | −.160*** |
| Civic permissiveness | −.013 | −.221*** |
| Traditional family pattern | .016 | .282*** |
| Traditional parent-child relationships | .011 | .192*** |
| Post-materialism | −.005 | −.084*** |

*** p < .001

Young Dutch people are indeed less traditional than older Dutch people. The effect of age seems particularly important with regard to family issues, moral orientations, and religiosity. Young people are less religious, and also more permissive with regard to both sexual and civic issues and behavior.

However, the differences between the youngest age group (18–26 years of age) and those between 63 and 71 years of age are declining when it comes to religiosity and sexual permissiveness. This is demonstrated in Tables 7.3 and 7.4, where we have displayed the means and standard deviations for these two age groups respectively. With regard to civic permissiveness, the difference between the youngest age group and the 63 to 71 age group is increasing, which is mainly the result of the older age group having become less permissive, while the level of this kind of permissiveness in the youngest age group did not change much.

Young Dutch people are less in favor of the traditional family structure, and less in favor of a traditional parent-child relationship. The differences between older and younger people are slowly declining, and, from 1981 to 1999, both age groups became less traditional with regard to family pattern. With regard to parent-child relationships, older age groups have become less traditional, whereas the youngest age groups appear to have become more inclined to favor more traditional viewpoints.

The effects of age are less important for trust in institutions and post-materialism. In fact, in 1981 and 1999, age has hardly any effect on the degree of post-materialism. Thus, in 1981 and 1999, young people are neither more nor less post-materialistic than older people. However, for the 1990 study, we found, as expected, that younger people are more post-materialistic than older people. The differences between the 63 to 71 year old age group and the youngest age group are slowly disappearing.

Age differences are important for the level of trust in 1999 and 1981, but not in 1990. In 1981 and 1999, older people appear to have more confidence in the traditional institutions than younger people. This is quite as expected (e.g., Inglehart, 1997), but the differences remained more or less the same from 1981 to 1999. What is remarkable is that the youngest age group in 1999 has more confidence than in 1981, while the level of trust among the 63–71 year old age group has declined.

The second part of the trendsetter hypothesis stated that young people will be more heterogeneous than older people. To test this idea,

Table 7.3. Mean scores for 18–26 years of age and 63–71 years of age on the seven dimensions.

| Dimension | Age group | Survey | | |
|---|---|---|---|---|
| | | 1981 | 1990 | 1999 |
| Trust | 18–26 | −.116 | .129 | .096 |
| | 63–71 | .204 | .257 | −.216 |
| Religiosity | 18–26 | −.184 | −.443 | −.195 |
| | 63–71 | .541 | .356 | .178 |
| Sexual permissiveness | 18–26 | .010 | .186 | .360 |
| | 63–71 | −1.037 | −.449 | −.018 |
| Civic permissiveness | 18–26 | .337 | .578 | .320 |
| | 63–71 | −.143 | −.391 | −.465 |
| Traditional family | 18–26 | −.187 | −.186 | −.457 |
| | 63–71 | .634 | .957 | .097 |
| Parent child relations | 18–26 | −.322 | −.146 | −.215 |
| | 63–71 | .287 | .502 | .198 |
| Post-materialism | 18–26 | 2.607 | 3.139 | 2.685 |
| | 63–71 | 2.083 | 2.302 | 2.462 |

Table 7.4. Standard deviations for 18–26 years of age and 63–71 years of age on the seven dimensions.

| Dimension | Age group | Survey | | |
|---|---|---|---|---|
| | | 1981 | 1990 | 1999 |
| Trust | 18–26 | .987 | .953 | .864 |
| | 63–71 | 1.208 | 1.148 | 1.025 |
| Religiosity | 18–26 | 1.003 | 1.028 | .879 |
| | 63–71 | .803 | .949 | .992 |
| Sexual permissiveness | 18–26 | .907 | .890 | .835 |
| | 63–71 | .908 | 1.044 | .955 |
| Civic permissiveness | 18–26 | 1.174 | 1.205 | .835 |
| | 63–71 | 1.156 | .504 | .905 |
| Traditional family | 18–26 | .912 | .942 | .956 |
| | 63–71 | .944 | 1.015 | .993 |
| Parent child relations | 18–26 | .942 | 1.032 | .930 |
| | 63–71 | .992 | .945 | .909 |
| Post-materialism | 18–26 | 1.071 | .911 | .907 |
| | 63–71 | .997 | .037 | .967 |

we have compared the standard deviations on the seven value orien-
ations for the age groups 18–26 years of age and 63–71 years of age.
The result of these comparisons makes clear that such a hypothesis
cannot be substantiated for all orientations.

On the contrary, it is the older age groups, not the younger, that
appear more heterogeneous with respect to trust in institutions, sexual
permissiveness, and traditional family pattern. These findings clearly
contradict the hypothesis. With regard to post-materialism, the hypothesis is confirmed for 1981, but not for 1990 and 1999, while, for civic
permissiveness and religiosity, the hypothesis is confirmed for 1981
and 1990, but not for 1999. As far as parent-child relationships, the
hypothesis is confirmed in 1990 and 1999, but not in 1981. The pattern
appears too diverse to conclude that the hypothesis is substantiated.
Of course, it is not easy to interpret or understand this mixed pattern;
why, for instance were older people in previous years indeed more
homogeneous in their religious beliefs than younger people, and why
have they become more diverse in their beliefs than young people? In
1990, the 63–71 year old age group was very homogeneous in being
not very permissive with regard to civic behaviors. Why the same age
group in 1999 turned out to be more diverse again, more even than
the youngest age group, is difficult to understand. In 1999, there is only
one dimension that is in line with the expectation and that is parent
child relations. Young people appear more heterogeneous with regard
to this dimension than people aged 63–71. On all other dimensions,
in 1999, the older people appear (slightly) more heterogeneous than
younger people, and that is opposite of what we expected to find.

## 5. *Conclusions*

In this chapter, we focused on values and value changes in Dutch
society. It is often argued that Dutch society is transforming as a result
of growing individualization, secularization, and globalization. The
dynamic of this transformation is slow and gradual, rather than very
radical, but is described in terms of de-traditionalization and increasing
heterogenization. We have explored whether values have changed in the
direction of more individualistic and less traditional preferences, and
whether this process of change took place in all value domains and age
groups in society. According to the generalization hypothesis, it should
be assumed that de-traditionalization took place in all life domains,

while as far as distinct age groups are concerned, we investigated the so-called trendsetter hypothesis, stating that young generations in particular will display individualistic values and will be more heterogeneous than older generations. We have focused on topics that seem to be changing most, not only in Dutch society, but in all Western and also probably in non-Western societies (see the other chapters in this book).

The de-traditionalization hypothesis is more or less confirmed. From 1981 to 1999, traditional views on religion, institutions, family and morality have declined. As others have noted before, the changes in the 1980s were not very substantial, but the 1990s showed a more pronounced move away from traditional views. Most significant are the changes with regard to the acceptance of different kinds of sexual behavior. Increasingly, sexual behavior is considered a personal matter that does not permit the interference of other people or institutions. This development does not necessarily mean that an ethos of anything goes has developed. Sexual permissiveness has to be clearly understood as the idea that one accepts and understands others to be engaged in such behavior, but this does not necessarily imply that people themselves prefer to behave in such ways. Thus, acceptance and acceptability of such behavior have grown. That an ethos of anything goes has not evolved in Dutch society also appears from the low level of acceptance of deviant and indecent behavior such as claiming state benefits illegally, cheating on taxes, joyriding and accepting bribery. Such behavior is hardly ever accepted by Dutch people and has become less acceptable by Dutch people during the last two decades.

According to the heterogenization hypothesis, we should find growing levels of diversity in Dutch society as a result of growing individualization and globalization. However, we cannot find much evidence to support such claims. We have seen that a growing diversity in the 1980s turned into a growing homogeneity in the 1990s; Dutch society seems to become more united in terms of values and wide differences seem to be slowly disappearing. It has been argued that the traditional sociological categories that divided society for such a long time can no longer define the dividing lines in contemporary society. Dutch society is a modern, highly educated, highly urbanized service oriented society in which gender, income, and level of education are of less importance for marked differences in values. Our analyses seem to confirm such ideas. The variation in value orientations is slowly declining.

The generalization hypothesis suggested that a similar process takes place in all value domains, and in different age groups in Dutch society.

As far as aggregate level changes in values are concerned, the hypothesis is more or less confirmed. In almost all orientations, we observed a shift away from traditional preferences towards more individualistic stances. Important exceptions were, in the eighties, concerning the orientations with regard to family patterns and parent child relations. As was observed, the views in this domain did not show dramatic changes in either direction. As such it was concluded that the old patterns persisted (Van den Akker, Halman & de Moor, 1994; Halman, 1998). The traditional pattern did not disappear despite the larger individual freedom, emphasis on openness of society, and extended range of opportunities in the domain of family and marriage. It seems as if most people still value the traditional patterns of family life, and thus it seems as if, in Dutch people's minds, the old patterns have survived the flows of modernity.

Finally, our trendsetter hypothesis was investigated by comparing the youngest age group (18–26 years of age) with the group aged 63–71. In most cases, the youngest age group showed the individualistic preferences, as expected, but, in many cases, the oldest age group changed more dramatically than the youngest. The 63–71 year old age group has become more lenient with regard to sexual behavior, less religious, less in favor of traditional family views and more post-materialistic.

As others have indicated before (Nauta, 1987; Felling, Peters & Scheepers, 2000; SCP, 2001), de-traditionalization continues gradually in Dutch society and is not a dramatic instantaneous development. Indeed, it seems as if more dramatic changes took place before the 1980s, during the 'exciting', 'turbulent' 1960s and 1970s. During these decades, the sexual revolution took place, and, together with unprecedented levels of existential security and increasing levels of welfare in Dutch society, peoples' views on many issues changed. In particular, the role and position of the traditional institutions were no longer taken for granted. The 1980s and 1990s do not show stability in values, and no dramatic value changes either. Instead, values are gradually changing into a more individualistic and less traditional direction, and it seems as if Dutch people are increasingly sharing similar values. The current popular view among Dutch people in general, and politicians and culture pessimists in particular, that Dutch society no longer maintains values, or that values are on the decline and slowly disappearing, cannot, however, be substantiated. As such, the answer to the question what happened to Dutch values can be answered very briefly: not much.

## References

Andeweg, R.B. 2000. From Dutch Disease to Dutch Model? Consensus Government in Practice. *Parliamentary Affairs* 52: 679–709.
Avineri, S. & A. De-Shalit 1992. 'Introduction'. Pp. 1–11 in S. Avineri & A. de-Shalit (eds.), *Communitarianism and Individualism*. Oxford: Oxford University Press.
Beck, U. 1992. *Risk Society. Towards a New Modernity*. London: Sage Publications.
Berger, P.L. 1967. *Het hemels baldakijn (The Sacred Canopy)*. Bilthoven: Ambo.
Birnbaum, P. & J. Leca. 1990. 'Introduction'. Pp. 1–15 in P. Birnbaum & J. Leca (eds.), *Individualism. Theories and Methods*. Oxford: Clarendon Press.
Crittenden, J. 1992. *Beyond Individualism. Reconstituting the Liberal Self*. Oxford: Oxford University Press.
Dobbelaere, K. 2002. *Secularization: An Analysis at Three Levels*. Brussels: P.I.E. Peter Lang.
Draulans, V. & L. Halman 2003. 'Religious and Moral pluralism in Contemporary Europe'. Pp. 371–400 in W. Arts, J. Hagenaars & L. Halman (eds.), *The Cultural Diversity of European Unity*. Leiden/Boston: Brill.
Elliot, F.R. 1996. *Gender, Family and Society*. Houndmills: Macmillan.
Ester, P., L. Halman & R. de Moor 1994. 'Value Shift in Western Societies'. Pp. 1–20 in P. Ester, L. Halman & R. de Moor (eds.), *The Individualizing Society*. Tilburg: Tilburg University Press.
Etzioni, A. (1993). *The Spirit of Community. Rights, Responsibilities, and the Communitarian Agenda*. New York: Crown.
Felling, A., J. Peters & P. Scheepers (eds.) 2000. *Individualisering in Nederland aan het einde van de twintigste eeuw*. Assen: Van Gorcum.
Fukuyama, F. 2000. *The Great Disruption: Human Nature and the Reconstitution of Social Order*. New York: Simon & Schuster.
Gabennesch, H. 1972. 'Authoritarianism as world view'. *American Journal of Sociology* 77: 857–875.
Giddens, A. 1991. *Modernity and Self-Identity*. Stanford: Stanford University Press.
Halman, L. 1998. Family patterns in contemporary Europe: Results from the European Values Study 1990. Pp. 99–122 in D. Kalekin Fishmann (ed.), *Designs for alienation. Exploring diverse realities*. Jyväskylä, Finland: SoPhi University of Jyväskylä.
Halman, L. & J. Kerkhofs 2002. 'Het Europese waardenonderzoek: enkele resultaten'. Pp. 11–54 in H. van Veghel (ed.), Waarden onder de meetlat.Budel: Damon.
Halman, L. & R. de Moor 1994. 'Religion, Churches and Moral Values'. Pp. 37–66 in P. Ester, L. Halman & R. de Moor (eds.), *The Individualizing Society*. Tilburg: Tilburg University Press.
Halman, L. & T. Pettersson (1996). Religion and Morality: A Weakened Relationship? *Journal of Empirical Theology* 9(2): 30–48.
—— (1996). 'The shifting soures of morality: From Religion to Postmaterialism?'. Pp. 261–284 in L. Halman & N. Nevitte (eds.). *Political Value Change in Western Democracies. Integration, Values, Identification and Participation*. Tilburg: Tilburg University Press.
HDR 2001. Human Development Report 2001. New York: United Nations.
Inglehart, R. 1977. *The Silent Revolution*. Princeton: Princeton University Press.
——. 1990. *Culture Shift in Advanced Industrial Society*. Princeton: Princeton University Press.
——. 1997. *Modernization and Postmodernization*. Princeton: Princeton University Press.
Jansen, M. 2002. *Waardenoriëntaties en partnerrelaties*. Utrecht: Proefschrift.
Jagodzinski, W. & K. Dobbelaere 1995. 'Religious and Ethical Pluralism'. Pp. 218–249 in J.W. van Deth & E. Scarbrough (eds.), *The Impact of Values*. Oxford: Oxford University Press.

Klages, H. 1985. *Werturientierungen im Wandel: Rückblick, Gegenwartsanalyse, Prognosen.* Frankfurt/New York: Campus Verlag.

Lesthaeghe, R. & D. van de Kaa 1986. 'Twee demografische transities?' *Mens en Maatschappij* 61:9–24.

Luckmann, T. 1967. *The Invisible Religion.* New York: MacMillan.

Manting, D. 1994. *Dynamics in Marriage and Cohabitation.* Amsterdam: Thesis Publishers.

Morgan, D.H.J. 1996. *Family Connections. An Introduction to Family Studies.* Oxford: Polity Press.

Nauta, A. 1987. 'De Europese waardenstudie: een terugblik.' Pp. 31–41 in: L. Halman & Felix Heunks (eds.), *De toekomst van de traditie.* Tilburg: Tilburg University Press.

Peters, J. 1995. 'Individualization: Fiction or reality?' *Sociale Wetenschappen* 38: 18–27.

Robertson, R. 1992. *Globalization. Social Theory and Global Culture.* London: Sage.

SCP 2001. *The Netherlands in a European Perspective. Social & Cultural Report 2000.* The Hague: Social and Cultural Planning Office.

Ultee, W., W. Arts & H. Flap 1992. *Sociologie. Vragen, uitspraken, bevindingen.* Groningen: Wolters-Noordhoff.

Van de Kaa, D. 1987. 'Europe's Second Demographic Transition.' *Population Bulletin* 42: 1–57.

Van den Akker, P., L. Halman & R. de Moor 1994. 'Primary Relations in Western Societies.' Pp. 97–127 in P. Ester, L. Halman & R. de Moor (eds.), *The Individualizing Society.* Tilburg: Tilburg University Press.

Wagner, P. 1994. *A Sociology of Modernity.* London and New York: Routledge.

Waters, M. 1994. *Modern Sociological Theory.* London: Sage.

# B. CENTRAL EUROPE

# CHAPTER EIGHT

## CIVIC VALUES AND VALUE CHANGE IN AUSTRIA AND GERMANY

Franziska Deutsch, Christian Welzel and
Julian Wucherpfennig

### 1. *Introduction*

Like most societies of the advanced industrial world, Austria and Germany are traversing fundamental changes linked with a process that Bell (1973) described as the rise of post-industrial knowledge societies. In many aspects, this process promotes an individualization trend that dissolves the mass-disciplined way in which industrial societies organized the workforce and other domains of society (Giddens 1990; Beck 1999). As a consequence of these changes, people have fundamentally different life experiences, which bring profound changes to their worldviews (Inglehart 1997; Inglehart and Baker 2000; Flanagan and Lee 2003).

In modern service economies, workers are increasingly autonomous in performing their tasks and they have to rely more and more on their own judgment. While the typical Fordist blue collar worker conducted standardized manual work on the assembly line, service professionals perform communicative, analytical, managerial and administrative tasks. They are less exposed to a mechanical world of physical products, but deal with information and symbols. The industrial world was a uniform world of huge, anonymous bureaucracies and party machines. The post-industrial world is a diverse place of smaller units and varied life styles. The industrial experience was based on mass discipline, group conformity, standardization and routine. The post-industrial experience is fundamentally different: it is based on diversity, creativity and individuality.

The fading of a standardized uniform world and people's growing individual autonomy have diminished the need for authority that had seemed necessary to discipline workers, voters, and consumers. Slowly but steadily, these processes have brought an emancipative change of authority orientations, giving rise to a broad syndrome of self-expression values.

This value change is pervasive. It affects all domains of life. The emancipative impulsion of self-expression values lets people place more emphasis on People Power, strengthening their adherence to democratic norms, and making them at the same time more critical of political authority (Norris 1999; Hofferbert and Klingemann 2001). People's working motivations seem to have changed correspondingly. Self-realization and identification with one's work became as important as merely materialistic concerns. Moreover, the goals of child education have changed; to the traditional emphasis on thrift and obedience comes a new emphasis on tolerance and imagination. Religious orientations have changed from an attachment to organized forms of dogmatic religion to individualized forms of spiritual religion, in which religion is no longer needed to provide rules of good conduct but to stimulate reflection about the meaning and purpose of life. This has given rise to a number of lifestyle concerns that nourish sensitivity to questions of ecological sustainability, gender equality and risk technologies. Political activities are leaving the narrow domain of electoral participation and are widening into an open field of lifestyle politics, in which expressive mass actions, such as boycotts and petitions, are becoming more widespread.

Finally, the most massive value changes are occurring in the domains of family, gender and sex. Traditionally, the family has been the basic reproductive unit of society. Family norms have always been particularly rigid against aberrations that threaten the family's basic reproductive function. Thus, abortion, divorce, and homosexuality have been seen as utterly wrong in most societies. Rising self-expression values, however, undermine this rigidity. Acceptance of abortion, divorce, and homosexuality has risen dramatically throughout post-industrial societies. In the same vein, women are nowadays less fixed in their traditional reproductive role and less tied to the households than ever before in human history. This is logical in a knowledge society in which the emphasis on cognitive work eliminates the advantage that sheer physical power has given to males.

Given that these are general trends in post-industrial societies, we expect to observe their manifestations in the following domains of the Austrian and German publics:[1]

---

[1] We use the available data from the World Value Surveys for our analyses. We pooled the 1997 and 2001 data for Germany in order to allow for equal time spans in longitudinal comparisons.

1. People should show strong commitment to democracy as a system of government, but precisely because of this they should be relatively critical in their evaluation of the actual performance of democracy, as measured by confidence in concrete institutions.
2. There should be a decline in attachment to ritual forms of organized religion, but an increase in spiritual forms of individualized religion.
3. Sexual norms once designed to protect the reproductive function of the family—namely rejection of divorce, abortion, and homosexuality—should erode, reflecting a trend of sexual liberation.
4. In child education, responsibility and tolerance should be increasing goals.
5. There should be a dominantly emancipative understanding of gender roles, which loosen women's ties to the household.
6. Due to generational replacement, there should be pronounced age group differences in the overall syndrome of self-expression values. Over time, these values should rise.

We will present separate analyses for East and West Germany. Due to 40 years of communist socialization, and based on previous empirical research (e.g. Kaase 1995; Fuchs 1999; Meulemann 2003), we assume that East German citizens show value orientations that are partly distinct from the prevailing mass attitudes in West Germany.

## 2. Democratic Values

Classical theories of political culture argue that the stability of a political system depends on the congruence of political institutions and political culture. More precisely, a long-lasting divergence between institutions and culture causes severe problems for maintaining a political order, especially in times of crisis (Eckstein 1961, 1966; Almond and Verba 1963).

Starting from this assumption, Almond and Verba conducted their ground-breaking study on the cultural prerequisites of democracy, "The Civic Culture" (1963). In this context, the case of Germany was a matter of substantial interest. Against the background of the Germans' traumatic experience with the Nazi regime, Almond and Verba observed a very distant orientation towards politics among the German public: "as if the intense commitment to political movements that characterized Germany under Weimar and Nazi era is now being balanced by a detached, practical, and almost cynical attitude towards politics" (Almond and Verba 1989 [1963]), 313).

Since then, tremendous changes in orientations, beliefs, and values have been observed. Until today, a huge body of literature documents the successful transition of mass attitudes in Germany from what Almond and Verba described as a rather passive subject culture to predominantly participatory orientations and to firm support for democratic norms (Conradt 1989 [1980]); Baker, Dalton and Hildebrandt 1981; Berg-Schlosser and Rytlewski 1993; Bauer-Kaase and Kaase 1996; Rohrschneider 1998).[2] In a follow-up of their study in 1980, Almond and Verba, and in particular Conradt, state that political skills and political interest as well as commitment to democratic norms among the German public have reached a level exceeding even those of the U.S. and Britain. Over the years, the economic prosperity, social security and political stability that came along with German democracy have contributed to a legitimization of this system in the eyes of most Germans.

In "The Civic Culture" Almond and Verba (1989 [1963]) argued that, although "there is relatively widespread satisfaction with political output, this is not matched by more general system affect. Germans tend to be satisfied with the performance of their government, but to lack a more general attachment to the system on the symbolic level" (p. 313). As the bar chart in Figure 8.1 shows, this is no longer the case.

In fact, this figure allows for three conclusions: First, German as well as Austrian citizens distinguish between democracy in general (that is, democracy as a system of governance), and its concrete performance (Easton 1965, 1975; Dalton 1999; Klingemann 1999). Second, among both publics, support for democracy in general exceeds by far the evaluation of its concrete performance. In other words, people strongly support democratic norms but, nevertheless, or precisely because of this, they are relatively critical with respect to its concrete performance (Norris 1999). Third, country differences become apparent. In particular the evaluation of the concrete performance of democracy is relatively

---

[2] Whereas Germany has been the focus of political culture research, the Austrian case has hardly been addressed in comprehensive studies (for exceptions, see Ulram 1990; Plasser and Ulram 2002; unfortunately, this literature is not available in English). The findings, however, indicate a shift in prevailing mass orientations similar to Germany.

Figure 8.1. Democratic Values.

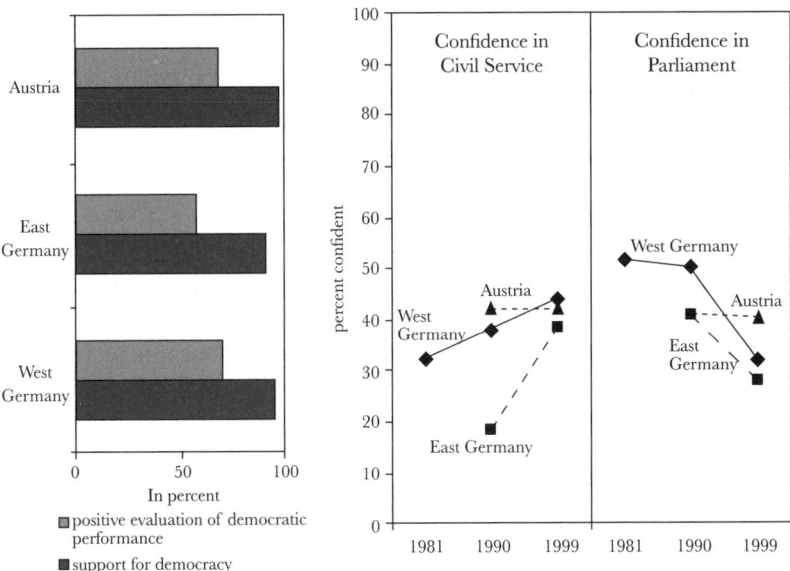

positive evaluation of democratic performance
support for democracy

*Support for Democracy*: additive scale, consisting of two items: (1) "Democracy is better than any other form of government", and (2) "Having a democratic system". The wording of the questions is as follows:
*(1)* I'm going to read off some things that people sometimes say about a democratic political system. Could you please tell me if you (1) agree, (2) strongly agree, (3) disagree or (4) strongly disagree? "Democracy may have problems but it's better than any other form of government."
*(2)* I'm going to describe various types of political systems and ask what you think about each as a way of governing this country. For each one, would you say that it is a (1) very good, (2) fairly good, (3) fairly bad or (4) very bad way of governing this country? "Having a democratic political system."
In a first step, the respondent's support for both items was added to form a 7-point scale. Second, the scale was recoded, so that now low scores on the scale also mean low support for democracy, whereas, correspondingly, high scores indicate high support. The figure shows the proportion of respondents with high support for democracy (scores: 5 to 7).
*Evaluation of Democratic Performance* is an additive scale, consisting of two items: (1) "Democracies are indecisive", and (2) "Democracies are bad in maintaining order." The wording of the questions is as follows: I'm going to read off some things that people sometimes say about a democratic political system. Could you please tell me if you agree, strongly agree, disagree or strongly disagree?
(1) "Democracies are indecisive and have too much quibbling."
(2) "Democracies aren't good at maintaining order."
The figure displays the proportion of respondents with a positive evaluation of democratic performance, and thus respondents who disagree or strongly disagree with the given statements.
*Confidence in Institutions*
Wording of the question: I am going to name a number of organizations. For each one, could you tell me how much confidence you have in them: is it a great deal of confidence, quite a lot of confidence, not very much confidence or none at all? (1) "Parliament"; (2) "The Civil Service".
The figure shows the proportion of respondents who indicate having a great deal or quite a lot of confidence.

high in West Germany and Austria and remarkably low in the former communist part of Germany.

Yet citizens do not blame a negative performance perception on democracy in general. This becomes even more obvious when we turn our attention to the line-chart of Figure 8.1. Confidence in the civil service and parliament are expressed by barely a majority of the population in each country. But, as was shown, support for democracy as a form of governance remains unaffected.

Furthermore, this figure reveals different trends for confidence in specific institutions, as well as apparent differences between societies. In Germany, confidence in the civil service used to be significantly lower than confidence in the national parliament, but this picture had changed by the end of the 1990s, when less than a third of the German population demonstrated confidence in its legislature. Interestingly, West and East Germany show parallel trends over time, with East Germany always scoring lower than the Western population. Austria, by contrast, appears to have maintained the same level of confidence in both institutions.

### 3. *Religious and Moral Values*

The processes of secularization and industrialization are interconnected. "The emergence of a sense of security among the economically more advanced societies diminishes the need for the reassurance that has traditionally been provided by absolute belief systems" (Inglehart 1997, 80). This has lead to a decline in the importance of traditional religious values in Western societies such as Germany and Austria.

However, it has been argued that modernization changes its direction. Industrialization brings a shift from sacred to secular values. Post-industrialization, by contrast, does not push further the secularization trend (Inglehart and Welzel, 2005). It brings another shift—from survival values to self-expression values—in which religion gains renewed relevance, though in a different form, namely as a source of reflection, meaning and purpose in one's life: "in some form or other, spiritual concerns will always be a part of the human condition" (Inglehart 1997, 80). As we know from other research, institutionalized forms of religious activity, such as church membership or service attendance, are declining (Jagodzinski and Dobbelaere 1995; Inglehart 1997). This indicates a decline in institutionalized forms of ritual religiosity. Nevertheless, more individualized and more expressive forms of spiritual religiosity are not necessarily declining in post-industrial societies. Insofar, one would not expect to find a straightforward trend in post-industrial societies. Figure 3.1 illustrates this expectation.

First of all, religious values between 1980 and 1999 have not been subject to much change; thus, whenever changes do occur, they are rather gradual. Second, thinking about the purpose and meaning of life seems to have become more important in West Germany and in Austria; yet, in East Germany, we find a decrease that also affects all other religious values. Third, whereas both the West German and Austrian societies show generally similar trends over time, the Eastern part of Germany is far less concerned with these issues. Forty years of communism left a largely secular imprint on the East German public. However, there is a functional equivalent for the lack of religiosity among East Germans: East German citizens think about the meaning of life more often than do West Germans and Austrians. Of all four religious items, "meaning of life" ranks highest in East Germany, whereas it gathers lowest support (compared to all other items) among the other two publics.

While post-industrialization shows ambiguous consequences on religious/spiritual values, it has straightforward and drastic consequences on other moral values. As we have already underlined above, a long period of political stability, economic prosperity and an extensive welfare state heavily contributed to an "unprecedented sense of security concerning one's own survival. (...) The same factors have weakened the functional basis of a pervasive set of norms linked with the fact that, throughout most of history, the traditional two-parent family was crucial to the survival of children, and thus, of society" (Inglehart 1997, 42). Figure 8.2 displays orientations towards those issues that threaten precisely the subsistence of the heterosexual nuclear family: divorce, abortion and homosexuality. Accordingly, as the survival value of the traditional family recedes, these formerly unacceptable behaviors become increasingly tolerated among all three publics.

This finding is not surprising. In Germany and Austria, societal trends point to the fact that survival norms, often linked with religion, become less formative. In 2002, for example, the German government passed the legal recognition of same-sex couples. Moreover, about 38% of all marriages in Germany end in divorce (Statistisches Bundesamt 2002, 44), and, in Austria, this rate is as high as 44%. These societal changes reflect an increasing trend towards self-actualization, which

Figure 8.2. Religious Values.

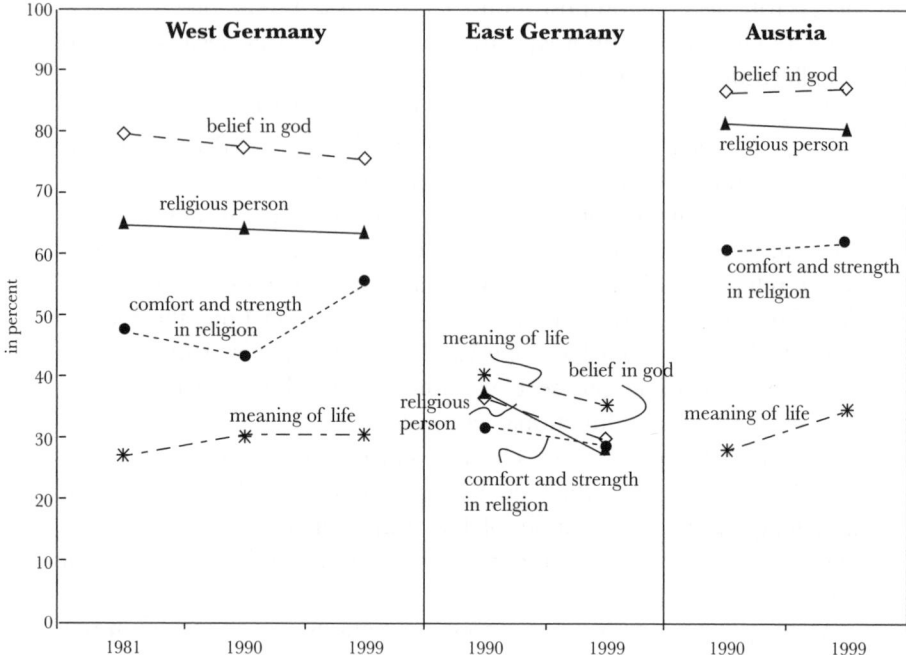

The figure shows the proportion of respondents who agree with one of the following items:

(1) "Do you believe in God?" (*Belief in God*)
(2) "Independently of whether you go to church or not, would you say you are...a religious person?" (*Religious Person*)
(3) "Do you find that you get comfort and strength from religion?" (*Comfort and Strength from Religion*)
(4) *Meaning of Life* shows the proportion of respondents saying that they often or sometimes think about the meaning of life: "How often, if at all, do you think about the meaning and purpose of life -often, sometimes, rarely, or never?"

is also reflected in Figure 8.2. Yet it is important to note that, for the case of Austria, due to the stronger role of traditional religious values, issues related to self-determination are less tolerated (see also Welzel and Deutsch 2007). The differences between Germany and Austria demonstrate the interaction between economic development and cultural traditions. Both societies are in the process of post-industrialization, which promotes rising self-expression values, but the cultural tradition of Catholicism retards this process in Austria, while the stronger imprint of Protestantism in Germany accelerates value change.

Figure 8.3. Moral Values.

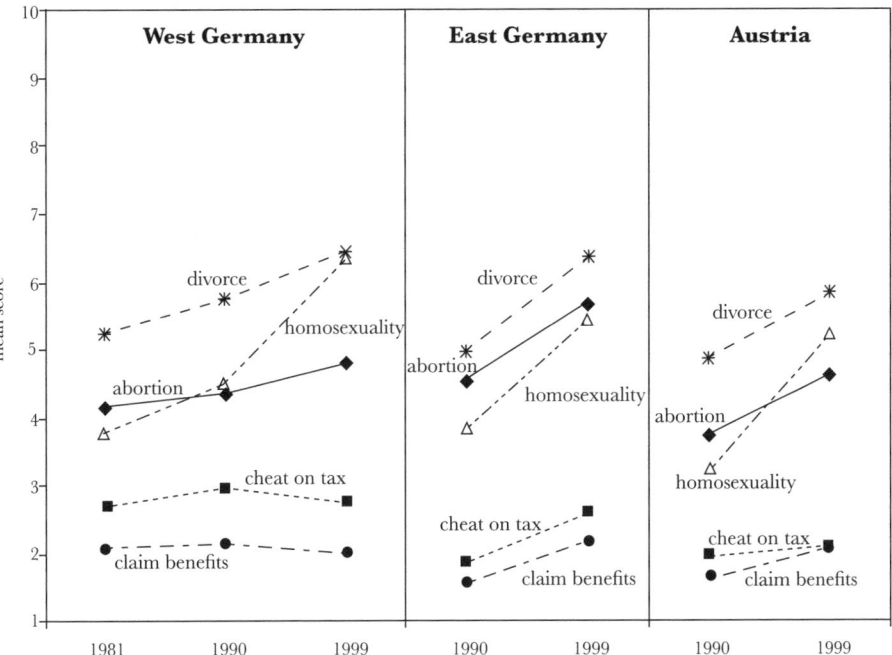

*Moral Values* are presented according to mean scores on a 10-point scale, with 1 always indicating that the statement is never justifiable, and 10 saying that it is always justifiable. The wording of the question is as follows:
    Please tell me for each of the following statements whether you think it can always be justified, never be justified, or something in between (scale from 1 = never justifiable to 10 = always justifiable).

(1) "Claiming government benefits to which you are not entitled."
(2) "Cheating on taxes if you have a chance."
(3) "Homosexuality."
(4) "Abortion."
(5) "Divorce."

Besides tolerance towards human diversity, Figure 8.3 also provides information about the moral acceptance of misbehavior that affects a community in general. Cheating on taxes and claiming benefits that one is not entitled to finds only minor support in both countries. Over time, their acceptance by the citizens is rather stable or increasing on a very low level. This might also indicate that people do not consider such misbehavior as a major problem in their societies. In general, these issues are not related to major trend of rising self-expression values. Accordingly, we do not observe any pronounced change.

## 4. *Individual and Community Responsibility*

Modernization has placed Austria and Germany among the wealthiest nations in the world, and their economic success is closely tied to the system of a corporatist market economy. These principles have been internalized by the masses, as Figure 8.4 indicates. The majority of the population regards competition as beneficial (instead of harmful), scoring above seven on a scale from one to ten, with ten indicating perfect competition. Likewise, private ownership of business is preferred over state ownership by only slightly fewer citizens. Yet, while the trends suggest considerable stability at rather high levels for Austria and West Germany, this is not the case for East Germany. In particular, we observe a negative trend concerning the preference for private ownership of businesses. This tendency may be explained by the particular experiences of East German citizens after the reunification. While "already shortly after the unification the East Germans supported the achievement principle of the market economy to the same degree as the West German" (Roller 1994, 115), considerable disappointment about the difficult economic situation was measured in the following years. Thus, feelings of relative deprivation probably account for these developments (Fuchs 1999, 143).

Moreover, during recent years, vehement debates on the role of the individual in society have marked the agenda of political and public discussion in Germany and Austria, mostly in the context of a restructuring of the welfare state and its social insurance system. As in most other Western democracies, problems of a financial nature are at the core of these discussions, questioning the current mechanisms of financing welfare services, and these developments have not gone unnoticed by the masses of Austria and Germany. While in 1990 the state was largely given the responsibility of providing welfare, we observe a sharp increase towards individual responsibility across Austria and both parts of Germany. Contrary to what politicians often claim, this trend indicates that citizens in both countries are indeed willing to concede, even accept, responsibility for their own pensions and provisions, simply because they have realized that the welfare state is heavily overstrained by citizens' demands. Finally, rising emphasis on individual responsibility for one's life is just another—in fact one of the strongest—indications of rising self-expression values, for these values emphasize individual choice and responsibility.

Figure 8.4. Capitalist Values.

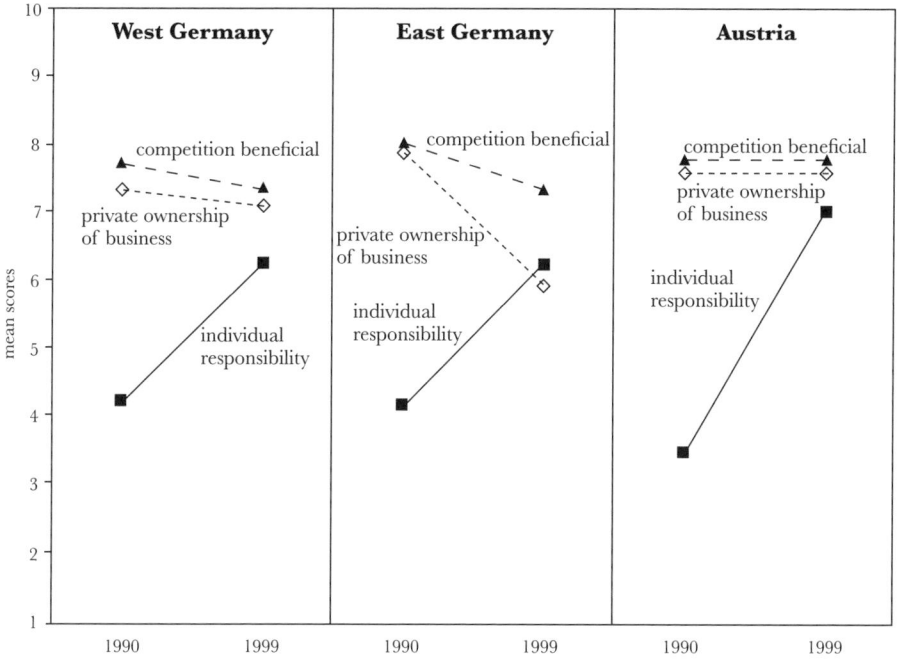

*Capitalist Values* is presented according to mean scores on a 10-point scale. The wording of the question is as follows: Now I'd like you to tell me your views on various issues. How would you place your views on this scale?

*Responsibility*: 1 = "The government should take more responsibility to ensure that everyone is provided for." 10 = "People should take more responsibility to provide for themselves."

*Ownership of Business*: 1 = "Private ownership of business and industry should be increased." 10 = "Government ownership of business and industry should be increased."

*Competition*: 1 = "Competition is good. It stimulates people to hard work and to develop new ideas." 10 = "Competition is harmful. It brings out the worst in people."

## 5. *Family Values*

Increasing individualization and rising self-expression values—displayed by higher levels of tolerance towards divorce, abortion and homosexuality—question the role of the traditional family as the core unit of community. Yet, as Figure 8.5 indicates, this is not necessarily true. For more than 70%, and, in Austria, for even more than 80% of the population, family is very important (though the understanding of

Figure 8.5. Importance in Life.

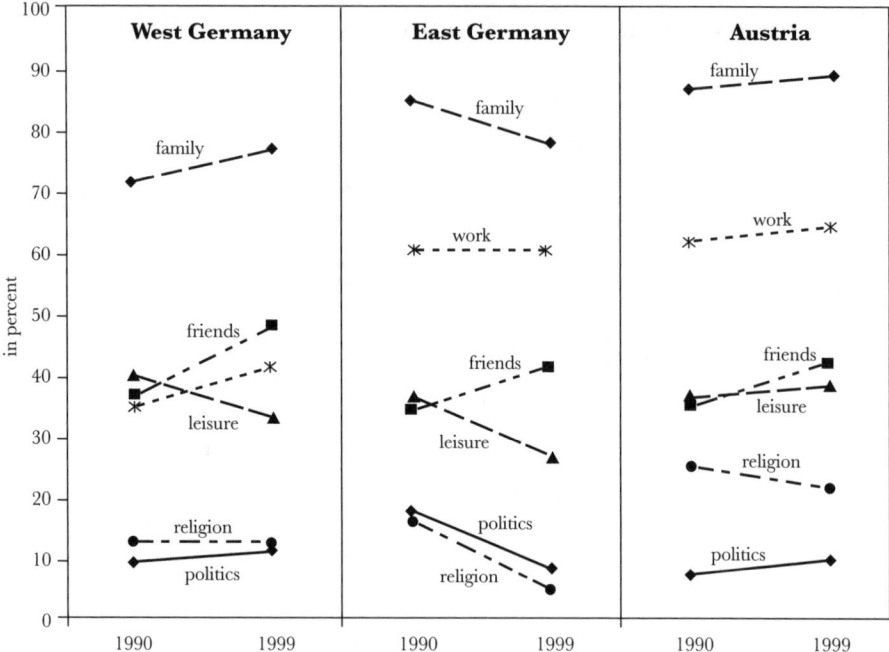

*Importance in Life.*
"Please say, for each of the following, how important it is in your life." (Scale from 1 = very important, to 4 = not at all important.) The figure shows the proportion of respondents answering 1 = very important.

what the family is and what it looks like is obviously changing). Again, compared to West and East Germany, Austria is more stable over time, showing a more traditional outlook.

During the past decade, about two-thirds of the citizens in East Germany and Austria considered work to be fundamental in their lives. However, this applied only to a third of all West Germans in 1990, with only little adjustment nine years later. By then, this had risen to 40%, thereby still remaining significantly below the level of Austria and East Germany.

Overall, each of the three publics assigns religion and politics the least importance. As indicated above, the relative significance of religion is highest in Austria. In East Germany this item falls even below politics, which, in turn, is considered least important by West German and Austrian citizens.

Figure 8.6. Child Qualities.

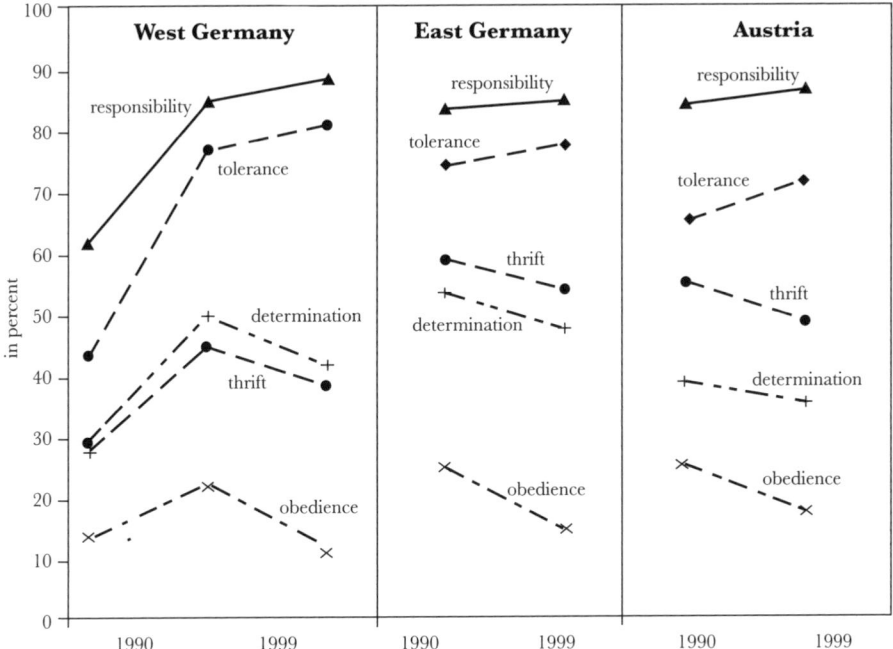

*Child Qualities*: "Here is a list of qualities that children can be encouraged to learn at home. Which, if any, do you consider to be especially important?"

Despite the consistently strong role of the family within the German and Austrian societies, one should keep in mind the observed shift towards self-determination with regard to the pluralization of lifestyles. Such broad value changes within society are also reflected in the transmission of values to new generations. An overview of value priorities in child education is depicted in Figure 8.6. For the past decade, distinct changes in both countries become apparent.

Values that help make children critical about authority are rising. By the same token, values that foster the adherence to authority (such as determination, thrift and especially obedience) are losing ground.

Emphasizing gender equality is part of a broader cultural change that is going on in post-industrial societies. It is, as Inglehart, Norris and Welzel (2002, 343) argue, "the most central component" in the rise of self-expression values. Figure 8.7 underlines that there is a value change happening with respect to gender roles.

Figure 8.7. Gender Roles.

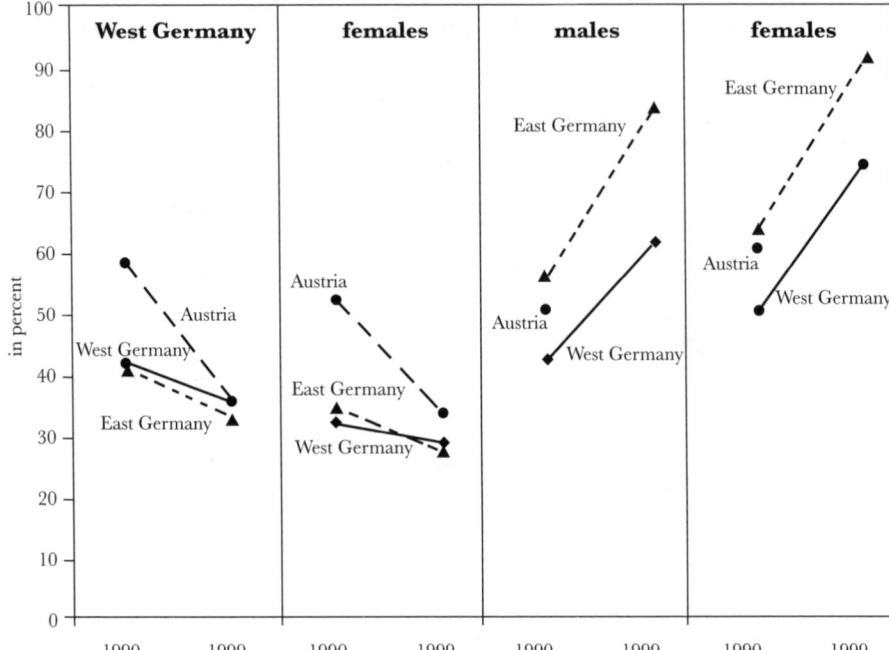

The figures show the proportion of female and male respondents who agree with one of the statements:

(1) "When jobs are scarce, men should have more right to a job than women." (*Men more right to job*)
(2) "A working mother can establish just as warm and secure a relationship with her children as a mother who does not work." (*Working mother*)

Since the beginning of the 1990s, support for preferring men to women when jobs are scarce has dropped. Though once having the highest acceptance of discrimination against women, Austria shows the most distinct decline. Today, differences between Germany and Austria have almost disappeared.

Changing gender roles can also be observed with regard to the role of mothers, especially when it comes to the compatibility of job and motherhood. As we can see in Figure 8.7, an accruing majority does not believe that, by definition, the employment of a mother does harm to the relationship with her children. Interestingly, within country differences based on gender are not very important. Naturally, items indicating discrimination against women find less support among women themselves (Davis and Robinson 1991). The same can be observed in Figure 8.7, where in all cases the male respondents of one society appear to be more patriarchal than women of the same society. However, the female and male citizens of the same society show parallel trends over time, meaning that gender equality has not only become a specific concern of women themselves, but is a more general societal phenomenon. Accordingly, men in East Germany have less dismissive attitudes towards women than women themselves in West Germany.

## 6. *Conclusion*

As our findings have shown, value changes in East Germany, West Germany and Austria follow broadly similar patterns. In fact, for the most part, whenever we observe value *change*, the trend is targeted at mainly one direction, that of self-expression.

Following Inglehart and Welzel (2005), we understand self-expression values as part of a two-dimensional phenomenon of value change. While the first dimension, a polarization between sacred versus secular values, is closely associated with the phase of industrialization, our focus here is on a polarization between survival versus self-expression values. This dimension is closely linked with the rise of the post-industrial society.

Interpersonal trust, tolerance of human diversity, emancipation, a sense of self-fulfillment—reflected in high rates of happiness, expressive forms of political action, and new gender-roles—comprise the syndrome of self-expression that is related to the emergence of the post-industrial society. At the opposite extreme of this dimension, survival values tap into insecurity, rigid material and intellectual constraints on human choice, as well as low well-being, intolerance towards homosexuals and other out-groups, such as foreigners. Thus, post-industrialization individualizes people by diminishing physical, material, organizational, social, educational and informal constraints on human choice, stimulating their striving for autonomy, self-realization and creativity, including a shift from materialistic to post-materialistic values. Instead of economic and physical security, subjective well being and the quality of life become the center of people's aspirations (Inglehart 1977, 1997; Inglehart and Welzel, 2005).

With the majority of the population growing up in existential security and in increasingly individualized working environments, people in Germany and Austria tend to tolerate more ambiguity (for instance, with regard to tolerance towards divorce or homosexuality). This hints at the importance of socialization and the formative years of life, and thereby suggests a gradual transformation of the value system in both Austria and Germany, shifting value orientations from survival to self-expression.

Figure 8.8 depicts self-expression values according to age groups in longitudinal comparison, with higher values indicating stronger emphasis on self-expression. The evidence shows that self-expression values are steadily increasing in Austria, as well as in both East and West German societies. Yet, at the same time, younger age groups across all waves show a stronger orientation towards self-expression, indicating that the trend is largely driven by generational replacement (Abramson, Ellis and Inglehart 1997). This was predicted explicitly by Inglehart in 1977: "The differences between the formative conditions of younger and older groups has been greater in *all* of the Continental countries, but one might expect Germany to show a particularly large amount of value change" (Inglehart 1977, 33). Furthermore, corresponding to the relative economic situation, and also with regard to its communist past, it is not surprising to observe lower levels of self-expression among the population of East Germany, whereas the Western part and Austria place comparably higher emphasis on these values. Again, this underlines the importance of both the formative years, as well as situational forces. Nonetheless, as the generational shift indicates, the former can certainly be assumed to be of stronger influence. Consequently, we can expect a future trend towards even further rising self-expression values among the masses of Austria and Germany.

In summary, we can conclude that wherever we observe straightforward trends in value change, they reflect various aspects of rising self-expression values, a phenomenon interpreted as human development (Welzel 2003; Welzel, Inglehart and Klingemann 2003; Inglehart and Welzel, 2005).[3]

---

[3] Available [online] at http://www.statistik.at/jahrbuch/pdf/k02.pdf

Figure 8.8. Self-expression Values.

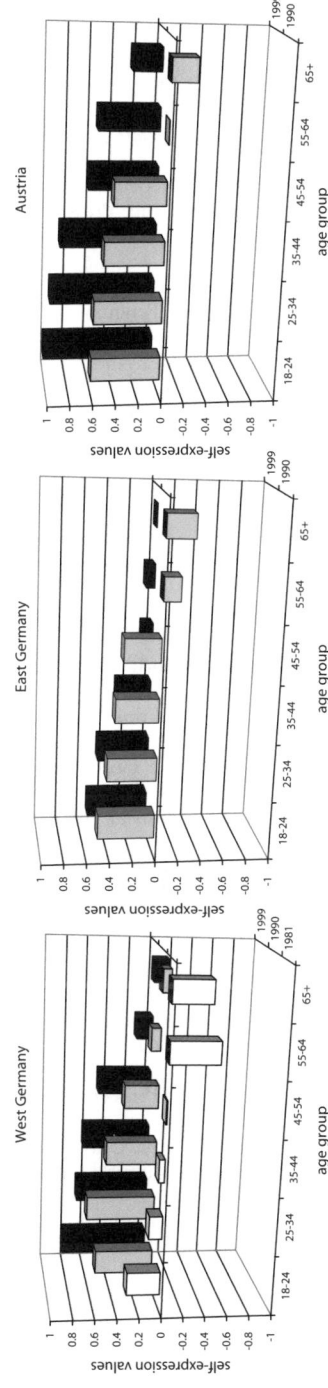

The figure shows mean factor scores based on the following items (two dimensional factor analysis with varimax rotation): Self-expression values emphasize the following:

(1) Respondent gives priority to self-expression and quality of life over economic and physical security [4 item materialist/ post-materialist values index].
(2) Respondent describes himself as happy.
(3) Respondent has signed a petition.
(4) Respondent considers homosexuality as always justifiable.
(5) Respondent thinks that most people can be trusted.

Survival-values take opposite position on all of the above.

## References

Abramson, Paul R., Susan Ellis and Ronald Inglehart. 1997. "Research in Context: Measuring Value Change," *Political Behavior*, 19, 41–59.

Almond, Gabriel A. and Sidney Verba. 1989 [1963]. *The Civic Culture. Political Attitudes and Democracy in Five Nations*. Newbury Park: Sage.

Baker, Kedall L., Russell J. Dalton and Kai Hildebrandt. 1981. *Germany Transformed. Political Culture and the New Politics*. Cambridge: Harvard University Press.

Bauer-Kaase, Petra and Max Kaase. 1996. "Five Years of Unification: The Germans on the Path to Inner Unity?" *German Politics*, 5 (1), 1–25.

Beck, Ulrich. 1999. *World Risk Society*. New York: Blackwell Publishers.

Bell, Daniel. 1973. *The Coming of Postindustrial Society*. New York: Penguin.

Berg-Schlosser, Dirk and Ralf Rytlewski (eds.). 1993. *Political Culture in Germany*. London: MacMillan.

Conradt, David P. 1989 [1980]. "Changing German Political Culture," in *The Civic Culture Revisited. Political Attitudes and Democracy in Five Nations*. eds. Gabriel A. Almond and Sidney Verba. Newbury Park: Sage.

Dalton, Russel J. 1999. "Political Support in Advanced Democracies," in Critical Citizens: Global Support for Democratic Government. ed. Pippa Norris. Oxford: Oxford University Press.

Davis, Nancy J. and Robert V. Robinson. 1991. "Men's and Women's Consciousness of Gender Inequality. Austria, West Germany, Great Britain, and the United States," *American Sociological Review*, 56, 72–84.

Easton, David. 1965. *A Systems Analysis of Political Life*. New York: John Wiley & Sons.

———. 1975. "A Re-Assessment of the Concept of Political Support," *British Journal of Political Science*, 5, 535–457.

Eckstein, Harry. 1961. *A Theory of Stable Democracy*. Princeton: Princeton University Press.

———. 1966. *Division and Cohesion in Democracy*. Princeton: Princeton University Press.

Flanagan, Scott C. and Aie-Rie Lee. 2003. "The New Politics, Culture Wars, and the Autoritarian-Libertarian Value Change in Advanced Industrial Democracies," Comparative Political Studies, 36, 235–270.

Fuchs, Dieter. 1999. "The Democratic Culture of Unified Germany," in Critical Citizens: Global Support for Democratic Government. ed. Pippa Norris. Oxford: Oxford University Press.

Giddens, Anthony. 1990. *The Consequences of Modernity*. Stanford: Stanford University Press.

Hofferbert, Richard I. and Hans-Dieter Klingemann (2001). "Democracy and Its Discontents in Post-Wall Germany," *International Political Science Review*, 22, 363–378.

Inglehart, Ronald. 1977. *The Silent Revolution: Changing Values and Political Styles among Western Publics*. Princeton: Princeton University Press.

———. 1990. *Culture Shift in Advanced Industrial Societies*. Princeton: Princeton University Press.

———. 1997. *Modernization and Postmodernization*. Princeton: Princeton University Press.

Inglehart, Ronald and Wayne E. Baker. 2000. "Modernization, Cultural Change, and the Persistence of Traditional Values," *American Sociological Review*, 65, 19–51.

Inglehart, Ronald, Pippa Norris and Christian Welzel. 2002. "Gender Equality and Democracy," *Comparative Sociology, Special Issue: Human Values and Social Change. Findings from the World Values Surveys*, 1 (3–4), 321–345.

Inglehart, Ronald and Christian Welzel. 2005. *Modernization, Cultural Change, and Democracy: The Human Development Sequence*. New York: Cambridge University Press.

Jagodzinski, Wolfgang and Karel Dobbelaere. 1995. "Secularization and Church Religiosity," in *The Impact of Values (Beliefs in Government, Volume Four)*. eds. Jan W. van Deth and Elinor Scarbrough. Oxford: Oxford University Press.

Kaase, Max 1995. "Die Deutschen auf dem Weg zur Inneren Einheit? Eine Längsschnittanalyse von Selbst- und Fremdwahrnehmungen bei West- und Ostdeutschen [The Germans on a Path to Inner Unity? A Longitudinal Analysis of Self- and Social Perceptions Among West and East Germans]," in *Geplanter Wandel, Ungeplante Wirkungen [Intended Change, Unintended Consequences]*. ed. Hedwig Rudolph. Berlin: Sigma.

Klingemann, Hans-Dieter. 1999. "Mapping Political Support in the 1990s: A Global Analysis," in *Critical Citizens: Global Support for Democratic Government*. ed. Pippa Norris. Oxford: Oxford University Press.

Meulemann, Heiner. 2003. "Transformation and Polarization: Attitudes towards Equality and Achivement and the Search for Losers and Winners of the East German Transformation 1990–1995," in *Political Culture in Post-Communist Europe*. eds. Detlef Pollack et al. Aldershot: Asgate.

Norris, Pippa (ed.). 1999. *Critical Citizens: Global Support for Democratic Government*. Oxford: Oxford University Press

Plasser, Fritz and Peter A. Ulram (2002): *Das österreichische Politikverständnis. Von der Konsens- zur Konfliktkultur [The Austrian Understanding of Politics. From a Consensus-Oriented to a Conflict-Oriented Culture]*. Wien: WUV Universitätsverlag.

Rohrschneider, Robert. 1998. *Learning Democracy: Democratic and Economic Values in Unified Germany*. Oxford: Oxford University Press.

Roller, Edeltraud. 1994. "Ideological Basis of the Market Economy: Attitudes toward Distributional Principles and the Role of Government in Western and Eastern Germany," *European Sociological Review*, 10, 105–17.

Statistisches Bundesamt [Statistical Office] (eds.) 2002. *Datenreport 2002. Zahlen und Fakten über die Bundesrepublik Deutschland/Information Report 2002*. [Data and Facts about Germany], Bonn: Bundeszentrale für politische Bildung.

Ulram, Peter A. 1990. *Hegemonie und Erosion. Politische Kultur und Politischer Wandel in Österreich [Hegemony and Erosion. Political Culture and Political Change in Austria]*. Wien et al.: Böhlau.

Welzel, Christian. 2003. "Effective Democracy, Mass Culture, and the Quality of Elites: The Human Development Perspective," *International Journal of Comparative Sociology*, 43 (3–5), 260–298.

Welzel, Christian and Franziska Deutsch. 2007. "Value Patterns in Europe and the United States. Is There a Transatlantic Rift?" in Conflict and Tensions. eds. Helmut Anheier and Yudhishthir Raj Iser. London: Sage.

Welzel, Christian, Ronald Inglehart and Hans-Dieter Klingemann. 2003. "The Theory of Human Development. A Cross-Cultural Analysis," *European Journal of Political Research*, 42 (3), 341–379.

# C. THE MEDITERRANEAN

# CHAPTER NINE

## FRENCH VALUES: BETWEEN SOUTHERN AND NORTHERN EUROPE

### PIERRE BRÉCHON

Synthesizing and summarizing the culture of a country is always extremely complex, particularly if we want to base our assertions on data rather than produce an interpretive essay. Data from quantitative surveys show that each culture and system of values is in fact very composite. There are many subcultures in each society, and these subcultures have not only relationships to each other, but also strong differences. In the same country, the values of some are not those of others. So, it is even possible to wonder if values really form a system at all. For France, correlations between all the responses to this survey are rather weak, even if there are some statistical consistencies between religious, political, family values, and more authoritative or liberal values. We will try to show the complexity of French data[1] and, at the same time, propose some interpretations of French values compared to those of other European countries.[2]

*Strong Secularization*

In terms of religious values, France is a Catholic country, but above all it is today one of the most secularized in Western Europe. Second only to the Netherlands (at 54%), France has the most people that say they

---

[1] On the French data, see Bréchon Pierre (ed.), *Les valeurs des Français*, Armand Colin, collection Sociétales, second edition, 2003; Galland Olivier, Roudet Bernard (eds.). *Les valeurs des jeunes. Tendances en France depuis 20 ans*, L'Harmattan, collection Débats Jeunesses, 2001.

[2] On European data, see

– Bréchon Pierre, Tchernia Jean-François (eds.). «Les valeurs des Européens. Les tendances de long terme,» *Futuribles*, special issue 277 (July–August 2002).

– Galland Olivier, Roudet Bernard (eds.). *Les jeunes Européens et leurs valeurs. Europe occidentale, Europe centrale et orientale*, La Découvete/INJEP, collection Recherches, 2005.

have no religious denomination (43%). Beyond this, 14% of the French even say they are 'confirmed atheists'. Thus, the opposition to religions is not really strong, even if it is in France that this rate of atheists is at its highest. The heavy trend of criticism of religious obscurantism at the end of the nineteenth and beginning of the twentieth centuries seems to have left some marks. France (along with Denmark and Belgium) is also the country where the rejection of the influence of religions on politics and policies is the most developed.[3]

In fact, it is not just rejection but religious indifference that dominates in France. Support for Catholicism has become weaker, and the loss of the Catholic system's hold over the culture and society is particularly evident. From this point of view, it is possible to compare the French and Danish situations.[4] Both of the two countries are very strongly secularized, and both have low levels of religious beliefs, but in Denmark the Lutheran church remains an important benchmark for the whole population (almost 90% of Danes are members of this church, compared to only 53% Catholic membership in France). This denominational association in Denmark is linked to national identity, which is not the case in France, where the church and State have been separated for a century. Comparing the data of Western European values surveys between 1981, 1990 and 1999, erosion is observed on many religious indicators. Catholic affiliation decreased from 71% in 1981 to 53% in 1999, monthly attendance at services from 17% to 12%, confidence in the Church from 54 to 44%, subjective feelings of religiosity from 51 to 44%, belief in God from 62 to 56%, and belief in a personal God from 26 to 21%.

The explanation of these changes lies above all in a phenomenon of replacement of generations: the older generations, still very much influenced by Catholicism, are progressively being replaced by much more secular younger ones (see Table 9.1). In 1981, the generational break is clear: the baby-boom generation (born between 1946 and 1954) was the first to distance itself from Catholic institutions. The two more recent survey waves show that, as they have grown older, pre-war gen-

---

[3] Only about 10% of the French prefer political leaders who believe in God or who have strong religious convictions. About 80% think that religious leaders should not influence government decisions.

[4] Cf. Riis Ole, Religion et identité nationale au Danemark, in Grace Davie, Danièle Hervieu-Léger (eds.), *Identités religieuses en Europe*, La découverte, 1996, 113–130.

Table 9.1. Non-denominational Affiliation in the Different Generations (in %).

| Generation born... | 1981 | 1990 | 1999 |
|---|---|---|---|
| from 1973 to 1981 | – | – | 53 |
| from 1964 to 1972 | – | 56 | 50 |
| from 1955 to 1963 | 40 | 47 | 46 |
| from 1946 to 1954 | 43 | 46 | 41 |
| from 1937 to 1945 | 23 | 28 | 38 |
| from 1928 to 1936 | 18 | 25 | 33 |
| from 1919 to 1927 | 13 | 18 | 28 |
| from 1910 to 1918 | 19 | 21 | – |
| from 1901 to 1909 | 9 | – | – |
| Average | 26 | 39 | 43 |

Table 9.2. Belief in Life after Death by Generation.

| Generation born... | 1981 | 1990 | 1999 |
|---|---|---|---|
| from 1973 to 1981 | – | – | 41 |
| from 1964 to 1972 | – | 41 | 44 |
| from 1955 to 1963 | 30 | 33 | 39 |
| from 1946 to 1954 | 30 | 34 | 40 |
| from 1937 to 1945 | 40 | 38 | 31 |
| from 1928 to 1936 | 38 | 34 | 33 |
| from 1919 to 1927 | 41 | 47 | 32 |
| from 1910 to 1918 | 38 | 38 | – |
| from 1901 to 1909 | 35 | – | – |
| Average | 35 | 38 | 38 |

erations have let themselves be influenced by secularized atmospheres and have also distanced themselves more from religion.[5]

Nevertheless small increases are observed on some less used religious indicators. For example, belief in the existence of life after death rose from 35 to 38% during the 18-year period under study. During the same period, belief in Hell increased from 15 to 18%, belief in Heaven from 27 to 28%, and belief in reincarnation from 22 to 25%. Table 9.2 allows us to evaluate the generational shift for the life after death belief.

[5] The thesis explaining that religious interest would be developed as quickly as adults age is here invalidated. On the contrary, it seems that older generations, even if they remain more religious than others, are increasingly influenced by the secularisation of French society.

This three-point average increase is the result of a double contradictory movement; the belief diminishes in the pre-war generations, but rises in generations born after the Second World War. Contrary to expectations linked to the secularization thesis, a rather clear rise on a religious indicator is observed here among the young. The interpretation of this is not easy, but, rather than interpreting it as a real return to religiosity among younger generations, it seems more correct to consider it as a rising trend of vague and floating beliefs on the borderline between religiosity and the psychological realm. The ISSP surveys in 1991 and 1998 (focusing on religion) also ask the question on life after death beliefs, but allow for people to indicate if they believe with certainty or only believe as a likelihood or possibility. The increase in this belief among the young comes from an increase in the answer 'likely,' while the answer 'certain' declines. Secularization, as a loss of the grip of the great religious institutions and of the failure of the sacred narratives to explain the world (its origin and meaning), can go together with a recomposition of floating and often very soft beliefs. The young who say they belong to no religious group may, at the same time, believe in the possibility of a more or less supernatural future afterlife. They probably have difficulty imagining that their very intense and rich life might have an end. This phenomenon of a new rise in some religious indicators among the young, although rare in the French data, is nevertheless more frequent in the other European countries.

*Moral Principles Relativized, Permissiveness but also Social Order*

The wide scale secularization that France has undergone helps to explain the prevailing conceptions of morality. To decide what is good or bad and guide their actions, the French do not particularly like strong principles. Only 25% come to a decision according to clear guidelines that should always be taken into account. Indeed, 64% think that it is not possible to apply clear and inviolable principles to decide what is good, that it depends entirely upon the circumstances at the time. We observe here an orientation that is found in all individualized societies; clear principles, often defined by tradition and institutions, are only reference points that must be interpreted and cannot be mechanically applied. What is good and bad must be decided taking into account the whole context. Percentages observed for 1999 are in fact very close to those found in 1981. It seems that the global conception of morality has evolved since the seventies, even if this shift has been faster in the younger generations than in the older ones.

The secularization of French society is also certainly an important element that explains the progression of permissiveness and tolerance concerning morals. In the long question on behaviors that are always or never justified, with notation from one to ten (one for behaviors never justified, and ten for those that are considered as always being right), the five practices most reproved (average notes between 1.35 and 2.13) and the five most recognized (between 4.31 and 6.33) have been selected (Table 9.3). The most recognized behaviors all concern private life and individual autonomy: sexuality, personal relationships, and power over one's own life are the choices of the individual, and society has no right to check or attempt to normalize them. Everyone chooses his/her behaviors in a dialogue only with the people involved (the other person in the relationship, close relations). The reproved practices on the contrary are subjects and problems of public order. Thus, for the French, even drug consumption is not simply an individual practice because it is perceived as leading to possible disorders for the neighborhood in the same way that driving a car under the influence of alcohol might.

Table 9.3. The Five Most Permitted and the Five Most Reproved Behaviors.

| | Average score | 18–29 years old | More than 60 years | Difference 99–81 |
|---|---|---|---|---|
| Stealing and driving a car (joyriding) | 1.35 | 1.53 | 1.22 | − 0.11 |
| Littering in a public place | 1.60 | 1.87 | 1.40 | − |
| Driving under the influence of alcohol | 1.87 | 2.14 | 1.57 | − |
| Accepting a bribe in the course of their duties | 2.07 | 2.61 | 1.80 | − 0.33 |
| Taking the drug marijuana or hashish | 2.13 | 2.77 | 1.40 | + 0.40 |
| Suicide | 4.31 | 4.36 | 3.72 | + 0.97 |
| Homosexuality | 5.26 | 6.19 | 3.91 | + 2.23 |
| Abortion | 5.66 | 5.92 | 4.63 | + 0.90 |
| Euthanasia | 6.17 | 5.98 | 5.74 | + 1.65 |
| Divorce | 6.33 | 6.54 | 5.46 | + 1.13 |

Liberalism about private morals is highly developed in France.[6] An index of permissiveness (constructed with the five indicators above) introduced in Table 9.7 (right column) shows that, in this domain, France is much closer to Northern than to Southern countries. Liberalism in morals is even in strong progression from 1981 to 1999, as the right column of Table 9.3 shows. In contrast, behaviors that affect public order are reproved strongly, with weak differences between young and old people. The former are almost as opposed as the latter to these practices. From 1981 to 1999, tolerance sometimes progresses slightly, sometimes regresses slightly. The tendency is thus clear: with regard to public order, the French are not particularly tolerant, even wishing for a reinforcement of controls and repression, all the more so as incivilities and minor delinquency are strongly on the increase. In contrast, with regard to issues related to one's private life, as society is not affected, individual liberty is absolute. The clearest change in this matter is about homosexuality, which was still rather largely reproved in 1981, and which has been largely legitimated since.[7] Table 9.4 shows that this process of recognition is not only due to the generational differences. Even if the older generations that are vanishing were very much opposed to homosexuality, and even if, contrarily, new ones accept it much more, a change in all generations can be observed. In 1981, only younger generations accepted homosexuality and discrepancies with the older generations were very large. Today, differences are much weaker, the older generations being converted to new more permissive values. For all these private behaviors, as the index of permissiveness analyzed by cohort shows (Table 9.5), discrepancies are now weak between generations from 18 to 60 years, much more so than in 1981.

---

[6] This can be seen as well with another question on abortion: approval or disapproval of abortion when the woman is unmarried or when the married couple does not want any more children. 34% disapprove in both cases, 19% in one case, 47% approve in both. Europe is highly divided on this question. Strong approval is only 9% in Ireland and 22% in Italy, but 47% in France, 63% in Denmark and 78% in Sweden. The latter three countries are the most favorable to abortion in Europe. The average is 37% for the European Union. This confirms France's belonging to those countries where permissivity is the greatest, abortion having been legalized there in 1974 in the wake of a strong public opinion movement encouraged particularly by feminist groups and associations.

[7] We measure in the survey the legitimation or condemnation of this sexual orientation. We do not measure the practice itself and do not know whether or not it is highly developed in French society.

Table 9.4. Percent Saying "Homosexuality is Never Justified' (1 on the 10-point scale).

|  | 1981 | 1990 | 1999 |
|---|---|---|---|
| From 1973 to 1981 | – | – | 11 |
| From 1964 to 1972 | – | 22 | 12 |
| From 1955 to 1963 | 28 | 31 | 16 |
| From 1946 to 1954 | 31 | 33 | 22 |
| From 1937 to 1945 | 50 | 38 | 31 |
| From 1928 to 1936 | 62 | 51 | 34 |
| From 1919 to 1927 | 64 | 56 | 34 |
| From 1910 to 1918 | 70 | 69 | – |
| From 1901 to 1909 | 64 | – | – |
| Average | 49 | 38 | 21 |

Table 9.5. Permissiveness Index[1] by Birth Cohort.

|  | 1981 | 1990 | 1999 |
|---|---|---|---|
| From 1973 to 1981 | – | – | 73 |
| From 1964 to 1972 | – | 67 | 77 |
| From 1955 to 1963 | 63 | 54 | 73 |
| From 1946 to 1954 | 57 | 57 | 72 |
| From 1937 to 1945 | 44 | 48 | 68 |
| From 1928 to 1936 | 29 | 41 | 55 |
| From 1919 to 1927 | 27 | 32 | 55 |
| From 1910 to 1918 | 26 | 31 | – |
| From 1901 to 1909 | 24 | – | – |
| Average | 43 | 51 | 68 |

[1] Sum of 10-point scale scores for justifiability of divorce, euthanasia, abortion, homosexuality and suicide. The scale values range between 5 and 50. The table gives percentage of those with scores between 24 and 50 (most permissive).

Table 9.6. Percent Selecting "Maintaining Order in the nation" as the Most Important Goal by Birth Cohort.

|  | 1981 | 1990 | 1999 |
|---|---|---|---|
| From 1973 to 1981 | – | – | 56 |
| From 1964 to 1972 | – | 39 | 53 |
| From 1955 to 1963 | 43 | 38 | 56 |
| From 1946 to 1954 | 36 | 40 | 58 |
| From 1937 to 1945 | 53 | 48 | 69 |
| From 1928 to 1936 | 53 | 45 | 73 |
| From 1919 to 1927 | 62 | 55 | 74 |
| From 1910 to 1918 | 64 | 72 | – |
| From 1901 to 1909 | 74 | – | – |
| Average | 52 | 44 | 61 |

The rise of permissive attitudes concerning one's private life goes along with an increasing demand for law and order. Table 6 shows this very clearly as it counts all those who consider the maintenance of order as a priority and have chosen it first or second in a set of four aims concerning the future. From 1990 to 1999, a period effect can be observed; all generations much prefer the maintenance of order as an important goal. The need for order affects all of society, as the 2002 French electoral campaign, of which one of the main issues was the struggle against delinquency and insecurity, is a strong reminder. Perhaps the most interesting phenomenon to notice in Table 9.6 is that the young are again less different from other generations than they were in 1981. The young seem to become less tolerant than in the past concerning deviations from public morality. Thus, all the generations would tend to act according to the axiom: 'Do what you want in your private life, but respect law and order.'

### Friendly Relationship, Trust in Others and Sociability

In terms of how the French experience their interpersonal relations, compared to people of other Western European countries (Table 9.7), they appreciate friendly relations: 50% consider friends and acquaintances as very important in their lives, which is a little above the mean for the European Union; friends seem to be valorized overall in the more Northern European countries while Southern countries seem to have a weak sensitivity for them. Contrary to often conveyed stereotypes, Southern European countries do not seem to seek out conviviality strongly; they are countries where solidarities are more family and community-oriented than society-oriented. In any case, 58% of the French say they spend time each week with their friends; here, France is again on an average level, but the northern-southern divide is less noticeable.

    It can be also observed that trust in others is very different across European countries, and that the divide between the north and the south of Europe is again apparent: Scandinavian countries and the Netherlands are countries where trust is spontaneous, while in other countries, people tend to be suspicious of those they meet. In the south of Europe, it is necessary to be acquainted in order to have confidence in others; there is no spontaneous trust, but rather a spontaneous distrust. In this, France is clearly a Southern European country. Trust in others has never been high in France (22% in 1981, 21% in 1990 and 21% in 1999).

Table 9.7. Relations with Others.

| | Friends (1) | Weekly Friend Time (2) | Trust in others (3) | Rejected neighbors (4) | Solidarity (5) | Association membership (6) | Permissiveness (7) |
|---|---|---|---|---|---|---|---|
| Sweden | 71 | 67 | 64 | 42 | 60 | 96 | 85 |
| Denmark | 55 | 60 | 64 | 36 | 31 | 84 | 71 |
| Finland | 51 | 60 | 57 | 54 | 24 | 80 | 58 |
| The Netherlands | 59 | 67 | 59 | 65 | 35 | 93 | 75 |
| Germany | 48 | 49 | 33 | 57 | 25 | 51 | 49 |
| Austria | 43 | 57 | 31 | 60 | 26 | 67 | 48 |
| Luxembourg | 47 | 62 | 25 | 49 | 39 | 59 | 60 |
| Belgium | 47 | 50 | 28 | 51 | 35 | 66 | 53 |
| France | 50 | 58 | 21 | 45 | 29 | 39 | 68 |
| Great Britain | 58 | 74 | 29 | 59 | 18 | 34 | 46 |
| Greece | 33 | 62 | 18 | 66 | 30 | 48 | 34 |
| Ireland | 61 | 72 | 35 | 57 | 49 | 57 | 27 |
| Spain | 39 | 67 | 36 | 42 | 35 | 31 | 47 |
| Portugal | 30 | 64 | 10 | 45 | 30 | 24 | 31 |
| Italy | 35 | 62 | 32 | 54 | 41 | 42 | 37 |
| Average | 47 | 61 | 32 | 53 | 30 | 46 | 51 |

1. Finding friends and relations very important in one's life.
2. % of people who say they spend time each week with their friends.
3. Thinking that most people can be trusted.
4. Half of the population (53%) who reject 14 kinds of dropouts from their neighborhood the most.
5. Index of solidarity (prepared actually to do something to improve the conditions of neighbors, elderly people, immigrants, sick or disabled people in your country).
6. Member of one association or more.
7. Half of population the more permissive (suicide + homosexuality + abortion + euthanasia + divorce).

Preferring friendly relations, but having no spontaneous trust in others, French people nevertheless are not among those Europeans who reject dropouts the most (Table 9.7, column 4). From the list of 14 categories of people for which interviewees say they would not like to have them as neighbors, for the whole European Union, we have taken into account the 53% who reject the greater number of categories. France is a little below the average. But in France, as in many European countries, people nowadays seem markedly more selective towards neighbors than in 1981, even if the young remain noticeably less selective than their elders. Most rejected is the neighbor who is likely to disturb public order. Repulsion based on principles is rare (9% of the French say they do not wish to have people of a different race as neighbors and 6% say this of Jews). However, 40% would not wish to have Gypsies as neighbors because they are often suspected of social deviance and of being a possible nuisance for the neighborhood. In other words, xenophobia is mainly linked to utilitarian and pragmatic concerns. Racism is not very widespread. Foreigners or people who are different are not rejected because of their difference (the French strongly believe in the ideas of equal dignity and of equality among all human beings); they are rejected because they are considered as generating disorder and problems for daily life. The idea of national priority in obtaining jobs (also an indicator of a utilitarian xenophobia) is rather highly developed: 52% of the French wish to keep jobs for French nationals. This percentage is close to the European mean, with very strong differences according to countries (11% in Sweden, 27% in the Netherlands, 33% in Denmark, but 60% in Italy, 62% in Portugal, 63% in Spain, 72% in Ireland, and 84% in Greece).

Concerning their aptitude for solidarity (Table 7, column 5), the French are situated in the European mean and thus do not seem very altruistic (national differences are strong, but cannot be explained only by the northern-southern divide). For France, there are no real differences in solidarity according to age, social position, level of education, or even income. Altruism simply seems more developed among members of associations or left leaning people.

Finally, contrary to what certain French observers often claim, associative sociability (Table 9.7, column 6) does not seem to be very widespread in France. Compared to Northern countries, France has a relatively weak associative membership. Only 39% of French people are members of an association, compared to 96% of the Swedish. From this point of view, France again seems rather to be a Southern European country.

*An Individualized Family*

In France, as everywhere in Europe and many other countries in the world, family is the most important thing in people's lives, and, for many people, the main aim is to succeed in their family lives. However, ideas concerning family have shifted a great deal. It is the marital family, more than kinship, which is subject to very strong expectations. The marital family, as the basic unit of society into which one enters at the beginning of one's conjugal life, to leave only with the death of one's spouse, is no longer considered an inviolable institution. Divorce thus must be a possibility (Table 9.3), and, in fact, in France, as in other countries, it is common: about one marriage in three ends in divorce. Single parent and second marriage families are numerous. Nowadays, family is not so much considered as mainly built on a legal contract, but on the rich relationship between partners, with communication and exchange between partners being the most important things for marital happiness.[8] Family is thus created progressively through relationships between husband and wife.[9] Partners also want an egalitarian relationship, and domination of the husband over his wife is a clearly rejected pattern. The couple wants to share occupational and educational roles, and this egalitarian conception of roles (desired, but not yet completely carried out) has become nearly consensual in the European Union, even if there are still nuances between countries (France is near the mean; Sweden, Denmark and Germany being the countries most in favor of equally shared roles; Greece and Ireland being, in contrast, a little more skeptical).

For couples, faithfulness is even an increasingly prized value: 80% consider it as important for a successful marriage (against 72% in 1981). In the same way, having an affair is considered as never justified by 36% (against 26% in 1981). This increase in faithfulness in France particularly comes from the young, who seem more attached to this value than twenty years ago.[10] Furthermore, marriage is only considered as outdated by 34% of the French.[11] Obviously, most of the young French have sexual relations before marriage and live together as a couple for some months or years before getting married. Yet, for many of them, marriage continues to be a kind of ideal model, a beautiful ceremony that allows them to celebrate mutual love and the will for faithfulness

---

[8] It is particularly noticeable in the answers to the question on what is most important for a successful marriage. At the top: mutual respect and appreciation (89%), faithfulness (80%), understanding and tolerance (79%), being willing to discuss the problems that come up between husband and wife (77%). In contrast, the less chosen items are: agreement on politics, shared religious beliefs, being of the same social background. Each individual in the couple being original, homogamy is not at all necessary. Material conditions are also secondary. The main thing is to communicate and to be in love. This ranking is about the same in almost all countries of Western Europe.

[9] This exalting ideal of a family built on rich subjective mutual relations perhaps explains also its fragility.

[10] 62% of the 18–29 years old asserted in 1981 that faithfulness was very important (for a successful marriage), they are now 85%, more than the average of the population. Only 15% of the young found an affair never justified in 1981, they are now 32%.

[11] It is nevertheless the highest rate of contesting marriage in Europe, the mean being 21%. Marriage is considered outdated by only 16% of Italians and Spaniards, 14% of Danes, 13% of Greeks.

and stability as an established couple. This family continues to desire children, and the fertility rate in France is now more than 1.9; even if this does not completely allow—over a long period—for the replacement of generations, it is one of the highest rates in Western Europe, much higher than the rate of Catholic Italy or Spain. This fact shows that the link between values and practices is complex. Catholic values regarding childbirth are not really applied in the southern societies where this religion nevertheless remains the most relevant.

*Modest Politicization but an Increase in Protesting Participation*

Contrary to what some observers of French society maintain, the survey shows there is *nowadays* no tendency to a depoliticization of the French. In 1981, 38% reported never discussing political matters with their friends, as opposed to 35% in 1999. This global stability comes from a double phenomenon: generations who have died since 1981 had very weak politicization. The generations who have since come to adulthood are also not highly politicized, even though they are far more educated than earlier generations.[12] In 1981, never discussing political matters with friends was the case in 37% of 18–26 years old, but the figure is 46% nowadays. Thus, there are concerns for the future: older generations who are approaching death are rather politicized and could be replaced by younger generations less sensitive to politics. However, it should be noted that the French were never strongly politicized. An index of politicization[13] shows that, on this matter, France is slightly below the European mean: politicization is the strongest in Germany, Austria, Denmark and the Netherlands, and the weakest in Spain and Portugal.

Politicization defines a level of familiarity with politics. Politicized individuals value this dimension of life, understand current debates, and are able to evaluate government decisions. Politicization is an internalized disposition, but political participation is not of the same nature; it depends on actions that people accomplish to influence public decisions such as voting, signing petitions, demonstrating, and supporting

---

[12] Education always favors politicization, but less strongly than before. The upper classes and people with high incomes are also more politicized.

[13] Built on political interest, asserting that politics is important in one's life, discussing politics with one's friends.

a political party. Even if politicization and political participation are linked statistically, the two dimensions are not at all redundant. Certain non-politicized people nevertheless can vote. Conversely, much politicized people sometimes engage in very little political activity, being only constant observers of political debate. Although, until now, politicization has not decreased for the mean of people, but only among the young, electoral participation is, on the contrary, clearly weakening, a phenomenon clear from electoral results.[14] The record of abstention for a first round of a presidential election—normally the most mobilizing one—was broken in April 2002 (28.4%), and records for the legislature were broken two months later (35.6% for the first round, and 39.7 for the second). For referenda, the record dates back to September 2000 (69.8% abstention for the vote on reducing the presidential mandate to five years), for regional elections to 1998 (42%), for the town council to 2001 (32.6% in the first round), and, for elections to the European Parliament, the record was broken in 2004 (57.2%). Thus, almost all records date back to the last election of each type. Registration on electoral lists is in fact rather stable; no increase in the constant abstention is recorded but, conversely, a rather clear growth in the intermittent one. The French seem to vote less according to principle and duty than to the perceived stakes in an electoral campaign. The meaning of the vote is changing: in this era of individualization, citizens tend to vote only if they feel the utility of their action and if they think they have good reasons to do so.

From the 1999 Values survey question on vote intention, if there was a general election tomorrow, an approximate measure of non-voting can be carried out (it is, however, a reduced measure because, despite the erosion of electoral duty, some people still feel guilty about admitting that they are non-voters). Table 8 shows that the propensity to abstain is stronger among the young. Furthermore, the effect of politicization on abstention is strong among the young, and weak among old people. Generally, old people seem to be disposed to vote even if they are not politicized. In contrast, the non-politicized young recognize much more clearly their non-voting behavior. These statistical observations are congruent with the hypothesis of a current evolution in the meaning of voting, from a principle vote to a conditional one, from a duty to vote to a simple right which the citizen may or may not exercise.

---

[14] See Bréchon Pierre. *La France aux urnes. Soixante ans d'histoire électorale*, La documentation française, Paris: 2003, 4ème edition.

Table 9.8. Level of Abstention According to Politicization and Age.*

| Level of politicization<br>Age | 0 | 1 | 2 | 3 | Average |
|---|---|---|---|---|---|
| 18–29 years old | 30 | 20 | 9 | 9 | 20 |
| 30–44 years old | 28 | 19 | 11 | 3 | 17 |
| 45–59 years old | 18 | 16 | 7 | 7 | 13 |
| 60 years and more | 12 | 13 | 7 | 7 | 10 |
| Average | 23 | 17 | 9 | 6 | 15 |

* Example of reading: if the level of registered abstention is 15% for all the sample, it rises to 23% among people with a 0 level on politicization index, and to 30% among these non-politicized people aged from 18 to 29 years old. On the contrary it is only to 7% among people of 60 years and more for the highest level of politicization.

Whereas electoral turnout appears to be decreasing, it is not the same thing for other kinds of political participation, noticeably for what is called protest participation. This concept takes into account all the kinds of action by which individuals put forward claims to the authorities, such as the simple signature of a petition, attending demonstrations, joining a product boycott, unofficial strikes, or occupying workplaces. These actions may concern social as well as political mobilizations. A Values survey question, asked since 1981, measures the percentage of those who have already been involved in this kind of activity in their lives.[15] The change in France over 20 years is high (Table 9.9): in 1981 half the population had never been involved in this kind of action during their lives, while nowadays the figure is only 28%. The number of petitions and demonstrations—that are legal and legitimate actions—is increasing. If 43% of participants had signed a petition in 1981, 67% had done so in 1999. The figure for attending demonstrations rose from 25% to 39%. Other kinds of protest actions (joining in boycotts, joining unofficial strikes, occupying building or factories) are probably not legitimate enough, or are too radical or violent, to be readily accepted by most people. The level of this kind of activity has remained stable during these last 20 years at between 8 and 12%.

---

[15] This question is inspired by the writings of Samuel Barnes, Max Kaase et al., *Political Action: Mass Participation in Five Western Democracies*, Sage, 1979.

Table 9.9. Protesting Participation from 1981 to 1999 (vertical %).

| Actions already done | 1981 | 1990 | 1999 |
|---|---|---|---|
| None | 50 | 43 | 28 |
| One | 27 | 25 | 33 |
| Two | 12 | 18 | 21 |
| Three or more | 12 | 14 | 18 |

A cohort analysis of the three surveys allows a better explanation of the progress of protest participation (Table 9.10), and a generational phenomenon is clearly perceptible. Contrary to what is often thought, the old and dying generations did not conduct many protest actions. Some famous strikes, particularly in 1936, had huge impact, but France remained largely conformist and respectful of authority. The post-war generations are more clearly protest oriented,[16] and a remarkable phenomenon is that this attitude seems to be maintained for the young generations since 40% of the 1999 youngest cohorts have already had two experiences of direct action while not yet being completely involved in the workplace. In fact, the young generations are socialized from their youth in an attitude of protest, particularly through demonstration experiences. The frequency of demands and demonstrations by young people in secondary schools has increased in France since the end of the sixties; they were almost non-existent before.

It is true that these political experiences are ephemeral; they involve many young people, not all of whom have a clear political awareness of the aims pursued by movements in which they participate. These teenagers often demonstrate as part of a group consensus and follow young leaders. But these demonstrating experiences probably socialize them in a certain critical and direct manner to practice politics. People do not often get involved in public matters, preferring instead to let their elites do the work, which also opens them up to criticism. But, sometimes, when they deem it useful and important, for a limited time and

---

[16] The specificity of the baby boom generation, which was the first to make a clear break with traditional ideas and living standards, and which was also the most active generation during the events of May 1968, clearly appears in the 1981 data: it was the generation with the strongest protest activity. This specificity is still perceptible in 1999, but it is lightened as a result of the increase in protesting actions in recent generations.

Table 9.10. Percent Who Have Participated in at least Two Protest Actions by Birth Cohort.

|  | 1981 | 1990 | 1999 |
|---|---|---|---|
| From 1973 to 1981 | – | – | 40 |
| From 1964 to 1972 | – | 29 | 35 |
| From 1955 to 1963 | 27 | 32 | 45 |
| From 1946 to 1954 | 38 | 44 | 47 |
| From 1937 to 1945 | 21 | 40 | 40 |
| From 1928 to 1936 | 23 | 27 | 36 |
| From 1919 to 1927 | 21 | 21 | 22 |
| From 1910 to 1918 | 16 | 17 | – |
| From 1901 to 1909 | 8 | – | – |
| Average | 24 | 32 | 39 |

for a specific action, people seem increasingly ready to directly defend their options on the social scene and to influence the authorities.

Protest participation is much higher among members of associations. While 32% of non-members have already participated in two protesting actions, it is the case for 60% of members of at least two associations.

If we look closely at the data, joining numerous kinds of associations (including, for example, being a member of a sports or leisure association) may lead to signing petitions more often, or to attending demonstrations. Those who protest the most, however, are members of trade unions and political movements. As for politicization, protest participation is more highly developed among men,[17] people with a higher education, those from the upper classes,[18] those with left-wing orientation, and those in favor of a secular culture. These statistical relations are about the same for the three waves of surveys, although with some modulations. Discrepancies have tended to narrow, and some until now very rarely politically active categories are beginning to become so, particularly professionals, farmers and rightist-oriented people. This culture of direct political action seems to have become more common, less specific, and less linked than before to a left-oriented

---

[17] It is known that electoral turnout is today as frequent among females as males. It is not the same thing for protest participation.

[18] Thinking that those who protest the most are not workers or the popular classes is accepted with difficulty by some French academics. Data from all surveys are nevertheless very corroborating.

culture.[19] In Western Europe (except Portugal), this protest culture is progressing everywhere, and France is among those countries which most often uses this kind of political practice (along with Sweden, Belgium, Denmark, and the Netherlands).

*The Ideological Universe: A Somewhat Nuanced Left-Right Divide*

The French continue to situate themselves on a ten level left-right scale. This political identity thus has meaning for the majority of them (the no answer rate to this question was 21% in 1990, and only 17% in 1999).[20] Much similarity can be observed in the results for the three survey dates: one-third chose the medium positions (5–6), which sometimes points to a centrist political identity, but more often a rather floating and wavering one; one-third chose the leftist positions (1–4); and only 16 to 17% the ones on the right. It seems, then, more difficult for people to describe themselves as right-wing than left-wing, the right rather meaning the principle of reality (the hard constraints that must be taken into account in political management), and the left the principle of pleasure and the utopia of a generous world.

To show that the left-right dimension goes on to structure the ideological universe of the French (but often in a more nuanced way), let us analyze the relations between this dimension and a set of values 18 years apart (Table 9.11). First, links between political and religious identity remain very strong. Today in France, there are fewer practicing Catholics and many more adhering to no religion than 20 years ago, and the former remain clearly right-oriented, while the latter very often identify themselves with the left. Concerning moral and family values, some links with the left-right scale are weakening. Claiming to guide one's action according to intangible principles is not very popular, but left-leaning people are a little less resistant to principles than in the past.

---

[19] In 1981, the rate of high political participation was 55% among leftist people (level 1 and 2 of the left-right scale) and only 11% among those on the right (level 9 and 10). Today, the rate is 58% for the left-wing, but 40% for the right-wing. The difference is no more than18 points.

[20] Many French people find that the concepts of left and right are outdated for evaluating the actions of the government because they think that left and right governments carry out similar policies, but they agree to define themselves with these words.

Table 9.11. Correlates of Left-Right Scale, 1981 and 1999*.

|  | 1981 | | | 1999 | | |
|  | Left | Right | Average | Left | Right | Average |
|---|---|---|---|---|---|---|
| Regular + non regular practicing Catholic | 18 | 52 | 29 | 13 | 40 | 22 |
| No religion + convinced atheist | 42 | 12 | 26 | 51 | 19 | 43 |
| For a morale of principle | 14 | 32 | 21 | 22 | 30 | 25 |
| Very in favor of family | 29 | 48 | 36 | 35 | 46 | 36 |
| Homosexuality, never justified | 41 | 58 | 49 | 15 | 33 | 21 |
| Marijuana or hashish, never justified | 72 | 83 | 79 | 55 | 81 | 68 |
| Maintain order in the nation | 32 | 74 | 52 | 47 | 77 | 61 |
| Giving people more say in government decisions | 52 | 24 | 35 | 53 | 36 | 43 |
| Fighting rising prices | 49 | 64 | 59 | 45 | 44 | 47 |
| Protecting freedom of speech | 61 | 29 | 47 | 51 | 39 | 45 |
| Preferring liberty to equality | 49 | 65 | 54 | 44 | 60 | 49 |
| In favor of companies ruled by employees | 32 | 6 | 17 | 17 | 4 | 12 |
| Confidence in major companies | 30 | 59 | 42 | 34 | 62 | 45 |
| Very nationalistic | 30 | 51 | 38 | 37 | 52 | 43 |
| Excluding other race and/or foreign workers | 7 | 17 | 9 | 9 | 22 | 14 |
| Rejection right-wing extremists | 21 | 17 | 14 | 55 | 39 | 44 |

* To avoid making the table heavy, the central category (position 5 and 6) of the left-right scale is not displayed here.

Similarly, differences between left and right concerning family values[21] have become weaker due to a strengthening on the left of attitudes in

---

[21] To identify a *family-oriented* attitude, an index was created with five questions in 1981 and six in 1999, four of them being identical. The 1999 scale is composed of the following items: a child needs a home with both a father and a mother to grow up happily; a woman has to have children in order to be fulfilled; marriage is not an outdated institution; to disapprove that a woman wants to have a child as a single parent; to strongly agree that a man has to have children in order to be fulfilled and that marriage is necessary to be happy.

favor of the traditional family. In contrast, discrepancies remain in the perception of homosexuality, and opinions about soft drug consumption seem even more divided according to political orientation. Left-wing people now accept this kind of consumption more often, while right-wing people still oppose it.

The classic question asking respondents to select two goals for the future out of four possible choices (maintaining order in the nation, giving people more say in important government decisions, fighting price increases, protecting freedom of speech)[22] shows a decrease (from 1981 to 1999) in the fight against inflation, which is not astonishing given that, nowadays, the latter seems to have been curbed. It is now an aim chosen with the same intensity by the left as the right-wing, whereas, in the past, the right put more stress on the fight against inflation, while the left defended a social policy (in spite of the rise in prices). If the demand for law and order has progressed (as we have shown above), it is due largely to an increase in this preoccupation on the left. Better participation in government decisions is desired, and, on this point, the shift of right-wing people explains the rise in the participative will. Freedom of speech remains more a goal of the left, but here also discrepancies between left and right-wing are softening. Thus, as far as grand political goals are concerned, the traditional ideological specificities of the left and right-wing seem to be slowly eroding. Conversely, the choice of liberty rather than equality remains rather an option of the right and, on this point, no noticeable weakening of differences can be observed over the past 18 years.

Next, Table 11 displays economic orientations. The idea that companies might be ruled by employees is even less supported than in 1981. People from the left-wing believe much less in this possibility than in the past. Distances between left and right-wing have thus been reduced due to a greater acceptation by the left of economic liberalism. In contrast, trust in major companies did not alter much between 1981 and 1999. It did increase dramatically between 1981 and 1990, in a context of triumphant liberalism, but now opinion seems to have become more

---

[22] As is well known, it is on this question that Ronald Inglehart elaborated his theory of the rise of post-materialist values. It is surprising to notice that, in 1999, the two post-materialist goals do not evolve in the same way. The aim of 'protecting freedom of speech' markedly regresses in relation to 1990, while the demand for participation in government decisions increases. The materialist aim of defense of social order also rises clearly. Due to these differentiated evolutions we do not use an index of post-materialism.

Table 9.12. Trust in Institutions (a great deal + quite a lot) Correlated with
Left-Right Orientation (in 1981, 1990 and 1999).

|  | 1981 | | 1990 | | 1999 | |
|---|---|---|---|---|---|---|
|  | Left | Right | Left | Right | Left | Right |
| Police | 50 | 80 | 61 | 74 | 61 | 76 |
| Army | 31 | 74 | 43 | 76 | 62 | 72 |
| Health care system | – | – | – | – | 77 | 77 |
| The education system | 47 | 55 | 68 | 48 | 72 | 64 |
| The social security system | – | – | 68 | 63 | 72 | 65 |
| The justice system | – | – | – | – | 42 | 44 |
| Civil service | 39 | 62 | 49 | 42 | 50 | 47 |
| Parliament | 39 | 68 | 49 | 44 | 42 | 48 |
| United Nations Organization | – | – | – | – | 50 | 57 |
| The European Union | – | – | 69 | 63 | 51 | 48 |

moderate. Nevertheless, it remains divided on this subject, the right-wing being very optimistic concerning companies, and the left pessimistic. The bottom of Table 11 shows that nationalism,[23] on the rise somewhat, remains markedly more developed on the right than on the left-wing. It is the same thing for xenophobia, here measured by the rejection as neighbors of people of a different race or foreign workers. Concerning right-wing extremism, this question did not divide the left and right-wing in 1981, but it divides them rather clearly nowadays. In a context of a rise of the National Front, the French have become aware of the danger represented by this political force.[24] Thus, the image of right-wing extremists has very much deteriorated, but clearly more on the left than on the right of the political field.

Table 12 allows us to complete the previous analysis. Trust in institutions, like all ideological dimensions, is a phenomenon that is also likely to separate left and right opinions. In 1981, hierarchical institutions were much more strongly supported by rightist than by leftists. Over the twenty years, leftist opinion has become more markedly accepting of the police and the army, leading to weakened differences between left and right.

---

[23] The nationalist attitude is evidenced with two questions: declaring pride in being French and being ready to fight for one's country in case of another war.
[24] Although Jean-Marie Le Pen's National Front party often obtains 15% of valid votes in elections (its leader even succeeded in being qualified in 2002 for the second round of the presidential election and in that round gained 17.8% of the vote), it is also the party most hated by the French, even more so than the Communist Party in the past.

The French are highly satisfied with their social and educational institutions. Whatever their political orientation, they are very much attached to the health care and social security systems. Moreover, even if they readily criticize the schools, they are aware of the value of their educational system. On education, in 1981, the left-wing was less enthusiastic than the right, a tendency that has since been reversed. The justice system engenders only medium trust, both on the left and on the right. Trust in the civil service and parliament was, in 1981, very strong on the right and very mitigated on the left-wing. Trust progressed on the left, whereas the conformism of the right was weakening. As a result, the tendency since 1990 has been to the near disappearance of ideological differences in these two areas.

The attachment to international institutions, and particularly to the European Union, is equally supported on the right and on the left. This is not surprising when one knows that the building of Europe has supporters and detractors in each political coalition.

Over the twenty years, the content of right and left identities has thus gone through curves that very often lead to a softening of the specificity of political cultures (Brechon *et al.* 2000),[25] even if it is not always the case. A clear ideological polarization however has appeared on at least two subjects (the rejection of the rightist extremists and soft drug consumption). Moreover, in some other areas, the differences in political culture have remained almost identical.[26]

*Strongly Rooted Democratic Values, But...*

If the Values survey had been carried out only in France, it certainly would not have been considered useful to ask questions concerning democracy insofar it goes fully unquestioned in France. The responses obtained are nevertheless astonishing. Even though 83% find democracy a very or fairly good system, one-third of the French find a political

---

[25] See Bréchon Pierre, Laurent Annie, Perrineau Pascal (eds.). *Les cultures politiques des Français*, Presses de sciences po, 2000.

[26] A question on the national preference (when jobs are scarce, giving priority to French people), asked in 1990 and 1999, shows a high difference according to political orientation for the two dates. In 1999, national preference was claimed by 38% on the left and 69% on the right. In 1990, it was 44% on the left and 81% on the right. On this indicator, a slight decrease in the attitude in favor of national preference is recorded, but links with the left right scale remain of the same intensity.

system ruled by 'a strong leader who does not have to bother with Parliament and elections' either very or fairly good. 44% would be very or rather satisfied with a system in which experts would make decisions concerning what is best for the country. Obviously a government by the army has very few supporters (4%). It appears that there exists a certain fragility in the actual attachment of the French to democracy.

One has the feeling that, in a troubled situation, a rather large part of the French population could be won over by more or less authoritative government formulae. Besides, French history is not devoid of examples of non-stability of the political system. Since 1789, republican and democratic ideals have not prevented the Terror (1793), two empires, some monarchical returns, five successive Constitutions in two centuries (judged in general wrong by a part of the French),[27] an exceptional régime during the second world war, and a fifth Republic born in 1958, embodied by general de Gaulle, whose dynamism a part of the French society praised, but whose authoritative drifts were feared by the other part. Moreover, as has been previously shown, the loss of credibility of the parliamentary institution, and the rise of the extreme right, have also weakened democracy.

An index measuring the level of anti-democratism of individuals can be elaborated: 25% of the French show an attraction for at least two non-democratic forms. No difference of age or gender can be detected in this phenomenon. On the contrary, links with education level, social position and income are important. The anti-democratic temptation seems to be all the stronger when an individual is on the fringe of society or in a precarious situation. Moreover, a strong correlation is also noticeable according to political orientation: anti-democratism rises from 13% in the most leftist group (position 1–2), to 50% in the most rightist one (position 9–10). The same index goes up to 47% among those who declare a vote intention in favor of the extreme right.

The anti-democratic people are also much less politicized, are more xenophobic, have less acceptance of delinquent neighborhoods, are not very often members of voluntary associations, and they fear others more than the French average. In other words, a culture of openness

---

[27] In a more positive way, it can be said that the 1958 Constitution has become more legitimate for the French since its use by the left with the accession of François Mitterrand to the presidential office (1981–1995). Today, some observers again criticize the Constitution and would like a Sixth Republic so that Parliament can again enjoy its former power.

to the world and to difference goes along with a democratic culture, whereas anti-democratism is accompanied by a culture of withdrawal into France and into national pride. Obviously France is not the only European country in which democratic weaknesses exist. The rise of the extreme right, criticism concerning parliament and politicians, and potential attraction to strong leaders or experts also exist elsewhere in the European Union. The index of anti-democratism is the highest (one quarter of the population) in France, Belgium and Portugal, while its minimum is found in Denmark and Greece.

### *France, a Point of Transition between Northern and Southern Europe*

The expression 'French exception' is often used as if France were comparable to no other one, as if its heritage of values were entirely original and only related to its particular history. In fact, each country has originality in part, but also common roots with other people. All countries are at the same time unique and nevertheless shaped by the same debates of society and major questions that have troubled Europe for centuries, a Europe in which exchanges between countries have always existed.

The concept of the French exception is thus excessive, and even a little ethnocentric. Each country has developed itself, in part, under the influence of others, noticeably in the context of powerful religions—actual international organizations—that have shaped the social order and strongly directed culture. But obviously religious factors have been mitigated by others (for example, the existence, at some periods, of transnational empires), producing in each country an original culture. There is no French exception, but a cultural dynamics exists, and is proper to each European country. What can be said about the French cultural dynamics compared to the dynamics of its neighbors? The French dynamics are the result of borrowings from different traditions; its originality is that of being both a country with an ancient Catholic tradition, and a country with an ancient secular one. Within this history can be discovered many keys to the understanding of French values.

Because it is a country of ancient Catholic tradition and of Southern Europe, France is characterized by a heavy emphasis on social hierarchies which can also be observed in the bureaucratic culture (the civil service works with the same attachment to hierarchy as the Catholic culture), in the political system (the Republican monarchy), in the management of organizations (decentralization and bottom up reform are not easily practiced in France), or even in everyday relations. Due to the Catholic mould of its culture, it is also a country in which expectations of central government are very strong; it must resolve all problems, and people leave it up to the State to take decisions even if they sharply criticize them afterwards. In other words, France has never much valued intermediary bodies. Government is in charge of carrying out the public good, and thus the initiatives of individuals and of the groupings of citizens do not have much legitimacy, as has been noticed with the weakness of associative links. We have also seen that France is a country in which politicization and electoral participation are not very intense, militantism in parties and trade unions is restricted, trust in others is very limited; incivility, contrarily, is highly developed, and societal pessimism is often stronger than in other countries, as is protest participation.

French culture is not only the product of its Catholic origins. France is also a country where the widespread contesting of Catholicism has generated a secular counter-pattern of values. The enlightened and reasonable man, freed from the ascendancy of the gods and of the Catholic religion, must be respectful of his brothers and show solidarity towards others. Nevertheless, this assertion of a secular humanism has not transformed French culture entirely. It has, however, contributed to the process of secularization, of the loosening of Catholicism's grip on society, and this process of secularization is at the root of the individualization of values. As previously seen, France today is one of the most secularized Western European countries (with the Netherlands, Sweden, Great Britain, Denmark, and even partly Belgium) and also one of the countries where the attachment to private liberties is highest. Each person must be able to live his private life as he desires, and the family has to be built on the interrelations of individuals who form it without having to fit into ready made molds; it is a place of strong expectations and of personal fulfillment, but very much an evolving place: the desired family stability is in the interest of the individual and of one's personal happiness. As far as the enhancing of the image of individual liberties is concerned, France no longer appears to be a country with a Catholic cultural matrix: it is closer to the countries of the Protestant matrix of Northern Europe.

A long history produces a culture, but the latter perpetually readjusts itself. Thus, there is no cultural fate: the religious and ideological matrices of a country constitute influences that are both assets and handicaps. Taking a closer look, we see that the cultural landscape is in fact much more complex than what we can explain here. Indeed, very many subcultures are at work within the same country. Thus, depending on regions or localities, culture may be different, between for example the Paris area (at the forefront of liberalism in morals) and a rural, traditional and remote area, or between the rich Alsace region, very proud of its traditions (but also very proud of belonging to the French nation) and the much poorer Corsica, whose people are often critical concerning the State and some of whom are desirous of obtaining independence. Certain subcultures correspond also to the different social groups, and inside the same group, there are still differences. There are, for example, several kinds of Catholic cultures. If the worship of hierarchy is what has dominated in the French Catholic legacy, this religion can also sometimes give birth to forms of social solidarity and to a feeling of national belonging. The culture of each country is thus modified with time. Twenty years of Values surveys show evolutions that might be breaks with or new orientations in what had constituted the French cultural originality until now. In light of this, two evolutions seem to emerge.

### The Worship of Private Liberties: A Threat to the Social Order?

Despite what the media sometimes put forward about the 'return of moral order,' the attachment to liberty in private life, far from being reduced, continues to progress. The acceptance of the right to abortion, or the tolerance of homosexuality, shows this clearly. On the other hand, real changes have occurred in attitudes concerning problems of authority and security. A spectacular rehabilitation of the principle of authority has been recorded, and this is a peculiarly French evolution. European countries as a whole have not been affected by a recovery of authoritarianizm. In fact, the return to the principle of authority in France is essentially a backlash following the events of 1968. So it is mainly in the young generations that the move can be observed: the under 40 year olds are today much more in favor of authority than was the same age group in 1981, being then still strongly imbued with the ideas of May 1968. This rising demand for authority does not mean in any case a demand for return to the past order concerning morals, nor a return to a rigid authoritarianizm in family, educational or occupational life. It seems to convey much more a reaction to the rise of outbreaks of disorder, violence and incivility, that is to say, to constitute a demand for public order.

If the French are very much attached to individual liberties, they might well also rediscover the meaning of public order. This new balancing in favor of the values of authority can obviously be explained by the rise in a feeling of insecurity (certainly rooted in reality), but it supposes a break with the impression of old-fashionedness, which was associated during the baby boom generation and May 1968 with expectations of order. Young people today are uninhibited about being in favor of order, authority, respect of conventions and forms in all social relations. They wish to be faithful to commitments and moral contracts made with a partner, for example, within a relationship, but they want also to save a sphere of private life where everybody can live as they want, as long as it does not infringe upon the liberty of others or does not become unfair towards them.

Two scenarios for the future seem in fact conceivable. The first of them is optimistic. If France learns again the meaning of order and authority, coupled with individualizing values, this country, a transitional one between Northern and Southern Europe, might in the future become closer to Northern Europe. Until now, in the French and European culture, the strong attachment to permissiveness has not led to a rise in individualizm. One can want the respect of private liberties and thus value also tolerance concerning the way of life of each individual, without adopting attitudes where the ego would be the only criterion of choice. One can want to decide for oneself about one's life and nevertheless take others into account and show solidarity with them. So, France may be on the way towards a new culture where principles of order and authority will no longer be in disgrace, but rather presented in a positive light as a principle of responsibility.

But a pessimistic scenario is possible as well. Individualization may, in the future, have effects on individualism. Indeed, it has been observed that the more people are attached to private liberties and individual values, the more they are also likely to lose the meaning of social links and collective belonging. It is true that, in the northern countries, the attachment to individual liberties coexists with a genuine sense of collective belonging. There is a real sense of social integration in these small countries that are also the most attached to tolerance and respect of individual life choices. France has never experienced this strong promotion of sociability and the social link. It has never succeeded in organizing as well as has the north of Europe a system of social protection and redistribution, so does the meaning of social relations risk being endangered with the rise of individual values?

# CHAPTER TEN

# VALUES AND GENERATIONS IN SPAIN

Juan Díez-Nicolás

*Modernization and Post-Modernization in Spain*

For the study of values, the case of Spain is particularly interesting because of the vast changes this country has experienced in only a few decades. One should take into account the fact that Spain stayed out of the two World Wars, something that contributed to its relative isolation from the rest of the European continent, an isolation that was reinforced by the Spanish Civil War (1936–1939) and the Franco dictatorship (1939–1975), which retarded the modernization process for several decades. In fact, economic modernization and full industrialization started in the 1960s, and was based on the increase of foreign currency that resulted from massive tourism into Spain, and from migrants' remittances to Spanish financial institutions. From 1939 to the late 1950s, Spain was an isolated and economically autarchic country ruled by a strong dictatorship based on a well defined "national-Catholicism." However, during the 15 years from 1960 to 1975, continuous economic development (as measured by high industrialization, high construction rates, and high per capita income increase) produced significant changes in the social structure (i.e., internal rural-urban migration flows, emergence of large urban middle classes, high rates of upward net social mobility, and a growing role of civic society), and changes in belief and value systems (i.e., rapid secularization and decline of Catholic practices and beliefs, growing disengagement from the fascist ideology prevalent during the 1940s, and emergence of a more pragmatic and technocratic life perspective), though political institutional change did not take place until the death of Franco in 1975. The so-called "peaceful political transition to democracy" took place in a very few years under the spirit of moderation and reform without real opposition from the remains of the Franco regime, and without recourse to revolutionary changes, as shown by the fact that, following two national elections (1977 and 1979), and the approval of a new Constitution (1978), during the seven years of a center party democratic rule (1975–1982), the socialist party PSOE was able to win the national elections of 1982 by a large absolute majority. We do not have sufficient space here to explain in detail the changes that have taken place in Spain during the 1980s and 1990s, but suffice it to say that it joined the European Union in 1986 and was one of the countries that adopted the common European currency from the beginning, that its rate of economic growth has steadily been above 2.5% and above the European average for at least two decades, and that in only a few years (since 2000) it has received more than three millions foreigners, three quarters of whom are from less developed countries. It seems fair to say that Spain has reached the status of a post-industrial society in economic, social and political terms, as demonstrated by any indicator one might prefer.

The main objective of this chapter is to trace the changes that have taken place in Spaniards' values during different recent decades, as well as generational change. Our main hypothesis is that one should find great differences in Spaniards' value orientations at different times during the past two decades due to changes in the economic, social and political structures and processes. One should also find great differences between the value orientation of different generations since each generation was socialized in their early years under very different economic, social and political structures and processes.

*The Concept of Generation*

The concept of generation has been widely used in the social sciences from its beginnings (Comte 1839, Cournot 1872, Ferrari 1874, Mannheim 1928, Eisenstadt 1956, Rintala 1963). A generation is not a cohort, but rather an aggregation of cohorts. A cohort refers to those who have been born in a specific year (Ryder 1965), The cohort is a well-accepted concept, especially in demography, because one can follow those born in a specific year (from January 1 to December 31) through their entire life, allocating demographic facts (which are generally reported on an annual basis) to the appropriate cohort according to the age that the cohort has in every particular year,. However, there is no general consensus on the number of cohorts that form a generation, nor on the starting date of a generation, nor even on whether all generations are of the same length, and there is certainly no agreement regarding the basis on which generations should be defined. Comte, Ferrari and Mannheim more or less agree that a generation comprises about 30 cohorts, and that it is defined on the basis of shared historical experiences. Ortega (1933) defined the generation as encompassing 15 cohorts, but Rintala thinks that, at present, generations last from 10 to 15 years, and even less.

Whatever the case, the concept of generation shares many of the limitations of any other abstract concept in terms of operationalization. For the purposes of this chapter, a generation will be defined on the basis of Ortega's 15 cohorts, while accepting that, in recent years, as a result of accelerated social change, generations may be approaching a 10 cohorts or even less. It seems more important, instead, to specify and justify from the very beginning the definition of the particular cohorts in contemporary Spain that will be used, in order to understand the change in value orientations that seems to have taken place in Spanish society in recent decades.

The following analysis has been based on data collected in Spain by the three waves of the European Values Study (1981, 1990 and 1999), and the three waves of the World Values Surveys (1990, 1995 and 2000), thus providing a total of more than 10,000 interviews over a period of 20 years.[1]

## Generations in Contemporary Spain

The main basis for the definition of Spanish generations has been the Civil War (1936–39). This is due to the impact it had in defining a "before" and "after", and because it influenced the life of Spaniards not only during the three years that it lasted, but for the following 40 years until Franco's death in 1975, when the restoration of democracy opened a new historical era through the process of peaceful political transition (Díez-Nicolás 1993, 1995, 1996b).

The cohorts used for this research replicate those defined and used to study the political preferences of Spaniards before the legislative elections in March 1996 (Díez-Nicolás 1996a), which provided a pre-electoral explanation of why the change of political preferences of the

---

[1] The aggregate data file used is the official data file: World Values Survey Association and European Values Study, xwvsevs_1981_2000_v20060423_por.sav produced by ASEP/JDS, Tilburg University and Central Archive.

youngest generation (1967–1981) towards a less leftist orientation might lead to the victory of the right Popular Party, putting an end to 14 years of Socialist government (1982–1996). The electoral results confirmed this forecast, providing some credibility to the instrumental definition of generations that had been used for that analysis.

The names given to cohorts have been based not on the historical facts of what was happening when they were born, but instead on the historical events that took place when they were in the middle of their adolescent years, the crucial years of socialization when individuals consolidate their beliefs and values. Thus, the central cohort of the "Republic-Civil War" generation, born in 1914, was 18 years old in 1932, only one year after the Second Spanish Republic was proclaimed, and it was 35 years old in 1949, one year before Spain was admitted to the United Nations, an event that put an end to the period of international diplomatic and economic isolation that the country had been suffering since 1946. The oldest cohort of this generation, born in 1907, reached 18 years of age in 1925, six years before the proclamation of the Republic, and was 35 years old in 1939, just as the Civil War ended and World War Two started. The youngest cohort, born in 1921, was 18 years old in 1939, the year the Civil War ended, and 35 years old in 1956, when the technocrats of the Opus Dei started the reforms of the economy that preceded the start of economic development in the 1960s. It seems that this generation lived and was influenced throughout the most important part of their lives by the Republic and the Civil War on the one hand, and the Post-war and the Isolation and Autarchy period on the other hand, about thirty years marked by deprivation and scarcity as well as by violence and war, and the toughest period of Franco's dictatorship, when the Phalangist party, the military and the Catholic Church controlled most of Spanish life.

The "Post-war-Isolation" generation[2] was exposed for the most important part of their lives to the post-war and isolation period of

---

[2] The central cohort of the "Post-war-Isolation" generation was born in 1929 (the year of the Great Depression after the New York stock market crash), reached the age of 18 years in 1947, two years after the end of World War Two and three years before Spain's admittance to the United Nations, and it reached the age of 35 years in 1964, when the first Economic and Social Development Plan (1964–68) was launched by the more liberal and technocratic government appointed in 1961. The oldest cohort of this generation was 18 years in 1940, only one year after the end of the Civil War, and it reached 35 in 1957, when the economic measures for stabilizing the economy

scarcity, but then experienced the benefits of economic and social development that took place during the 1960s. It is the generation that best experienced the significant economic and social changes that took place during the period 1955–1970: the change from an agricultural economy to an industrial economy, the great internal population movements from rural to urban-industrial centers, the migration flows to other more developed central and northern European countries, the reception of millions of tourists, the beginning of the secularization of Spanish society, the birth of television in Spain, a relative freedom of the press, the beginning of some relative political freedoms, the beginning of mass consumption, but also the beginning of important changes in value orientations that were the result of greater economic and personal security.

The "Economic development" generation has been the most central during the twentieth century in Spain, and it may be considered as the bridge between the previous more traditional generations and the subsequent and more modern ones.[3] For the most part, this generation

Table 10.1. Definition of contemporary Spanish generations.

| Generation | Central cohort | 18 years in: | Name of Generation | 35 years in: | Protagonists of: |
|---|---|---|---|---|---|
| 1907–21 | 1914 | 1925–39 | Republic-Civil War | 1942–56 | Post-war & Autarchy |
| 1922–36 | 1929 | 1940–54 | Post-war & Autarchy | 1957–71 | Economic development |
| 1937–51 | 1944 | 1955–69 | Economic development | 1972–86 | Transition to democracy |
| 1952–66 | 1959 | 1970–84 | Transition to democracy | 1987–01 | Democracy consolidation |
| 1967–81 | 1974 | 1985–99 | Democracy consolidation | 2002–16 | Globalization |
| 1982–96 | 1989 | 2000–14 | Globalization | 2017–31 | ? |

were adopted, while the youngest cohort was 18 years old in 1954 and 35 in 1971, only two years before the first oil crisis and five years before Franco's death.

[3] The central cohort of this generation was born in 1944 and turned 18 in 1962, one year after the appointment of a new more "open" cabinet and two years before the launching of the first Economic and Social Development Plan. It reached 35 in 1979, when the second legislative elections of the new democracy were held. It is therefore the generation that was definitely marked by the political transition to democracy. Its oldest cohort, born in 1937, was 18 in 1955, and 35 in 1972, while its youngest cohort, born in 1951, turned 18 in 1969, and 35 in 1986 (the year when the Socialist Party won its second legislative elections, the fourth elections since the beginning of democracy in 1976).

was born after the Civil War, and it therefore lived its most important adult years during a 30-year period experiencing the beginning of the economic reforms during the mid 1950s, the economic and social development during the 1960s, and the political changes of the transition to democracy during the 1970s and early 1980s. It has been central in more than one sense, as will be shown later, but it embodies, better than any other generation, the spirit of reform (economic, social and political) that characterized the late years of the Franco regime and the first two democratically elected governments of the UCD (Union of the Democratic Centre) in 1977 and 1979. This generation had a prominent role in leading the peaceful political transition from a dictatorship to a full democracy, showing a very visible change in their value orientations (religious, economic, political, family, work, moral, etc.).

The following generation, the "Transition to democracy" generation, was born during the years of economic development (1952–1966). Most of their members, reaching their young-adulthood more or less when the transition to democracy took place (1970–1984), and reaching 35 during the Socialist governments of the late 1980s and early 1990s,[4]

Figure 10.1. Percent Postmaterialists (12 items), Spain, 1988–2000

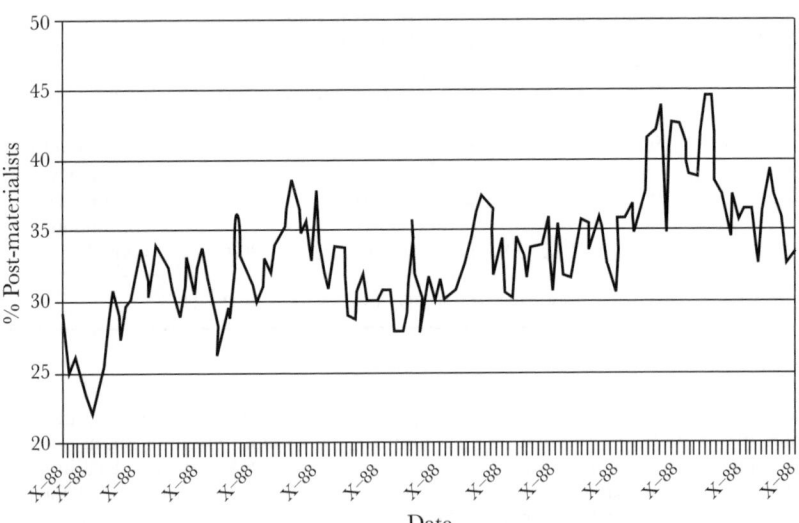

[4] Its central cohort, born in 1959, was 18 years old precisely the year that the first democratic elections were held (1977), and it was 35 in 1994, the year of great political scandals that led the Socialist Party to its first defeat in the 1996 elections, when the Popular Party won its first elections.

never knew what scarcity and deprivation really meant. This generation collectively experienced the events that took place between 1970
and 2000, 30 years that were marked by the transition to democracy
after Franco's death in 1975, the UCD governments of 1977 and 1979,
and the Socialist governments of 1982, 1986 and 1993, and, later, the
Popular governments of 1996 and 2000. This generation, therefore,
has lived for the most part in a democratic political system, and can
be considered as the first to have almost no memory of the Franco
regime (the oldest cohort reached 18 years of age only five years before
the Franco era ended). It did not participate actively in the process
of change, but benefited fully from the economic, social and political
changes that had already taken place. From an economic perspective,
this generation took advantage during its childhood of the affluence
of the 1960s and early 1970s; it had to cope in young adulthood with
the high inflation rates of the late 1970s, but then experienced the
economic boom of the 1980s and the uncertainties of the 1990s. In
addition, this generation has had to compete with greater number of
peers, since the cohorts of the first part of the 1960s have been the
most numerous of the twentieth century in Spain, due to very high
fertility rates during the period 1960–1965.

The "Democracy consolidation" generation is the last one that will
be considered here, since it was born during 1967–1981 and, therefore,
none of its cohorts had reached the age of 35 by 2000 (the year of the
last wave of surveys that will be analyzed here). This is the generation,
however, that arrived at its young adulthood during the final years of
Socialist governments, and probably voted for the first time in 1996,
when the Popular Party won its first elections. They experienced the
great economic and political scandals of the last Socialist governments
when they were young, and have lived under Popular governments most
of their young-adulthood, since the oldest of them were 37 when the
last legislative elections were held in 2004. About half of the cohorts of
this generation were already born after Franco died, and the other half
was at most eight years of age when he died. It is very likely that this
generation will be the first one to really experience the consequences
of globalization, since they were mainly in their "teens" when Spain
joined the Economic European Community in 1986, and when the
Berlin Wall came down in 1989. This cohort has not known post-war
poverty and scarcity, but, after having experienced the extraordinary
economic affluence and mass consumption of the 1980s when they
were children, they experienced high unemployment rates amongst

the young during the early 1990s. Therefore, they have experienced the fear of not reaching the economic levels of their families of origin, of not finding jobs that will be in accordance with their higher than ever educational achievements, of not being able to finance adequate housing, and of having to compete with a greater number of peers that have also acquired a higher education. This generation, finally, seems to rely more on their "social networks" than on their own personal merits to get ahead in life.

There is also another generation, here denominated the "Globalization" generation, which has not yet begun to play a role in Spanish life. Born between 1982 and 1996, their oldest cohort was 20 years old in 2002; thus only the cohort of 1982 was able to vote in the 2000 legislative elections, and only the five oldest cohorts were able to vote in the last elections of 2004. The oldest cohort of this generation was 14 years old when the Popular Party won the 1996 elections, and so this generation has only experienced this party in power, but had no direct experience of Socialist governments (until the PSOE won the last elections in 2004), just as they have no direct knowledge of the "cold war". Given the rather small number of individuals belonging to this generation in our surveys, it will not be included in the analysis presented below.

For the sake of brevity, one could say that the "Republic-Civil War" generation members experienced deprivation and scarcity during most of their lives, from childhood to late adulthood although they have benefited from the higher retirement pensions of a more prosperous and comprehensive welfare state. Politically speaking, some minority groups within this generation were either very "pro-Franco" or very "anti-Franco", but most of them would claim to be "apolitical." The "Post-war and Isolation" generation lived through childhood in deprivation and poverty, but in their adulthood they personally experienced the meaning of economic development and the benefits of a new consumption society, as well as the benefits of the welfare state when they reached retirement. Politically speaking this generation was mainly "pro-Franco", or apolitical, because opposition to the regime was not allowed, so only the politically very conscious ones risked taking an active role against the dictatorship. The "Economic development" generation only had a short experience of years of scarcity, but soon began to experience the benefits of the economic and social development of the 1960s and 1970s, along with the difficult years of long unemployment and early retirement during the late 1980s and early 1990s. In political terms, this generation was very conscious of the need to promote political change. It was attracted by the ideal of building the bridge from Franco's authoritarian (or late soft dictatorship) regime to democracy, and therefore was for the most part supportive of the "reform" process that President Suarez, as the leader of the centre party UCD, and the constitutional King Juan Carlos, represented. This generation, as with the previous one, experienced generally harder economic conditions when they were younger, but better economic conditions as they grew older. As for the "Transition to democracy" generation, it experienced economic development during childhood and youth, it achieved higher educational levels than previous generations, and it had to compete more for jobs, due to higher collective educational levels and to greater numbers resulting from the high fertility rates during the early 1960s. This generation also had to face high unemployment rates during the early 1990s. Therefore, and unlike the previous generation, this generation has experienced relatively good economic conditions throughout most of their lives. Politically speaking, they were, for the most part, supportive of the Socialist Party, and so contributed greatly to its electoral victories in 1982, 1986, 1989, and 1993. Finally, the "Democracy consolidation" generation is the first one to have experienced better economic conditions during childhood and youth than at later ages, to the point that, given the more competitive conditions they have to face, as well as their higher expectations for good jobs and housing derived from increasingly higher life-style standards, they have postponed their separation from their parents until after the age of 30, and they have reduced their fertility to the lowest rates ever known in Spain and in most other developed countries. In political terms they seem to have contributed significantly to the first victory of the Popular Party in 1996 and to the next one in 2000.

Table 10.2. Distribution of each Spanish wave's sample by generation.

|           | 1981    | 1990    | 1995    | 2000    | Total    |
|-----------|---------|---------|---------|---------|----------|
| 1907–1921 | 20.4%   | 8.9%    | 7.3%    | 4.1%    | 10.2%    |
| 1922–1936 | 23.9    | 20.6    | 21.7    | 18.6    | 21.0     |
| 1937–1951 | 24.3    | 23.5    | 20.5    | 20.9    | 22.7     |
| 1952–1966 | 31.4    | 32.6    | 26.8    | 25.2    | 29.8     |
| 1967–1981 | –       | 14.5    | 23.6    | 30.3    | 16.1     |
| 1982–1996 | –       | –       | –       | 1.0     | .2       |
| Total     | (2,303) | (4,147) | (1,211) | (2,409) | (10,070) |

*Value Change in Spanish Society: Generation Effects and Period Effects*

Monthly data collected by ASEP (Análisis Sociológicos Económicos y Políticos, Madrid) from 1988 to the present (more than 200 national surveys with samples of about 1,200 persons each, representative of the Spanish population 18 and over), using Inglehart's 12-item scale (Inglehart 1990:74–5), show a steady increase of post-materialist values from 1988 to 1999, though a change of trend seems to have taken place since the beginning of 2000, a change that has persisted in the following years (not shown here since the present analysis will be carried to 2000, the year of the last WVS wave conducted in Spain).

In view of the summary given above, it should be expected that value-orientation changes in Spain should be related both to period and age, that is, to generation. Data from the World Values and the European Values surveys, and from other surveys conducted in the last two decades, seem to confirm a general trend from scarcity-survival values towards self-expression values. On the basis of data collected through the four waves conducted in 1981, 1990, 1995, and 2000, it is clear that the Spanish population seems to have changed systematically from a relatively more scarcity-survival value orientation in 1981, to an increasingly self-expression value orientation in 1990, 1995, and 2000, thus following the expected direction of change.

However, the change in the other dimension seems to have had a temporal backward change in 1995, although the general trend from 1981 to 2000 seems to follow the expected direction from traditional to secular-rational values. This reversal of the trend in 1995, which implies a certain return to more traditional values, might be a consequence of various factors, including methodological or sampling differences, but, after a close examination of the data, it seems that these factors must be discarded. The only possible methodological explanation might be the fact that the sample in 1995 is the smallest of all waves, and considering that the number of respondents who answer all the items to build the traditional/secular-rational scale is generally about a third of the total sample, this may well have affected the index for this wave. However, a more plausible explanation is that the events that took place in Spain during the previous years (very high unemployment rates in 1992–94, great economic scandals attributed to Government officials and to the party in power, a certain disenchantment with how democracy was working, and great uncertainties about the future) may have jointly contributed to a certain return to more traditional

Figure 10.2. Values in Spain, by Wave.

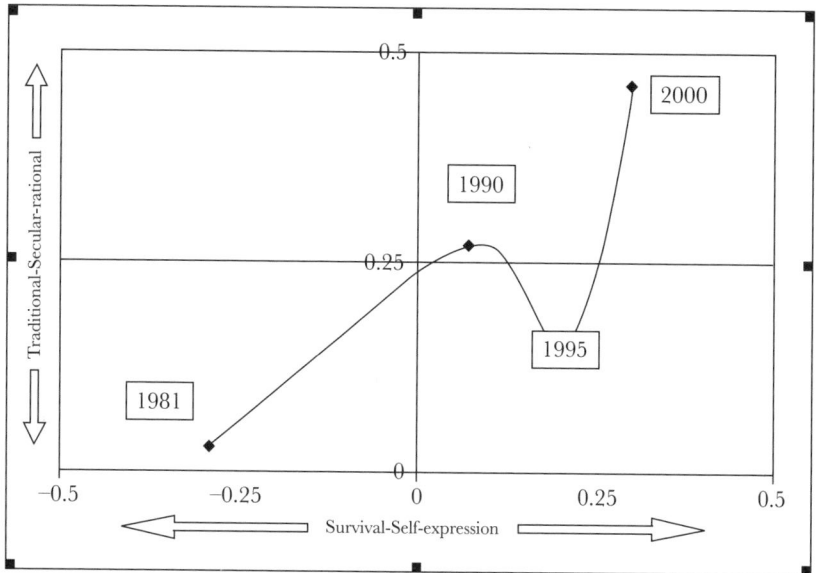

(conservative) values as a reaction to the progressive values that were encouraged during the fourteen years of socialist government. Had the 1995 wave be conducted in a different year, it probably would have obtained different results, proving the importance of the social context in which a survey is conducted. Whatever the explanation, however, the fact is that, in 1999–2000, the plot of the combined position of the traditional/secular-rational value and the survival-self expression value is in line with the 1981 and 1990 values, showing a very steady rate of change consistent with theoretical expectations.

On the other hand, without exception, the change of values between generations follows the pattern that was predicted by Inglehart's theory of postmaterialism that we have already referred to. However, there are some points that must be emphasised. First, it may be noticed that the difference between the two oldest generations is smaller than the difference between the second oldest and the generation that has been considered central, the "Economic development" generation (born between 1937 and 1951), which, as was noted above, was the generation that supported the greater responsibility in carrying out the political transition to democracy. It may also be noticed that the difference in values between the two youngest generations is also smaller than the

Figure 10.3. Values in Spain, by Generation.

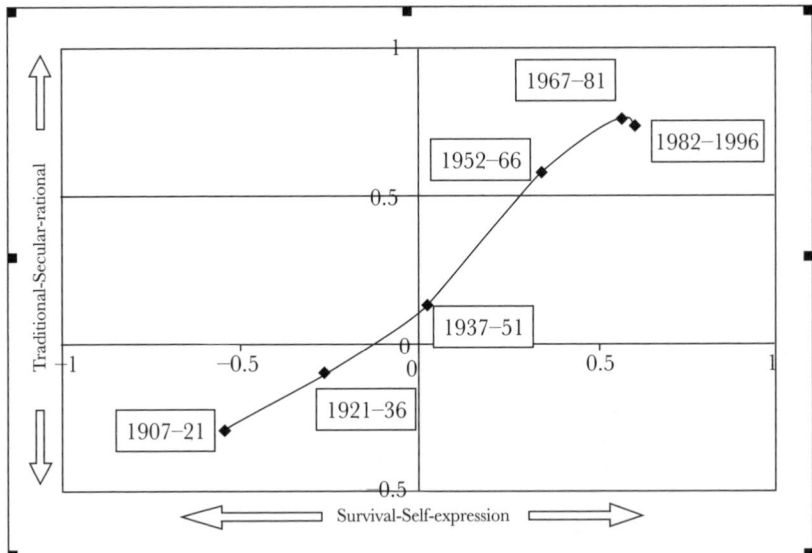

difference between the less young one and the "Economic development" generation. In other words, the central generation, i.e. the "Economic development" generation, seems to have been the one breaking away more significantly with the past (that is, with preceding generations that are more directly influenced by the Civil War and the Franco regime). But, at the same time, this generation also differs significantly from the subsequent generation. The data seems to confirm the very distinctive role played by the "Economic development" generation as a bridge between the past and the future. This generation buried the "old regime", gave birth to democracy and to the 1978 Constitution, and supported a political party, the UCD, which carried on a centrist and reformist program equidistant from the left and the right. In so doing, they facilitated the task of the following generations, which broke away even more profoundly with the value systems of the past, adopting a more secular-rational and a more self-expressive orientation.

As has been said, the change of values between the five generations that have coexisted in twentieth century Spain is consistent with the theory. But there seems to be an inconsistency regarding a certain drawback in traditional values in 1995 for which a plausible interpretation has been given above. However, it seems appropriate to examine the change in values by wave and generation simultaneously.

Table 10.3. Values in Spain by wave and generation.

|  | 1097–21 | | 1922–36 | | 197–51 | | 1952–66 | | 1967–81 | |
|---|---|---|---|---|---|---|---|---|---|---|
|  | Surv-Self | Trad-Rat | Surv-Self | Trad-Rat | Surv-Self | Trad-Rat | Surv-Self | Trad-Rat | Surv-Self | Trad-Rat |
| 1981 | −.64 | −.31 | −.37 | −.04 | −.22 | −.06 | .05 | .49 | – | – |
| 1990 | −.56 | −.21 | −.25 | −.17 | .07 | .18 | .36 | .65 | .44 | .74 |
| 1995 | −.42 | −.50 | −.29 | −.22 | .20 | .07 | .41 | .35 | .69 | .57 |
| 1999–00 | −.11 | −.30 | −.11 | .01 | .07 | .26 | .56 | .69 | .62 | .89 |

As the data in Table 3 show, traditional-secular rational values vary from one generation to the next in the expected manner in each of the four dates for which data were collected. In each one of the four dates, older generations show more traditional values, while younger generations show more secular-rational values. There is not one single exception. But, following each generation through the four waves, the expected pattern of decreasing traditional values (and increasing secular-rational values) with time is irregular. They all show a certain return to more traditional values in 1995, following the pattern already established for the Spanish population as a whole. But all generations also show a recovery towards more secular-rational values in 1999–2000 as compared with 1995. Therefore, save for a methodological error in the 1995 data, the only possible explanation seems to be that there were certain events that had such great impact on people's attitudes as to significantly change their value orientations. The only possible events that seem to meet those requirements is the relative discredit of progressive (as opposed to traditional) attitudes that resulted after a period of three years of political and economic scandals attributed to the incumbent national government at the time, together with economic difficulties not experienced in the preceding years. In this respect, public opinion data collected monthly by ASEP demonstrates that an indicator that is included every month, measuring satisfaction with how democracy works in Spain, obtained its lowest values from the beginning of 1994 to the end of 1995, in a monthly time series running from October 1986 to the present. During those two years, satisfaction with how democracy was working not only reached its worst ratings, but for several months the number of those unsatisfied was higher than those who were satisfied.[5]

---

[5] The data for this and other permanent monthly political and economic indicators, such as satisfaction with the Government's performance, or the consumer sentiment

Figure 10.4. Value Change in Spain by Generation.

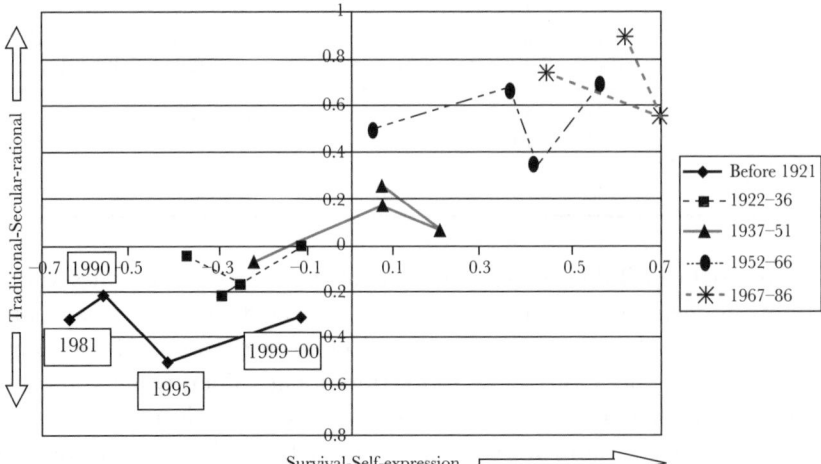

In general terms, therefore, Spanish data for four waves and five generations confirm the expected trend of value change towards more secular-rational (less traditional) values, and towards more self-expression (less survival or scarcity) values. The evidence, however, seems to show that generation change has been greater than period change, a finding that, excluding very important events such as those mentioned for Spain prior the 1995 wave, is also frequent in other societies that have experienced rapid social change, as has been the case for Spain. To find further evidence for this assertion, an analysis of the influence of generation and period (wave) on different sets of values regarding the family, socialization of children, religion, politics, ethics and other similar aspects of life has been conducted in order to verify that generational rather than period effects are more important in explaining values change among Spaniards, and that the change has always been in the direction towards more self-expression, and in general, too, towards more secular-rational, values.

*Generations and Family Values*

Spaniards, like citizens of many other countries, attribute more importance to the family than to other aspects of their life: work, friends,

---

index and its main components, (evaluation of the national and personal economic situations) may be found in ASEP's surveys collection on Spaniards' Public Opinion, in ASEP/JDS Data Bank (www.jdsurvey.net).

leisure, religion and politics. The average importance attributed to the family (3.8 points on a four point scale) has not varied at all between 1990 and 2000, and in general has been somewhat higher among the three oldest generations and lower among the two youngest generations, but the differences are very small.

Eight items regarding attitudes towards the family have been used to construct an index of traditional values towards the family.[6] This index varies between 0 and 7 with higher scores indicating higher levels of traditional family values. As expected, this index is positively correlated with the importance attributed to the family (r = .16) and has a rather high negative correlation with the rational-secular values (r = −.44) as measured by the traditional-secular/rational values index.

The index calculated for each wave and generation shows that traditional values towards the family are always higher for the oldest generation and lowest for the youngest generation in each of the four periods. But these values seem to have increased from the initial wave of 1981 to the wave of 1995, and then to have decreased. The first relationship seems to fit the expected pattern, in the sense that, at any particular point in time, Spaniards' values towards the family are more traditional in the older generations. But the second relationship suggests that, as the members of a particular generation grow older, their values regarding the family become more traditional, though they

Table 10.4. Index of orientation towards traditional family's values, by wave and generation.

|  | 1981 | 1990 | 1995 | 2000 |
|---|---|---|---|---|
| 1907–1921 | 4.57 | 5.58 | 5.86 | 5.79 |
| 1922–1936 | 4.15 | 5.42 | 5.53 | 5.51 |
| 1937–1951 | 3.78 | 4.85 | 5.07 | 5.01 |
| 1952–1966 | 2.96 | 4.01 | 4.33 | 4.20 |
| 1967–1981 | – | 3.93 | 4.11 | 3.73 |

---

[6] The index was constructed on the basis of agreement with the following statements: "regardless of what the qualities and faults of one's parents are, one must always love and respect them"; "parents' duty is to do their best for their children even at the expense of their own well-being"; "a child needs a home with both a father and a mother to grow up happily" and "a woman has to have children in order to be fulfilled"; and disagreement with these other statements: "marriage is an out-dated institution"; "a woman wanting to have a child as a single parent"; "a working mother can establish just as warm and secure a relationship with her children as a mother who does not work"; and "being a housewife is just as fulfilling as working for pay".

have decreased slightly, but consistently, for each generation, between 1995 and 1999–2000. Considering the comment regarding the return to more traditional values in 1995, it could well be that the apparent decrease in traditional values towards the family in 1995 was a result of it having reached a peak in 1995. A regression analysis in which the dependent variable is the index of traditional values towards the family, and the predictors are wave and generation, shows that generation is inversely and more significantly related to traditional values than wave, which in turn is related positively to it. But, when several socio-demographic variables are controlled for, the effect of wave disappears, while completed education is the only other predictor that shows a significant, and negative, relationship with traditional values towards the family.[7] In other words, this analysis suggests that Spaniards who have a higher education and belong to younger generations have a less traditional concept of the family than those with a lower education and belonging to older generations.

Related to family values are values regarding gender equality. An index of favorable attitudes towards gender equality has been constructed on the basis of four items that seem to be part of the same factor, according to a principal component analysis.[8]

Again, the differences among generations in each of three dates are remarkable, showing attitudes increasingly more favorable to gender equality among the youngest generations, and less favorable among the oldest generations. But the time sequence does not match with what is expected, as respondents in 1995 seem to be more favorable to gender equality than those in 1999–2000. Generation and wave are significantly related to gender equality attitudes, even when controlling for gender, education, employment status, and social class. The relationship with generation is positive, meaning that the younger the generation the more favorable their attitudes are towards gender equality, but it is negative with wave, and this may be explained by the fact that the social and

---

[7] The control variables in the regression model were sex (male), highest completed education, employment status, and social class.

[8] The index was constructed on the basis of agreement with the statements that "both husband and wife should contribute to the household income", and disagreement with the statements that "men make better political leaders than women," that "university education is more important for men than for women," and that "when jobs are scarce men have more right to a job than women."

Table 10.5. Index of attitudes towards gender equality, by wave and generation.

|           | 1981 | 1990 | 1995 | 2000 |
|-----------|------|------|------|------|
| 1907–1921 | –    | 1.00 | 2.33 | 1.80 |
| 1922–1936 | –    | 1.24 | 2.54 | 1.95 |
| 1937–1951 | –    | 1.30 | 2.84 | 2.14 |
| 1952–1966 | –    | 1.52 | 3.16 | 2.38 |
| 1967–1981 | –    | 1.64 | 3.38 | 2.47 |

political context in which the 1995 sample was taken was exceptional, as has been explained. The trend from 1990 to 2000 goes in the expected direction, but gender equality attitudes seem to have been much more pronounced in 1995 than in 1990 and 2000, accounting for the negative relationship. The regression model explains 14% of the total variance, and it is important to underline that women are significantly more in favor of gender equality than men, and that education and employment status are positively related to favorable attitudes towards gender equality, but social class is negatively related. Social class has been defined in this analysis by combining two different indicators used by EVS and WVS in their surveys: subjective social class and an index of socio-economic status. But the relationships of the two variables and the combined variable used in this analysis on the one hand, and the gender equality index constructed for this purpose are all negative, a result that implies that the upper social strata are more conservative. To confirm this assertion, the traditional-rational/secular values (trad-rat index) correlates positively and significantly with the gender equality index ($r = .17$), implying that more secular-rational individuals are more favorable to gender equality than more traditional individuals, but it correlates negatively and significantly ($r = -.11$) with subjective social class, and shows no significant relationship with the other two social class indicators.

*Generations and Social Exclusion*

According to the theoretical framework of cultural change which has been adopted for this analysis, social exclusion is more characteristic of traditional societies, and it should decrease in more industrial and post-industrial societies. Exclusionist attitudes have generally been measured by asking about different social groups one would not like as neighbors, so that thirteen of these groups have been included in the different waves, though not all of them were included in all surveys.[9] A principal component analysis shows that there are three different types of socially excluded groups by Spaniards. One is composed (in order of saturation) of immigrants/foreign workers, people of a different race, Jews, Muslims and people with large families. The second component includes (also in order of saturation) drug addicts, people who have AIDS, homosexuals, people with a criminal record and heavy drinkers. And the third component includes right wing extremists and left wing extremists. Emotionally unstable people do not seem to correspond to any of these three groupings.

Four indexes of social exclusion have been calculated, one including all twelve items (all but the emotionally unstable), and one for each of the three components mentioned above. The correlation coefficients among the four indicators are all high and statistically significant, and the four of them are significantly and negatively correlated with rational values on the traditional-rational/secular scale, implying that the more traditionally oriented individuals tend to hold more exclusionist attitudes than the more rational/secular oriented.

Exclusionist attitudes have been very infrequent among Spaniards . When all 13 groups in the "neighbors battery" of the questionnaires are taken into account, the highest average of groups mentioned as not being desirable as neighbors is always below five. When only the five racial/ethnic groups included in the first component are considered, the average of groups mentioned is always below one. The data in Table 6 also demonstrate that social exclusion of minority groups characterized by some particular behavior as those in component two (drug addicts, people with AIDS, homosexuals, former criminals and heavy drinkers) are more socially excluded than ethnic or racial minorities (immigrants/foreign workers, people of a different race, Jews, Muslims and also people with large families, probably assimilated to foreign or ethnic groups). In fact, when the 1990 and 1999–2000 waves are compared, it is evident that, although both types include five groups each, ethnic-racial minority groups are less rejected as neighbors (averages below one) than social minority groups (averages between 1.21 and 2.72).

---

[9] Muslims, people with AIDS, drug addicts, homosexuals and Jews were omitted in the 1981 wave, while Jews, left extremists, right extremists and people with large families were omitted in the 1995 wave. Many other social groups that were included in only one wave have also been omitted in this analysis, as they did not allow a time comparison.

Table 10.6. Indicators of social exclusion, by wave and generation.

| | 1981 | | 1990 | | 1995 | | 2000 | |
| | Total | 1 | Total | 1 | Total | 1 | Total | 1 |
|---|---|---|---|---|---|---|---|---|
| 1907–1921 | – | – | 4.57 | .97 | – | – | 3.43 | .71 |
| 1922–1936 | – | – | 3.86 | .60 | – | – | 3.61 | .64 |
| 1937–1951 | – | – | 3.44 | .50 | – | – | 3.18 | .53 |
| 1952–1966 | – | – | 2.62 | .34 | – | – | 2.65 | .50 |
| 1967–1981 | – | – | 2.47 | .32 | – | – | 1.97 | .22 |

| | 1981 | | 1990 | | 1995 | | 2000 | |
| | 2 | 3 | 2 | 3 | 2 | 3 | 2 | 3 |
|---|---|---|---|---|---|---|---|---|
| 1907–1921 | – | .56 | 2.72 | .63 | 2.57 | – | 2.01 | .46 |
| 1922–1936 | – | .51 | 2.38 | .62 | 2.28 | – | 2.11 | .67 |
| 1937–1951 | – | .48 | 2.14 | .53 | 1.81 | – | 1.82 | .59 |
| 1952–1966 | – | .43 | 1.54 | .50 | 1.35 | – | 1.52 | .55 |
| 1967–1981 | – | – | 1.53 | .39 | 1.38 | – | 1.21 | .43 |

However, although averages for the third type of groups are also below one, one should remember that only two extremist groups are included in this third component (left and right extremists), so that an average of 0.5 is 25% of the maximum possible average, and comparatively they seem to be more excluded than the five social groups mentioned on the second component, and much more excluded than the five racial/ethnic groups included in component one.

The data in Table 6 also shows that social exclusion of any type of groups has decreased among Spaniards with time, and it has also decreased in younger generations as compared to the older ones. Thus, if the total indicator is taken into account, it is evident that all averages have declined for each generation between 1990 and 2000 (with the only minor exception of the 1952–1966 generation). And in both waves, without exception, the younger the generation is, the lower the level of exclusion. Similar trends are found when comparing generations on the average for the first component (racial/ethnic groups) in 1990 and 2000, but there are some exceptions when comparing the values for the same generation in the two waves (probably because exclusion is so low). The generation and wave comparisons for 1990, 1995, and 2000 also show similar trends in general when referring to the social groups in the second component, exceptions being few and very small. But, when one compares the groups in the third component (left and right extremists) in waves 1981, 1990 and 2000, the generation pattern is also maintained (exclusionism decreases the younger the generation is, with the sole exception of the older generation, 1907–1921 in 2000 as compared with the 1922–36 generation), but the comparison of each generation in the three waves shows in general an increase, and not a decrease, in exclusionism of the two groups. This implies that Spaniards of any generation have been increasing their rejection of political extremist groups, no matter whether they are right or left.

Generation explains a greater proportion of the variance in social exclusion attitudes than wave (in each of the four indicators of exclusion), but, as was seen above, both are negatively related to exclusionism. The power of generation as predictor is maintained even when other socio-demographic variables are controlled (gender, education, employment status and social class), none of which adds significantly to the explanation in the presence of generation (with the only exception of education when the dependent variable is social exclusion of social minority groups, in which case the more educated are less exclusionists of drug addicts, people with AIDS, homosexuals, former criminals and heavy drinkers, than the less educated).

The results of this analysis confirm results of more than fifteen annual surveys since 1991, all national representative samples of the Spanish population, that show a very low level of racism, xenophobia or social exclusion among Spaniards, especially regarding immigrants (Díez-Nicolás 2005). Results of those surveys also show lower exclusion of immigrants than of other social minority groups (drug addicts, homosexuals, etc.).

## Generations and Political Values

Change in cultural values in Spain has been greatly influenced by the political transition to democracy that started in 1975 with the death of Franco. This is something that must be taken into account when examining value change in any domain, but especially when analyzing political values. Political attitudes had certainly developed before the political transition, but they manifested themselves more openly when the dictatorship disappeared. Contrary to what many politicians and analysts expected, Spaniards faced the political transition with great moderation, disengaging themselves from nostalgic desires to maintain the old regime as well as from revolutionary ideals. Reform and change were the mottos of the centrist governments of 1977 and 1979, and the socialist governments of 1982, 1986, 1989, and 1993, respectively.

Table 10.7. Position on the Left (1) and Right (10) Scale by
Wave and Generation: Mean Scores.

|           | 1981 | 1990 | 1995 | 2000 |
|-----------|------|------|------|------|
| 1907–1921 | 5.69 | 5.31 | 5.45 | 5.43 |
| 1922–1936 | 5.09 | 5.25 | 5.10 | 5.32 |
| 1937–1951 | 4.86 | 4.73 | 4.95 | 4.96 |
| 1952–1966 | 4.24 | 4.16 | 4.38 | 4.59 |
| 1967–1981 | –    | 4.60 | 4.79 | 4.34 |

That is why Spaniards' ideological center of gravity was at the very centre at the beginning of the political transition and, since 1982, has maintained itself between the center and the center left.

Using a 10-point self placement scale of left-right ideology (where the higher the scale value the more to the right the individual places himself/herself), the means for Spaniards range between a minimum of 4.16 and a maximum of 5.69 (i.e., between the center-left and the center right, and the results are the same when we use a seven-point scale with labels. As expected, young generations always place themselves a little to the left, while older generations place themselves a little more to the right. Only on two occasions, in 1990 and 1995, the 1967–1981 did a generation place itself slightly to the left but closer to the centre than the previous generation, probably marking distances with a socialist government that had lasted for eight or 13 years, respectively, for these two generations. On the other hand, variations between consecutive waves were probably affected by the political context in which each wave was conducted and by the proximity of elections. Thus, all generations seem to have changed a little towards the left between 1981 and 1990, probably reflecting the impact of the large absolute majorities of the socialist party in the 1982, 1986, and 1989 elections. Then, there was a small but consistent change towards the right in 1995, announcing the victory of the conservative party in the 1996 elections, and a continuing small change towards the right again in 2000, when the conservative party won the elections by an absolute majority. Only the very young 1967–1981 generation turned more significantly towards the left in 2000, probably because they aimed again for a new change.

This well known preference of Spaniards for a center ideological position also manifests itself in the overwhelming preference for the statement "our society must be gradually improved by reforms," as against the opinion of very small minorities which express that "our society must be radically changed" or "the existing social order must be valiantly defended." But, at the same time, it must be stressed that, in the 1981 and 1990 waves, when the government was socialist; equality was preferred to freedom by the three oldest generations, while freedom was preferred by the two youngest generations. However, in 2000, when the government became conservative, freedom was preferred to equality by all generations.

Regarding preference for democracy, in the last two waves, 1995 and 2000, respondents were asked to show the importance they attributed, using a four point scale, to four different types of government: strong leader, a government of experts, having the army rule, and having a democratic government. Democratic government is clearly preferred by all generations, and in the two waves, to the other three forms of government, but a government of experts is preferred to having a strong leader, and even more to having the army rule. In general, each generation has shown less preference for any of those three forms of government in 2000 than in 1995, but it must be noted that a democratic system of government enjoys somewhat less support in 2000 when compared with 1995.

Finally, with regard not to attitudes, but to behavior, five political action items (signing a petition, joining in boycotts, attending lawful demonstrations, joining unofficial strikes, and occupying buildings or factories) have been aggregated on a political action index that could vary between 0 and 15 points (since there were three optional responses for each item, "have done", "might do" and "would never do".

The data suggest that political action score is always greater in younger generations, although the level of political action is generally low (always below six points when the maximum number of points possible is 15). Political action in each generation, however, decreased from 1981 to 1990, increased in 1995, and diminished again in 2000. These fluctuations are probably related to the events around each wave.

Table 10.8. Political action, by wave and generation.

|           | 1981 | 1990 | 1995 | 2000 |
|-----------|------|------|------|------|
| 1907–1921 | 5.42 | 4.48 | 5.09 | 5.22 |
| 1922–1936 | 6.30 | 5.42 | 5.72 | 5.58 |
| 1937–1951 | 6.97 | 6.18 | 7.00 | 6.47 |
| 1952–1966 | 8.05 | 7.52 | 7.45 | 7.34 |
| 1967–1981 | –    | 7.11 | 7.76 | 7.66 |

Using a regression model it has been possible to show that political action is related positively to generation (younger generations show more political action) and negatively related to wave (each generation shows decreasing political action with time). But these relationships are maintained when controlling for sex, education, social class and employment status, although males, those who have full employment, and those with more formal education also show more participation through political action.

*Generations and Religious Values*

The political transition in Spain implied not only a great change in political institutions and processes, but, as was said at the beginning of this chapter, a great and significant change regarding the role of the Catholic Church in Spain. With respect to political values, the change had already started during the 1960s, although it manifested itself more clearly after 1975. The secularization process has affected religious beliefs and practices.

An index of religious beliefs has been constructed on the basis of eight beliefs which are common to both Catholics and Protestants: belief in God, in life after death, in the existence of a soul, in hell, in heaven, in sin, in reincarnation and in the devil. It is observed that, in each of the four waves with only one exception, religious beliefs are greater among the oldest generations, and lower among the youngest generations. Moreover, the religious beliefs of different generations diminished between 1981 and 1990, but have increased between 1990 and 1995, something that was already anticipated at the beginning of this chapter when trying to explain the reasons for the decline in secular/rational values (and therefore the increase in traditional values) in 1995. Religious values in 2000 for each generation are the lowest of the whole period.

Table 10.9. Index of religious beliefs, by wave and generation.

|           | 1981 | 1990 | 1995 | 2000 |
|-----------|------|------|------|------|
| 1907–1921 | 4.94 | 4.65 | 4.76 | 3.48 |
| 1922–1936 | 4.45 | 4.30 | 4.52 | 3.26 |
| 1937–1951 | 3.95 | 3.56 | 3.91 | 2.71 |
| 1952–1966 | 3.10 | 2.88 | 3.60 | 2.39 |
| 1967–1981 | –    | 2.96 | 3.41 | 2.08 |

Table 10.10. Importance of God in one's life, by wave and generation.

|  | 1981 | 1990 | 1995 | 2000 |
|---|---|---|---|---|
| 1907–1921 | 7.47 | 7.41 | 7.98 | 7.42 |
| 1922–1936 | 6.75 | 7.14 | 7.59 | 7.06 |
| 1937–1951 | 6.36 | 6.39 | 7.35 | 6.44 |
| 1952–1966 | 5.19 | 5.19 | 6.25 | 5.63 |
| 1967–1981 | – | 5.16 | 6.16 | 4.86 |

A second, widely used indicator of religious beliefs is the 10-point scale that measures the subjective importance attributed to God in one's life. The data show, in all four waves, and without any exception, that the importance of God in one's life is less in each generation when compared with its predecessor. And, when examining the changes in time for each generation it is observed again that the importance of God decreases from 1981 to 1990, but increases in all generations in 1995 and decreases again in 2000.

It must be underlined that the rise in the importance of God in one's life in 1995 confirms once more that the reasons given to explain the change of trend in the traditional-rational/secular index were not mere artifact or justification. The "trad-rat" index dropped in 1995 towards the traditional axis, and many of the data examined here have confirmed that change in the trend with an increase in different traditional measurements. This indirect validation of the value change provides confidence in the data.

To summarize, it is important to measure both the change in religious practice or behavior, and not only the change in beliefs. The usual measure of religious practice is attendance at religious services, an indicator that, in Protestant countries, refers to church attendance for religious services generally on Sunday, and, in Catholic countries, generally refers to attendance at mass on Saturday or Sunday.

Once more, in all four waves and without exception, church attendance has decreased from the oldest to the youngest generations, a finding that is consistent with secularization theory. Also, in accordance with this theory, church attendance of each generation has declined consistently from 1981 to 1995, but it is evident that all generations seem to have increased their church attendance in 2000, with the sole exception of the youngest generation (1967–1981), which has continuously reduced its church attendance since 1990. There is not, at least at this time, a particular explanation for this increase in church attendance in 2000, a finding that will have to be followed up in future surveys.

Table 10.11. Attendance at religious services, by wave and generation.

|           | 1981 | 1990 | 1995 | 2000 |
|-----------|------|------|------|------|
| 1907–1921 | 5.90 | 5.46 | 5.12 | 5.32 |
| 1922–1936 | 5.23 | 5.16 | 4.80 | 5.10 |
| 1937–1951 | 4.44 | 4.45 | 4.19 | 4.52 |
| 1952–1966 | 3.52 | 3.10 | 3.31 | 3.48 |
| 1967–1981 | –    | 3.10 | 3.04 | 2.87 |

## Concluding Remarks

The main hypothesis of this chapter has been that change in the two values dimensions defined by Inglehart as accompanying the processes of modernization and post-modernization—the traditional-rational/secular dimension and the scarcity/survival-self-expression dimension—may be observed in Spain not only in time, comparing data for four waves (1981, 1990, 1995 and 1999–2000), but also comparing the five generations from that born in 1907 to that born in 1981, grouped in 15 cohorts for each generation. Results seem to confirm this main hypothesis. Younger generations are generally more secular/rational oriented and more self-expression oriented, while older generations are generally more oriented towards traditional and scarcity/survival values. In general, the same pattern of change is observed when comparing values of each generation since 1981 to 2000, though here an exception is usually found in 1995, when a return to traditional values is observed.

To confirm and validate this twofold trend, a great deal of data on attitudes towards the family, gender equality, social exclusion, ideology, societal change, preference between equality and freedom, preference for different forms of government, political action, religious beliefs and religious practice have been examined. For the most part, the reported trends of change have been confirmed, and a modest return to more traditional values in 1995 has also been confirmed by many of these indicators, thus demonstrating that it is not a deviation that could be attributed to an error in sampling or in the items that form the traditional-secular/rational values index, but is a fact that is confirmed when using many other indicators.

As a concluding test, regression models have been estimated to test the predictive value of the two values dimension, the traditional-secular/rational values index, and the survival/scarcity-self-expression values index, as predictors of the different dependent variables already tested against generation and wave as independent-predictive variables. Thus, the two value dimensions explain 21% of the variance in the index of traditional family orientation, so that traditional family orientation is positively related to traditional values and to scarcity values; they explain 9% of the gender equality index, so that gender equality is related to self-expression values and secular/rational values; they explain 6% of the total social exclusion index, implying a relation of this index with traditional and survival/scarcity values; they explain 18% of ideological self-anchoring, so that leftism is related to traditional and survival/scarcity values while rightism is related to rational/secular and self-expression values; they explain 4% of the variance in the preference for a democratic government, in such a way that it is related to self-expression and rational/secular values; they explain 29% of political action, implying a strong relationship with self-expression and rational/secular values; they explain 26% of religious beliefs, 48% of God's importance in one's life, and 25% of religious practice, so that they are related to traditional and survival/scarcity values. All these relationships are maintained when one controls for gender, education, employment status and social class.

## References

Comte, Auguste. 1839. *Cours de Philosophie Positive*. Vol. IV. Paris: Bachelier.
Cournot, Antoine. 1872. *Considerations sur la marche des idées et des évenéments dans les temps modernes*. Paris: Boivin.
Díez-Nicolás, Juan. 1993. «Una Sociedad en Transición». *Telecomunicaciones y Sociedad. Libro Aniversario de los XXV años de FUNDESCO*. Madrid: FUNDESCO.
——. 1994. "Postmaterialismo y Desarrollo Económico en España», in *Tendencias Mundiales de Cambio en los Valores Sociales y Políticos*. J. Díez- Nicolás and R. Inglehart ed. Madrid: FUNDESCO.
——. 1995. "A Permanent Victory of Moderation". *Public Perspective*. (February). University of Connecticut: The Roper Center.
——. 1996a. "Generaciones y Preferencias Políticas", *Investigaciones Políticas VIII*, Madrid: AEDEMO.
——. 1996b. "Completing the Cycle: The End of Spain's Political Transition", *Public Perspective*. (August). University of Connecticut: The Roper Center.
——. 2000. "La Escala de postmaterialismo como medida del cambio de valores en las sociedades contemporáneas", in *España 2000, entre el Localismo y la Globalidad. La Encuesta Europea de Valores en su Tercera Aplicación, 1981–1999*. F. Andrés Orizo and J. Elzo ed. Madrid: Editorial Santa María.
——. 2005. *Las Dos Caras de la Inmigración*. Madrid: IMSERSO.
Eisenstadt, Samuel. 1956. *From Generation to Generation. Age Groups and Social Structure*. Glencoe, Ill.: Free Press.

Ferrari, Giuseppe. 1874. *Teoria dei periodici politici*. Milano: Hoepli.
Inglehart, Ronald. 1977. *The Silent Revolution*. Princeton: Princeton University Press.
———. 1990. *Culture Shift in Advanced Industrial Society*. Princeton: Princeton University Press.
———. 1997. *Modernization and Postmodernization*. Princeton: Princeton University Press.
Mannheim, Karl. 1928. "Das Problem der Generationen". *Kölner Vierteljahrshefte für Soziologie* 7. Jahrg., Hefte 2–3.
Norris, Pippa and Inglehart, Ronald. 2003. *Human Values and Social Change*. R. Inglehart. ed. Leiden-Boston: Brill.
Ortega y Gasset, José. 1933. *En Torno a Galileo*. Obras Completas, vol. V. Madrid: Revista de Occidente.
Rintala, Marvin. 1963. "A Generation in Politics: A Definition", *Review of Politics*, 25, 509–522.
Ryder, N.B. 1965. "The Cohort as a Concept in the Study of Social Change". *American Sociological Review*, 30, 843–861.

# CHAPTER ELEVEN

# ISLAM, GENDER, DEMOCRACY AND VALUES: THE CASE OF TURKEY, 1990–2001

## Yilmaz Esmer

Turkey is the only predominantly Islamic country that has participated in every wave of the World Values Surveys since 1990. Although some other Islamic countries have been in and out of the study, unfortunately, they have failed to provide time series WVS data for all four or even three of the waves of surveys conducted around the years 1990, 1996, 2000 and 2006. Similarly, the International Social Survey Program (ISSP) and the Eurobarometers, the two other long term international social survey programs, have not included any predominantly Islamic societies in a systematic manner until very recently. Looking back a decade and a half, one can only wish that such had not been the case and that the world had realized the crying need for such data long before the profound shock caused by September 11, 2001 and the developments subsequent to this tragic event. Nonetheless, the only longitudinal data set on the values of predominantly Islamic societies comes from Turkey, a country with a population that is over 95 percent Muslim.

For the study of value change in Islamic societies, the Turkish case is beset by at least two disadvantages. First, the story, for reasons of data availability, covers a period of less than two decades—an extremely short span of time for studying value change. Second, and more important, Turkish society is hardly representative of the Islamic world by any stretch of the imagination. With its long history of Westernization attempts, its strictly secular constitution, its transition to a competitive multi-party system way back in 1946, its long term military alliance with the West, and its intense economic, cultural and political relations with Western Europe as well as North America, Turkey is a truly unique case within the Islamic world. Nevertheless, by and large, the overwhelming majority of its population are devout Muslims and a good proportion practice their religion on a daily basis. So much so that, many see this cultural (translate: religious) difference as the main barrier to Turkey's full membership in the European Union. Indeed, this concern about admitting an Islamic society into the EU has been raised time and again by politicians, researchers, journalists and academics. Commenting on the subject, *The Financial Times* (Quentin Peel, September 16, 2004:15) wrote that "...the technical challenges are manageable. The real challenges are cultural. Is Europe prepared to accept such a large Islamic country into its midst?" *The Economist* (18–24 September 2004:36) agreed: "...the biggest issue of all is Islam. Few people now insist that the EU is a Christian club, but *the feeling that it should be is widespread*, especially among Christian Democratic parties. September 11th, Iraq and the war on terror have all focused renewed attention on whether the EU is right to consider admitting a Muslim country." [emphases original]

In brief, despite all its differences with the rest of the Islamic world, many still see Islam as an outstanding if not the defining characteristic of Turkey and the Turkish people. Why is this of any relevance for the present chapter? Why should religion be the focus of attention in a study of value change in Turkey in the 1990s? The question has an obvious answer which has only been amplified by Huntington's thesis on "the clash of civilizations." Islam is a distinct civilization, it is said, which fosters values quite different from other civilizations. According to Huntington (1998), these profound value differences, often referred to as a "cultural fault line," between the West and Islam are highly likely to clash in the post-communist era.

The crucial question is, then, what is so different about Islam and Islamic values that is assumed to set Islamic societies miles apart from the West. After all, Islam is a monotheist religion that originated in the same geographic region as Judaism and Christianity—the two religions explicitly recognized by its Prophet. Any discussion of this question inevitably centers around gender issues and the status of women in Islam, at least as it is understood and practiced by a vast majority of its adherents. Both macro and micro level data show clearly that Islamic societies lag far behind the rest of the world with respect to the equal treatment of women in all spheres of life. And this is not just a question of economic development and welfare. The relationship holds even after income is controlled for.

## Human Development, Gender Equity and Islamic Societies

No matter which one of the available measures of gender equity or the status of women one prefers, Islamic societies perform rather poorly and almost invariably rank at the bottom of the list. A glance at the available statistics will suffice to verify this fact.

The United Nations Development Programme calculates a "Gender Empowerment Measure" which is a composite index of i) seats in parliament held by women as percent of total, ii) female legislators, senior officials and managers as percent of total, iii) female professional and technical workers as percent of total, and iv) ratio of estimated female to male earned income. It is worth noting that among the 80 countries ranked in the *2005 Human Development Report* (UNDP, 2005:306) on this measure, the first 50 do not include a single country with a Muslim majority population. Among the first 50, Tanzania ranks 42nd and has the highest proportion Muslims in this group. Yet, only little over 30 percent of the Tanzanian population is Islamic. Among the 80 countries for which data and rankings are available, the highest ranking completely or predominantly[1] Islamic country is Bahrain which occupies the 62nd position in the list. More significantly, the last six countries (Iran, Turkey, Egypt, Saudi Arabia, Bangladesh and Yemen) are all overwhelmingly Islamic.

Further analysis shows that almost all countries with zero percent women in their lower houses are Islamic (UNDP, 2005). These countries are Bahrain, Kuwait, Saudi Arabia, the United Arab Emirates and Yemen with the two exceptions (i.e. non-Islamic) in this group being Saint Kitts and Nevis (a Caribbean island with a population of around 50,000) and Solomon Islands (Pacific islands with a population of less than 500,000). The list of countries with less than five percent women in their parliaments (UNDP, 2005) presents a very similar picture. There are 13 such countries with nine of them being overwhelmingly Muslim and the remaining four being Vanuatu (population less than 200,000), Papua New Guinea, Haiti and Sri Lanka. Statistics related to female/male schooling ratios and female economic activities do not point out to an optimistic outlook for Islamic societies either.[2]

---

[1] The highest rated Muslim-majority country is Malaysia with a rank of 51.

[2] For detailed data analysis, readers are referred to Arab Human Development Reports published by the UNDP. 2000 and 2005 Reports are of particular relevance.

It is beyond the scope of this chapter to go into a detailed analysis of the relationship between Islam and gender issues (see, for example, Inglehart 2003; Norris and Inglehart 2004). But one point is reasonably clear: Islamic societies do not reflect a favorable image with respect to the macro level international statistics regarding the status of women. This conclusion is generally true for a variety of indicators of gender equity.

## *Values, Religion and Gender*

Another strategy for tackling the problem is to look at the values of individuals from a comparative perspective and try to answer the question of whether or not Muslims are indeed different with respect to major value dimensions. From this approach, if Muslims as individuals think and behave similarly as non-Muslims sharing similar socio-economic and demographic characteristics, then macro level differences can safely be attributed to factors other than individual faith.

We are aware of three approaches within the WVS tradition to test the hypotheses concerning Islamic/non-Islamic value differences at the individual level. Norris and Inglehart (2002) have compared societies which are considered to be within the "Islamic civilizational zone" with others. Thus, in their analysis, a country is classified as Islamic if the majority of its population is Muslim. Esmer (2002), on the other hand, compared the values of Muslims with non-Muslims within the same societies. The Norris-Inglehart approach assumes that if a country is predominantly Muslim (or Protestant, Catholic, etc.) its non-Muslim (or non- Protestant, non-Catholic, etc.) citizens will hold more or less similar values. In other words, the country's dominant tradition will be the major independent variable. Esmer's analysis tries to uncover differences in the value systems of the adherents of different religions within the same society. Pettersson (2003) employs an innovative strategy and, using European survey data, matches the socio-demographic characteristics of Muslims with non-Muslims. He then compares these "social twins" with respect to their attitudes towards the United Nations.

All three studies fail to find major differences in political values (especially attitudes towards democracy) and attitudes towards the U.N. between Muslims and non-Muslims. However, Norris and Inglehart, and Esmer agree that there is a significant cleavage between Muslims and non-Muslims in values and beliefs about gender equality and sexual freedoms. As aptly put by Norris and Inglehart (2002:236) "*The cultural gulf separating Islam from the West involves Eros far more than Demos.*" [our emphases]

The conclusions reached by these studies indicate that one would be well-advised to focus on gender and religion in a study of value change in an Islamic society. Thus, the following analyses will track values and attitudes related to gender issues in Turkey and will explore the link between these and religiosity. But first, we present a very brief historical background for our analyses.

## *The Ottoman Legacy and the Republican Revolution*

Turkish conversion to Islam started about a century and a half after the Prophet established his religion and the process continued for about 300 years. By and large, the conversion was completed by the middle of the 10th century. Islam entered the Asia Minor through Seljuk Turks who established a short-lived state in the region. However, Islam's glorious centuries and far-reaching conquests started with the Ottoman Turks. It is generally agreed that the year 1299 marks the founding of the Ottoman state, which quickly developed into a powerful world empire and lasted for over six centuries. Like any other empire, the citizens of the Ottoman State belonged to a wide variety of ethnic *groups and religions*. Nevertheless, it is beyond doubt that the ruling ideology of the Empire was Islam and the founding *element* was Muslim Turks. The ruling elites were Muslims, although many were converts to the faith, and the Ottoman Sultans (many of whose mothers were born as Christians but later converted to Islam) ruled in the name of Allah and Mohammad.

Europeans made little or no distinction between Ottomans and Turks and very often referred to the territory simply as the 'Turkish Empire.' Furthermore, for the Christendom, the major defining characteristic of the Ottoman State was its religion. Thus Europe, for the most part, defined itself with reference to the 'other' which was Islam. The unmistakably Islamic character of the Ottoman Empire acquired its symbolic seal in the first quarter of the 16th century. In 1516, the Ottomans conquered the holiest cities of Islam—Mecca, Medina and Jerusalem. Thus they not only became the trustees and the defenders of the material/cultural heritage of early Islam but also gained control of the annual holy Hajj. A year later, Sultan Selim declared himself the Caliph, that is, the spiritual and political leader of all Muslims. From then on, and until the Republic, Ottoman Sultans were proud to bear that title.

As is true for most other religious traditions, Islam, as a faith dealing with every conceivable aspect of human existence, played a major role in shaping the value systems of its adherents everywhere. Thus Inglehart (Inglehart, 1997; Inglehart and Welzel, 2005) has been able to show that similar religious traditions tend to cluster together on a map of major value dimensions. Keeping in mind that "The Ottomans were a people of faith. Their worldviews were based on the Koran, Hadith, and the text that sought to interpret these" (Timur, 1994: 16), it should not come as a surprise to anyone that Islam has had a profound impact on Turkish culture. Even today, one can observe the effects of the centuries-old tradition of classifying the whole world into two distinct categories: dar-ul Islam (land of Islam) and dar-ul harb (land of war).

The crucial importance of particularly the three monotheistic religions and their major denominations in molding the worldviews and the value systems of their adherents is indisputable. In Huntington's (1998:47) words "of all the objective elements which define civilizations, however, the most important is usually religion." But it is equally true that religion is not the only factor in defining a civilization. There is a host of other variables such as geography, political history, economic welfare and many others, that could also play a role. In the Turkish case, the long, arduous and still ongoing process of Westernization is perhaps equally important in understanding the contemporary Turkish culture.

The first few centuries of the Ottoman Empire were a period of glory indeed. Almost every military campaign was victorious and ended in further territorial expansion. There was much reason to believe that Islam was superior to all other faiths, and societies organized in accordance with Islamic principles were to prevail over their rivals. Starting with the 16th century, however, the fortunes of the Ottoman Empire seemed to be taking a turn for the worse. At an accelerating pace, the Ottomans started to experience the bitter taste of defeat and territorial loss. Questioning the superiority of one's way of life is not easy for anyone and change is universally a painful process. The easy way out under such circumstances is accepting the need to import new and more advanced technologies while rejecting the value systems that produce those technologies. This attitude is present in most modernizing societies with Japan and Russia being the two most prominent examples.

The Ottoman elites were not an exception in this regard. It was becoming harder to deny that European military technology was proving to be superior and the process of Ottoman modernization started with the army. However, maintaining a "customs" policy of letting technology in, while "confiscating foreign and harmful ideas" is not an easy proposition. Inevitably, the Empire embarked on a process of modernization that certainly went beyond just military technology or technology in general. To be sure, the process met with a great deal of resistance and was seen as a threat both to Islamic values and also to vested interests.

The year 1839, when the so called *Tanzimat* (the word itself means reorganizing or putting to order) was proclaimed, is usually regarded as the 'official beginning' of the reforms extending to the legal, administrative and political spheres. With this Proclamation, the Ottomans were declaring their adoption of a number of legal and administrative practices from Europe. As this author put it elsewhere "the wheels of Westernization had started turning; they squealed and screeched, and the coefficient of friction was very high, but the process proved irreversible. The second cultural pillar of contemporary Turkish society was being erected." (Esmer, 2006:222)

This gradual and piecemeal process of modernization took a radical and swift turn as the Turkish Republic replaced the Ottoman Empire. The Republic, more than anything else, was a large scale modernization project that left hardly any aspect of social, political and even cultural life untouched. From the alphabet to the dress code, from civil and criminal law to the educational system, from the calendar and measures to the court system things were changed dramatically and almost overnight. And perhaps the most important of all was the adoption of a rather strict and rigorous version of secularism. This not an easy or simple accomplishment in any society even in today's world, let alone in the Turkey of the 1920s. Nevertheless, the country that had been the leader of the Islamic world for centuries was now eliminating all references to religion and even to Allah from its constitution and laws. Such revolutionary change was bound to have a significant impact on values.

Against this historical background, it is only natural to expect that the values of the contemporary Turkish society will have both Islamic and Western shades. This much is beyond dispute. The important question, however, is whether the present day culture is an amalgam of these two sets of values or whether these two sets of values exist more or less separate from and independent of each other. If the latter is the case, then one can talk about a cultural fault line within the Turkish society as well—a fault line that runs between the secular/Western values and Islamist values.


## Value Change in Turkish Society since 1990

The first Turkish WVS survey was fielded in October 1990 with a sample size of 1,030.[3] Subsequent WVS surveys were conducted in December 1996–January 1997 (number of completed interviews = 1,907),[4] and then in November 2000 to February 2001 when the sample size was 3,401.[5] Finally, the European Values Survey was fielded in Turkey in September and October 2001 with a total of 1,206 interviews completed.[6] The following analyses are based on data from these surveys.

Like all Islamic publics, Turkish citizens display very high levels of religiosity and score very highly on indicators of both practice and faith. For instance, according to data from the 2000 wave, 10 out of 14 countries which had a mean of over 9.5 on a 1 to 10 'importance of God' scale were Islamic and the top ranking were all predominantly Muslim (Inglehart, et al. 2004). Similarly, Islamic societies always have the highest proportions of those who believe in life after death, in heaven, in hell, and in sin.

The data summarized in Table 1 show that a great majority of the Turkish population are believers and God is important in their lives. Over 90 percent say that 'they derive comfort and strength from religion.' Furthermore, the findings have stayed remarkably consistent over the years. Table 2 indicates a slight increase from 1990 to 1996 in indicators of faith (as opposed to practice) and a leveling off after 1996. As expected, 2000 and 2001 results are almost identical—a fact that increases our confidence in the reliability of our findings. With

---

[3] Along with the present author, Ustun Erguder and Ersin Kalaycioglu directed the 1990 survey which was supported by a grant from the Turkish Industrialists' and Businessmen's Association (TUSIAD).

[4] Yilmaz Esmer and Ersin Kalaycioglu were the principal investigators of the 1996 survey which was supported by the Friedrich Ebert Stiftung in Istanbul and two dailies, *Milliyet* and *Sabah*.

[5] The 2000 Turkish WVS study was directed by Yilmaz Esmer and was supported by TOFAS, the maker of Fiat automobiles in Turkey.

[6] The Turkish European Values Survey was supported by the Scientific and Technological Research Council of Turkey (TUBITAK), grant no. SEB-3004.

Table 11.1. Indicators of Religiosity (Faith): 1990–2001.

| Year of Survey | Considers oneself religious (%) | Believes in God (%) | Believes in life after death (%) | Believes in heaven (%) | Importance of God in Life (arithmetic mean) | Derives comfort and strength from religion (%) |
|---|---|---|---|---|---|---|
| 1990 | 75 | n.a. | 80 | 87 | 8.8 | 88 |
| 1996 | 78 | 98 | 89 | 92 | 9.3 | 93 |
| 2000 | 81 | 98 | 90 | 94 | 9.2 | 93 |
| 2001 | 80 | 98 | 91 | 93 | 9.3 | 92 |

Figure 11.1. Religious Practice (Mosque Attendance)

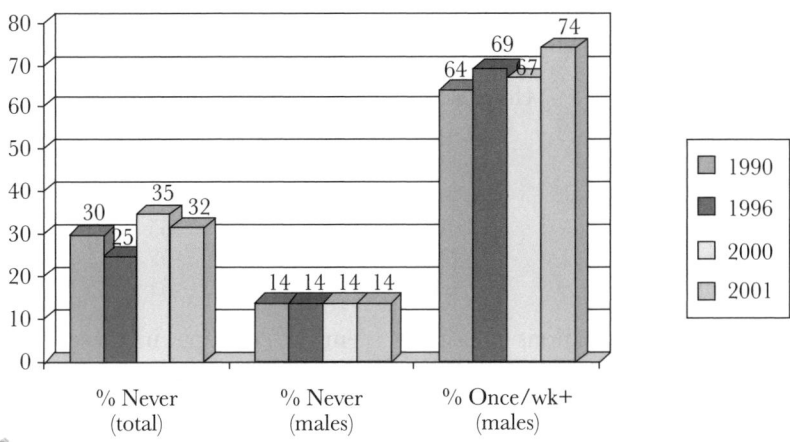

respect to the faith aspect of religiosity, Turkish society does not score the highest points within the Islamic world but it emerges as one of the most religious in Europe.

The findings about the faith aspect of religiosity seem to be valid for practice as well. As seen in Figure 1, the proportion of males who never go to mosque (except for funerals, etc.) has remained amazingly stable between 1990 and 2001 (14 percent for all four surveys). However, a slight increase is observed in the proportion of males who attend mosque at least once a week or more during the same period. (Since Islam requires only men to attend mosque services on Fridays and gives women the choice of not attending if they so desire, it is meaningful to observe mosque attendance data for males only.)

Tables 2 and 3 summarize our findings regarding the role of religion in different spheres of life and particularly in politics. About a third of the respondents express a preference for observing religious principles in education, government, inheritance laws (an area the Koran treats in some detail) and criminal law (more specifically, deciding on the penalties for certain crimes). However, some of these respondents who seemed to be in favor of divine interference in these areas probably interpreted 'religious principles' in this question as a 'code of good conduct' rather than a strict observance of the Sharia law. Together with the findings that about three fourths are opposed to religious leaders influencing government decisions and roughly four fifths do not want them to have an impact on how people vote, one can perhaps conclude that, despite the very high levels of religiosity, secularism has also taken root in Turkish society. To put things in a comparative perspective, one may look at the following findings from selected few Western countries (Inglehart *et al.*, 2004).

Religion leaders should not influence:

|  | How people vote | Government decisions |
| --- | --- | --- |
| Turkey | 78 | 72 |
| Canada | 77 | 67 |
| Germany | 75 | 71 |
| G. Britain | 70 | 65 |
| Sweden | 68 | 52 |
| United States | 64 | 51 |

Assuming the questions measured identical concepts in these countries, compared to some of the most advanced Western democracies, Turkish citizens are more critical of the influence of religious leaders on electoral choice and government affairs. Are Turks more secular in this respect (that is, religious intervention in government and politics) than, for instance, Canadians, Germans or Swedes? That would be a hasty and rather counter-intuitive conclusion. Some other possible explanations are:

a. Although very religious and devout at the personal level, most Turkish citizens can draw a line between individual faith and affairs of the state.
b. Turkish population is rather skeptical of its religious leaders.
c. Because of the absence of an official clergy or a church leader or any formal hierarchy, Turks had difficulty in interpreting this question.

There is probably some truth in all of these three interpretations of the findings. Nevertheless, it would not be unfair to say that a sizeable proportion of the Turkish population does espouse secular values, that is, the separation of the state and religion. Indeed, it is worthy of

Table 11.2. Religion and Politics: Percent saying "......should be conducted in accordance with religious principles" (survey year: 2000).

| | Educational System | Government Affairs | Inheritance Rules | Criminal Code |
|---|---|---|---|---|
| Total | 31 | 23 | 32 | 30 |
| Male | 31 | 20 | 30 | 29 |
| Female | 32 | 25 | 34 | 31 |

Table 11.3. Religion and Politics: Percent agreeing with the statement.

| | Politicians **not** believing in God unfit for office | Religious leaders should **not** influence how people vote | Religious leaders should **not** influence government decisions | Better if people with strong religious beliefs held public office |
|---|---|---|---|---|
| 2000 Total | 60 | 79 | n.a. | 56 |
| 2000 Male | 62 | 81 | n.a. | 57 |
| 2000 Female | 59 | 79 | n.a. | 54 |
| 2001 Total | 63 | 78 | 72 | 58 |
| 2001 Male | 64 | 81 | 72 | 58 |
| 2001 Female | 62 | 79 | 74 | 56 |

consideration that a good 40 percent of the population (sum of those who disagree with or are indifferent about the statement that "politicians who do not believe in God are unfit for office") is comfortable with politicians who do not believe in God. On the other hand, we do not observe a rise in secularization in the sense of the decreasing role of religion in one's life (that is, lower levels of the faith dimension of religiosity). In fact, if anything, some indicators reveal higher levels of individual religiosity in 2000 compared to 1990.

To sum up our findings concerning religious values in Turkey in the 1990s:

a. Although some rise in religiosity is observed in the first half of the decade, basically levels of religiosity have not shown dramatic changes during this period.

b. Like other Islamic societies, Turkish people are among the most devout in the world.

c. Turkish and Western publics display very similar attitudes with respect to the interference of religion and in religious leaders in political matters.

d. However, a sizeable minority in Turkey (approximately one fourth to one fifth) are in favor of organizing such areas as educational system, criminal law, government affairs or inheritance rules along religious lines.

Having sketched religious values in the last decade of the 20th century, we now turn our attention to a major focus of this paper, namely gender roles and the status of women. As we have noted in the beginning, previous research has suggested that this is *the* area where the major differences between Western and Islamic societies lie. It is a common assumption that the fault line dividing the two civilizations is defined by male-female relations and sexuality. Our question is whether or not this is true for the Turkish society as well. If the answer to this question is yes, that will provide strong evidence for the gender hypothesis because it will mean that even in a society with a tradition of secularism, Islam can still determine, or at least strongly affect, values on gender and sexuality.

Tables 4 and 5 summarize our findings on attitudes related to gender roles and gender equality. Table 4 draws a rather mixed picture. On the one hand, we observe overwhelming support (over 90 percent among female respondents but also very high among males) for the statement that 'both the husband and wife should contribute to household income.' Thus there is no objection whatsoever for the wife to be gainfully employed. On the other hand, there seems to be a preference for women to assume their traditional roles and responsibilities. For instance, close to 80 percent feel that women have to have children for fulfillment in life. 81 percent of men but also 68 percent of women believe that the husband should be the head of the household. Around 80 percent of respondents think that 'being a housewife is as fulfilling as working for pay.' These somewhat contradictory findings remind one of the well known line from the musical, *Fiddler on the Roof:* "I know it is not a shame to be poor, but it is no great honor either!" It seems like our respondents think that 'it is not a shame for a woman to work and earn money, but it is not a shame to be a good housewife and

Table 11.4. Gender Roles: Percent agreeing with the statement.

|  | Working mother can have warm and secure relationship with her children | Being a housewife as fulfilling as working for pay | Husband and wife should both contribute to household income | Woman has to have children in order to be fulfilled | In our society, men should be the head of household |
|---|---|---|---|---|---|
| 1990 Total | 55 | 80 | 86 | 74 | n.a. |
| 1990 Male | 53 | 79 | 80 | 72 | n.a. |
| 1990 Female | 58 | 81 | 92 | 76 | n.a. |
| 1996 Total | 44 | 80 | 88 | 78 | n.a. |
| 1996 Male | 41 | 82 | 82 | 79 | n.a. |
| 1996 Female | 48 | 78 | 94 | 77 | n.a. |
| 2000 Total | 70 | 79 | 88 | 78 | 75 |
| 2000 Male | 68 | 71 | 82 | 76 | 81 |
| 2000 Female | 72 | 75 | 93 | 80 | 68 |

raise children either.' In fact, the majority of both males and females think men should have priority when jobs are scarce. However, only about one fourth of the women agree that university education is more important for boys than girls. (Table 5) Thus, at least a sizeable majority is of the opinion that women should get a university education (girls have as much right to university education as boys) and contribute to household incomes when necessary. However, at the same time the majority agree that men have priority when jobs are scarce, that the husband is the head of the household, that men are expected to make better politicians and that women should keep their virginity until their wedding day at all costs (Table 5) as if to prove Norris and Inglehart that the problem is "*Eros* far more than *Demos*."

Tables 4 and 5 show that, like religiosity, gender values have also been noticeably stable during the decade of study with the possible exceptions of i) 'working mothers can have warm secure relationship with their children' and ii) 'when jobs are scarce, men should have

Table 11.5. Gender Equality: Percent agreeing with the statement.

|  | Men make better political leaders than women | When jobs scarce, men should have more right to a job | University education more important for boy | Important for women to be virgin at first marriage |
|---|---|---|---|---|
| 1990 Total | n.a. | 52 | n.a. | n.a.. |
| 1990 Male | n.a. | 60 | n.a. | n.a. |
| 1990 Female | n.a. | 45 | n.a. | n.a. |
| 1996 Total | 65 | 67 | 34 | n.a. |
| 1996 Male | 65 | 73 | 41 | n.a. |
| 1996 Female | 66 | 61 | 27 | n.a. |
| 2000 Total | 62 | 60 | 30 | 89 |
| 2000 Male | 66 | 67 | 34 | 91 |
| 2000 Female | 59 | 53 | 24 | 87 |

more right to a job.' Both questions relate to women's employment and one can speculate that attitudes about employment are deeply affected by the fluctuations in the job market.[7] It is also quite possible that the increase from 52 to 67 percent in the proportion of those who believe that 'when jobs are scarce, men should have priority over women' is related to the 1994 economic crisis in the country which resulted in great numbers losing their jobs.

Another remarkable observation one makes from data summarized in Tables 4 and 5 is the relative insignificance of the differences between males and females. Although the differences between male and female proportions are all in the expected direction, it is surprising that these differences are rather minor. To give but one example, two thirds of men agree with the statement that 'men make better political leaders then men.' On the other hand, the proportion of women who share this view is no less than 59 percent.

---

[7] Of course, one can never rule out the possibility of sampling error and/or imperfections in question wording.

To what extent are the Turkish values related to gender a product of Islam? Clearly, it is not easy to answer this question with certainty. Nevertheless, outcomes of a few simple regression equations do give us some idea. Table 6 summarizes the results of regression analyses with four dependent variables. These are:

a. University education is more important for boys then girls.
b. Wives should always obey their husbands.
c. Men make better political leaders than women.
d. It is more appropriate in our society for the husband to be the head of the household.

The independent variables included as control variables are income and education and, as expected, both have significant effects on all of the four dependent variables. More specifically, the higher the income and education, the higher the support for gender equality. What is of more interest for our purposes is the fact that our two measures of religiosity (Is the respondent a religious person—coded as yes or no, and the importance of God in one's life, coded on a 10-point scale) also had significant effects net of income and education effects. Put differently, religiosity does have a negative effect on values related to gender equality after controlling for income and education.

### Democratic Values in the 1990s

The compatibility of Islam with democracy is an intensely debated topic. There are a number of factors that lend support to the arguments that Islam and a democratic system of government are mutually exclusive. First of all, Turkey is the sole Islamic country which has been able to sustain a parliamentary democracy for a reasonable period of time and which has been able to change governments through free and competitive elections starting in 1950. But even Turkey has had problems with its democracy from time to time. Thus, clearly, there is very strong negative correlation between Islamic societies and democratic regimes. This is an empirical fact that is hard to deny. Some argue that this state of affairs is not a consequence of a particular faith, in this case Islam, but rather of a unique combination of historical, economic and political circumstances. On the other hand, others point out that the system of values generated by the Islamic religion contradicts the basic principles

Table 11.6. Effects of Religiosity on Gender Equality Attitudes: Regression Results.

| Dependent variable | University education more important for boys | | Wife should always obey her husband | | Men make better political leaders | | Men should be the head of household | |
|---|---|---|---|---|---|---|---|---|
| Independent vars | Beta | Sig | Beta | Sig | Beta | Sig | Beta | Sig |
| Income | .131 | .000 | .126 | .000 | .074 | .000 | .141 | .000 |
| Education | .169 | .000 | .198 | .000 | .178 | .000 | .190 | .000 |
| Importance of God | −.042 | .022 | −.111 | .000 | −.037 | .000 | −.109 | .000 |
| Is R religious? | .087 | .000 | .141 | .000 | .108 | .000 | .136 | .000 |

of democracy thus making it impossible to sustain the democratic system of government for long periods of time. In addition, it is contended that the Sharia law contains numerous canons that contradict principles of democracy in a very direct and blatant fashion.

We have already mentioned studies (Esmer 2002; Norris and Inglehart 2002; Pettersson 2003) comparing value systems of Islamic societies as well as individuals with non-Islamic ones. We also noted that these studies, by and large, have failed to demonstrate any appreciable differences with respect values directly or indirectly related to democracy. We now turn our attention to the level of, and changes in, democratic values in the Turkish context.

At the very minimum, one can distinguish between two dimensions of democratic values. First, one can directly probe approval or disapproval of the democratic system. Second, and perhaps more meaningfully, one can measure the prevalence of values that are assumed to support and sustain a democratic regime. Tolerance of differences, participation, support for basic freedoms and trust are some of the value dimensions that are likely to support democracy. One can also mention high levels of confidence in democratic institutions such as elected parliaments or political parties. Finally, it is also important to know how individuals define democracy to be able to meaningfully interpret their support or lack of support for democracy.

*Support for Democracy*

In the 1990s it has become highly unlikely, if not impossible, for an individual to say that one is against democracy in any part of the globe. Juan Linz coined the phrase "democracy is the only game in town" (Linz

1990) and argued that a country's democratic regime could be said to be "consolidated" when there is widespread consensus that democracy must be the 'only game in town' (Linz and Stepan 1996). It is debatable that everywhere democracy has become the only game in town in the way Linz meant it—that is, there is no significant opposition or threats to the democratic regime. However, the status and popularity enjoyed by the term 'democracy' itself is undeniable. Therefore, survey findings quoting very high levels of support for democracy in every corner of the globe should be taken with a grain of salt. Indeed, in countries surveyed by WVS/EVS around 2000, an average of 91 percent agreed that having a democratic political system would be very good or good. The two lowest proportions are found in Russia and Moldova, with 63 and 75 percent, respectively. The proportions in all other countries are above 80 percent and obviously Turkey is no exception with 89 percent in 1996 and 92 percent in 2000. Meanwhile, the proportions are 89 percent in the United States, 88 percent in Canada and 88 percent in Great Britain. Thus, it is debatable that these findings have any significance other than the fact that democracy is perceived to be the 'correct' system of government in Turkey and elsewhere.

In the WVS/EVS questionnaires, the battery on democracy has a number of additional questions to tap attitudes on various aspects of democratic systems. Answers given to these questions by the Turkish respondents are summarized in Table 7. These findings indicate that the Turkish public finds a number of faults with the democratic system but supports it despite these faults. Indeed, a majority of Turks think that democracies are indecisive. But we hasten to add that the Turkish public is in 'distinguished company' in that respect. Indeed, 82 percent in Iceland, 66 percent in Germany, 64 percent in Spain and 61 percent in the United States are also of the same opinion.

As can be seen from Table 7, results show some minimal fluctuation between 1996 and 2000 but not in a consistent manner. Therefore, we hesitate to call these differences a change in values. Rather, we believe these fluctuations reflect satisfaction or dissatisfaction with policies regarding the economy or law and order at the time of the survey. Additionally, it seems like the differences between the two survey years occur in the agree/disagree categories but the strongly agree and strongly disagree categories are remarkably stable.

One aspect of Turkish democracy that is often puzzling for Western observers of Turkish politics is the role of the armed forces in government affairs. It is puzzling because from a conventional Western point of view such prominence enjoyed by the military in Turkish political

Table 11.7. Attitudes towards Democracy
(% of respondents who strongly agree or agree with the statement).

|  | In a democracy, economy runs badly | Democracies are indecisive and have too much squablling | Democracies are not good in maint- aining order | Democracy better than all other systems despite faults |
|---|---|---|---|---|
| Turkey 1996 | 24 | 65 | 30 | 92 |
| Turkey 2000 | 31 | 57 | 37 | 89 |

life is in contradiction with the basic principles of democracy, and therefore unacceptable. On the other hand, the stated—and for many the also the true—objective of the Turkish military is the preservation of the democratic system and particularly of secularism. Ever since the founding of the Republic, a sizeable minority of the masses and perhaps the majority of the ruling elites have felt that Islamists continue to pose a threat to the secular system and that they would try to establish a government more along religious lines if they had the chance. What concerns us in this chapter is not the status and the role of the military in Turkey and whether or not this is compatible with the democratic system from a theoretical or legal perspective. This chapter is about values and attitudes. And from that perspective, two of the most stable findings about the Turkish public are their high levels of religiosity as we have already noted and their positive feelings about the Turkish armed forces. In countless surveys conducted in Turkey in the last couple of decades, the military emerged as the institution with the highest levels of confidence. This statement holds true for all social classes and demographic groups. Turkish values surveys have also confirmed this finding a number of times. For instance, in 1990, 91 percent of the respondents said they had 'a great deal' or 'quite a lot of' confidence in the armed forces. The figures were 94 percent in 1996 and 86 percent in 2000. No other institution in Turkey comes even close to these levels of confidence and there is evidence that there has not been much change in these figures since 2000. On the other hand, Turkey is certainly not unique in this respect. The proportions of those who have 'a great deal' or 'quite a lot of' confidence in the armed forces in some highly developed Western democracies are quite comparable to Turkey (for example, Finland 84 percent, G. Britain 84 percent, United States 82 percent).

Having very high levels of confidence in one's military is one thing but supporting army rule is quite another thing. And it is the feelings about the latter that perhaps sets the Turkish public unique in this respect. Would it be very good, good, bad or very bad to have the army rule the country? In 1996, a third of the Turkish respondents answered this question in the positive (i.e. very good or good). The figures were 30 percent in 2000 and 25 percent in 2001. Clearly, these are very high proportions not to be found in Western democracies. For comparison, the average for the year 2000 for all WVS/EVS countries is 16 percent (Inglehart, *et al.* 2004) and for EVS countries only 7 percent (Halman 2001). There are, however, a couple of European countries, even EU countries, that approach or even match these proportions (e.g. Romania 28 percent, Russia 19 percent, Poland 17 percent). How various populations interpret 'army rule' is an open question. It is not impossible that many Turks read this question as 'the army should continue to play the role it has played in the past.' This, we feel, is a topic that warrants further and in-depth research. For the time being, however, we conclude that the military is held in very high esteem in the eyes of the Turkish public.

### Values that Sustain Democracy

It may be assumed that the feelings about a specific political system can be performance related and therefore rather volatile. It is a well known fact that when there is a great deal of political turmoil and violence in a society and when physical security becomes a key issue, people start favoring authoritarian forms of government. Under such circumstances, it is not a surprise to observe increases in the proportion of those supporting strong leadership and even army rule. Similarly, during periods of economic failure or crises, one would expect that the percentage of those who agree that 'in democracies, the economy runs badly' would rise considerably. Therefore, these direct questions concerning the political system are, at least to some extent, 'context contaminated.' Are there more profound and more stable values that are supportive of a given system of government? Political culture tradition goes back all the way to Plato and Aristotle to answer this question in the affirmative. And systematic comparative empirical studies of 'the civic culture' (Almond and Verba 1963) in the second half of the 20th century have provided ample evidence to support this centuries-old observation. There is also strong evidence that the effects of economic prosperity on the stability of democratic regimes are not direct but rather indirect through cultural factors (Inglehart 1990).

A number of cultural variables have been suggested as correlates of democracy with the implicit or the explicit assumption that they are very useful if not essential in sustaining stable and long lasting democratic regimes. I propose to discuss two of these variables in the Turkish context: interpersonal trust and tolerance.

It was Putnam (1993) who forcefully argued about a decade and a half ago that trust was an indispensable component of social capital which, in turn, largely determined economic and political performance in Italy. In recent years, both social capital and trust have become rather popular topics in all branches of the social sciences and the number of articles and books dealing with these topics continue to increase at rapid rates. Inglehart (1997:173–4) calculated the correlation coefficient between the level interpersonal trust and the number of years of unin-terrupted democracy for 43 societies and found it to be remarkably high at 0.72. However, he assumes a reciprocal relationship between the two rather than a cause and effect relationship. He writes: "It seems likely that democratic institutions are conducive to interpersonal trust, as well as trust being conducive to democracy." (Inglehart 1997:173–4). No matter which direction(s) the causal arrow(s) go, the magnitude of the relationship between trust and enduring democracy is rather impressive with China as the outstanding exception.

Values surveys conducted since 1990 have all shown that Turkey is an extremely low trust society with one of the lowest levels of interpersonal trust among all societies surveyed. The proportion of those who say that 'most people can be trusted' are always below 10 percent and sometimes as low as half of that. Thus, when interpersonal trust is measured with that one dichotomous question, there is almost no variance within the Turkish population. This being the case, it is impossible to correlate trust levels with age, education or income. However, some elite studies show that political, media and economic elites all have higher levels of interpersonal trust compared to the general public. For instance, the figures were 39 percent for the economic elites and 19 percent for a representative sample of Bogazici University[8] students.

Fortunately, the European Social Survey (www.europeansocialsurvey. org) has three 11-point scales which allow a more detailed analysis

---

[8] The survey of economic elites was conducted in 2002 and of Bogazici Univer-sity, one of the most prestigious institutions of higher education in Turkey, students in 2003.

of interpersonal trust. One of these questions is worded in exactly the same way as the WVS/EVS question we have mentioned above but requires placement on an 11-point scale rather then a simple yes or no answer. The distribution of the answers given to this question[9] only confirms that Turkey is a very low trust society. A fourth of the respondents marked '0' on this scale and one half chose 0, 1 or 2. The mean score for Turkey was 3.01, the lowest among the 25 European countries for which data were reported.

These findings indicate that if interpersonal trust is related to democracy (and we have just seen that it is indeed) then we can draw the following conclusions:

a.  If trust is an independent variable affecting the stability and quality of democracy, Turkey is in a rather disadvantaged position due to this cultural factor.
b.  If, on the other hand, trust is a dependent variable with democratic institutions fostering higher levels of trust, Turkey will have to live under democratic rule for a long period of time before it can claim a 'trusting culture' since cultural change is a slow process.
c.  If there is a non-recursive relationship and if lower levels of trust produce lower levels of democracy, which in turn will have further negative effects on trust levels, at least one more variable is needed (economic prosperity, perhaps?) in the equation to break this self-reinforcing system.

Our next question is whether or not this situation, that is, such low levels of interpersonal trust is related to Islam within the Turkish context. Once again, the ESS has turned the dichotomous WVS/EVS question of 'do you consider yourself to be a religious person?' into an 11-point scale. The Pearson correlation coefficient between these two scales (trust and religiosity) is a mere 0.05. Thus, we can comfortably assert that, at least in contemporary Turkish society, there is no linear relationship[10] between Islam and interpersonal trust. Norris and Inglehart's (2002) conclusions are confirmed within the Turkish society with respect to

---

[9]  Fieldwork was completed in May 2006 (n=1856).
[10]  Actually, further analysis reveals that there is no non-linear relationship either between the two variables.

interpersonal trust. Devout Muslims do not appear to have either lower or higher levels of interpersonal trust.

It would not be an exaggeration to state that democracies depend on the explicit recognition and mutual toleration of differences—not only political and ideological but racial, ethnic religious, etc. as well. This is easier said than done, however, and throughout history, humankind has found it most difficult to accept differences. Human species seems to have a special gift for immediately creating the 'other', based on whatever characteristic is available at hand, and then it is only a short step to various forms of discrimination, oppression or even physical violence. Even the most advanced contemporary societies are not immune to widespread manifestations of intolerance and no society can yet claim that racism is completely a thing of the past.

The WVS/EVS questionnaires have a classical 'would you like [. . . .] as your neighbor?' battery to measure levels of tolerance for different or marginal or deviant groups. The battery has been kept in all rounds of the surveys although the items included have not been exactly the same. Comparative data indicate that the Turkish society, usually proud of its assumingly tolerant past, has rather low levels of tolerance for differences, at least as measured by the WVS/EVS battery.

The proportions of those who said that they would *not* want certain groups as their neighbors in 1990 (WVS), 2000 (WVS) and 2001 (EVS) are as follows:

|                                           | 1990 | 2000 | 2001 |
|-------------------------------------------|------|------|------|
| People of a different race or color       | 39   | 31   | 34   |
| People who drink too much                 | 88   | 87   | 88   |
| Emotionally unstable people               | 73   | 76   | 77   |
| People of a different religion            | na   | 35   | na   |
| Immigrants, foreign workers               | 32   | 37   | 45   |
| People with AIDS                          | 91   | 84   | 81   |
| Homosexuals                               | 93   | 91   | 90   |
| Christians                                | 59   | 45   | 52   |
| Extreme rightists                         | na   | na   | 68   |
| Extreme leftists                          | na   | na   | 67   |

These figures indicate rather high levels of intolerance. Furthermore, they have been rather stable in the 1990s. In fact, some proportions are almost identical after 10 or 11 years. There seem to be two exceptions, however: tolerance for immigrants and foreign workers has decreased considerably during this period while it has increased somewhat for people with HIV/AIDS. Proportions of unwanted neighbors are usually much lower in Western countries. Contesting the conclusion that this is due to higher levels of tolerance, two arguments have been offered as alternative explanations. First, it is argued that the more educated segments of any population know the 'right' answers to these questions. This is the well known social desirability effect in survey research. Since the levels of education are much higher in advanced societies, it follows that their populations will offer the 'right' answers more frequently. Second, it is pointed out that the meaning of a neighbor is very different in traditional as opposed to modern and postmodern societies. Indeed, a neighbor in downtown Manhattan is quite a different thing from a neighbor in Monticello, Utah. Similarly, people in rural Anatolia feel much closer to a neighbor than apartment dwellers in Paris or London. Thus, in a traditional environment, a neighbor is more like part of the family. Therefore, it is only natural that people are much more selective and demanding about their neighbors in these societies.

It is very likely that both the methodological and the sociological explanations outlined above have some truth in them. However, it is highly improbable that it is only these two explanations that account for these findings. It is also a fact that the levels of intolerance are generally high in the Turkish society which, by the way, is certainly not alone in the world in this respect. Indeed, 28 percent of Bulgarians, 24 percent of Romanians, and 20 percent of Croatians, for instance, do not want neighbors of a different race.

Returning to our original question, is the level of tolerance related to religiosity in general and Islam in specific? Cross tabulations between the religiosity question ('Are you a religious person?') and the items in the neighbors battery show rather strong and significant relations between the two, indicating that the higher the level of religiosity, the lower the level of tolerance. However, it is quite possible that this is a spurious relationship reflecting the effects of income and education rather than religiosity. To control for these variables, we run a multiple regression with the level of tolerance (a total tolerance scale constructed by adding up the items in the battery with high scores indicating higher levels of tolerance) as the dependent variable and income, education and age as the independent variables. The results are not surprising: while the coefficients for all four independent variables are statistically significant, a comparison of betas shows that the order of importance is education, religiosity, income and age (betas are 0.279, 0.149, 0.137, and 0.045, respectively). Like gender equality values, tolerance values are also impacted by religiosity controlling for demographics. Higher levels of religiosity translate into lower levels of tolerance as measured by the neighbors battery.

*Change or Stability?*

Finally, we take a very brief look at selected values in 1990 and 2000 to assess the degree of change or stability in various spheres. Table 8 summarizes our findings for 1990 and 2000 in a number of value dimensions[11] covering basic areas included in WVS/EVS questionnaires. Of the 36 questions listed in Table 8, only 9 have changed by at least five percentage points[12] in this ten-year period. The changes relate to:

a.  A moderate increase in tolerance for people with HIV/AIDS and a moderate decrease in tolerance for immigrants and foreign workers.
b.  A rather significant shift from the center of the political spectrum to the right while the proportion of the left is unchanged.
c.  An increasing emphasis on economic development and stability as asked in the materialism-postmaterialism batteries. However, fighting rising prices seems to have decreased in importance.
d.  A moderate increase in the proportion of those who have signed a petition.

Overall, the decade of the 1990s has been a period of value stability and certainly not a period of change in Turkey.

*Conclusions*

Turkey is the only Islamic society that has provided time series data for the values studies since 1990. However, it is a rather atypical Islamic society with its long tradition of a secular government and a history of modernization and Westernization. Nevertheless, Turks are, for the most part, devout Muslims and levels of religiosity, be it faith or practice, have maintained their very high levels throughout the 1990s. Drawing upon research which argues that the main cultural difference between Muslims and others is in the area of gender and sexuality, we looked

---

[11] In order to avoid repetition, values related to gender and women's status have been omitted from Table 8 since these have been analyzed in some detail in the previous section.

[12] Obviously, the meaning of a five percentage point change for a proportion of, say eight percent, is very different from a five percentage point change in a proportion of 50 percent.

Table 11.8. Turkish Values in the 1990s: Change or stability?.

| Values related to: | Question | 1990 (%) | 2000 (%) | Minimum 5 percentage points change? |
|---|---|---|---|---|
| Happiness; life satisfaction | Very happy or happy | 81 | 78 | No |
| | Average life satisfaction (4,5,6 or 7 on the scale) | 53 | 52 | No |
| Family; marriage; sexual freedom | Family very important or quite important | 100 | 99 | No |
| | Marriage is an outdated institution (agree) | 12 | 9 | No |
| | Approve of single women having children | 6 | 6 | No |
| | Individuals should have complete sexual freedom (agree) | 23 | 26 | No |
| | Make parents proud aim in life (strongly agree or agree) | 97 | 94 | No |
| Important values for children (top 3 items on the list) | Good manners | 92 | 92 | No |
| | Hard work | 74 | 74 | No |
| | Responsibility | 64 | 63 | No |
| Work; employment | Work very important or important | 87 | 88 | No |
| | Good pay important | 89 | 91 | Yes (+) |
| | Interesting work important | 48 | 49 | No |
| | Fair for a more efficient secretary to get higher salary | 70 | 77 | Yes (+) |
| Religion; religiosity | Religiosity important value for children | 46 | 44 | No |
| | Believe in God | 98 | 98 | No |
| | R a religious person | 78 | 81 | No |
| | God is important in R's life (8,9 or 10 on the scale) | 83 | 90 | Yes (+) |
| | Mosque attendance once/week or more (males only) | 64 | 67 | No |
| Tolerance of differences (do not want as neighbor) | Immigrants, foreign workers | 32 | 37 | Yes (+) |
| | People with AIDS | 91 | 84 | Yes (-) |
| | Homosexuals | 91 | 91 | No |
| Left-Right ideology | Left (0,1 or 2 on the scale) | 18 | 17 | No |
| | Right (8, 9 or 10 on the scale) | 17 | 29 | Yes (+) |
| Politics; political participation | Never discuss politics with friends | 44 | 48 | No |
| | Not interested in politics at all | 30 | 34 | No |
| | Have or may sign a petition | 37 | 42 | Yes (+) |
| Materialism-postmaterialism | Most important in battery 1: economic development | 60 | 66 | Yes (+) |
| | Most important in battery 2: fighting rising prices | 34 | 27 | Yes (-) |
| | Most important in battery 3: stable economy | 35 | 42 | Yes (+) |
| Identity; nationalism; patriotism | Above all, belong to Turkey | 46 | 43 | No |
| | Above all, belong to region/city/town | 34 | 32 | No |
| | Above all, belong to whole world | 7 | 10 | No |
| | Above all, belong to Europe | 1 | 1 | No |
| | Very proud to be a Turk | 68 | 67 | No |
| | Not proud to be a Turk (not proud or not proud at all) | 8 | 11 | No |

at values in this sphere and have confirmed the previous findings in the Turkish context. Furthermore, we have found that gender values are linked to religiosity in addition to demographic characteristics such as income and education. Similarly, intolerance is also related to levels of religiosity, a finding that is probably valid for Catholic, Protestant and Jewish communities as well. So the causal chain is likely to be as follows: the higher the level of religiosity, the lower the level of tolerance in monotheist cultures. Islamic societies have very high levels of religiosity. Therefore, Islam has an indirect effect on tolerance/intolerance—a value which is very conducive to democracy.

We have found no correlation between religiosity and support for democracy or interpersonal trust.

Finally, Turkish society did not experience any significant value changes in the 1990s.

## References

Almond, Gabriel A. and S. Verba. 1963. *The Civic Culture*. Princeton: Princeton University Press.
Esmer, Yilmaz. 2002. "Is There an Islamic Civilization?" *Comparative Sociology*, vol. 1, no. 3–4, 26–98.
Esmer, Yilmaz. 2006. "Turkey: Torn Between two Civilizations." in Harrison, Lawrence E. and P. L. Berger, eds., *Developing Cultures: Case Studies*. New York: Routledge. pp. 217–231.
Halman, Loek. 2001. *The European Values Study: a Third Wave*. Tilburg: Tilburg University.
Huntington, Samuel, P. 1998. *The Clash of Civilizations and the Remaking of the World Order*. London: Touchstone Books.
Inglehart, Ronald. 1990. *Culture Shift in Advanced Industrial Society*. Princeton: Princeton University Press.
———. 1997. *Modernization and Postmodernization: Cultural, Economic and Political Change in 43 Societies*. Princeton: Princeton University Press.
———, ed., 2003. *Islam, Gender, Culture, and Democracy*. Ontario, Canada: de Sitter Publications.
——— et. al., eds., 2004. *Human Beliefs and Values*. Mexico: Siglio Veintiuno Editores.
Inglehart, Ronald and C. Welzel. 2005. *Modernization, Cultural Change and Democracy: The Human Development Sequence*. Cambridge: Cambridge University Press.
Linz, Juan. 1990. "Transitions to Democracy." *Washington Quarterly*. vol. 13.
Linz, Juan and Stepan, Alfred. 1996. *Problems of Democratic Transition and Consolidation*. Baltimore: The Johns Hopkins University Press.
Norris, Pippa and R. Inglehart. 2002. "Islamic Culture and Democracy: Testing the 'Clash of Civilizations' Thesis." *Comparative Sociology*, vol. 1, no. 3–4, 235–664.
———. 2004. *Sacred and Secular: Religion and Politics Worldwide*. Cambridge: Cambridge University Press.
Pettersson, Thorleif. 2003. "Muslim Orientations toward Global Governance: The United Nations between Islam and the Secularized West." Paper presented at the

conference on "Explaining the Worldviews of the Islamic Publics: Theoretical and Methodological Issues." Cairo, Egypt, February 2–6, 2003.

Timur, Taner. 1994. *Osmanli Kimligi*. 2nd ed. Istanbul: Hil Yayin.
Putnam, Robert D. 1993. *Making Democracies Work: civic traditions in modern Italy*. Princeton: Princeton University Press.
UNDP. 2005. *Human Development Report*. New York: UNDP.

PART FOUR

ASIA

CHAPTER TWELVE

# VALUE CHANGE AND DEMOCRATIZATION IN SOUTH KOREA

Soo Young Auh

## I. *Introduction*

South Korea has undergone dramatic change in almost all fields in the last decades. Following its liberation in 1945 from 35 years of Japanese colonial rule, South Korea experienced a bloody war for three years, and authoritarian military dictatorships for more than two decades. However, since the 1987 grand compromise between authoritarian rulers and democratic forces, the South Korean people have enjoyed democratic political systems, peaceful power transfers have occurred, and, in 1997, the opposition political party took power in a competitive and free presidential election. The local political autonomy systems have been restored.

After the Korean War, the South Korean people suffered poverty, with a per capita income of only around a hundred dollars until the early part of 1960s. The South Koreans did, however, achieve the "Miracle of Han River," achieving around ten thousand dollars per capita income in the middle of the 1990s. An economic crisis in 1997 due to the shortage of foreign currency resulted in the IMF bailout, but, after three years of hard work, South Korea was able to overcome the economic crisis, achieving again the previous level of economic prosperity. In the early part of 2000, South Korea had the 12th largest export-import trade by volume in the world. In this respect, South Korea is one of the best countries to test the relationship between environmental factors and value changes.

According to the political socialization theory, people's value systems are dependent on the environment they were exposed to during the character formation stage of their lives. Those who grew up in a materialistically abundant and physically secure environment are likely to prefer post-materialist values to materialist values. Comparative research conducted in 18 countries in Europe demonstrates that this pattern of value change, in turn, brings about a change in politics (Inglehart 1971, 981–1017; 1977, 21–71; 1990).

From empirical research done in 1990, it was found that South Korea, too, is experiencing a pattern of value change, and thus political change, similar to that of many European societies. The empirical research revealed that there are many post-materialists in South Korea, especially in the 20 to 30 age group (Soo Young Auh 1992, 137–159; 1997, 24–31). Postmaterialists stressed active involvement in their work-places and in politics, and expressed a keen interest in freedom of speech and the enhancement of quality of life. They have contributed to the process of democratization, and it seems that they will remain as a powerful force for the future in sustaining democracy in South Korea.

This chapter, then, attempts to analyze the following questions: In what ways have the South Korean people's basic values changed given the rapid institutional change in South Korean society? With the process of prosperity, has there been an increase in the size of the postmaterialist population in South Korea? How have changes in values affected attitudes towards democratic values such as civic tolerance, trust and participation? These questions will be analyzed using World Value Survey data collected in South Korea in 1990, 1996, and 2001.

## II. *Theoretical Framework*

According to Abraham Maslow's value priority thesis, people first select the value that best satisfies essential conditions for survival (Maslow 1954). Only when essential biological needs are met, will people then choose values that satisfy the need for physical safety. Although physical safety is as important as biological needs, an average person's value priority is such that a starving person will compromise his or her life in order to satisfy his or her hunger. It is when physical and economic needs are satisfied to a certain degree that people will pursue non-materialistic values of self-esteem such as love, belonging and respect, along with the pursuit of intellectual and aesthetic values. Although it is difficult to clearly distinguish the value priority order of non-materialistic values, the fact remains that materialistic values must be satisfied to certain extent for there to be a pursuit of non-materialistic values (Inglehart 1990, 67–69; James Davies 1963).

When the above theory is supplemented by socialization theory, the relationship between value change and generation on cohort effects can be understood. It is argued that the value priorities established during a person's character-formation years (hereafter referred to as formation period) will, to a great extent, continue to prevail into adulthood. In other words, basic character structures formed during the pre-adulthood period will not dramatically alter even after adulthood is reached. This argument can be traced back to Plato, and is present in the writings of contemporary social scientists. It should be noted, however, that the argument does not necessarily imply that people's personality structures do not change at all in their adulthood. Rather, character structures formed during pre-adulthood last for many years, possibly a lifetime (Block 1981, 27–43; Jennings and Niemi 1981; Jennings and Markus 1984, 1000–1018).

From the two theories, it can be understood that there will be a big difference in value-formation depending on different generations. According to Maslow's theory, in the generation that has experienced deprivation, poverty and war, there will be many who would consider materialistic values to be of great importance. Conversely, in the generation that experienced materialistic abundance and physical security, there will be many who would consider post-materialistic values to be of importance. According to early socialization theory, because the character-structure or value priority formed during the formation period does not change overnight, but rather lasts for a long time, the value system that places importance on materialistic/post-materialistic values will not dramatically alter in people's adulthood.

From the perspective of its historical environment, it can be said that South Korea's population consists of both a generation that is likely to hold materialistic values, as well as a generation that is likely to hold post-materialist values. After experiencing war, deprivation and poverty under Japanese colonization (1915–1945), and again during the Korean War (1950–53), the process of extremely rapid industrialization in the 1970s enabled South Korea to experience economic growth and, with it, improvements in the standard of living, and freedom from poverty and deprivation. In addition, even with the possible threat from North Korea, South Korea has continuously maintained peace and stability. Especially in the 1990s, with increased per capita income, with freedom of travel increasing contacts with other civilizations, and with the ongoing development of communications technology, there has been a great change in the lives of every South Korean.

It could be said that such a contrasting short-term historical experience will enhance the difference in value preferences between different generations. In other words, it might be assumed that the generation that has experienced war, poverty and deprivation will predominantly be materialists, while the generation that has experienced material abundance, peace and stability will be post-materialists.

What must not be overlooked, however, is the possibility that the value preference formed during a person's formation period may change as he or she reaches adulthood. Furthermore, there is also the possibility that a person may have value priority that is different to the general trend, as well as the possibility that the value preference may alter due to a change in the historical condition. Hence, it must be kept in mind that post-materialists may, and do, exist in the older generation or age cohorts.

### III. *Measurement of Materialistic and Post-Materialistic Value*

Can people's values be measured by mass surveys? Philip Converse (1964, 201–261; 1970) argued that, because public value priorities are extremely volatile, measuring their systems of value priorities remains a difficult task. Furthermore, people generally tend to answer superficially and according to convenience because they often lack a definite attitude. Therefore, when the same question is asked again after a given time interval, there is a low correlation between responses to the first and second round of questions (Sydney Verba 1967, 317–334; Inglehart 1977, 24–26). In addition, there are other difficulties arising from the fact that the general public does not always have a concrete or definite attitude toward a given issue. Mostly, however, the difficulty lies with errors in the questionnaires, resulting in a failure to accurately assess people's attitudes.

As previous research has indicated (Frank Andrews & Stephen Withey 1974, 1–26; Robert Lane 1962; Inglehart 1997, 26–7), the difficulties of accurate measurement of people's attitude can be overcome by using scientifically evaluated and sophistically designed questionnaires. In an in-depth interview, unlike a questionnaire that consists of several questions, people's attitudes can better be measured. However, although depth interviewing is naturally most effective, because of the drain on finances and time needed to implement a depth interview, in reality, it is rarely used. Therefore, the best option in conducting research that aims to assess people's attitudes is to refine and increase the reliability and validity of the questions asked. This research survey will make use of the following twelve-item value index to measure people's material-istic/post-materialistic values:

"Choose what you consider to be the most and second most important long-term goal of a nation."

| | A. The most important | B. Second most important |
|---|---|---|
| 1–1. Attaining a high level of economic growth | ( ) | ( ) |
| 1–2. Maintaining strong defense forces | ( ) | ( ) |
| 1–3. More say in their jobs and in their communities | ( ) | ( ) |
| 1–4. Make our cities more beautiful | ( ) | ( ) |

"Choose what you consider to be the most important and second most important goal of a nation."

| | A. The most important | B. Second most important |
|---|---|---|
| 2–1. Maintaining order | ( ) | ( ) |
| 2–2. More say in government decisions | ( ) | ( ) |
| 2–3. Fighting rising prices | ( ) | ( ) |
| 2–4. Protecting freedom of speech | ( ) | ( ) |

"Choose what you consider to be the most important and the second most important national goal."

| | A. The most important | B. Second most important |
|---|---|---|
| 3–1. Stable economy | ( ) | ( ) |
| 3–2. Less impersonal and more humane society | ( ) | ( ) |
| 3–3. Ideas count more than money | ( ) | ( ) |
| 3–4. Fighting crime | ( ) | ( ) |

By repeatedly asking respondents about the twelve-item value index, the questionnaire tried to accurately determine their value system. If, from items 1–1 to 1–4, a certain respondent chose "the maintenance of high economic growth" as the most important goal of a nation, and "national defense reinforcement" as the second, it can be inferred that the respondent considers materialistic values to be important. Conversely, if a certain respondent chose "active involvement in the work place and community" as second most important, it can be inferred that the respondent considers post-materialistic values to be important.

If a respondent chooses 6 materialistic values—economic growth, defense reinforcement, social order, price and inflation control, fight against crime—it can be inferred that the person is a pure materialist. On the other hand, if a respondent chooses 6 post-materialistic values—active involvement in the work place and community, improvement of the environment, active participation in politics, freedom of speech, development towards a humane society, and development towards an idea-oriented society—it can be inferred that the person is a pure post-materialist.

Respondents' attitudes are analyzed using the factor analysis method to determine whether public value preferences between materialistic and post-materialistic values vary as suggested in theory. The results are shown below as Table 1.

As can be seen in Table 1, for the 1990 data, the six materialistic values show a trend of negative factor loading, while the six post-materialistic values show a trend of positive factor loading. This trend holds for both the 1996 and 2001 data. As explained by the theory, the materialistic/post-materialistic values clearly divide the priorities of materialists and post-materialists. Among the post-materialistic values, only the "development towards an idea-oriented society" variable shows a factor loading of .18, whereas all the other values show a factor loading above .33.

We will now make a distinction between a materialist and post-materialist. A respondent who chose all six materialistic values out of twelve-item value will be considered as a pure materialist. However, in reality, a respondent choosing all six of these values is uncommon, and thus we will consider even those who have chosen one post-materialistic value and five materialistic values as being a materialist. Likewise, those who chose one materialistic value and five post-materialistic values will be considered a post-materialist. Those who chose less than either four post-materialistic values or materialistic values will be considered as holders of mixed values (hereafter referred to as mixed-type).

Table 12.1. "Value Priorities of South Koreans: Materialistic and Post-materialistic Values".

| Variables | Loadings on First Principle Component | | |
|---|---|---|---|
| | 1990 | 1996 | 2001 |
| Price/inflation control | −.41 | −.54 | −.52 |
| Economic stability | −.59 | −.46 | −.45 |
| Fighting against crime | −.38 | −.46 | −.43 |
| High economic growth | −.60 | −.45 | −.45 |
| Maintenance of social order | −.47 | −.44 | −.45 |
| National defense reinforcement | −.45 | −.43 | −.49 |
| Improvement of the environment | .40 | .33 | .35 |
| Development towards an idea-oriented society | .18 | .46 | .39 |
| Development towards a humane society | .72 | .46 | .39 |
| Protection of freedom of speech | .57 | .48 | .38 |
| Active public participation in policy decision-making | .46 | .51 | .61 |
| Active involvement in the workplace and community | .61 | .53 | .50 |

• Data were weighted.

Table 12.2. The Distribution of Materialists and Post-Materialists.

| | 1990 | N | 1996 | N | 2001 | N |
|---|---|---|---|---|---|---|
| Materialists | 31.3% | 378 | 23.9% | 295 | 23.4% | 281 |
| Mixed-type | 64.1 | 773 | 71.2 | 878 | 71.7 | 864 |
| Post-Materialists | 4.6 | 55 | 4.9 | 61 | 4.5 | 55 |
| Total | 100% | 1206 | 100% | 1234 | 100% | 1200 |

For comparison, Table 2 shows the outcomes of the 1990, 1996 and 2001 surveys. In the 1990 survey, there are more than six times more materialists than post-materialists in South Korea: 31.3% were materialists, 4.6% post-materialists, and most were mixed-type (64.1%). According to the 1996 survey, 23.9% were materialists, 4.9% post-materialists, and 71.2% mixed-types. In the 2001 survey, 23.4% were materialists, 4.5% post-materialists, and 71.7% mixed-type. When the three surveys are compared, there is a small decrease in materialists in 1996, but there is almost no change in post-materialists, the figures remaining steady at 4.6% in 1990, 4.9% in 1996 and 4.5% in 2001. Because the South Korean people suffered an economic crisis for several years at the end of the 1990s, it might be expected that the number of materialists would increase considerably, while the number of post-materialists would decrease sharply. However, it emerges that there was a very slight decrease in post-materialists, only 0.4 percent points from 4.9 percent in 1996 (when South Korea enjoyed economic prosperity), to 4.5 percent in 2001 (when the South Korean economic situation began to improve after the economic crisis). For the materialists, rather than an increase, there was a very small decrease, from 23.9 percent in 1996, to 23.4 percent in 2001. It can be said that the number of materialists and post-materialists has remained constant over the 10 year period, even though South Korean society experienced economic instability during these years.

## IV. Value Change: Is it Life Cycle Effect or Generational Change?

Is materialism/post-materialism the outcome of the political and economic environment under which a person has been socialized? Is an environment in which constant threats to the physical well-being of a person exist—an environment of poverty, destitution, and war—likely to encourage materialists? Are those who have been socialized in conditions of relative prosperity without threats to physical well-being likely to be post-materialists? In order to verify these hypotheses, diverse analysis and verifications are needed, but, in this study, we will focus on examining the political and economical differences in relation to differences in age.

The difference in the level of poverty and prosperity experienced by South Koreans since 1945 can be understood in relation to age cohorts. In 1990, when the first survey was administered, those now in their 50s were born in the 1940s, just after South Korea gained its independence, and grew up in the period of the Korean War and the hard times that followed. On the other hand, those now in their 30s were in their teens in the post-1970s period, when South Korea began to step out of poverty and move towards economic development. Those now in their 20s were teenagers in the 1980s, when the South Korean economy reached the highest point of growth, free from a substantial threat of war. We will analyze the data in Table 3 with these major political and economic changes in mind.

The 1990 data show that 15.6% were materialists and 10% post-materialists in their 20s, 28.2 % materialists and 3.1% post-material-

Table 12.3. Distribution of Value Types by Age Cohort—1990 Survey.

| Age<br>Year of birth | 20s<br>1962–72 | 30s<br>1952–61 | 40s<br>1942–51 | 50s<br>1932–41 | 60s<br>before 1931 |
|---|---|---|---|---|---|
| Materialists | 15.6% | 28.2 | 34.4 | 38.0 | 65.4 |
| Mixed-type | 74.4 | 68.7 | 63.9 | 59.5 | 34.5 |
| Post-materialists | 10.0 | 3.1 | 1.7 | 2.5 | 0.2 |
| Total | 100% | 100 | 100 | 100 | 100 |
| N | 374 | 319 | 197 | 162 | 147 |

Table 12.4. Distribution of Value Types by Age Cohort—1996 Survey.

| Age<br>Year of Birth | Early 20s<br>after 1973 | 20s<br>1962–72 | 30s<br>1952–61 | 40s<br>1942–51 | 50s<br>1932–41 | 60s<br>before 1931 |
|---|---|---|---|---|---|---|
| Materialists | 4.3% | 13.2 | 19.5 | 29.8 | 42.4 | 69.0 |
| Mixed-type | 82.6 | 79.9 | 76.6 | 66.9 | 57.3 | 31.0 |
| Post-materialists | 13.1 | 6.9 | 3.8 | 3.3 | 0.3 | 0.0 |
| Total | 100% | 100 | 100 | 100 | 100 | 100 |
| N | 126 | 379 | 276 | 204 | 175 | 74 |

Table 12.5. Distribution of Value Types by Age Cohort—2001 Survey.

| Age<br>Year of Birth | Early 20s<br>after 1979 | 20s<br>1973–78 | 30s<br>1962–72 | 40s<br>1952–61 | 50s<br>1942–51 | 60s<br>before 1941 |
|---|---|---|---|---|---|---|
| Materialists | 4.2% | 13.1 | 23.0 | 19.3 | 34.6 | 39.9 |
| Mixed-type | 82.1 | 78.3 | 72.4 | 77.3 | 63.5 | 60.1 |
| Post-materialists | 13.7 | 8.6 | 4.7 | 3.4 | 1.9 | 0.0 |
| Total | 100% | 100 | 100 | 100 | 100 | 100 |
| N | 95 | 175 | 322 | 264 | 162 | 183 |

ists in their 30s, and 34.4% materialists and 1.7% post-materialists in their 40s. Those in the 50s and 60s age cohorts show an even greater distribution gap; materialists are the majority of the population, while post-materialists are virtually non-exist. The 1996 data in Table 4 show a similar pattern, as does the 2001 data shown in Table 5. In South Korea, there is a noticeable difference in the age cohorts and difference in their socialization environment. Whereas post-materialists exist to some extent in the 20s and 30s age cohorts, having been socialized in conditions of relatively prosperity, post-materialists are rare in the 40s and above age cohort, having been socialized under much tougher conditions.

It is uncertain whether the above distribution pattern of value types in relation to age is due to differences in the environment in which the people were raised, or if it is merely due to the conservative characteristic attributed to the aging process. In order to examine this problem in depth, comparisons will be made among the 3 survey data in Tables 3, 4, and 5.

In the 20s age cohort, those born in the years between 1962 and 1972, there were 15.6% materialists in 1990, 13.2% in 1996, and 23% in 2001. Although the number of materialists in the youngest cohort fluctuates with changes in economic situation, the 30s age cohort shows more consistency, and for those born between 1952 and 1961, there were 28.2% materialists in 1990, 19.5% in 1996, and 19.3% in 2001. In the 40s cohort, those born between 1942 and 1951, there were 34.4% materialists in 1990, 29.8% in 1996, and 34.6% in 2001. In the 50s cohort, those born between 1932 and 1941, there were 38.0% materialists in 1990, 42.4% in 1996, and 39.9% in 2001. We found in the three surveys that the five age cohorts show a little change in their values with the increase in age. Materialists decreased slightly in 1996, when South Koreans experienced economic prosperity, and increased in 2001, when the economic situation deteriorated.

The post-materialists, on the other hand, show a slightly different pattern to that of the materialists. In the 20s cohort, 10% were post-materialists in 1990, 6.9% in 1996, and 4.7% in 2001. This cohort shows a noticeable change in their values with the increase in age. In contrast to the decrease of post-materialists among the youngest cohort, the 30s cohort showed a different pattern. The number of post-materialists did not decrease as time passed, remaining almost constant: 3.1% in 1990, 3.8% in 1996, and 3.4% in 2001. In the 40s cohort, 1.7% were post-materialists in 1990, 3.3% in 1996, and 1.9% in 2001. For those in their 50s, 2.5% were post-materialists in 1990, 0.3% in 1996, and 0% in 2001. The youngest age cohort in the 1996 survey, those in their early 20s who were born after 1973, showed the sharpest decrease among all cohorts, from 13.1% in 1996 to 8.6% in 2001.

The data show that a decrease of post-materialists is most vivid among those in their twenties. However, there is no sharp rise of materialists among those in their thirties and forties. We found that those in their twenties tend to be influenced greatly by the economic situation, while those in their thirties and forties tend to be less affected. Why are the youngest age cohort most influenced by the nation's economic condition? This phenomenon might be related to the special condition of the youngest cohort in finding jobs; when economic condition worsen, they face a harder time in finding jobs. Therefore, they are more likely to prefer materialistic values.

The data shown above do not clearly support the hypothesis that, as one ages, the more conservative and, thus, more materialistic one becomes. Furthermore, neither can the hypothesis that the post-materialist population uniformly decreases as age increases be supported. The data disproves the hypothesis that the increase in materialists, or decrease in post-materialists, is due to conservativeness of age (life cycle difference). Therefore, it can safely be said that the noticeable distribution difference of value types in relation to age cohort in South Korea is due to the different environment experienced during the character formation period (generation difference).

The findings of our study is in accord with Inglehart (1990, 71–103). Although the controversial point in many of the studies on the nature of value change is whether it is due to the difference in life cycle rather than that of political generation, our data validate the latter argument.

## V. *The Effect of Value Change on Democratic Values*

What kind of impact is there on the development of democracy when there is an increase in the people who prefer post-materialist values? Do post-materialists prefer democratic values more than do materialists?

It can be assumed that the appearance of a generation that endorses post-materialistic values has a positive impact on the democratization of South Korea. This is because the concept of post-materialism itself is comprised of the essential political principles of democracy. Post-materialistic values, as explained before, consist of values that emphasize protection of freedom of speech, active participation in the policy decision-making, active involvement in the work place and community, development toward a humane society, improvement of the environment, and development toward an idea-oriented society. The fact that post-materialists regard these values as important is equivalent to the fact that they consider the political principle of democracy to be important. Therefore, we could even go as far as to say that, to brighten the future of democracy in South Korea, the move toward post-materialism is required.

An important question to be asked now is whether or not post-materialists prefer democratic values other than those preferred by materialists or mixed-types. Our study will now be to comparatively analyze the differences in attitudes of post-materialists and materialists in relation to important democratic values such as civic tolerance, critical outlook, and trust in the political institutions as well as social institutions, and, finally, political participation.

## 1. *Civic Tolerance*

One of the basic values essential for the growth of democracy is tolerance, specifically political tolerance and civic tolerance. Political tolerance refers to open attitudes toward different political ideologies, beliefs and minority opinions, while civic tolerance means that citizens show open minds toward minorities, alienated groups and fellow citizens whose behavior is not usual (Paul Abramson 1983, 241–259). The question of how much tolerance is practiced toward minority or minority opinion is a critical indicator of the smooth operation of democracy, for democracy can be realized by respecting differences in opinion, especially minority views. Therefore, the level of civic tolerance in relation to the different value types will be examined.

Respondents were asked if they are likely to accept people such as drug addicts, alcoholics, people with criminal records, emotionally unstable people, and foreign workers as a neighbor. In order to make a scale for civic tolerance, we give 1 point to those respondents who refuse to accept one of the five categories of people, and 2 points to those respondents who accept one of them. We add up each respondent's scores for the five categories. For easy comparison, the scale has been standardized. The population mean is zero on the scale. Positive numbers indicate that a person shows a more tolerant attitude than the average of all respondents, while negative numbers show a less tolerant attitude than the average. The scores of the scale have been multiplied by 100 for easy visual display.

Table 6 shows that post-materialists demonstrated the highest civic tolerance among the three value types. They showed the highest willingness to accept people who are not generally well received in society, such as violators of the law, drug-addicts, and the emotionally unstable. This pattern is visible in all three surveys data. An important finding is that civic tolerance among post-materialists increases over time: 38 in 1990, 49 in 1996, and 66 in 2001. Materialists, on the other hand, showed far less civic tolerance. This trend does not change much as the data show: –23 in 1990, –7 in 1996, and –23 in 2001. Even after

Table 12.6. Civic Tolerance by Value Types, Education, Age, Gender and Urbanization.

|  | 1990 | 1996 | 2001 |
|---|---|---|---|
| Materialists | −23 (−22)*** | −7 (−6) | −23 (−22) |
| Mixed type | 10 (10) | −1 (−1) | 4 (3) |
| Post-materialists | 38 (36) | 49 (48) | 66 (65) |
| Men | 14 (21)*** | 11 (10) | 10 (6) |
| Women | −13 (−12) | −10 (−10) | −8 (−5) |
| 20s | 29 (21)* | 12 (12) | 31 (18) |
| 30 | 4 (0) | 11 (11) | 7 (0) |
| 40 | −23 (−21) | −7 (−7) | −4 (−3) |
| 50 | −36 (−27) | −12 (−12) | −22 (−12) |
| 60+ | −11 (7) | −24 (−23) | −36 (−14) |
| Primary education | −26 (−25)** | −7 (−6) | −28 (−27) |
| Secondary education | 8 (8 ) | −2 (−2) | −7 (−13) |
| Higher education | 18 (17) | 11 (10) | 29 (23) |
| Rural areas | −21 (−19)*** | −7 (−6) | −15 (−14) |
| Mid cities | 30 (30) | 20 (19) | 0 (0) |
| Large cities | 7 (−0.5) | 6 (5) | 6 (6) |

* Control for education only
** Control for age only
*** Control for education and age

controlling for the effect of education and age on civic tolerance, the wide gap between materialists and post-materialists does not decrease as shown in the figures in parentheses.

It is a noticeable that there is a wide gap between genders in civic tolerance. Male respondents show far more tolerant attitudes than their female counterparts. This pattern holds true in data from the three surveys. Male respondents scored 14 in 1990, 11 in 1996 and 10 in 2001, while females scored −13 in 1990, −10 in 1996, and −8 in 2001, showing a welcome increase in civic tolerance over time. However, even after controlling for the effect of education and age, a wide gap still remains, although with a slight decrease.

What is the relationship between age and civic tolerance? Does civic tolerance increases when people get old? Table 6 shows that the youngest age cohort demonstrated the highest civic tolerance among all age groups. This trend is visible in data from all three surveys. The 20s and 30s age groups have maintained positive scores, while the over

40s cohorts have shown negative scores in all three surveys. In other words, the young age cohorts, the under 30s, are far more tolerant than the middle age cohorts or older cohorts. Even after controlling for the effect of education, these patterns still hold.

This phenomenon of senior respondents' intolerance seems to be related to their conservative attitude. A study of South Korean political culture found that there is a strong negative relationship between tolerance and conservative attitude (Bae-ho Hahn and Soo Young Auh 1987, 130–4; Soo Young Auh & Bae-ho Hahn 1996). The oldest age cohort, the over 60 year olds, shows that their tolerance decreases with the passage of time: −11 in 1990, −24 in 1996, and −36 in 2001. Reasons for such a decrease in tolerance among the oldest age group are not clearly offered, and another depth analysis may be needed to explain this phenomenon.

When a person receives a higher level of education, does she or he show a more tolerant attitude? Table 6 reveals that there is a strong positive relationship; the higher the education people receive, the more tolerant they are. Those with only primary education scored −26 in 1990, −7 in 1996, and −28 in 2001, while those who received a college education showed much higher tolerance, scoring 18 in 1990, 11 in 1996, and 29 in 2001. Even after allowing for the effect of age, the wide gap remains. There is also a positive relationship between urbanization and tolerance; urban dwellers are much more tolerant than those who reside in rural areas. This pattern is visible in all three surveys, even after controlling for the effect of education and age.

## 2. Trust in Political and Social Institutions

There are many different types of trust: trust in fellow citizens, trust in politicians, trust in political systems, and trust in social systems (Paul Abramson 1983, 193–208; Easton 1965, 1975). This study deals only with trust in political and social institutions.

If politics is to run its normal course in a democratic society, citizens have to be able to trust their political institutions. If political institutions are well operated, and the outcomes are positive, citizens will naturally trust in their political institutions. On the other hand, when they do not function properly, that is, if there is corruption and incompetence, the citizens will distrust the political institutions. Likewise, when the social systems work properly and perform their proper role, people do trust in their social institutions, but, if social systems do not work well, their members are not likely to trust in them.

In order to examine the relationship between trust and value types, a political trust scale has been constructed using five variables: executive branches, parliament, judicial systems, the police, and the military. A social trust scale has also been made using the three variables of the mass media, big business, and labor unions. Respondents are asked as to their confidence in the above institutions, and to reply with one of the following choices: a great deal of confidence, quite a lot, not very much and not at all. The scales have been constructed like those used for tolerance.

Table 7 shows that there is a wide gap in political trust among value types. Post-materialists showed the lowest trust in political institutions, whereas materialists showed the highest. Mixed-types also exhibited distrust in political systems. This pattern is visible in all three surveys

Table 12.7. Trust in Political Institutions by Value Types, Gender, Education, and Urbanization.

|  | 1990 | 1996 | 2001 |
|---|---|---|---|
| Materialists | 24 (16)*** | 20 (10) | 33 (24) |
| Mix-type | −5 (−2) | −4 (−2) | −6 (−4) |
| Post-materialists | −90 (−70) | −36 (−23) | −69 (−55) |
| Men | −6 (−5)*** | −4 (−2) | −5 (−7) |
| Women | 7 (6) | 4 (2) | 5 (6) |
| 20s | −25 (−9)* | −26 (−11) | −31 (−18) |
| 30 | −4 (2) | −13 (−5) | −23 (−17) |
| 40 | 9 (4) | 4 (2) | 8 (6) |
| 50 | 5 (−12) | 18 (4) | 32 (22) |
| 60+ | 54 (27) | 53 (25) | 52 (30) |
| Primary education | 38 (16)** | 38 (11) | 28 (34) |
| Secondary education | −4 (3) | 1 (7) | 4 (11) |
| Higher education | −44 (−33) | −39 (−26) | −26 (−19) |
| Rural areas | 36 (23)*** | 38 (27) | 19 (9) |
| Mid cities | −3 (0) | −10 (−8) | −1 (1) |
| Big cities | −21 (−15) | −14 (−10) | −7 (−4) |

* Control for education only
** Control for age only
*** Control for education and age

data. Post-materialists scored −90 in 1990, −36 in 1996, and −69 in
2001, while materialists scored 24 in 1990, 20 in 1996, and 33 in
2001. Mixed-types also had low scores: −5 in 1990, −4 in 1996, and
−6 in 2001. These are huge differences in evaluating political systems,
and the wide gaps remain even after making a control for the effect
of education and age.

It is interesting to find that value priority makes a sharp difference
in evaluating political systems. Those who have chosen values such as
national security, economic growth, and law and order as important
national goals have maintained a trusting attitude toward political
institutions, whereas those who have chosen values such as freedom,
participation, environment and humanity have presented a distrustful
attitude. Why do post-materialists remain critical of the performance
of political systems? Why do materialists have positive views on the
operation of political institutions? Is this unique to the South Korean
case? The analysis of these problems is beyond this study, although some
explanations could be offered to the question of different evaluation
of political systems by the value types. However, before proceeding,
another interesting phenomenon should be noted; post-materialists
presented the highest tolerance attitude among the three value types,
but, in contrast, they showed the lowest trust attitude toward political
institutions. How could we explain the contradictory attitudes of post-
materialists? Because these two questions are closely related, we want
to provide a combined explanation.

The reasons may be related to the wide gap between their democratic expectation and stark reality. When we compare the confidence
level of five political institutions, we find that the parliament receives
the lowest trust rate from post-materialists. Their approval rate for the
parliament (a combination of the two categories, trust "a great deal"
and trust "quite a lot") remained less than 20 percent in the three
surveys. For mixed-type and post-materialists, the parliament's role is
insignificant and negative. The high distrust arises from the fact that
the parliament is either constantly preoccupied with partisan strife, or
is acting as a "servant" of an authoritarian government. The South
Korean parliament tends to be a place where violence and physical
fighting are frequently visible, something which remains a disappointment to the citizens, even under civil government. The police tend
to be regarded as a political arm serving the power holder, and the
undemocratic operation and role of political institutions such as the
parliament and police cause disappointment among post-materialists

who know how the political systems should operate in a democratic society, most post-materialists being young and college-educated. These young intellectuals have a strong tendency to emphasize freedom and fairness in politics in order to achieve democracy in South Korea.

Table 7 shows that there is a wide gender gap in the evaluation of political systems. Men tend to have far less trust in political institutions than do women. Male respondents' trust rates were −6 in 1990, −4 in 1996, and −5 in 2001, whereas female trust rates were 7 in 1990, 4 in 1996, and 5 in 2001. These gaps remained even after controlling for the effect of education and age. Men have maintained a far more critical attitude toward the performance of political institutions than women, and this trend has been found by other studies (Doh C. Shin 1999, 152–8; Soo Young Auh 1994, 124–8).

We found that age makes a big difference in evaluation of political institutions. Table 7 shows that the younger the age cohort, the more criticism of political systems. The youngest age cohort shows the lowest trust rates in the three surveys: −25 in 1990, −26 in 1996, and −31 in 2001. Those in their 30s also show low trust; −4,−13,−23. In contrast to this response, the middle and old age cohorts show confidence in political institutions; the older a person is, the more trust there is in political systems. Those in their fifties scored 5 in 1990, 18 in 1996, and 32 in 2001, while those in their sixties scored 54 in 1990, 53 in 1996, and 52 in 2001. These patterns are visible in the three surveys data even after controlling for the effect of education. It was found that the source of older respondents' high trust in political institutions is related to their conservative attitude when they become older (D. Shin 1999, 82–6; Bae-ho Hahn & Soo Young Auh 1987, 76–82).

In respect of young respondents' low trust, we found an interesting phenomenon; that is, their distrust increases with age. In the older age cohorts, there is no such increase of distrust. Why did the 20s and 30s age cohorts show increasing distrust? Several explanations could be offered. First, the young generations have encountered tough job markets; youth unemployment increased yearly following the extended economic slump. In the eyes of the 20s and 30s, the performance of political institutions, especially parliament was very disappointing. Second, governments have changed the methods of college entrance so frequently that young people could not trust in government policies. Third, various political scandals have emerged in the civilian governments. Citizens believe that political scandals increase rather than decrease as time goes on. The sons of civilian presidents, Kim Young

Sam, and Kim Dae Jung, have been involved in corruption and bribery scandals and jailed. Fourth, the mass media and civil society have been increasingly active in finding and revealing political corruption, and the younger age cohorts have easy access to the internet and electronic newspapers covering all kinds of political scandals.

Is there any relation between urbanization and political trust? Table 7 shows that the relationship is negative. Rural residents tend to be more trustful than urban dwellers. Rural residents show the highest trust among three types of residents, while dwellers in the large cities have the lowest trust, a pattern visible in the all three surveys even after controlling for the effect of age and education.

What is the relationship between the level of education and trust in political institutions? Does education make a difference in evaluating political systems? Table 7 shows that the more educated a person is, the more distrust there is in political systems. The trust index scores for those with only primary education are 38 in 1990, 38 in 1996, and 28 in 2001, whereas scores for respondents with secondary education are −4, 1 and 4. The scores from college-educated respondents are much lower than these two groups, scoring −44 in 1990, −39 in 1996, and −26 in 2001. In South Korean society, intellectuals have presented the lowest trust in political institutions, a pattern found by other empirical studies, too (D. Shin 1999, 159, 224). Even though the intellectuals' trust level is very low in the three surveys, their trust increases over time, which is a welcome sign. The trust level of young generations decreases, whereas that of the college-educated increases, which is an interesting contrast since it is closely related to the increasing high trust attitude of the middle or old age cohorts, especially those of 50s, as shown in Table 7.

Is there any relationship between value types and trust in social institutions? Table 8 shows that post-materialists have far less trust in social systems than do materialists. Materialists scored 6 in 1990, 5 in 1996, and 19 in 2001, while post-materialist scored −43, −19 and −43. Such a huge gap between materialists and post-materialists remains even after controlling for the effect of age and education. Post-materialists have a strong distrust not only of political institutions, but also of social institutions. In contrast, materialists have strong trust in both political and social systems. Why do post-materialists have such critical attitudes? As we have already observed, post-materialists are composed mainly of young and college-educated people. The young age cohorts of 20s and 30s are very critical of social institutions, scoring −3, −8,

Table 12.8. Trust in Social Institutions by Value Types, Age, Gender, Education and Urbanization.

|  | 1990 | 1996 | 2001 |
|---|---|---|---|
| Materialists | 6 (6)*** | 5 (−5) | 19 (14) |
| Mix-type | 0 (0.4) | 0 (3) | −2 (−2) |
| Post-Materialists | −43 (−43) | −19 (−4) | −43 (−32) |
| Men | −4 (−4)*** | −8 (−6) | −14 (−13) |
| Women | 5 (4) | 7 (5 ) | 13 (12) |
| 20s | −3 (−3)* | −8 (2) | −17 (−6) |
| 30 | −9 (−9) | −2 (3) | −15 (−10) |
| 40 | 5 (5) | 2 (1) | 13 (10) |
| 50 | 5 (4) | −8 (−18) | 13 (5) |
| 60+ | 17 (16) | 26 (6) | 29 (10) |
| Primary education | 9 (9)** | 18 (16) | 31 (39) |
| Secondary education | 1 (1) | 8 (9) | 1 (1) |
| Higher education | −17 (−16) | −34 (−34) | −23 (−16) |
| Rural areas | 17 (17) *** | 21 (15) | 1 (−5) |
| Mid cities | −2 (−2) | 3 (−3) | 2 (3) |
| Large cities | −10 (−10) | −11 (−6) | −1 (0) |

\* Control for education only
\*\* Control for age only
\*\*\* Control for education and age

and −17, while college-educated respondents have far more distrust, scoring −17, −34 and −23 in the three surveys. The young generations and urban intellectuals have also maintained a very critical attitude toward the performance of big business, the mass media and labor organizations. Even though big business has made a big contribution to South Korean economic development, their moral position has been severely criticized by various civic organizations. In the eyes of young intellectuals, the mass media's role in criticizing power holders has not been viewed as proper; newspapers and television tend to be seen as pursuing their own interests, instead of playing a role as fair, public organizations.

In the same way that there is a wide gender gap in the evaluation of political institutions, there is also a sharp difference in evaluating social systems. Male respondents maintained low trust in social institutions, whereas females showed high trust in them. The former scored −4 in 1990, −8 in 1995, and −14 in 2001, while the latter scored 5 in

1990, 7 in 1996, and 13 in 2001. This huge gap still remains even after controlling for the effect of education and age. As we have already discussed, male respondents show very low trust in political systems as well as social systems. In contrast, female respondents have high trust in both institutions. This is an interesting contrast in evaluating political and social systems.

Residents in rural areas showed a high trustful attitude toward social systems in the two surveys, except in the 2001 survey data. In contrast, dwellers in the mid and large cities maintained distrustful attitudes toward them, except for in the 2001 survey. For the 1990 and 1996 surveys, we found a uniform pattern of rural dwellers maintaining a higher trust in social systems than urbanities. However, in the 2001 survey, we found a different pattern; rural residents began to show distrustful attitude when we control for the effect of education and age. Before controlling for education and age, rural residents maintained low trust, scoring 1, while mid city residents scored 2, and big city resident −1. The wide gaps between rural residents and urbanities in the two survey data have decreased drastically. When we correct for education and age, rural residents began to show a distrustful attitude toward social institutions, which is a new phenomenon. More longitudinal studies are needed in order to provide explanations for this new development.

## 3. *Protest Participation*

Materialists and post-materialists exhibit profound differences in their perception of politics. Post-materialists show more respect for the political principles of democracy, and are also more tolerant of differences in social minorities than Materialists. Furthermore, they show a higher distrust and a more critical attitude toward the present political and social institutions. Is there any relationship between such a tendency and protest participation? How does such a tendency reveal itself in attitudes toward protest participation? There is a high degree of correlation between political attitude and political behavior because political activity is largely determined by political attitude (Bae-ho Hahn & Soo Young Auh 1987, 266–270). Taking these findings into consideration, post-materialists, who emphasize democratic principles, are likely to participate in various political activities. In order to confirm this hypothesis, respondents were asked: 1 whether they have an experience of protest participation; 2. whether there is a possibility of protest participation in the future; 3. whether there is an intention to participate in the four protest-types of political participation—petition, boycott, demonstration and strike. The index of protest participation has been constructed in the same way as mentioned earlier. The results are presented in Table 9.

Table 9 shows that post-materialist protest participation has been the most active among the three types of value holders. Materialists were far less active, scoring −27 in 1990, −31 in 1996, and −34 in 2001. In contrast, post-materialists were very active, scoring 101, 65, and 45 respectively in the three surveys. This is a sharp difference in protest activities, and such a huge difference remains even after controlling for education and age. With regard to post-materialist protest activities, an interesting pattern emerged; their protest activities decrease to a considerable degree over time. This trend is also found in college-educated respondents, with scores of 60 in 1990, 43 in 1996, and 17 in 2001. The youngest age cohort shows a similar pattern, although the trend is not clear. Why did the post-materialists and young college-educated participate less in protest activities over time? This phenomenon is clearly related to the progress of democratization after the establishment of a civilian government in 1987. During the military-authoritarian regimes, the young college students were the major force in protesting

Table 12.9. Protest Participation by Value Types, Gender, Age and Education.

|  | 1990 | 1996 | 2001 |
|---|---|---|---|
| Materialists | −27 (−22)*** | −31 (−20) | −34 (−32) |
| Mix-type | 8 (6) | 6 (3) | 7 (7) |
| Post-materialists | 101 (92) | 65 (51) | 45 (43) |
| Men | 8 (7)*** | 6 (3) | 8 (8) |
| Women | −8 (7) | −5 (−3) | −8 (−8) |
| 20s | 31 (21)** | 36 (24) | 22 (10) |
| 30 | 11 (7) | 9 (3) | 21 (15) |
| 40 | −9 (−7) | −13 (−12) | 0 (−1) |
| 50 | −26 (−16) | −22 (−10) | −30 (−21) |
| 60+ | −59 (−41) | −50 (−27) | −53 (−27) |
| Primary education | −44 (−20)* | −42 (−39) | −54 (−51) |
| Secondary education | 2 (−1) | −1 (−2) | 4 (4) |
| Higher education | 60 (31) | 43 (41) | 17 (16) |

* Control for age only
** Control for education only
*** Control for education and age

undemocratic rules and policies, actively participating in various
nationwide demonstrations, rallies and strikes. College campuses were
the stronghold for the organization of protest activities. However, after
the establishment of democratic governments, such protest activities
have gradually decreased, college campuses have become calm, and
the smoke of tear gas has gradually disappeared. This trend has also
been found by many other studies (Doh C. Shin 1999; Sunhyuk Kim
2000; Soo Young Auh & Jin-young Kwak 2001).

Protest activity is closely related to age, decreasing to a large extent
in the older age cohorts in all three surveys. The younger age cohorts,
the 20s and 30s, participated in protest activities far beyond the average, whereas the over 40s began to participate much less. The rapid
decrease of protest activities in the old age groups is related to physical
weakness because protest participation requires physical strength (Sidney
Verba, Nie & Kim 1978; Inglehart 1990; M. Kent Jennings & van Deth
1990). Women are far less active in protest activities than men, and
although the gap decreased slightly, it remained over the three surveys,
even after controlling for education and age data. This phenomenon is
readily found in other societies, too (Sidney Verba, Nie & Kim 1978;
Inglehart 1990; Jennings & van Deth 1990).

## VI. *Comparison of Influence on Democratic Values*

So far, we have examined the impact of value changes, gender, age,
education and urbanization on such democratic values as civic tolerance, trust in political and social institutions, and political participation.
In the next analysis, we add occupation as an independent variable.
Only the 2001 survey data will be analyzed.

Table 10 shows the beta coefficients of six independent variables
and, in parentheses, correlation coefficients. For civic tolerance, mate-
rialism/post-materialism has the largest beta coefficient (.143), which is
statistically significant at .001 level. Value change has the most powerful influence on the tolerance attitude of respondents. In the analysis,
we have made a cline from low to high. Age, for instance, is arranged
from 20s to 60s; education from primary education to college education; gender from women to men; occupation from lower to higher;
urbanization from rural areas to big cities. Table 10 shows a positive
relationship between value changes and civic tolerance attitude, which
means that post-materialists are more tolerant than mixed-types or

Table 12.10. Comparison of Influence on Democratic Values-Comparison of Beta (2001).

| | Tolerance | Trust in Political Systems | Trust in Social Systems | Protest Participation |
|---|---|---|---|---|
| Mat/Post-Mat. | .143** (r=.197) | −.120** (r=−.174) | −.084* (r=−.087) | .139* (r=.172) |
| Age | −.130* (r=−.261) | .302** (r=.214) | .123* (r=.062) | −.170* (r=−.263) |
| Education | .111* (r=.236) | −.027 (r=−.138) | −.038 (r=−.069) | .067 (r=.227) |
| Gender | −.094* (r=−.070) | −.003 (r=.023) | .022 (r=.052) | −.108* (r=−.081) |
| Occupation | .015 (r=.036) | −.115* (r=.095) | −.006 (r=.008) | .093 (r=.137) |
| Urbanization | .003 (r=.067) | .067 (r=−.003) | .149** (r=.088) | −.169** (r=−.016) |
| | R square=.346 | R square=.375 | R square=.109 | R square=.120 |

* P<.05   ** P<.001   r = correlation coefficient

materialists. Age ranks second in influence on civic tolerance attitudes, although the correlation coefficient between the two is the biggest. The beta coefficient and correlation coefficient are negative, meaning that civic tolerance attitudes decrease with a rise in age. Education ranks third, and urbanization has the weakest impact.

For trust in political systems, age is the most powerful variable among the six independent variables, showing the largest beta coefficient (−.130). The second most influential variable is materialism/post-materialism. The third is occupation, while gender shows the weakest influence on trust in political institutions. For trust in social systems, urbanization is the most powerful variable, with the second most influential independent variable being age, and the third being materialism/post-materialism. For political protest activities, age is the most powerful variable in influence (−.170), with the negative beta coefficient meaning that protest activities decrease with a rise in age. Urbanization ranks second (−.169), and this negative beta coefficient also indicates that protest activities are more visible in rural areas than in mid-sized or large cities. During the democratization movement times of the 1970s and 1980s, urban dwellers, especially young college students or college-educated citizens, had actively participated in protest activities. However, such a political protest movement has gradually decreased since the establishment of civilian governments. On the other hand, farm unrest has increased in rural areas in recent years because the life of farmers has been worsening. Since South Korea joined the WTO, the government has had to open domestic markets to foreign farm products, and farmers began to protest government policies, especially export liberalization of farm products, by staging intensive mass rallies and demonstrations.

In sum, value change plays an import role in influencing democratic values, although it does not rank first in all cases: for tolerance, it ranks first, for trust in political institutions it ranks second, for trust in social systems it is third. For protest participation it ranks third. The six independent variables explanation of tolerance is about 35 percent (R square =.346), and of trust in political systems about 38 percent (R square =.375). For trust in social systems and protest participation, the six variables explain far less: 11 percent and 12 percent respectively. This means that other factors besides the six variables have a more powerful impact on democratic values.

## VII. *Conclusion*

With South Korea's middle- and old-aged cohorts having grown up during social and economic difficulties of poverty, colonization and war, and with the younger age cohort experiencing a relatively better social economic climate due to major economic development in the 1970s and 1980s, it is one of the best societies for verifying theories of value change. The economic crisis from 1997 to 2000 became another good environment for testing the theories.

Our most general conclusion is that materialists are the dominant group in the former age cohort, while post-materialists can mainly be found in the latter. Materialists do not increase in large number, except for the youngest cohort, even, after South Koreans faced economic crisis. Thus, the validity of both the scarcity hypothesis and the early socialization hypothesis can be verified by examining South Korean society.

What is controversial about the nature of value change is whether or not it is attributed to the change in life cycle or in political generation. Do people become materialists due to the conservatization process involved in aging, as claimed by the life cycle argument? The comparative analysis of the data outcomes of the three surveys indicates that the life cycle hypothesis cannot be supported. The vast difference between the materialists and the post-materialists in relation to age is, in fact, the result of generational differences experienced by people in their formation periods.

On the basis of the above analysis, we could conclude that the generation that prefers post-materialistic to materialistic value is growing due to the improved political and economic conditions that foster prosperity and security, which, in turn, has contributed to the democratization process in South Korea.

Post-materialists are, in their behavior, tolerant of social minorities and their opinions, and are politically very active. They have remained critical of the performance of various political and social institutions, and it can be expected that they will continue to contribute to protecting and promoting democracy in the future as they have done in the past. If prosperity and security continues to prevail in South Korea, it can also be expected that democracy will flourish as the post-materialist population increases and their democratic principles are actively pursued.

The point that must not be overlooked is that the post-materialists' democratic tendency does not mean the opposite for the materialists. The materialists, too, have rendered service to the growth of democracy in South Korea; it is simply that the post-materialists' role has been greater in the past, and is expected to be so in the future.

A problem that can be raised about post-materialists is that its numbers are small and concentrated in the younger generation. Hopefully, as South Korea takes steps toward greater material prosperity and a more sophisticated democracy, the number of post-materialists will increase, and with it their influence in society. Although the comparison of 1990, 1996 and 2001 data illustrates that there is yet to be a sufficient increase in the post-materialist population, there is certainly an increase in the number of mixed-types, which leaves room for the possibility of value change toward post-materialism.

However, there is also a darker side to value change. This study reveals that there is a sharp difference between the young age cohorts, the 20s and 30s, and the old age cohorts, the 50s and 60s, in value change as well as all democratic values such as civil tolerance, trust in political and social institutions, and protest participation. These sharp differences are likely to disturb social stability and hinder dialogue among generations. Furthermore, the differences are likely to increase conflicts in the socio-political field as well as all others. The huge gap is not likely to decrease in the near future.

## References

Abramson, Paul R. 1983. *Political Attitudes in America*. San Francisco: Freeman and Company.

Andrews, Frank and Stephen Withey. 1976. *Social Indicators of Well-being In America*. New York: Plenum.

Auh, Soo Young. 1992. "Value Change and Democracy in Korea." *Korean Political Science Review*. Vol.25, No.2.

———. 1997. *The Impact of Value Change on Politics and Life in Korea, Japan, Mexico and the U.S.A.*. Seoul: Ewha Womans University Press.

——— and Bae-ho Hahn. 1987. *Korean Political Culture*. Seoul: Bupmoonsa.

———. 1999. "Value Change and Continuity in Korea and its Democratization." *Korean Political Science Review*. Vol. 33, No. 3.

——— and Bae-ho Hahn. 1996. "Change and Continuity of Korean Political Culture." *Korean Political Science Review*. Vol. 30, No. 3.

——— and Jin-Young Kwak. 2001. "Change and Continuity of Political Participation in Korea." *Korean Political Science Review*. Vol. 35, No. 4.

Block, J. 1981. "Some Enduring and Consequential Structures of Personality." In Albert I. Rabin, et al., eds. *Further Explorations in Personality*. New York: Wiley-Interscience.

Cole, David C. and Princeton N. Lyman. 1971. *Korean Development: the Interplay of Politics and Economics*. Cambridge, Massachusetts: Harvard University Press.

Converse, Philip E. 1964. "The Nature of Belief Systems in Mass Publics." In David E. Apter ed., *Ideology and Discontent*. New York: Free Press.

Cotton, James, ed. 1993. *Korea Under Roh Tae-Woo: Democratization, Northern Policy and Inter-Korean Relations*. Canberra: Allen & Unwin.

Davies, James C. 1963. *Human Nature and Politics*. New York: Wiley.

Han, Sung-joo. 1974. *The Failure of Democracy in South Korea*. Berkeley: University of California Press.

———. 1989. "South Korea: Politics in Transition." In Larry Diamond, Juan Linz and Seymour Lipset, eds., *Democracy in Developing Clountries*. Boulder, Colorado: Lynne Rienner Publishers.

Henderson, Gregory. 1968. *Korea: The Politics of Vortex*. Cambridge, Massachusetts: Harvard University Press.

Hinton, Harold C. 1983. *Korea under New Leadership*. New York: Praeger.

Inglehart, Ronald. 1990. *Culture Shift in Advanced Industrial Society*. Princeton: Princeton University Press.

———. 1977. *The Silent Revolution: Changing Value and Political Styles among Western Publics*. Princeton: Princeton University Press.

———. 1975. "The Silent Revolution in Europe: Intergenerational Change in Post-Industrial Societies." *The American Political Science Review*. Vol. 65, No. 4.

Jennings, M. Kent and Gregory Markus. 1984. "Partisan Orientations over the Long Haul: Results from the Three Waves Socialization Panel." *The American Political Science Review*. Vol. 78.

——— and Richard Niemi. 1981. *Generation and Politics*. Princeton: Princeton University Press.

Kihl, Yong Whan. 1980. *Politics and Policies in Divided Korea*. Boulder, Colorado: Westview Press.

———. 1980. "Linkage and Democratic Orientation of Party Elites in South Korea." In Kay Lawson, ed., *Political Parties and Linkage: A Comparative Perspective*. New Haven, Connecticut: Yale University Press.

Kim, Alexander. 1975. *Divided Korea: The Politics of Development*. Cambridge, Massachusetts: Harvard University Press.

Kim, Chong Lim, ed. 1980. *The Political Participation in Korea: Democracy, Mobilization, and Stability.* Santa Barbara, California: Clio Press.

Kim, Sunhyuk. 2000. *The Politics of Democratization in Korea: The Role of Civil Society.* Pittsburgh Pa.: Univ. of Pittsburgh Press.

Lane, Robert. 1962. *Political Ideology.* New York: Free Press.

Maslow, Abraham K. 1954. *Motivation and Personality.* New York: Harper and Low.

Shin, Doh C. 1999. *Mass Politics and Culture in Democratizing Korea.* New York: Cambridge University Press.

Verba, Sidney, Norman Nie & Jae-on Kim. 1978. *Participation and Political Equality.* New York: Cambridge University Press.

Wright, Edward, ed. 1975. *Korean Politics in Transition.* Seattle: University of Washington Press.

PART FIVE

AFRICA

# THE CONSTANT OF TRANSFORMATION: ELEVEN YEARS OF VALUE CHANGE IN SOUTH AFRICA, 1990–2001

## Hennie Kotze

## 1. *Introduction*

This chapter presents an exploratory and descriptive examination of the changes in value orientations within South Africa, from the period of "formal transition" that started in 1990 until well into the consolidation period (1994 until 2001). During this period, South Africa was characterized by intense political, social, cultural and economic restructuring, and this extensive transformation had a varied impact on South African society.

Political development in South Africa dramatically reflects different patterns of socialization amongst the various sections of society. This can be described as the "socialization of isolation", due to the codification of racial discrimination under Apartheid, leading to the creation of nearly watertight, socially-constructed divisions of the population. The resulting groups all experienced a different political socialization. Although the cornerstone of this "compartmentalization" policy, the Population Registration Act, was scrapped in the late 1980s, the implications of these racial categories continue to influence South Africans' lives and their value orientations. Although value orientations tend to change gradually, in the case of South Africa, it is reasonable to expect that, during a period of dramatic regime change such as the one the country went through in the last decade of the twentieth century, some significant changes, especially in value orientations, will be noticeable.[1]

---

[1] This notion is shared by Van Deth and Scarbrough (1995, 46), who state that "changing attitudes about government and politics originate in changing values." The process of "rooting" institutions in the society, or alternatively the process of democratic consolidation, will take a decade or two. But, the process of institutionalisation will in turn be determined by the changing value orientations of South Africans during this period.

The aim of this chapter, therefore, is to determine whether South African value priorities are indeed changing, and, if so, what the direction and magnitude of this change is. For the analysis of value shifts, it is important to give a brief background sketch of the macro-level political circumstances that have shaped socio-political orientations. In this way, an analytical link can be established between value orientations and behavioral intentions measured in the survey research. For this reason, the point of departure in this chapter is an overview of the transition, initiated in February 1990, followed by a brief description of the economic, political and social environment preceding, during and following the political transition. The second part of the chapter deals with the value orientations of South Africans. Particular focus will be placed on materialist and post-materialist value orientations, the individualization of work values, religious and social values, and, finally, democratic values and confidence in the state. Three surveys serve as the main data sources: the 1990, 1995 and 2001 South African WVS. Some additional data has been gleaned from the 1981 World Values Survey.[2]

## 2. Socio-Political Setting of Value Orientations

### 2.1. Transition

South Africa is possibly one of the most racially and culturally divided societies in the world, leading to a continuous struggle between the forces that bind society together and those that tear it apart. A further complicating factor is the unequal distribution of wealth, over which racial divisions are currently super-imposed, exacerbating chances of

---

[2] Research design of World Values Surveys: Markinor, a South African market research company, conducted all four surveys between September and October 1981, 1990 and 1995, and in March and April in 2001. They were administered to probability samples in South Africa—the realized sample sizes were 1,596 (1981), 2,736 (1990) 2,935 (1995) and 3,000 (2001). From 1990 onwards, the universe of sample designs consisted of all South African residents, 16 years and older. In 1995 and 2001, a probability sample was stratified according to the nine provinces (in 1981 and 1990, only four provinces existed), population groups and community size. Within each stratum, sampling points were selected at random. From each sampling point, 10 interviews were done based on random selection, and marked on maps which were given to the interviewers. In 1981, the people living in the "homelands" were not included in the sampling frame.

potential conflict. In South Africa, these conditions have been historically induced by the white minority, which deprived other groups of
voting rights in order to create state-institutionalized white privilege.
This was a deliberate and sustained exclusion of the majority from
political decision-making process.

Burdened by the financial cost of Apartheid, increased pressure from
the resistance movements such as the African National Congress (ANC),
and the socio-economic challenges of urbanization, unemployment,
housing and education, the National Party (NP) government under De
Klerk initiated a political transition on 2 February 1990. Black resistance
movements were unbanned, and Nelson Mandela was released, leading
South Africa away from apartheid (read white) domination.

From the beginning of 1990, this political process has been characterized by pact-formation between the most important contenders
for power.[3] During November 1991 to late 1993, the foundations
for a negotiated political settlement were laid by these main political
groupings, those most dominant being the ANC and the NP. Three
years of constitutional negotiations came to an end in December 1993,
and South Africa's first truly democratic elections were held in April
1994.

These election results resembled a racial census, with overwhelming support from the African[4] population for the historically black
parties and movements, including the ANC, Pan African Congress
(PAC), and Inkatha Freedom Party (IFP). Similarly, the traditionally white parties—NP, Democratic Party (DP), and Freedom Front

---

Within the qualifying households, all males/females were listed, and the qualifying
respondent selected according to a random system. If the selected person could not
be interviewed, even after three calls, including evening calls, the person was substi-
tuted in a prescribed way. A minimum back-check of 20% was administered on each
interviewer's work. The questionnaire was available in all the major languages, and the
interview was conducted in whatever language the respondent preferred. In each survey,
samples were weighted and projected onto the universe, and are thus representative
of the universe from which it was drawn.

[3] Higley and Gunther (1992, 13–17) call this type of transition an "elite settlement"
characterized by the following distinct features:
- speed—it appears that elite settlements are carried through rapidly;
- face-to-face, largely secret, negotiations among leaders of the major elite
  factions;
- formal written agreements; and
- the predominance of experienced political leaders—"new men" played only a
  peripheral role.

[4] Although the country has 11 official languages, the main historically designated
groups are Africans 77%; Whites 12%; Coloreds 8.5%; and Asians 2.5%.

(FF)—garnered the majority of white support, with majority support from the colored and Indians going to the NP.[5] Of South Africa's 37.9 million inhabitants (1996 Census),[6] of which an estimated 21.6 million voters were qualified to vote, more than 86% of those qualified participated in the election. The election results came as no surprise, with the ANC obtaining an almost two-thirds majority, and the NP coming second with one fifth of the vote. The results were as follows: ANC—62.65%; NP—20.39%; IFP—10.54%; FF—2.17%; DP—1.73%; PAC—1.25%; ACDP—0.45%; and other parties (not represented in Parliament)—0.82%.[7] In the second democratic election in 1999, the ANC came within one seat of obtaining a two-thirds majority in Parliament, indicating the possible onset of a one-party dominant state. This majority was achieved in 2004 general elections, with the ANC obtaining 69.69% of the vote.[8]

### 2.2. *Socio-economic Transformation*

Economic aspects clearly influence political decision making and the development of value orientations. The South African economy consists of various elements, including a first-world industrial component, an informal sector, typical of developing economies, and a subsistence economy, typical of rural societies. Having developed from a heavy dependence on gold and other minerals, it is now broadly based, with manufacturing constituting one of the largest sectors (18.9% of GDP), although mining (7.1% of GDP) remains the largest source of foreign exchange (*South Africa Survey*, 2003/04, 42). South Africa is classified as a middle income country, with an estimated per capita GDP (PPP) of around US$ 10,346 in 2003 (World Bank, 2005).

During the 1960s, South Africa maintained an exceptionally high growth rate of nearly 9%. During the 1970s, however, this slumped,

---

[5] For an estimated distribution of the voter support from the different ethnic groups, see Reynolds (1994, 190–199). Notwithstanding the strong racial and ethnic identities found among the supporters of most parties, these divisions are not necessarily "frozen".

[6] The census data found that there were 10% fewer people than previously estimated, and a range of organisations questioned the accuracy of the figures.

[7] See Independent Electoral Commission, 2004, <http://www.elections.org.za/Elections94.asp>

[8] See Independent Electoral Commission, 2004, <http://www.elections.org.za/Elections2004_Static.asp>

and, from 1980 to 1990, the average growth rate was less than 1%. It was only in the mid-nineties that it increased again to around 3% (*South Africa Survey*, 2001/02, 147–148).

Although financial indicators are important, the significance of overall development levels should not be underestimated. In 1995, South Africa ranked 86th on the Human Development Index (HDI), whilst, in 2000, its ranking was 103rd (United Nations Development Program, 2000). Despite this apparent drop in standards of living, the quality of life of many South Africans has improved through the provision of free or affordable basic goods and services, examples of which include the provision of water, electricity and shelter. Evidence of the quality of health care and education provision nevertheless seems contradictory. The superficial signs of prosperity in South Africa can possibly be attributed to the skewed distribution of wealth.[9] About 10% of the population receives about 50% of the income, whereas the lower half of the population gets only about 7% of the income (*SA 1996–97*, 86–88).

Political transformation impacted heavily on the labor front, where large numbers of black South Africans who were previously excluded from full participation in the production, distribution and consumption circuits were integrated into it. According to Webster (1999, 32), the introduction of the Labour Relations Act, the Employment Equity Act, and the Basic Conditions of Employment Act substantially reduced what has been referred to as "racial despotism" and "racial Fordism". Furthermore, various initiatives that support Black Economic Empowerment have given rise to a corporate class of young black entrepreneurs (Gevisser 1997, 26).

Similarly, since 1994, a number of reforms aimed at gender redress have also been instituted (UNDP 2000, 67). These developments include the adoption of a Charter for Effective Equality (1994), the participation of a number of South African delegations at regional and international human rights conferences, women's development conferences, and, in 1995, the Convention on the Elimination of all Forms of Discrimination against Women (Commission on Gender Equality South Africa 1999, 3).

---

[9] According to the Development Bank of Southern Africa (1991,1) the Gini coefficient is 0.69, and the distribution occurs along racial lines. The Gini coefficient can vary from 0 (income distributed absolutely equally) to 1 (income concentrated in a small group in society).

Steyn and Kotzé (2003) indicated that research on the South African labor market suggests that South African firms are moving in the same direction as organizations in developed countries. Statistics show a greater use of flexi-workers, casual labor, contract labor, home workers, out-workers and agency workers (Webster 1999, 33). Furthermore, the service sector of the South African economy is expanding rapidly. Transport and communication services, finance, real estate and business services, as well as general government services have increased, while agriculture, mining, quarrying and manufacturing make up less of the GDP share (Marais 2001, 171).

All in all, socio-economically, it is quite clear that the major challenge facing the new government is essentially the problem of distribution. A democratic government, voted into power by the "have nots" on the basis of promises that this issue would receive attention, thus has an obligation to make redistribution a priority.

## 3. *Value Orientations*

### 3.1. *A South African Three Index Model: Pre-materialist/materialist/ post-materialist*[10]

The design of the WVS has been influenced by, among others, a theory of intergenerational value change (Inglehart 1977, 1990). Inglehart and his colleagues maintain that the formative experiences of the younger birth cohorts in most industrial societies differed from those of the other birth cohorts due to the rapid economic development and the expansion of the welfare state that followed World War II. This unprecedented degree of economic security experienced by the former has led to a gradual shift from materialist values (that stress economic and physical security) towards post-materialist value priorities (that emphasize self expression and quality of life).

Although the South African population has undergone a number of unprecedented political, economic and social changes over the last decade, the high prevalence of poverty in the country may render Inglehart's materialist/post-materialist continuum inappropriate to

---

[10] This section relies heavily on Kotzé and Lombard (2002).

the socio-economic and historical context of South Africa. Kotzé and Lombard (2002, 414) hypothesized that the pre-materialist/materialist continuum they offer will "prove more applicable than Inglehart's original materialist/post-materialist dimension, rendering it a better instrument for the measurement and consequent analysis of South Africa's, and potentially other developing countries', values." Similarly, Lategan (2000, 410) maintained that the principal investigators' inclusion of the six extra pre-materialist items in the 1995 WVS in South Africa[11] can be justified by "the complexity and diversity of the South African population as far as values are concerned and the extent that poverty is affecting value orientations."

As a result, value change in South Africa was measured in terms of both the materialist/post-materialist dimension between 1990 and 2001, and a separate pre-materialist/materialist continuum between 1995 and 2001, after which a comparison was drawn to determine which dimension proved more pertinent.

An important motivation for the inclusion of a pre-materialist continuum was that very little of the research conducted by Inglehart and his colleagues has been undertaken outside the industrialized world. Kotzé and Lombard (2002, 417) argued as follows: "Although some recent adaptations have allowed, to a limited degree, for the developing world to be included in the research (Abramson and Inglehart 1994, 11), a classification that only allows for a materialist/post-materialist dimension does not prove very relevant for most of the developing world, where basic survival needs are often not even met." In an effort to measure the "survival needs", the 12 original items included in the 1995 and 2001 South African WVS were extended by an extra six items that are concerned with basic survival needs. The pre-materialist items are as follows: "Providing shelter for all People," "Providing clean water for all people," "Making sure that everyone is adequately clothed," "Making sure that everyone can go to school," "Providing land for all people," and "Providing everyone with enough food to eat."

Chart 1 gives an indication of the location of the South African population along the original dimension first proposed by Inglehart in

---

[11] They were: Mari Harris (Markinor, Johannesburg), Hennie Kotzé (Stellenbosch University), Bob Mattes (University of Cape Town) and Johann Mouton (Stellenbosch University).

1973. (See Kotzé and Lombard 2002, 433–434 for information on the construction of the indexes.) The chart can be interpreted in terms of a score of −10 and 10 denoting 'highly polarized' materialist or post-materialist types, with scores of between −2 and 2 denoting neutral or 'mixed' types who express both materialist and post-materialist values in roughly equal proportions. Those scoring between 4 and 8 (or −4 and −8) can be thought of as mixed types with greater emphasis on either materialist or post-materialist needs. From Chart 1, it becomes clear that there has been very little shift in the portion of pure materialists and pure post-materialist between 1990 and 2001, whilst a substantial increase in the number of mixed type materialists (i.e. those scoring −6 and −8) is discernible.

The increased prioritization of materialist values is inevitably paralleled by an overall reduction of respondents on the more neutral and post-materialist side of the scale. Any further analysis of the data in the above format shall be foregone in favor of analysis according to the pre-materialist/materialist dimension, primarily on the grounds of the previously described socio-economic situation in the country.

Chart 2 portrays the value orientations of the South African population between 1995 and 2001. Overall there is a higher portion of respondents that prioritize pre-materialist needs in 1995, than in 2001, appearing to be compensated for by the large percentage of respondents with weak to medium materialist underpinnings in 2001.

Figure 13.1. Scores on the Materialist/Post-materialist Continuum.

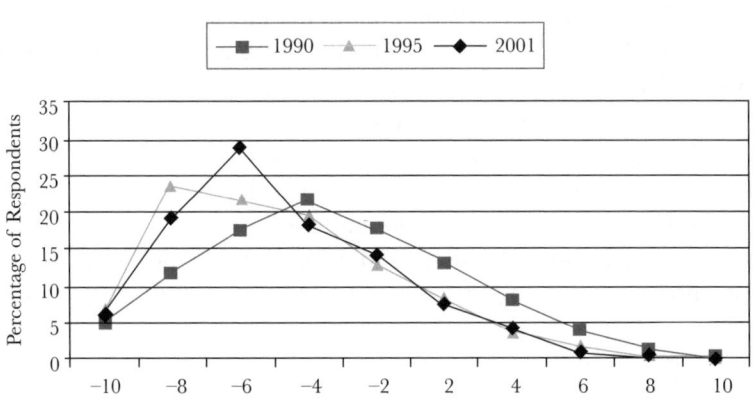

Figure 13.2. Scores on the Pre-materialist/Materialist Continuum.

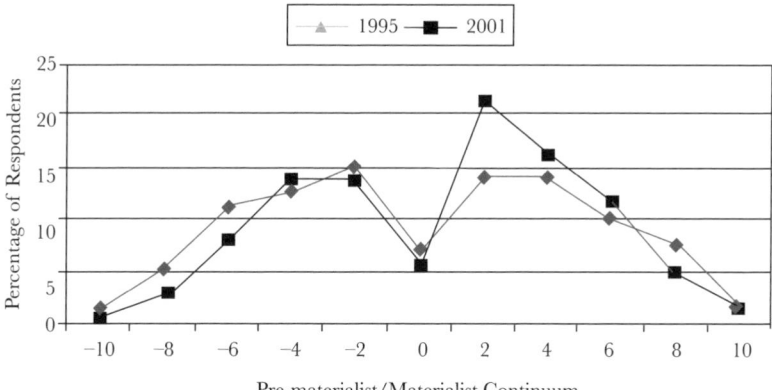

Taken as a whole, there does appear to be a slight decrease in the needs of pre-materialists, as opposed to materialists, over the last five years. This could be attributed to a number of factors.

The first plausible rationale involves a general perception that the basic survival needs are being catered for through a real improvement in state delivery of basic services and infrastructure, rendering their provision a progressively less pre-occupying need. Evidence suggests that primary needs are increasingly being met, allowing other values to be prioritized. Statistics quoted in Moller (2000, 22) imply that a large portion of South Africans feel that their basic needs are being fulfilled to greater satisfaction now than was the case six years ago. The perception of improvements in other fields, such as the creation of jobs or increased crime prevention, is far smaller, leaving much room for improvement.

An alternative explanation is based on a more even distribution of basic social services and infrastructure, independent of the increasing income inequality gap. This would mean that, although people do not have more income available, they have experienced a higher standard of living due to benefits handed out in kind not cash. Examples include free education (Van Den Berg 2000, quoted in Nattrass and Seekings 2001, 56), free health care to pregnant women and children under the age of 6, as well as food stamps or producer subsidies (*Indicator SA* 2000, 82).

Despite this, critics could easily find information suggesting that increasing financial and personnel allocation does not guarantee better social services output. The decline of the prioritization of pre-materialist needs could, therefore, also be based on completely different factors, with one possibility being that the poor and needy are increasingly looking for, and finding, other sources for the provision of basic needs. Superior social networks, facilitating community and family delivery of perfunctory goods and services, as well as other non-state actors, such as NGO's, churches, community and foreign aid organizations, may be fulfilling the needs of people more successfully now than in 1995.

Equally plausibly, one could reconceptualize the de-prioritization of pre-materialist values since 1995. The latter could also be due to the ever-escalating levels of crime and employment, meaning that pre-materialists would select items relating to crime prevention, rather than other important pre-materialist items. Although crime levels in South Africa are exceptionally high by international standards, various factions (such as the media and political parties) have utilized crime to realize political agendas and maintain existing support bases.

Another reason as to why materialist values are not being prioritized may be the phrasing of the question. Possibly, people interpreted it not in terms of what the national needs are, but in terms of government policy weaknesses. It would seem, then, from the statistics discussed in the paragraphs above, that most South Africans feel that the government has focused to a greater extent (and with more success) on items of a pre-materialist foundation, and that the 'materialist' items need to be accorded more attention in the future, despite the fact that pre-materialist needs are not being adequately met.

Another alternative could be that South Africans are undergoing a mind shift, exemplified by the policy move from the Reconstruction and Development Program (RDP) to Growth, Employment and Redistribution (GEAR). This would entail that people no longer think in the order of needs as postulated by Maslow (1954), whereby the fulfillment of basic survival is a pre-requisite for the prioritization of security. It is possible that South Africans are increasingly re-organizing their needs, whereby to fulfill basic survival needs is to have economic and physical security and safety. High levels of economic growth, low inflation, and full employment may thus be prioritized ahead of items such as the provision of food, clothing, land and water, as people could rationalize that these can be bought once money has been earned. The item regarding shelter, and to a greater degree that regarding education, would probably be exceptions; unsurprisingly, these are the two most mentioned pre-materialist items.

It becomes clear that there are a multitude of motivations for the visible decrease in the emphasis of pre-materialist values in favor of low-polarized materialist items. Most probably, it is the dynamics of the duel effects of decreasing pre-materialism and increasing materialism that can be held liable for these findings. The fact that most of the increase is experienced amongst the least-polarized materialists (those scoring 2) highlights the fact that the results have been altered by just one or two fewer pre-materialist, and one or two more materialist, items being selected in 2001 than in 1995. Thus, it would seem that this change is very short-term, and that the orientations in the South African case are still very fluid and far from any kind of crystallization.

## 3.2. *Work values in South Africa*[12]

In 2002, a study by Steyn (2002), Work Value Change in South Africa, attempted to measure the extent to which work values in South Africa have changed in the direction of individualization between 1990 and 2001. Two dimensions of work values were used to measure the rate, direction and nature of this change: the centrality of work to other life domains, and the distribution of power within the work place. The study hypothesized that work values in South Africa would display a change in the direction of individualization due to the high number of systemic level changes that had taken place in the South African working dynamics since 1990.

The position of work relative to other life domains can provide some insightful findings associated with the individualization thesis. Scholars in the field postulate that work will decline in importance in relation to the family, due largely to the blurring of the distinction between work and family life associated with the new world of work (Beck 1992; Beck and Beck-Gernsheim 2001). In industrial society, work was largely regarded as the mechanism used to define the individual's place in society. With the rapid increase of women in the labor market, the decline of the patriarchal family, and the rapid disintegration of the boundaries between work and family life, the importance of work should display a slight decline, while the importance of the family as a life domain should increase.

---

[12] This section is based on Steyn and Kotzé (2003).

The position of work relative to other life domains was measured in the 1990, 1995 and 2001 components of the South African WVS using the following question: "For each of the following, indicate how important it is in your life. Would you say it is: very important, important, not very important, not at all important, or don't know."[13] The life domains evaluated included family, work, religion, friends and acquaintances, politics and leisure.[14]

In 1990, 1995 and 2001, family was regarded as the most important life domain, followed by work, religion, leisure, friends and politics (see Table 1). Between 1990 and 1995, however, the importance of family displayed an increase, while the importance of work remained relatively unchanged. The importance of religion and leisure displayed a slight increase, whilst the importance of friends and politics decreased slightly.

In 2001, the order of the value priorities expressed by the respondents remained relatively unchanged. Family was still regarded as the most important life domain, followed by the same sequence of domains. Between 1995 and 2001, the importance of family increased, again indicating a trend in the direction of individualization in South Africa. The importance of work remained relatively unchanged between 1990 and 2001, while religion displayed a steady increase in importance. The South African population therefore reflects a slight shift in the direction of individualized work values. Although the position of work remained relatively unchanged between 1990 and 2001, the position of family has increased slightly since 1990.

Work values relating to the distribution of power in the organization were also measured using all three waves of the South African WVS. Respondents were asked the following question: "There is a lot of discussion about how business and industry should be managed. Which of these four statements comes closest to your opinion:

1. The owners should run their business or appoint the managers (Capitalist orientation)
2. The owners and the employees should participate in the selection of managers (Participatory orientation)

---

[13] The response categories were recoded so as to exclude "don't know." This enables the data to be categorized as interval data, and allows for the comparison of means.

[14] The 2001 WVS contained an additional category, "service to others", which was excluded for the purposes of comparison.

Table 13.1. Comparison of Means- Work Centrality, 1990–2001.

| Domain | 1990 | 1995 | 2001 |
|---|---|---|---|
| Family | 1.11 | 1.09 | 1.06 |
| Work | 1.27 | 1.28 | 1.27 |
| Religion | 1.49 | 1.44 | 1.40 |
| Friends | 2.17 | 2.23 | 1.94 |
| Politics | 2.33 | 2.62 | 2.05 |
| Leisure | 2.07 | 2.04 | 2.45 |
| N | 2736 | 2899 | 3000 |

(Range 1–4, 1 = very important; 4 = not at all important)

3. The government should be the owner and appoint the managers (Socialist orientation)
4. The employees should own the business and should elect the managers (Collectivist orientation)
5. Don't know

The individualization theory suggests that support for participatory and capitalist models of power distribution will increase as societies become increasingly individualized.

According to the data presented in the study, South African respondents do indeed display a shift towards individualized values relating to the distribution of power in the work place between 1990 and 2001. In both 1990 and 1995, the majority of respondents regarded the participatory model as the most appropriate form of power distribution. There was, however, a slight increase in support for the socialist and collectivist modes of power distribution. Between 1995 and 2001, support for the capitalistic model increased and became the majority in 2001.

The trends reflected in Chart 3 may better be explained through reference to the changing political climate in South Africa between 1990 and 2001. During the apartheid era, the dual system of labor relations in South Africa was characterized by the "racially exclusive" capitalism of the white upper classes, and the "social democracy" of the black under classes (Human 1991, 96). During apartheid, black employees used their industrial rights as an instrument through which to attack the apartheid government, resulting in strong socialist tendencies that were captured in the relationship between the ANC and COSATU. According to Bendix (1996, 74), "South Africa had, not by

Figure 13.3. Power Distribution, 1990–2001.

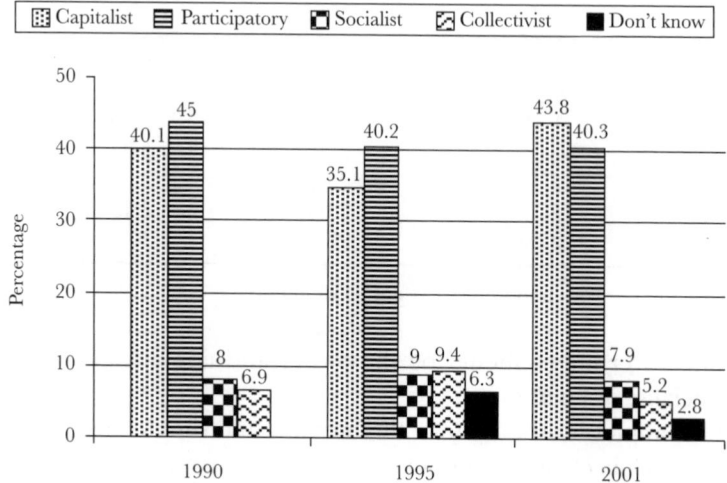

consent or consensus but by political expediency, an unusual mixture
of raw capitalism and the free market enterprise on the one hand, and
of socialism, targeted at white Afrikaners, as well as a large number of
institutionalized controls on the other."

The rise in socialist and collectivist modes of power distribution
between 1990 and 1995 can therefore be explained by reference to
the political system, where the liberation struggle, spearheaded by the
ANC and COSATU, and propelled by ideologies of social democracy,
brought an end to white minority rule in South Africa. This further
explains the effect on work values relating to the distribution of power
in the work place when comparing these values across the various
racial groupings in South Africa (see Table 2). In 1990, black respondents displayed the strongest support for the socialist and collectivist
modes of power distribution in comparison to the other groupings.
Support for the capitalist model of power distribution was relatively
low amongst the black respondents in comparison to the other racial
groupings, while white respondents displayed the strongest support for
the capitalist model.

Between 1990 and 1995, black and colored respondents displayed a
decline in support for both the capitalistic and participatory forms of
power distribution, and an increase in support for socialist and collectivist models. Between 1995 and 2001, however, black respondents reflected
an increase in support for the capitalist model of power distribution,

Table 13.2. Power distribution and race, 1990–2001.

| | White | | | Indian | | | Black | | | Colored | | |
|---|---|---|---|---|---|---|---|---|---|---|---|---|
| | 1990 | 1995 | 2001 | 1990 | 1995 | 2001 | 1990 | 1995 | 2001 | 1990 | 1995 | 2001 |
| Capitalist | 54.5 | 61.3 | 62.3 | 45.7 | 46.5 | 61.8 | 34 | 27.8 | 39.1 | 45.8 | 45.7 | 46.7 |
| Participatory | 41.1 | 32.7 | 29.9 | 41.3 | 40.7 | 30.0 | 46.1 | 42.4 | 42.2 | 47.6 | 35.0 | 44.2 |
| Socialist | 0.6 | 0.9 | 1.0 | 4.3 | 4.3 | 0.5 | 11.8 | 11.7 | 10.6 | 1.2 | 2.9 | 0.5 |
| Collectivist | 3.9 | 3.6 | 0.8 | 8.7 | 6.9 | 0.2 | 8.1 | 10.9 | 3.5 | 5.4 | 7.5 | 6.3 |
| Don't know | 0 | 7.2 | 0.2 | 0 | 7.2 | 1.4 | 0 | 1.5 | 3.3 | 0 | 8.9 | 2.3 |
| N | 1196 | 725 | 899 | 181 | 196 | 299 | 1031 | 1592 | 1303 | 166 | 386 | 499 |

and a slight decrease in support for the socialist and collectivist models. According to Gevisser (1997, 24), the trade unionism, characterized by the ideology of social democracy, used by left-wing South Africans as a political tool in the struggle against apartheid, is fast transforming into a new form of unionism characterized by labor capitalism. The growth of black economic empowerment, and the rapid emergence of a neo-liberal black bourgeoisie, have transformed the face of industrial unionism in South Africa and altered the nature and distribution of work values relating to the distribution of power in organizations. Gevisser (1997, 26) maintains that these trends have been "...without a doubt, one of the quietest and most profound revolutions of post-apartheid South Africa: not just that former militants like Ramaphosa and Golding have become captains of industry, but that the ideology of this transformation is so radical a departure from traditional labor values. It reflects, many are beginning to say, a profound crisis in the South African labor movement".

## 3.3. *Religious Values*

There are a number of general theories explaining the role of religiosity in the modern world,[15] the essence of which can be encapsulated in the proposition that, as societies become more industrialized, religious values will become more eroded and rationalism more wide-spread.

Van Deth and Scarbourgh (1995, 11) summarize the above proposition as follows: "The rise in secular value orientations can be conceptualized as a process—originating in occidental rationality—of detachment from the beliefs, values, and practices of traditional churches. The

---

[15] See for instance Van Deth and Scarbrough, *op. cit.*, pp. 77–83.

Figure 13.4. Religiosity in South Africa, 1990–2001.

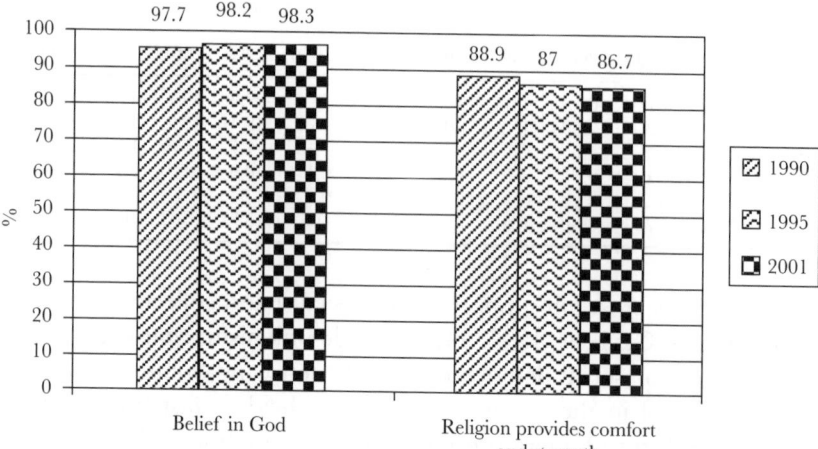

process has become evident in many West European countries in the last few decades. From one point, if churches lose their monopoly to define religious and moral norms, the whole moral system of a society; or generally accepted norms and fundamental values, might break down. A less dramatic scenario points to the gradualness of change, to the diversity and more flexible interpretation of norms, within which individuals arrange their own private set of religious beliefs".

Since South Africa is a semi-industrialized society with a predominance of pre-materialist value orientations, one can expect that there will be a relatively high level of religiosity in the country. According to the data provided in Chart 4, South Africans do display a high level of religiosity. In 1990, 1995 and 2001, over 97% of respondents believed in God, while over 86% felt that religion provided them with strength and comfort.

When comparing the levels of religiosity across the three waves of surveys, evidently South Africans have become slightly more religious over the ten year period. The importance of religion relative to other life domains (family, friends, work, politics etc.) displayed an increase (Table 1), while the importance placed on God also increased slightly between 1990 and 2001 (see Chart 5).

Of interest, however, is the fact that the percentage of respondents that believed in God increased between 1990 and 2001, while the percentage of respondents that found comfort and strength in religion simultaneously decreased slightly. This may be explained by the fact

Figure 13.5. Importance of God (Means on a 10-point scale).

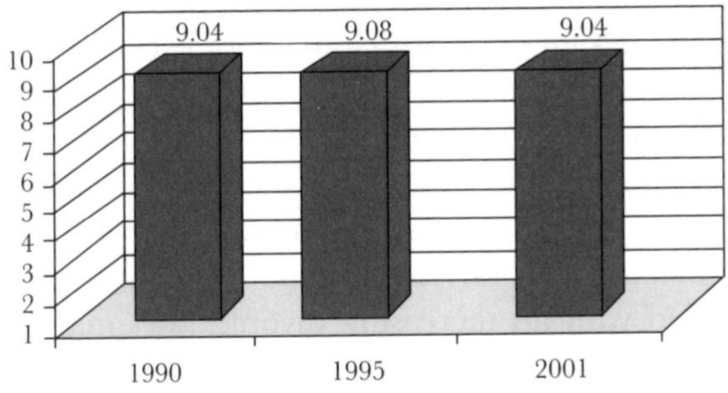

(Range: 1 = not at all important; 10 = very important)

that the church played a prominent political socialization role during the apartheid regime and democratic transition. The diversity of cultural identity in South Africa was replicated in the church, religion and theology, and the church was often used as an instrument to either legitimize the doctrine of apartheid or fight for liberation. Loader (1985) distinguishes three broad religious traditions in South Africa: passive participants, critical churches, and pro-apartheid churches. Passive participants included churches such as the Pentecostal churches, conservative gospel churches, charismatic churches, and the independent black churches. The critical churches were all those affiliated to the South African Council of Churches, along with the Roman Catholic Church. The pro-apartheid churches included the Nederduits Gereformeerde Kerk (NG Kerk), the Nederduits Hervormde Kerk, and the Gereformeerde Kerk (three white Afrikaans-based protestant churches). The latter in particular made a significant attempt to defend racial divisions under apartheid and promote ethnic distinctiveness.

3.4. *Family values*

According to Castells (1997), Izzo and Withers (2001) and Grantham (2000), excessive individualization in modern society has led to the decline of the traditional patriarchal family. Global trends point towards an increase in the number of unmarried couples, co-habitation, divorces, extra-marital births, dual income families and smaller families. These trends are largely due to society's changing needs as more women enter the workforce, thereby challenging traditional gender roles and promoting women's societal liberation.

An analysis of family structures and patterns in South Africa poses somewhat of a problem, as declining fertility rates and an increase in single parent families in South Africa may not exclusively point to the liberation of women in society. Such statistics may instead point to the poor socio-economic conditions of the majority of South African women. Furthermore, South Africa has experienced a legacy of divided families resulting from the migrant system and domestic labor (largely amongst the black and colored communities.) These flexible family patterns, coupled with an increasing divorce rate, may not point to liberation, but rather to social fragmentation.

Fertility rates in South Africa are still amongst the highest in the world, although statistics show a marked decline. Between 1950 and 1970, the fertility rate was at its peak and stood at between six and seven children per woman. Between 1980 and 1995, it dropped to approximately 4.5 children per women, and currently stands at 3.2 children per woman (Henderson 2002, 30).

The reason for this high fertility rate is largely attributable to traditional African culture, captured within the notion of "ubuntu". Community, communality, and family play an important role in the African culture, expressed as follows: 'Umutu ke mutu ke batu' (Zulu), which basically means, 'a person is a person because of other people.' Other aspects contained in the concept of 'ubuntu' are 'uzwelo', or empathy, and 'inhlonipho' (respect and dignity). The underlying assumption of 'ubuntu' is that the primary political entity is not necessarily the individual, but rather the community. Traditional African values emphasize the importance of the group, and the promotion of many children to preserve the status and well-being thereof as they are seen as objects of pride that provide a social security network to parents in their old age (Van Aardt 1994, 18).

Complicating matters further is the fact that "marriage as an institution" has a cultural meaning vastly different to that espoused by the West. In the latter, fertility rates mostly correlate with marriage rates. A decline in marriage rates due to the liberation of women consequently leads to a decline in fertility rates. In sub-Saharan Africa, especially amongst the black population, this is not the case. Marriage is not highly valued amongst the black and colored population in South Africa, since only a small difference between marital and non-marital fertility exists. The high fertility rates amongst unmarried, single mothers, (especially within the African and colored population) is in response to disempowering, patriarchal economic and cultural structures (National Popula-

Figure 13.6. Family values in South Africa, 1990–2001 (percentage in agreement).

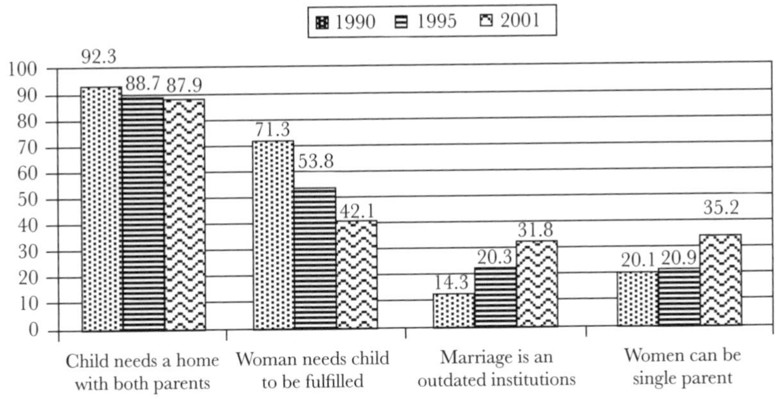

| ▓ 1990   ▤ 1995   ▨ 2001 |

tion Unit 2000, 45). As a result, there is a high prevalence of single, women-headed households in South Africa. In 1995, for instance, 29 percent of all women who had given birth at some time in their lives had never been married. Twelve percent of children under seven years of age were not living with either of their parents, and 42 percent of children under seven years of age were living only with their mother (SSA 1999, 9). Research shows that, amongst the Asian and white populations, "consensual and co-habitative" unions are still preferable (Jones 1996, 7).

Although the importance of family, relative to other life domains, increased slightly amongst South Africans between 1990 and 1995 (See Table 1), South Africans seem to show increasing tolerance of alternatives to the traditional nuclear family (Chart 6). Although the majority of respondents in 1990 (92.3%) believed that a "child needs a home with both a father and a mother to grow up happily," this percentage decreased to 87.9 percent in 2001. Although a minority, the percentage of respondents that believed marriage to be an outdated institution increased from 14.3 percent in 1990, to 31.8 percent in 2001. Similarly, the percentage of respondents that felt that a woman has the right to be a single parent if she so chooses increased by 15 percent between 1990 and 2001, while the percentage of respondents that felt that a woman needs a child in order to be fulfilled decreased by 29.2 percent for the same period.

South Africa has also experienced a notable shift in perceptions of ideal family size, as the percentage of respondents wanting smaller families has increased significantly. In 1990, for instance, around 30 percent of respondents felt that two or fewer children were ideal. By 2001, the percentage of respondents who felt that two or fewer children were ideal rose to well over 50 percent.

Looking at the spread of orientations regarding elements of family and religious life, it thus becomes clear that South Africans regard themselves as very religious and pro-family.

### 3.5. *Moral Permissiveness*[16] *(Ethics Index)*

Bearing the family and religious orientations discussed above in mind, it is not surprising that South Africans are also very "conservative" as far as moral issues are concerned. The following issues from the 1990, 1995 and 2001 WVS, on which respondents could indicate on a 10-point scale whether they find it always or never justifiable, were combined in an 'ethics index' ('homosexuality, prostitution, abortion, divorce, suicide and euthanasia') to gauge the reaction of respondents (See Chart 7). The classification represents a continuum from very liberal to very conservative. Respondents were asked to react, on a ten point scale, to statements that in each instance could "always be justified, never be justified or something in between" (where ten indicated the former and one indicated the latter). Respondent categories comprised: "Very liberal, liberal, neither liberal nor conservative, conservative and very conservative."

The data reflected in chart 7 suggests that South Africans have become less conservative and increasingly neutral towards the ethical issues included in the index. Those that can be regarded as quite liberal displayed a slight increase, while those regarded as very liberal decreased slightly.

Nevertheless, there has been increased support for the reintroduction of the death penalty -more than 70% of the people supported this in 1995– and growing public opinion against the abolition of corporal punishment in schools, and the legalization of gambling (Kotzé 1996, 15).

This hardening of attitudes contradicts the "softening" of official positions on these two issues, thus flying in the face of the South Africa's new Constitution with its liberal interpretation of the "right to life" and "individual freedoms". Research has indicated that there exists a

---

[16] Moral permissiveness refers to the acceptance of multiple moral standards concerning sexual and bio-ethical behaviour and is indicated by an acceptance of homosexuality, prostitution, euthanasia, divorce.

Figure 13.7. Ethics in South Africa, 1990–2001.

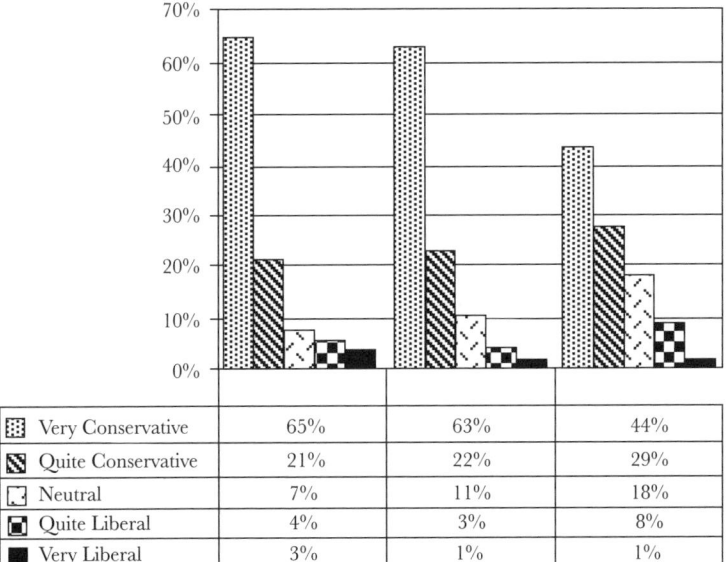

| | | 65% | 63% | 44% |
|---|---|---|---|---|
| | Very Conservative | 65% | 63% | 44% |
| | Quite Conservative | 21% | 22% | 29% |
| | Neutral | 7% | 11% | 18% |
| | Quite Liberal | 4% | 3% | 8% |
| | Very Liberal | 3% | 1% | 1% |

significant ideological gap between the general population and their leaders, especially within the ANC, who have much more "liberal" value orientations than their followers. It seems that the public feels that individual freedoms, especially those related to moral issues, should be more strongly controlled, thus demanding a "strong state" to protect them against criminal elements; hence, the overwhelming support for the death penalty.

On the political front, these value orientations certainly pose a major threat to the present government's efforts to legitimize very liberal legislation on public policies, such as legislation on abortion, and the introduction of euthanasia.

### 3.6. *Democratic values in South Africa*

Since the ANC won a majority in the country's first democratic elections in 1994, the country has experienced impressive economic gains and improvement regarding the provision of basic amenities. Two democratic constitutions have been negotiated, and the country's third multi-party election held in 2004. But, Mattes (2002, 22) maintains that successful democratic consolidation depends on three factors: a growing economy that reduces inequality, stable and predictable institutions, and a supportive political culture. The following section will therefore examine two key areas of political culture crucial to the consolidation of democracy in South Africa; namely, value orientations regarding the workings of democracy, and public levels of confidence in the institutions of state.

### 3.6.1. *Perceptions of Democracy*

Although, in many instances, South Africa's democracy appears relatively healthy, supportive orientations regarding the democratic regime and political system have been eroded over the last five years. Public opinion indicators collected by the Institute for Democracy in South Africa in Cape Town (www.idasa.co.za) reveal that South African political culture is, as yet, not mature enough to consolidate democratic practices; there seems to be a significant increase in "nostalgia" for the way the country is perceived to have been governed under apartheid, especially among the white, colored and Indian respondents, and support for democracy has not increased since 1995, corroborated by data from the 1995 and 2001 South African WVS. When asked to rank the political system as it is today on a scale of one to ten, (1 = very bad; 10 = very good), mean scores dropped considerably from 6.13 in 1995, to 4.29 in 2001. Interestingly, the black population in South Africa displays the strongest drop in support for the democratic system. In 1995, black respondents boasted a mean of 6.99, slightly higher that the national mean. By 2001, however, this mean had dropped to 3.8.

When asked whether having a democratic political system is a very good, fairly good, bad, or very bad way of governing the country, the extreme response percentage decreased, while the percentage that ranked it fairly good and fairly bad increased slightly (see Chart 9). When asked to what extent they agreed with the statement that "democracy may have its problems but it's better than any other form of government," respondent disagreement increased by over ten percent between 1995 and 2001 (see Chart 10).

### 3.6.2. *Confidence in institutions*[17]

Sustainable economic growth is one of the core factors needed to maintain political and economic stability in South Africa (Mattes 2002,

---

[17] This section draws heavily on Kotzé (2001).

Figure 13.8. Satisfaction with democracy in South Africa
(means on a 10-point scale).

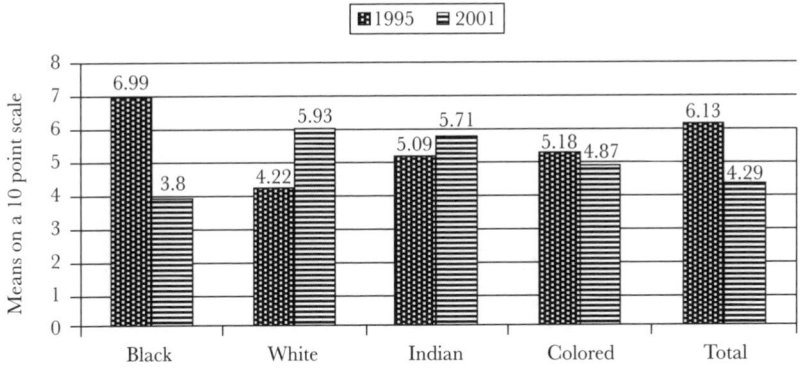

(Range: 1 = very bad; 10 = very good)

Figure 13.9. Support for a democratic political system.

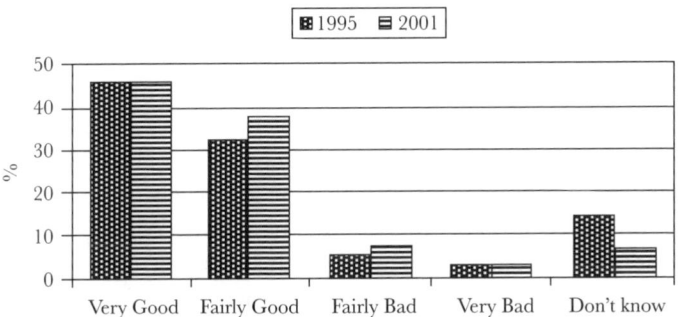

22), and is very much linked to orientations towards democracy and
democratic consolidation. There is little disagreement that economic
growth can only be brought about by a "virtuous circle" of investment
that will hopefully lead to an increase in employment opportunities that,
in turn, should ultimately bring about the above. The expectations during the Mandela-era of a large increase in local and foreign investments
never really materialized, and, under Mbeki, who succeeded Mandela
in 1999, this trend continued. A compelling argument can be made
that the reasons for this, and the consequent weak economic growth,
must be sought in the levels of confidence in the state.

Figure 13.10 Democracy may have its problems, but it's better than any other form of government.

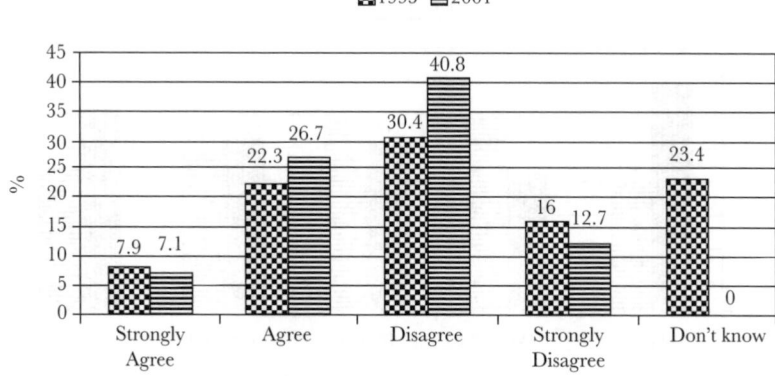

A number of writers are of the opinion that it is very difficult to measure legitimacy (Linz 1988[18] and Widmaier 1988). Thus, a different approach is taken in this chapter. Using Linz (1988, 85) as a point of departure, the assumption is made that "confidence" in state institutions, although only one element of legitimacy (albeit an important one), may give an indication as to the direction legitimacy is moving, making it an indicator of potential legitimacy problems. However, this approach is not entirely unproblematic because there are no absolute standards as to what should be regarded as high or low levels of confidence. In "lieu of unequivocal benchmarks" (Listhaug and Wiberg 1995, 298), a longitudinal approach, as is used in this chapter, may indicate the direction in which confidence levels are moving.

The following five items were used for a "state confidence index": (1) Parliament; (2) the armed forces; (3) the legal system; (4) the police; and (5) the civil service.[19] The index was built up by allocating 4 points for "a great deal", 3 points for "quite a lot", 2 points for "not very

---

[18] Linz (1988, 65) states that, "to avoid the many complexities of the notion of legitimacy, I shall use a minimalist definition: the belief that in spite of shortcomings and failures, the political institutions are better than any others that might be established and therefore can demand obedience."

[19] The question posed to respondents was as follows: "I am going to name a number of organisations. For each one, could you tell me how much confidence you have in them: is it a great deal of confidence, quite a lot of confidence, not very much confidence or none at all?"

much", and 1 point for "not at all." Thus, scores on the index ranged from a minimum of 5, to a maximum of 20.[20]

The use of racial categories remains a very sensitive issue in South Africa, and it should be noted that the choice of race as an explanatory variable in the analysis was not only based on the nature of the context, but also on an exploratory analysis (the percentage variance explained by race emerged as highly significant in various regression analyses), indicating the former to be a most significant predictor. Race also remains one of the best analytical categories in analyses that look at attitudes towards the political process. Nevertheless, it must be mentioned here that the use of terms such as black, white, colored and Indian does mean that this categorization of people is endorsed.

In the 1981 survey –completed during the zenith of the apartheid era—87% of whites have a high level of confidence ("a great deal" and "quite a lot" are combined), the corresponding figures for blacks is 31%, for Indians 46% and coloreds 45%. The figures for those respondents that were excluded from the political system –blacks, coloreds and Indians—are relatively high considering the political climate in the early 1980s.

Table 13.3. Confidence index by race, 1981.

| | A great deal | Quite a lot | Not very much | None at all | Mean | Standard deviation | n |
|---|---|---|---|---|---|---|---|
| All South Africans | 14.8 | 29.6 | 31.2 | 23.9 | 2.35 | 1.0 | 1 582 |
| Black | 9.0 | 21.6 | 35.5 | 34.0 | 2.06 | 0.96 | 589 |
| White | 50.4 | 36.4 | 9.4 | 0.9 | 3.20 | 0.70 | 593 |
| Indian | 16.7 | 33.3 | 37.5 | 12.5 | 2.55 | 0.96 | 193 |
| Colored | 9.7 | 35.0 | 40.8 | 14.6 | 2.40 | 0.85 | 202 |

Table 13.4: Confidence index by race, 1990.

| | A great deal | Quite a lot | Not very much | None at all | Mean | Standard deviation | n |
|---|---|---|---|---|---|---|---|
| All South Africans | 20.0 | 52.0 | 21.0 | 7.0 | 2.85 | 0.82 | 2 653 |
| Black | 20.5 | 49.1 | 21.0 | 9.5 | 2.81 | 0.87 | 1064 |
| White | 22.7 | 58.3 | 17.4 | 1.7 | 3.02 | 0.68 | 1206 |
| Indian | 31.3 | 39.6 | 25.0 | 4.2 | 2.98 | 0.87 | 191 |
| Colored | 9.9 | 59.4 | 26.6 | 4.2 | 2.75 | 0.69 | 192 |

---

[20] Responses to these five items were also highly inter-correlated, forming a reliable index with Cronbach's Alpha for the four items as follows: 1981 = 0.8679; 1990 = 0.7835; 1995 = 0.7741; and 2001 = 0.7664.

The 1990 WVS data shows that there had been some marked shifts since 1981 (see Tables 3 and 4). What emerges particularly clearly in Table 4 is the relatively sharp rise in confidence in institutions amongst blacks (from 31 percent to 70 percent, if we combine the first two categories), coloreds (45 percent to 69 percent), and Indians (50 percent to 71 percent) in comparison with the 1981 figures. This is probably related to the onset of political transition and heightened expectations of a "better deal" from the state. Had the survey been conducted in mid-1989, rather than late 1990, the results might have been very different. There was a slight decline in confidence among whites from 87 percent to 81 percent, although these levels of confidence still remained higher than among other South Africans. Confidence amongst the white population, therefore, seems to have held up, despite the protest rhetoric of right-wing parties and the uncertainty associated with transition, suggesting that white respondents may have perceived that they were still firmly in control of the state and its institutions.

One would expect confidence in state institutions amongst the black majority to rise after 1994, whilst confidence amongst other South African groupings might decline. After 1994, and particularly under President Mbeki's leadership after the 1999 elections, the South African state institutions underwent a far-reaching transformation, with rapid changes in the composition of the bureaucracy, and legislation such as the Employment Equity Act affecting the private sector similarly. The rapid pace of restructuring seems to have resulted in state institutions' decline in capacity. An increase, or the perception of an increase, in crime, corruption, the misapplication of power, the undermining of property rights, and the inefficiency of the criminal justice system, all fuelled the perception of a weakened state. This could ostensibly affect confidence levels, especially amongst those groups supporting the opposition Democratic Alliance.

Table 13.5. Confidence Index by race, 1995.

| | A great deal | Quite a lot | Not very much | None at all | Mean | Standard deviation | n |
|---|---|---|---|---|---|---|---|
| All South Africans | 21.9 | 46.9 | 25.6 | 5.7 | 2.73 | 0.84 | 2 809 |
| Black | 27.3 | 50.2 | 19.3 | 3.3 | 3.02 | 0.77 | 1528 |
| White | 5.1 | 34.3 | 47.6 | 13.1 | 2.31 | 0.76 | 712 |
| Indian | 11.1 | 51.2 | 33.1 | 4.7 | 2.69 | 0.73 | 194 |
| Colored | 10.6 | 40.6 | 36.7 | 12.1 | 2.50 | 0.84 | 375 |

Table 13.6. Confidence Index by race, 2001.

| | A great deal | Quite a lot | Not very much | None at all | Mean | Standard deviation | n |
|---|---|---|---|---|---|---|---|
| All South Africans | 13.4 | 37.1 | 39.4 | 10.1 | 2.54 | 0.85 | 2 858 |
| Black | 21.3 | 52.9 | 21.8 | 4.0 | 2.91 | 0.76 | 1293 |
| White | 1.3 | 21.0 | 49.4 | 28.3 | 1.95 | 0.74 | 861 |
| Indian | 15.5 | 27.6 | 49.5 | 7.4 | 2.51 | 0.84 | 276 |
| Colored | 7.6 | 35.5 | 50.1 | 6.8 | 2.44 | 0.73 | 482 |

Tables 4 and 5 show that, between 1990 and 1995, there was a further rise in confidence in state institutions amongst black people. After 1995, this trend was reversed, although confidence remained at a higher level than pre-1990 data. Opinion polls show, and the 1999 election results suggest, a high level of satisfaction among black South Africans with the overall performance of state institutions. The opposite occurred among whites, who recorded a significant decline in confidence. The very high confidence level of 81 percent in 1990 halved to 40 percent in 1995, and then almost halved again to 22 percent in 2001. A similar, though less dramatic, trend is seen among coloreds and Indians from 1990 to 1995, where the confidence index recorded a decline of 18 percent and 9 percent respectively in comparison with the 1990 figures. However, a notable further decline took place between 1995 and 2001, as the confidence level for coloreds dropped another 8 percent, while those for Indians dropped by nearly 20 percent. Reflecting more or less the same levels of 1981, this suggests that whites, coloreds and Indians do not perceive the state's performance as very efficient. Overall, confidence levels rose from 44 percent in 1981, to 73 percent in 1990, declining to 69 percent in 1995, and 63 percent in 2001.

Confidence levels have been highly fractured in South Africa over the past 20 years (with the exception of 1990), and the 1995 and 2001 surveys reveal a low level of confidence among the (mainly white) minority who have disproportionate influence over investment decisions and hence the country's economic growth prospects. (Chart 11 summarizes the trends in confidence levels). In 2001, respondents earning more than R10,000 per month ($1,500, at December 2003 exchange rates), a relatively high income, had an average confidence level of 20 percent, whilst confidence amongst the poorest 70 percent was slightly over 73 percent.[21] Simply put, those who have the money to invest

---

[21] There is a negative correlation (Pearsons −.3222, significant at 0.01 level) between income and the confidence index.

Figure 13.11. State Confidence Index by race, 1981–2001.

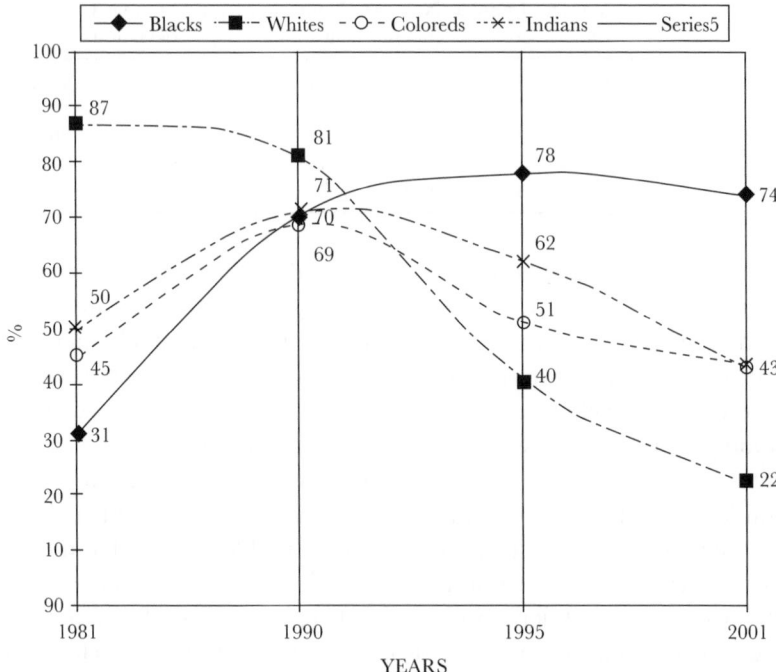

YEARS

have too little confidence in the state to invest their money locally. It is entirely probable that this situation is, at least partially, responsible for recent disinvestment in local markets, ostensibly under the banner of globalization.[22]

The key conclusions that can be drawn from the WVS data in this regard suggest that confidence in the state (and thus this particular element of legitimacy) has risen and then stabilized above the 70 percent level among black people since the transition, while it has declined

---

[22] A concomitant liberalisation of exchange controls made it easier for the high-income groups with a great deal of capital to take billions of Rands out of the country. In the four years after July 1997, when the concession that private individuals could invest abroad was introduced, more than R17 billion was taken out of the country (*Business Day*, 1 August 2001). Between 1995 and 2001, when an asset swap mechanism was in place, more than R100 billion was invested abroad by institutional investors, including pension funds and the unit trust industry (See the statement by Mr T. Mboweni, Governor of the S.A. Reserve Bank, 21 February 2001).

among most whites, coloreds and Indians. It also seems that confidence does not necessarily measure perceptions of the effectiveness and performance of institutions as the literature suggests. The high confidence levels amongst blacks, coloreds and Indians in 1990 is surely less of an assessment of the institutions against which many of them had been protesting actively, as a belief in the prospective legitimacy of these institutions following democratization. In the longer term, the decline in confidence among the minority groups may spell danger, and it is evident that the sustainability of political institutions will be severely tested during the period of democratic consolidation. Not only will the institutions have to exhibit responsiveness to the various interests and address inequalities, especially in terms of wealth, but they will also have to stabilize the confidence in state institutions for domestic and foreign investment.

One of the most important challenges facing the current government at the institutional level is the weakening of state structures after 1995. The relative strength of the state is important in the consolidation of democracy because democratic institutions and practices are embedded in its institutional network. Strong states are able to enforce social control on negative elements (such as warlords and drug barons), whereas weak states typically have high levels of crime and civil disobedience. Competing organizations impose their own networks and civil servants are drawn into corruption networks. The police are challenged, and violence becomes an increasingly prevalent feature. These are all elements that we observe presently in South Africa, and which can probably be ascribed to the fragmented nature of confidence in the important institutions of the state.

## 4. *Concluding Remarks*

WVS data is not only of value in tracking changes in value orientations in South Africa, but is also helpful in shedding light on the potential adherence of South Africa to global value patterns and processes.

As is so often the case with middle-income or semi-peripheral countries, the nature of South Africa's political and socio-economic situation is paradoxical in that it displays characteristics of both the industrialized North and the developing world. Nevertheless, from the above analysis of WVS data, it can be seen that, especially following the disintegration of Apartheid-induced global isolation, and despite its very unique historical context, South Africans' values are slowly changing to reflect more global trends.

It has been seen that South African society has a strongly religious and family orientated aspect, fostered presumably not only by the important role of the church, whether African Independent or NG, as an instrument of political socialization, but also by the influence on the ethnic majority of the population of the concept '*ubuntu*.' Furthermore, it has been seen that, despite the initial correlating conservative moral values, South Africans are becoming increasingly neutral towards erstwhile ethical taboos. Although it is recognized that the influence of the church has declined as a tool of political mobilization since the end of apartheid, South African values can also be seen to slowly follow the general global trend of secularization independently of this. This is especially so as acceptance of the non-nuclear family, as well as racial and gender liberation, approaches global standards. In addition, although, during Apartheid, ideologies which informed attitudes to labor were distinctly polarized along racial lines -blacks tending towards a collectivist and socialist orientation and whites to a capitalist and participatory orientation, with the rise of the black elite[23] following the scrapping of discriminatory labor legislation- South African values have swung steadily in support of a capitalist orientation, reflecting the ideological dominance of the industrialized North, and the emphasis laid on the economic individual. This goes hand in hand with the South African service industries increased share in the GDP, and the corresponding transformation of labor relations and skills in an attempt to reflect global trends.

On a more national level, the South African WVS also plays an important role in assessing the prospects of democratic consolidation in South Africa, as it reveals public attitudes regarding the performance or worth of state institutions. The levels of political confidence in the state play an important part in the assessment of the consolidation process in South Africa. Thus, studies like the World Values Survey render an invaluable service in tracking these changing perspectives on the state, having been able to give empirical evidence with regards to support of the majority for the prospective democratization on the eve of

---

[23] Using WVS data, Rivero, Kotzé and Du Toit (2003) indicated that the South African middle class grew from 7% to over 11% in the period 1990–2001, while the black component nearly doubled from 29% to 50% of the middle class.

transition, as well as decreases in support due to the high expectations of many previously disadvantaged South Africans not being fulfilled. This reflects attitudes towards both democracy as an institution and its physical manifestation in terms of the state structures.

Analysis of the WVS data is only just beginning. Indeed, its continuation will be specifically beneficial in the South African context in that it will allow the continuation of analysis of value orientations towards the adopted economic policies which signaled a dramatic policy shift on the part of the government away from the ANC's erstwhile socialist orientations. Indeed, it is to be hoped that the WVS will be used in future both to inform an understanding of South African politics and society, and to use the South African case to inform comparative social and political analysis.

## References

Abramson, P.R. and R. Inglehart. 1994. *Value Change in Global Perspective.* Ann Arbor: University of Michigan Press.

Beck, U. 1992. *Risk Society. Toward a new modernity.* Translated by Mark Ritter. London: Sage Publications.

Beck, U. and E. Beck-Gernsheim. 2001. *Individualization: Institutionalized individualism and its social and political consequences.* London: Sage.

Bendix, S. 1996. *Industrial Relations in the New South Africa.* Cape Town: Juta and Company.

Castells, M. 1997. *The Information Age: Economy, Society and Culture, Vol. 2: The Power of Identity.* Malden, Mass: Blackwell Publishers.

Commission on Gender Equality South Africa. 1999. *Conference on Gender and the Private Sector.* Braamfontein, South Africa.

Development Bank of South Africa. 1991. *South Africa: An International Profile.* Halfway House: DBSA.

Gevisser, M. 1997. "Ending Economic Apartheid: Is Labour Capitalism Risking the Legacy of SA's Liberation Struggle," *Nation,* 265(9), 24.

Grantham, C. 2000. *The Future of Work: The promise of the new digital work society.* New York: McGraw Hill.

Henderson, J. 2002. "Demographics," in *South Africa Survey, 2002/2003.* Kane-Berman, J. *et al.* (eds.) Johannesburg: South African Institute of Race Relations.

Higley, J. and R. Gunther. 1992. *Elites and Democratic Consolidation in Latin America and Southern Europe.* Cambridge: Cambridge University Press.

Human, P. 1991. "Managerial Beliefs and Attitudes and Change in South Africa," in *Educating and Developing Managers for a Changing South Africa.* L. Human. (ed.) Kenwyn: Juta.

*Indicator SA.* 2000. "Education: Achieving Equality?" 17(2), 40–44.

Inglehart, R. 1977. *The Silent Revolution: Changing Values and Political Styles among Western Publics.* Princeton: Princeton University Press.

—— 1990. *Culture Shift in Advanced Industrial Society.* Princeton: Princeton University Press.

366    HENNIE KOTZE

Izzo, J.B. and P. Withers. 2001. *Values shift: the new work ethic and what it means for business.* Vancouver: Fairwinds Press.

Jones, M. 1996. *Marriage and Family Life in South Africa: Research Priorities.* Pretoria: Human Sciences Research Council.

Kotzé, H.J. 1996. 'The Working Draft of South Africa's 1996 Constitution: Elite and Public Attitudes to the "Options"', Johannesburg: Konrad-Adenauer-Stiftung.

—— 2001. "Unconventional Political Participation and Political Confidence in South Africa", *Social Dynamics*, 27(2), 134–155.

Kotzé, H.J. and K. Lombard. 2002. "Revising the Value Shift Hypothesis: A Descriptive Analysis of South Africa's Value Priorities between 1991 and 2001". *Comparative Sociology.* 1 (3–4), 413–437.

Lategan, B.C. 2000 "Extending the Materialist/Post-materialist distinction: Some remarks on the classification of values from a South African perspective," *Scriptura.* 75, 409–420.

Linz, J. 1988. "Legitimacy of democracy and the socio-economic system," in *Comparing Pluralist Democracies: Strains on Legitimacy.* M. Dogan. (ed.) Boulder, C.O.: Westview Press.

Listhaug, O. and M. Wiberg. 1995. "Confidence in Political and Private Institutions," in *Citizens and the State.* H. Klingemann and D. Fuchs. (eds.) London: Oxford University Press.

Loader, J.A. (1985): "Church, theology and change in South African," in Van Vuuren, DJ *et al.* (eds.), *South Africa: A Plural Society in Transition*, Durban: Butterworths.

Marais, H. 2001. *South Africa limits to change: the political economy of transition.* 2nd edition. Cape Town: University of Cape Town Press.

Maslow, A. 1954. *Motivation and Personality.* New York: Harper.

Mattes, R. 2002. "South Africa: Democracy without the people," *Journal of Democracy,* 13(1), 22–37.

Moller, V. 2000 "Democracy and Happiness: Quality of Life Trends," *Indicator South Africa,* 17(3), 26–36.

National Population Unit. 2000. *State of South Africa's Population Report: Population, poverty and vulnerability.* Pretoria.

Nattrass, N. and J. Seekings. 2001. "Race and Economic Inequality in South Africa," *Daedalus,.* (Winter), 45–72.

Public Opinion Service Report. 1996. "The Public's View of Parliament". Cape Town: IDASA

Reynolds, A. (ed.). 1994. *Election 1994: South Africa.* Cape Town: David Philipp.

Rivero, C. Kotzé H.J., and du Toit, P. 2003. "Tracking The Development Of The Middle Class in Democratic South Africa", *Politeia,* 22(3) 56–79.

*SA 1996–97.* 1996. *South Africa at a Glance.* Johannesburg: Editors Inc.

*South Africa Survey 2001/02.* Kane-Berman, J. *et al.* (eds.) Johannesburg: South African Institute of Race Relations.

*South Africa Survey 2003/04.* Kane-Berman, J. *et al.* (eds.) Johannesburg: South African Institute of Race Relations.

SSA (Statistics South Africa). 1999. *South Africa in Transition: selected findings from the October Household Survey of 1999 and comparisons between 1995 and 1999.* Pretoria: Government Printers.

Steyn, C. 2002. *Work Value Change in South Africa.* Unpublished MA Thesis, University of Stellenbosch.

Steyn, C. and H.J. Kotzé. 2003. "Work Value Change in South Africa between 1990 and 2001: Race, gender and occupations compared", *South African Journal of Labour Relations.* 28(1):4–33.

United Nations Development Programme. 2000. *South Africa: Transformation for Human Development.* Pretoria.

Van Aardt, 1994. *The Future South Africa: issues, options and prospects.* Pretoria: Van Schaik.

Van Deth, J. and E. Scarbrough. 1995. *The Impact of values.* New York: Oxford University Press.

Webster, E.C. 1999. "Race, Labour Process and Transition: The Sociology of Work in South Africa," *Society in Transition.* 30(1), 28–42.

Widmaier, U. 1988. "Tendencies toward the erosion of legitimacy". *Comparing Pluralist Democracies: Strains on Legitimacy.* M. Dogan. (ed.) Boulder, CO.: Westview Press.

World Bank, 2005. *World Development Indicators 2005.* Washington, DC: World Bank.

# REFERENCES

Abramson, P.R. (1983). *Political attitudes in America*. San Francisco: Freeman and Company.

Abramson, Paul R., Ellis, S. & Inglehart, R. (1997). Research in context: Measuring value change. *Political Behavior*, 19, 41–59.

Abramson, P.R., & Inglehart, R. (1994). *Value change in global perspective*. Ann Arbor: University of Michigan Press.

Almond, G.A., & Verba, S. (1963). *The civic culture*. Boston: Little, Brown and Company.

—— (1989). *The civic culture. Political attitudes and democracy in five nations*. Newbury Park: Sage. (Original work published 1963).

Alwin, D.F., Cohen, R.L., & Newcomb, T.M. (1991). *Political attitudes over the lifespan. The Bennington women after fifty years*. Newbury Park: Sage.

Andersen, P.A., & Riis, O. (2002). Religionen bliver privat. In P. Gundelach (Edt.). *Danskernes værdier 1981–1999* (76–98). København: Hans Reitzels Forlag.

Anderson, B. (1991). *Imagined communities: Reflections on the origin and spread of nationalism* (Revised Edition). Verso Books.

Andersson, A. (1998). *Framtidens arbete och liv*. Stockholm: Natur och kultur.

Andeweg, R.B. (2000). From Dutch disease to dutch model? Consensus government in practice. *Parliamentary Affairs*, 52, 679–709.

Andrews, F., & Withey, S. (1976). *Social indicators of well-being in America*. New York: Plenum.

Aronsson, Peter. (1992). *Bönder gör politik. Det lokala självstyret som social arena i tre sm Dlandssocknar, 1650–1850*. Lund: Lund University Press.

Ashford, S. & Timms, N. (1992). *What Europe thinks. A study of Western European values*. Aldershort: Dartmouth.

Auh, S.Y., & Hahn, B. (1987). *Korean political culture*. Seoul: Bupmoonsa.

—— (1992). Value change and democracy in Korea. *Korean Political Science Review*, Vol. 25 (2).

Auh, S.Y., & Hahn, B. (1996). Change and continuity of Korean political culture. *Korean Political Science Review*, 30 (3).

—— (1997). *The impact of value change on politics and life in Korea, Japan, Mexico and the U.S.A.* Seoul: Ewha Womans University Press.

—— (1999). Value change and continuity in Korea and its democratization. *Korean Political Science Review*, Vol. 33 (3).

Auh, S.Y., & Hahn, B., & Kwak, J. (2001). Change and continuity of political participation in Korea. *Korean Political Science Review*. 35 (4).

Avineri, S., & De-Shalit, A. (1992). Introduction. In S. Avineri & A. De-Shalit (Eds.), *Communitarianism and individualism* (pp. 1–11). Oxford: Oxford University Press.

Baker, K.L., Dalton, R.J., & Hildebrandt, K. (1981). *Germany transformed. Political culture and the new politics*. Cambridge: Harvard University Press.

Baker, W.E. (2004). *America's crisis of values: Reality and perception*. Princeton, NJ: Princeton University Press.

Barnes, S.H., Kaase, M. et al. (1979). *Political action: Mass participation in five Western democracies*. Beverly Hills: Sage.

Basáñez, M., (1986). Tradiciones combativas y contemplativas: México mañana. *Revista Mexicana de Ciencias Políticas y Sociales*, 32 (125). Mexico: UNAM.

—— (1987). Elections and political culture in Mexico. In J. Gentleman (Edt.), *Mexican politics in transition*. Boulder and London: Westview Press.

—— (1990). *El Pulso de los sexenios: 20 años de crisis en México*. México: Siglo 21.

—— (1992). Encuestas de opinión en México. In C. Bazdresch et al., (Eds.), *México: Auge, crisis y ajuste*. México: Fondo de Cultura Económica.

—— (1993). Is México headed toward its fifth crisis?. In R. Roett, (Edt.), *Political & economic liberalization in México: At a critical juncture?*. Boulder and London: Lynee Rienner Publishers.

—— (1993). Protestant and Catholic ethics: An empirical comparison. Paper presented at the 1993 World Values Survey Conference, El Paular, Spain, September.

—— (1995). Public opinion research in Mexico. In Smith, P.H. (Edt.), *Latin America in comparative perspective: New approaches to methods and analysis*. Boulder, San Francisco, Boulder, Co. Westview Press.

—— (1996). Polling and the 1994 election results. In Camp, R.A. (Edt.), *Polling for democracy: Public opinion and political liberalization in Mexico*. Washington: Scholarly Resources.

Basáñez, M., & Camp, R.A. (1984). La Nacionalización de la Banca y la opinión pública en México. *Foro Internaciona, Vol. 25*. Mexico: Colegio de México.

Basáñez, M., & Moreno, A. (1994). México en la encuesta mundial de valores 1981–1990. In J.D. Nicolás and R.F. Inglehart (Eds.), *Tendencias mundiales de cambio en los valores sociales y políticos*. Madrid, Spain: Fundesco.

Basáñez, M., & Parás, P. (2001). Color and democracy in Latin America. In Roderic Ai Camp (Edt.), *Citizen views of democracy in Latin America*. Pittsburgh: University of Pittsburgh Press.

Bauer-Kaase, P., & Kaase, M. (1996). Five years of unification: The Germans on the path to inner unity?. *German Politics*, 5 (1), 1–25.

Bauman, Z. (1999). *Liquid modernity*. Cambridge: Polity Press.

Beaujot, R. (2003). Effect of immigration on the Canadian population: Replacement migration? Paper presented at the meetings of the Canadian population Society: Halifax.

Beck, U. (1992). *Risk society. Towards a new modernity.* (M. Ritter, Trans.). London: Sage Publications.

—— (1999). World risk society. New York: Blackwell Publishers.

Beck, U., & Beck-Gernsheim, E. (2001). *Individualization: Institutionalized individualism and its social and political consequences*. London: Sage.

Belah, R.N. (2000). The protestant structure of American culture: Multiculture or monoculture? Fall lecture in Culture and Social Theory, Institute for Advanced Studies in Culture, University of Virginia.

Bell, D. (1973). *The coming of postindustrial society*. New York: Penguin.

—— (1978). *The cultural contradictions of capitalism*. NY: Basic.

Bendix, S. (1996). *Industrial relations in the new South Africa*. Cape Town: Juta and Company.

Berg-Schlosser, D., & Rytlewski, R. (Eds.). (1993). *Political culture in Germany*. London: MacMillan.

Berger, P.L. (1967). *Het hemels baldakijn (The sacred canopy)*. Bilthoven: Ambo.

Bilodeau, A., & Nevitte, N. (2003). *Trust, tolerance, and confidence in institutions: Evidence from the Canadian world values surveys, 1990–2000*. Report prepared for Canadian Heritage.

Birnbaum, P., & Leca, J. (1990). Introduction. In Birnbaum, P., & Leca, J. (Eds.), *Individualism. Theories and methods*. Oxford: Clarendon Press, 1–15.

Block, J. (1981). Some enduring and consequential structures of personality. In Rabin, A.I. et al., (Eds). *Further explorations in personality*. New York: Wiley-Interscience.

Borre, O., & Andersen, J.G. (1997). *Voting and political attitudes in Denmark*. Århus: Aarhus University Press.

Brechon, P. (2000). *Les valeurs des Francaise. Evolutions de 1980 a 2000*. Armand Colin Editions. Paris.

Bréchon, P. (2003). *La France aux urnes. Soixante ans d'histoire électorale*, La documentation française, Paris: 4ème edition.

—— (Édt.). (2003). *Les valeurs des Français*. Armand Colin, collection Sociétales, second edition.

Bréchon, P., Laurent A., & Perrineau, P. (Eds.). (2000). *Les cultures politiques des Français*, Presses de sciences po.

Bréchon, P., Tchernia, J.F. (Eds.). (2002, July–August). Les valeurs des Européens. Les tendances de long terme. *Futuribles*, (Special Issue), 277.

Carballo, M. (1987). *Qué pensamos los argentinos? Los valores de los argentinos de nuestro tiempo*. Buenos Aires: Ed. El Cronista Comercial.

Castells, M. (1997). *The information age: Economy, society and culture: The power of identity, Vol. 2*. Malden, Mass.: Blackwell Publishers.

—— (1997). *The power of identity*. Oxford: Blackwell.

—— (2000). The rise of the network society. *The information age: Economy, society, and culture, Vol: 1*, (Second Edition). Oxford: Blackwell.

Catterberg, G., & Moreno, A. (2002). The individual bases of political trust: Trends in established and new democracies. Paper presented at the 58th Annual Conference of the American Association for Public Opinion Research (AAPOR), Nashville, Tennessee, May 15–18, 2003.

Censo nacional de población y vivienda 2001, Buenos Aires, Instituto Nacional de Estadísticas y Censos.

Citrin, Jack, and Christopher Muste. 1999. Trust in government. In J.P. Robinson, P.R. Shaver & L.S. Wrightsman (Eds.), *Measures of political attitudes*. San Diego, Ca. Academic Press.

Cole, D.C., & Princeton, N.L. (1971). *Korean development: The interplay of politics and economics*. Cambridge, Massachusetts: Harvard University Press.

Coleman, J.S. (1988). Social capital in the creation of human capital. *American Journal of Sociology*, 94, (Supplement), 95–120.

Commission on gender equality South Africa. (1999). *Conference on gender and the private sector*. Braamfontein, South Africa.

Comte, A. (1839). *Cours de philosophie positive. Vol. IV*. Paris: Bachelier.

Conradt, D.P. (1989). Changing German political culture. In G.A. Almond, and S. Verba (Eds.), *The civic culture revisited. Political attitudes and democracy in five nations*. Newbury Park: Sage. (Original work published, 1980).

Converse, P.E. (1964). The nature of belief systems in mass publics. In David E. Apter (Edt)., *Ideology and discontent*. New York: Free Press.

Copleston, Frederick (1993). *A history of philosophy*, vol. 1. New York: Doubleday Books.

Cotton, J. (Edt). (1993). *Korea under Roh Tae-Woo: Democratization, Northern policy and inter-Korean relations*. Canberra: Allen & Unwin.

Cournot, A. (1872). *Considerations sur la marche des idées et des évenéments dans les temps modernes*. Paris: Boivin.

Crittenden, J. (1992). *Beyond individualism. Reconstituting the liberal self*. Oxford: Oxford University Press.

Dalton, R. (2000). Value change and democracy. In S. Pharr & R. Putnam, *Disaffected democracies*. Princeton: Princeton University Press.

—— (2002). *Citizen politics: Public opinion and political parties in advanced industrial democracies*. Third Edition. Seven Bridges Press, Inc.: Chatham House Publishers.

Dalton, R.J. (1988). *Citizen politics in Western democracies: Public opinion and political parties in the United States, Great Britain, West Germany and France*. Chatham: Chatham House.

—— (1999). Political support in advanced democracies. In P. Norris (Edt.), *Critical citizens: Global support for democratic government*. Oxford: Oxford University Press.

Davies, James C. (1963). *Human nature and politics*. New York: Wiley.

Davis, N.J., & Robinson, R.V. (1991). Men's and women's consciousness of gender inequality. Austria, West Germany, Great Britain, and the United States. *American Sociological Review*, (56), 72–84.

Davis, N.J., & Robinson, R.V. (1996). Are the rumors of war exaggerated?. *American Journal of Sociology*, 102.

Demerath III, N.J., & Yang, Y. (1997). What American culture war? A view from the trenches as opposed to the command posts and the press corps. In R.H. Williams (Edt.), *Cultural wars in American politics* (17–38). NY: Aldine de Gruyter.

Development Bank of South Africa. (1991). *South Africa: An international profile*. Halfway House: DBSA.

Díez-Nicolás, J. (1993). Una sociedad en transición. *Telecomunicaciones y sociedad. Libro aniversario de los XXV años de FUNDESCO*. Madrid: FUNDESCO.

—— (1994). Postmaterialismo y desarrollo económico en España. In J. Díez-Nicolás and R. Inglehart (Eds). *Tendencias mundiales de cambio en los valores sociales y políticos*. Madrid: FUNDESCO.

—— (1995, February). A permanent victory of moderation. *Public Perspective*. University of Connecticut: The Roper Center.

—— (1996 a, August). Completing the cycle: The end of Spain's political transition. *Public Perspective*. University of Connecticut: The Roper Center.

Díez-Nicolás, J. (1996 b). Generaciones y preferencias políticas, *Investigaciones Políticas VIII*, Madrid: AEDEMO.

—— (2000). La Escala de postmaterialismo como medida del cambio de valores en las sociedades contemporáneas. In F. Andrés Orizo and J. Elzo (Eds.). *España 2000, entre el localismo y la globalidad. La encuesta Europea de valores en su tercera aplicación, 1981–1999*. Madrid: Editorial Santa María.

—— 2005. *Las dos caras de la inmigración*. Madrid: Imserso.

—— (2005). *Value systems of elites and publics in the Mediterranean: Convergence or divergence*. Madrid: Asep and Complutense University.

DiMaggio, P., Evans, J., & Bryson, B. (1996). Have Americans' social attitudes become more polarized? *American Journal of Sociology* (102), 690–755.

Dobbelaere, K. (1981). Secularization, a multidimensional concept. *Current Sociology* 29 (2), 1–216.

—— (2002). *Secularization: An analysis at three levels*. Brussels: P.I.E. Peter Lang.

Draulans, V., & Halman, L. (2003). Religious and moral pluralism in contemporary Europe. In W. Arts, J. Hagenaars & L. Halman (Eds.), *The cultural diversity of European unity* (371–400 ). Leiden/Boston: Brill.

Durkeim, E. (1958). *The rules of sociological method* (S.A. Solovay & J.H. Mueller, Trans.). Glencoe, IL: The Free Press.

—— (1960). *The division of labor in society*, (G. Simpson, Trans.). Glencoe, IL: The Free Press.

Easton, D. (1965). *A systems analysis of political life*. New York: John Wiley & Sons.

—— (1975). A re-assessment of the concept of political support. *British Journal of Political Science*, (5), 535–457.

Eckstein, H. (1961). *A theory of stable democracy*. Princeton: Princeton University Press.

—— (1966). *Division and cohesion in democracy*. Princeton: Princeton University Press.

Eisenstadt, S. (1956). *From generation to generation. Age groups and social structure*. Glencoe, Ill: Free Press.

Eisenstadt, S.N. (1982). The axial age. *European Journal of Sociology* (23), 294–314.

Elkins, D., & Simeon, R.E.B. (1980). *Small worlds: Provinces and parties in Canadian political life*. Toronto: Methuen.

Elliot, F.R. (1996). *Gender, family and society*. Houndmills: Macmillan.

Erikson, K.T. (1966). *Wayward puritans*. NY: John Wiley and Sons.

Esmer, Y. (2002). Is there an islamic civilization?. *Comparative Sociology*, *Vol. 1*, (3–4). 265–298.

—— (2006). Turkey: Torn between two civilizations. In Harrison, L.E., &. Berger, P.L. (Eds)., *Developing cultures: Case studies*. New York: Routledge. 217–231.

Esping-Andersen, G. (1994). Jämlikhet, effektivitet och makt. In P. Thullberg and K. Östberg (Eds.). *Den svenska modellen*, Lund: Studentlitteratur.

Esping-Andersen, G. (1996). *Three worlds of welfare capitalism*. Cambridge: Polity Press.

Ester, P., Halman, L. & De Moor, R. (1993). *The individualizing society. Value change in Europe and North America*. Tilburg: Tilburg University Press.

Ester, P., Halman, L. & De Moor, R. (1994). Value shift in Western societies. In P. Ester, L. Halman & R. de Moor (Eds.), *The individualizing society* (1–20). Tilburg: Tilburg University Press.

Etzioni, A. (1993). *The spirit of community. Rights, responsibilities, and the communitarian agenda*. New York: Crown.

—— 2001. *The monochrome society*. Princeton, NJ: Princeton University Press.

Felling, A., Peters, J. & Scheepers, P. (Eds.). (2000). *Individualisering in Nederland aan het einde van de twintigste eeuw*. Assen: Van Gorcum.

Ferrari, G. (1874). *Teoria dei periodici politici*. Milano: Hoepli.

Fletcher, J. (1966). *Situation ethics: The new morality*. Louisville, KT: Westminster John Know Press.

Fogarty, M., et al. (1984). *Irish values and attitudes. The Irish report of the European values systems study*. Dublin, Dominican Publications.

Fogel, R.W. (2000). *The fourth great awakening and the future of egalitarianism*. Chicago: University of Chicago Press.

Franklin, M. (1985). *The decline of class voting in Britain: Changes in the basis of electoral choice 1964–1983*. Oxford: Oxford University Press.

——, et al. (1992). *Electoral change: Responses to evolving social and attitudinal structures in Western countries*. Cambridge: Cambridge University Press.

Fryklund, B., Himmelstand, U., & Peterson, T. (1988). Folklighet, klass och opinion i svensk politik under efterkrigstiden. In U. Himmelstrand & G. Svenssson (Eds.), *Sverige—vardag och struktur*. Stockholm: Nordstedts.

Fuchs, D. (1999). The democratic culture of unified Germany. In P. Norris (Edt.), *Critical citizens: Global support for democratic government*. Oxford: Oxford University Press.

Fukuyama, F. (2000). *The great disruption: Human nature and the reconstitution of social order*. New York: Simon & Schuster.

Gabennesch, H. (1972). Authoritarianism as world view. *American Journal of Sociology*, (77), 857–875.

Galbraith, J.K. (1996). *The good society*. Boston, MA: Houghton Mifflin Co.

Galland, O., & Roudet, B. (Eds.). (2001). *Les valeurs des jeunes. Tendances en France depuis 20 ans*. L'Harmattan, collection Débats Jeunesses.

Galland, O., & Roudet, B. (Eds.). (2005). *Les jeunes Européens et leurs valeurs. Europe occidentale, Europe centrale et orientale*. La Découvete/INJEP, collection Recherches.

Gallup, G. Jr., & Lindsay, D.M. (1999). *Surveying the religious landscape: Trends in U.S. beliefs*. Harrisburg, PA: Morehouse Publishing.

Galtung, J. (1964). Foreign policy opinion as a function of social position. *Journal of Peace Research*, 34.

—— (1976). Social position and the image of the future. In H. Ornauer, et al. (Eds.), *Images of the world in the year 2000*, Paris: Mouton.

Geertz, C. (1973). *The interpretation of cultures*. NY: Basic.

Gevisser, M. (1997). Ending economic apartheid: Is labour capitalism risking the legacy of SA's liberation struggle. *Nation, Vol. 265* (9), 24.

Giddens, A. (1987). Structuralism, post-structuralism and the production of culture. In A. Giddens & J. Turner, *Social theory today*, California: Stanford University Press.

—— (1990). *The consequences of modernity*. Stanford: Stanford University Press.

—— (1991). *Modernity and self-identity*. Stanford: Stanford University Press.

—— (1993). *Modernity and self-identity. Self and society in the late modern Age*. Cambridge: Polity Press.

Grantham, C. (2000). *The future of work: The promise of the new digital work society*. New York: McGraw Hill.

Guillén, M.F. (2001). *The limits of convergence*. Princeton, NJ: Princeton University.

Guinness, O. (1993). *The American hour: A time of reckoning and the once and future role of faith*. NY: Free Press.

Gundelach, P. (Edt.). (2002). *Danskernes værdier 1981–1999*. København: Hans Reitzels Forlag.

—— (Edt.). (2004). *Danskernes særpræg*. København: Hans Reitzels Forlag.

Gundelach, P., & Riis, O. (1992). *Danskernes værdier*. København: Forlaget Sociologi.

Habermas, J. (1998). *The inclusion of the other*. In C. Cronin and P. De Grieff (Eds.). Cambridge, MA: MIT Press.

Hagenaars, J., Halman, L., & G. Mors. (2003). Exploring Europe's basic values map. In W. Arts, J. Hagenaars & L. Halman (Eds.), *The cultural diversity of European unity*. Leiden: Brill.

Hägg, G. (2003). *Svenskhetens historia*. Stockholm: Wahlström & Widstrand.

Halman, L. (1992). *Scandinavian values. How special are they?*. Institute for Social Research Tilburg University.

—— (2001). *The European values study: A third wave*. Tilburg: Tilburg University.

—— (1998). Family patterns in contemporary Europe: Results from the European values study 1990. In D. Kalekin Fishmann (Edt.), *Designs for alienation. Exploring diverse realities*, (pp. 99–122). Jyväskylä, Finland: SoPhi University of Jyväskylä.

Halman, L., & De Moor, R. (1994). Religion, churches and moral values. In P. Ester, L. Halman & R. de Moor (Eds.), *The individualizing society* (pp. 37–66). Tilburg: Tilburg University Press.

Halman, L., & Kerkhofs, J. (2002). Het Europese waardenonderzoek: enkele resultaten. In H. van Veghel (Edt.), *Waarden onder de meetlat* (pp. 11–54). Budel: Damon.

Halman, L., & Pettersson, T. (1996). Religion and morality: A weakened relationship? *Journal of Empirical Theology, Vol. 9* (2), 30–48.

—— (1996). The shifting soures of morality: From Religion to postmaterialism?. In L. Halman & N. Nevitte (Eds.), *Political value change in Western democracies. Integration, values, identification and participation* (pp. 261–284). Tilburg: Tilburg University Press.

Halman, L., & Riis, O. (1999). *European values studies*. Tilburg: Tilburg University Press.

Han, Sung-joo. (1974). *The failure of democracy in South Korea*. Berkeley: University of California Press.

—— (1989). South Korea: Politics in transition. In Larry Diamond, Juan Linz & Seymour Lipset (Eds.), *Democracy in developing clountries*. Boulder, Colorado: Lynne Rienner Publishers.

HDR 2001. *Human Development Report 2001*. New York: United Nations.

Henderson, G. (1968). *Korea: The politics of vortex*. Cambridge, Massachusetts: Harvard University Press.

Henderson, J. (2002). Demographics. In J. Kane-Berman, et al., (Eds.), *South Africa Survey, 2002/2003*. Johannesburg: South African Institute of Race Relations.

Higley, J., & Gunther, R. (1992). *Elites and democratic consolidation in Latin America and Southern Europe*. Cambridge: Cambridge University Press.

Himmelfarb, G. (2001). *One nation, two cultures*. NY: Alfred A. Knopf.

Himmelstrand, U. (1988). Den sociologiska analysen av Sverige. In U. Himmelstrand & G. Svenssson (Eds.), *Sverige-vardag och struktur*. Stockholm: Nordstedts.

Hinton, H.C. (1983). *Korea under new leadership*. New York: Praeger.

Hofferbert, R.I., & Klingemann, H.D. (2001). Democracy and its discontents in post-wall Germany. *International Political Science Review* (22), 363–378.

Human, P. (1991). Managerial beliefs and attitudes and change in South Africa. In L. Human (Edt.), *Educating and developing managers for a changing South Africa*. Kenwyn: Juta.

Hunter, J.D. (1991). *Culture wars: The struggle to define America*. NY: Basic.
—— (1994). *Before the shooting begins: Searching for democracy in America's culture war*. NY: Free Press.
Hunter, J.D., & Bowman, C. (1996). *The state of disunion*. Ivy, VA: In Medias Res Educational Foundation.
Huntington, S.P. (1998). *The clash of civilizations and the remaking of the world order*. London: Touchstone Books.
*Indicator SA*. (2000). Education: Achieving Equality?. 17 (2), 40–44.
Ingelstam, L. (1988). *Framtidstron och den svenska modellen*. Linköpings universitet: Tema T.
Inglehart, R. (1971). *The silent revolution in Europe: Intergenerational change in post-industrial societies*. Indianapolis, Ind.: Bobbs-Merrill.
—— (1975). The silent revolution in Europe: Intergenerational change in post-industrial societies. *The American Political Science Review*, 65 (4).
—— (1977). *The silent revolution: Changing values and political styles among Western publics*. Princeton: Princeton University Press.
—— (1990). *Cultural change in advanced industrial society*. Princeton: Princeton University Press.
—— (1990). *Cultural shift in advanced industrial society*. Princeton, N. J.: Princeton University Press.
—— (1997). *Modernization and postmodernization: Cultural, economic, and political change in 43 societies*. Princeton, N.J.: Princeton University Press.
—— (1998). Postmodernism erides respect for authority, but increases support for democracy. In P. Norris (Edt.), *Critical citizens global support for democratic governance*. Oxford: Oxford University Press.
—— (2000). Culture and democracy. In Lawrence E. Harrison & Samuel P. Huntington (Eds.), *Culture matters: How values shape human progress*. New York: Basic Books.
Inglehart, R. (Edt.). (2003). *Human values and social change*, Leiden, Brill.
—— (Edt.). (2003). *Islam, gender, culture, and democracy*. Ontario, Canada: de Sitter Publications.
—— et al., (Eds.). (2004). *Human beliefs and values*. Mexico: Siglio Veintiuno Editores.
Inglehart, R., & Baker, W.E. (2000). Modernization, cultural change, and the persistence of traditional values. *American Sociological Review*, (65), 19–51.
Inglehart, R. & Baker, W. (2000). Modernization, globalization, and the persistence of tradition: Empirical evidence from 65 Societies. *American Sociological Review*.
Inglehart, R., Basanez, M., & Mareno, A. (1998). *Human values and beliefs: A cross cultural sourcebook*. Ann Arbor: University of Michigan Press.
Inglehart, R., Basanez, M., Diez-Medrano, J., Halman, L., & Luijkx, R. (2005). *Human beliefs and values. A cross-cultural source-book on the 1999–2000 values surveys*.
Inglehart, R.F., & Catterberg, G. (2003). Trends in political action: The developmental trend and the post-honeymoon decline. Paper presented at the Annual Meeting of the Midwest Political Science Association, Chicago, April.
Inglehart, R., Nevitte, N., & Basáñez, M. (1996). *The North American trajectory: Cultural, economic, and political ties among the United States, Canada, and Mexico*. New York: Aldine de Gruyter.
Inglehart, R., & Norris, P. (2003). *Gender equality and cultural change*. New York and Cambridge: Cambridge University Press.
—— (2004). *Rising tide: Gender equality and cultural change around the world*. Cambridge University Press.
Inglehart, R., Norris, P., & Welzel, C. (2002). Gender equality and democracy. *Comparative Sociology, Vol. 1* (Special Issue: Human values and social change. *Findings from the world values surveys*), (3–4), 321–345.
Inglehart, R., & Welzel C. (2003). Democratic institutions and political culture: Misconceptions in addressing the ecological fallacy. *Comparative Politics*. (Forthcoming).
Inglehart, R., & Welzel, C. (2005). *Modernization, cultural change, and democracy: The human development sequence*. New York: Cambridge University Press.

Izzo, J.B. & Withers, P. (2001). *Values shift: The new work ethic and what it means for business.* Vancouver: Fairwinds Press.

Jagodzinski, W. & Dobbelaere, K. (1995). Religious and ethical pluralism. In J.W. van Deth & E. Scarbrough (eds.), *The Impact of Values*, (pp. 218–249). Oxford: Oxford University Press.

—— (1995). Secularization and church religiosity. In Jan W. van Deth and Elinor Scarbrough (Eds.), *The impact of values. Beliefs in Government, Vol. 4.* Oxford: Oxford University Press.

Jansen, M. (2002). *Waardenoriëntaties en partnerrelaties.* Utrecht: Proefschrift.

Jaspers, K. (1953). *The origin and goal of history.* (Michael Bullock, Trans.). London: Routledge & Kegan Paul.

Jennings, M.K. & Markus, G. (1984). Partisan orientations over the Long Haul: Results from the three waves socialization panel. *The American Political Science Review.* Vol. 78.

Jennings, M.K. & Markus, G., & Richard Niemi. (1981). *Generation and politics.* Princeton: Princeton University Press.

Jones, M. (1996). *Marriage and family life in South Africa: Research priorities.* Pretoria: Human Sciences Research Council.

Kaase, M. (1995). Die Deutschen auf dem Weg zur Inneren Einheit? Eine Längsschnitttanalyse von Selbst- und Fremdwahrnehmungen bei West- und Ostdeutschen [The Germans on a Path to Inner Unity? A Longitudinal Analysis of Self- and Social Perceptions Among West and East Germans]. In Hedwig Rudolph (Edt.), *Geplanter Wandel, Ungeplante Wirkungen [Intended Change, Unintended Consequences].* Berlin: Sigma.

Kihl, Y.W. (1980). Linkage and democratic orientation of party elites in South Korea. In Kay Lawson, (Edt.), *Political parties and linkage: A comparative perspective.* New Haven, Connecticut: Yale University Press.

—— (1980). *Politics and policies in divided Korea.* Boulder, Colorado: Westview Press.

Kim, A. (1975). *Divided Korea: The politics of development.* Cambridge, Massachusetts: Harvard University Press.

Kim, C.L. (Edt.). (1980). *The political participation in Korea: Democracy, mobilization, and stability.* Santa Barbara, California: Clio Press.

Kim, S. (2000). *The politics of democratization in Korea: The role of civil society.* Pittsburgh Pa.: Univ. of Pittsburgh Press.

Kingdon, J.W. (1999). *America the unusual.* NY: St. Martin's/ Worth.

Klages, H. (1985). *Werturientierungen im wandel: rückblick, gegenwartsanalyse, prognosen.* Frankfurt/New York: Campus Verlag.

Klein, J., Keiding, N., & Kreiner, S. (1995). Graphical models for panel studies, Illustrated on Data. *Statistics in Medicine,* (14), 1265–1290.

Klingemann, H.-D. (1999). Mapping political support in the 1990s: A global analysis. In Pippa Norris (Edt.) *Critical citizens: Global support for democratic government.* Oxford: Oxford University Press.

Kluckholn, F.R., & Strodtbeck, F.L. (1961). *Variations in value orientations.* Evanston, IL: Row, Peterson and Co.

Kotzé, H.J. (1996). The Working draft of South Africa's 1996 constitution: Elite and public attitudes to the "options". Johannesburg: Konrad-Adenauer-Stiftung.

—— (2001). Unconventional political participation and political confidence in South Africa. *Social Dynamics, Vol. 27* (2), 134–155

Kotzé, H.J., & Lombard, K. (2002). Revising the value shift hypothesis: A descriptive analysis of South Africa's value priorities between 1991 and 2001. *Comparative Sociology.* 1 (3–4), 413–437.

Kreiner, S. (1986). Computerized exploratory screening of large-dimensional contingency Tables. In F. de Antoni, H. Lauro, and A. Rizzi (Eds.). Compstat. *Proceedings in Computational Statistics.* 7th Symposium held at Rome 1986. Heidelberg, Wien: Physica Verlag: 355–359.

—— (1987). Analysis of multidimensional contingency tables by exact conditional tests: Techniques and strategies. *Scandinavian Journal of Statistics* (14), 97–112.

—— (1989). User guide to digram. A program for discrete graphical modeling. Univ. of Copenhagen, Statistical Research Unit. Research report 89/10.

Lane, R. (1962). *Political ideology.* New York: Free Press.

Lategan, B.C. (2000). Extending the materialist/post-materialist distinction: Some remarks on the classification of values from a South African perspective. *Scriptura* (75), 409–420.

Lesthaeghe, R., & Van de Kaa, D. (1986). Twee demografische transities?. *Mens en Maatschappij* (61) 9–24.

Linz, J. (1990). Transitions to democracy. *Washington Quarterly.* Vol. 13.

—— (1988). Legitimacy of democracy and the socio-economic system. In M. Dogan, *Comparing pluralist democracies: Strains on legitimacy.* Boulder, C.O.: Westview Press.

Linz, J. & Stepan, A. (1996). *Problems of democratic transition and consolidation.* Baltimore: The Johns Hopkins University Press.

Lipset, S.M. (1996). *American exceptionalism.* NY: W. W. Norton.

Lipset, S.M., & Rokkan, S. (1967). Cleavage structures, party Systems, and voter alignments: An introduction. In Lipset & Rokkan (Eds.), *Party systems and voter alignments: Cross-national perspectives.* New York: Free Press.

Listhaug, O., & Wiberg, M. (1995). Confidence in political and private institutions. In H. Klingemann and D. Fuchs, *Citizens and the state.* London: Oxford University Press.

Loader, J.A. (1985). Church, theology and change in South African. In Van Vuuren, DJ *et al.* (Eds.), *South Africa: A plural society in transition.* Durban: Butterworths.

Luckmann, T. (1967). *The invisible religion.* New York: MacMillan.

Mannheim, K. (1928). Das problem der generationen. *Kölner Vierteljahrshefte für Soziologie* 7. Jahrg., Hefte 2–3.

—— (1952). *Essays on the sociology of knowledge.* London: Routledge & Kegan Paul.

—— (1952). The Problem of Generations. In P. Kecskemeti (Eds.) *Essays on the Sociology of Knowledge* (276–332). London, England: Routledge and Kegan Paul. (Original Work Published 1928).

Manting, D. (1994). *Dynamics in marriage and cohabitation.* Amsterdam: Thesis Publishers.

Marais, H. (2001). *South Africa limits to change: The political economy of transition.* 2nd edition. Cape Town: University of Cape Town Press.

Maslow, A.K. (1954). *Motivation and personality.* New York: Harper and Low.

Mattes, R. (2002). South Africa: Democracy without the people. *Journal of Democracy, Vol 13* (1), 22–37.

Mattes, R., & Bratton, M. (2003). Learning about democracy in Africa: Performance, awareness and history. Paper presented at the WAPOR Regional Conference, Cape Town, South Africa, May.

Maybury-Lewis, D. (1989). The quest for harmony. In David Maybury-Lewis and Uri Almagor (Eds.), *The attraction of opposites: Thought and society in the dualistic mode* (1–17). Ann Arbor, MI: The University of Michigan Press.

Maybury-Lewis, D. and Almagor, U. (Eds.). (1989). *The attraction of opposites: Thought and society in the dualistic mode.* Ann Arbor, MI: The University of Michigan Press.

McNeill, W. (1982). The care and repair of the public myth. *Foreign Affairs* (Fall).

Meulemann, H. (2003). Transformation and polarization: Attitudes towards equality and achivement and the search for losers and winners of the East German transformation 1990–1995. In Detlef Pollack et al. (Eds.) *Political culture in post-communist Europe.* Aldershot: Asgate.

Moller, V. (2000). Democracy and happiness: Quality of life trends. *Indicator South Africa,* Vol. 17 (3), 26–36.

Moreno, A. (1999). *Political cleavages: Issues, parties, and the consolidation of democracy.* Boulder, Co. Westview Press.

—— (2002a). Mexican public opinion toward NAFTA and FTAA. In Edward J.

Chambers and Peter H. Smith (Eds.), *NAFTA in the new millenium*. La Jolla: Center for U.S.-Mexican Studies, University of California, San Diego, and Edmonton: The University of Alberta Press.

—— (2002b). La sociedad mexicana y el cambio, *Este País 134,* April.

—— (2003). *El votante mexicano: Democracia, actitudes políticas y conducta electoral*. México, D.F. Fondo de Cultura Económica.

Moreno, A., & Méndez, P. Forthcoming. Attitudes toward democracy: Mexico in comparative perspective. *The international journal of comparative sociology* (Special Issue). Edited by Ronald F. Inglehart.

Morgan, D.H.J. (1996). *Family connections. An introduction to family studies*. Oxford: Polity Press.

Mouw, T., & Sobel, M.W. (2001). Culture wars and opinion polarization: The case of abortion. *American Journal of Sociology*, 106, 913–943.

National Population Unit. (2000). *State of South Africa's population report: Population, poverty and vulnerability*. Pretoria.

Nattrass, N., & Seekings, J. (2001, Winter). Race and economic inequality in South Africa. *Daedalus*, 45–72.

Nauta, A. (1987). De Europese waardenstudie: een terugblik. In L. Halman & Felix Heunks (Eds.), *De toekomst van de traditie* (31–41). Tilburg: Tilburg University Press.

Nevitte, N. (1996). *The decline of deference: Canadian value change in cross-national perspective*. Peterborough: Broadview Press.

Nevitte, N., & Kanji, M. (2003). *Immigrant orientations towards sustainability: Evidence from the canadian world values surveys, 1990–2000*. Report prepared for Citizenship Canada.

Nevitte, N., & Kanji, M. (2003). Immigrants and work: findings from the 1990 and 2000 World Values Surveys (Canada). Report prepared for Citizenship Canada.

Newton, K., & Norris, P. (2000). Confidence in public institutions: Faith, culture, or performance?. In S. Pharr & R. Putnam, *Disaffected democracies: What's troubling the trilateral countries?*. Princeton, N.J.: Princeton University Press.

Noelle-Neumann, E. (1993). *The spiral of silence*. 2nd ed., Chicago and London: The University of Chicago Press.

Norris, P. (1999). Introduction: The growth of political citizens. In P. Norris, *Critical citizens: Global support for democratic governance*. Oxford: Oxford University Press.

—— (Edt.). (1999). *Critical citizens: Global support for democratic government*. Oxford: Oxford University Press.

—— (2003). *Democratic phoenix*. Princeton: Princeton University Press.

Norris, P., & Inglehart, R. (2002). Islamic culture and democracy: Testing the 'clash of civilizations' thesis. *Comparative Sociology, Vol. 1* (3–4), 235–263.

—— (2003). *Human values and social change*. R. Inglehart. (ed.). Leiden: Brill.

—— (2004). *Sacred and secular: Religion and politics worldwide*. Cambridge: Cambridge University Press.

—— (2003). Islamic culture and democracy: Testing the 'clash of civilizations' Thesis. *Comparative Sociology, Vol.1* (3), 235–263.

Ogburn, William F. (1973). "The Hypothesis of Cultural Lag" in Etzioni-Halevy, Eva and A. Etzioni, eds., *Social change: Sources, patterns, and consequences*. New York: Basic Books, 477–480.

Ole, Cf. Riis (1996). Religion et identité nationale au Danemark, in Grace Davie, Danièle Hervieu-Léger, eds., *Identités religieuses en Europe*, La découverte. 113–130.

Orrù, Marco. (1987). *Anomie: History and meanings*. Boston: Allen & Unwin.

Ortega y Gasset, José. (1933). *En torno a Galileo*. Obras Completas, *Vol. 5*. Madrid: Revista de Occidente.

—— (1961). The concept of the generation. *The modern theme*. NY, 1961.

Palme, J., et al. (2002). *Welfare in Sweden: The balance sheet for the 1990s. Reports from the Government* (Ds), 32. Stockholm: Fritzes.

Peters, J. (1995). Individualization: Fiction or reality?. *Sociale Wetenschappen* 38, 18–27.

Pettersson, T. (1988). *Bakom dubbla lås. En studie av små oh långsammavärderingsförändringar.* Stockholm: Allmänna förlaget.

—— (1992). Folkrörelsefolk och samhällsförändring. In S. Axelson & T. Pettersson (Eds.), *Mot denna framtid,*. Stockholm: Carlssons. 1992.

—— (2003). Muslim orientations toward global governance: The United Nations between Islam and the secularized West. Paper presented at the conference on "Explaining the Worldviews of the Islamic Publics: Theoretical and Methodological Issues." Cairo, Egypt, February (24–26), 2003.

Petersson, O., Hermansson, J., Michelotti, M., Teorell, J., & Westholm, A. (1988). *Demokrati och medborgarskap. Demokratirådets rapport 1998.* Stockholm: SNS.

Petersson, O., Westholm, A., & Blomberg, G. (1988). *Medborgarnas makt.* Stockholm: Carlssons.

Plasser, F., & Ulram, P.A. (2002). *Das österreichische Politikverständnis. Von der Konsens zur Konfliktkultur [The Austrian Understanding of Politics. From a Consensus-Oriented to a Conflict-Oriented Culture].* Wien: WUV Universitätsverlag.

Poponoe, D. (1988). *Disturbing the nest: Family change and decline in modern societies.* New York: De Gruyter.

Public Opinion Service Report. (1996). The Public's View of Parliament. Cape Town: IDASA.

Putnam, R. (2000). *Bowling Alone: The collapse and revival of American Community.* New York: Simon and Schuster.

—— (1993). *Making democracy work: Civic traditions in modern Italy.* Princeton: Princeton University Press.

Religion and Public Life Survey. (2002). Pew Research Center for the People & the Press and Pew Forum on Religion and Public Life. Survey conducted by Princeton Survey Research Associates. Available at http://www. people-press.org/.

Reynolds, A. (Edt.). (1994). *Election 1994: South Africa.* Cape Town: David Philipp.

Riffault, H. (1994). *Les valeurs des francais.* Saint Germain, Presses Universitaires de France.

Rintala, Marvin. (1963). A generation in politics: A definition, *Review of Politics,* 25, 509–522.

Rivero, C., Kotzé, H.J., & du Toit, P. (2003). Tracking the development of the middle class in democratic South Africa, *Politeia, Vol. 22* (3), 56–79.

Robertson, R. (1992). *Globalization. social theory and global culture.* London: Sage.

Rohrschneider, R. (1998). *Learning democracy: Democratic and economic values in unified Germany.* Oxford: Oxford University Press.

Roller, Edeltraud. (1994). Ideological basis of the market economy: Attitudes toward distributional principles and the role of government in Western and Eastern Germany. *European Sociological Review,* 10, 105–17.

Rosenberg, M. (1968). *The logic of survey analysis.* New York: Basic Books.

Russell, B. (1979). *History of Western philosophy.* London: Unwin Paperbacks.

Ryder, N.B. (1965). The cohort as a concept in the study of social change. *American Sociological Review,* 30, 843–861.

*SA 1996–97.*1996. *South Africa at a glance.* Johannesburg: Editors Inc.

Scarbrough, E. (1995). Materialist-postmaterialist value orientation. In Jan W. van Deth & E. Scarbrough (Eds.), *The impact of values,* (pp. 123–159).

SCP 2001. *The Netherlands in a European perspective. Social & Cultural Report 2000.* The Hague: Social and Cultural Planning Office.

Schultz, P.W., Unipan, J.B. & Gamba, R.J. (2000). Acculturation and ecological worldview Among Latino Americans. *The Journal of Environmental Education Vol. 31* (2), 22–27.

Schuman, H., & Scott, J. (1989). Generations and collective memories. *American Sociological Review, Vol. 54* (3), 590–381.

Seligman, Adam B. (1989). The comparative study of utopias. In Adam B. Seligman

(Edt.), *Order and transcendence: The role of utopias and the dynamics of civilizations*, (pp. 1–12). Leiden: Brill.

Shanahan, D. (1992). *Toward a genealogy of individualism.* Amherst, MA: University of Massachusetts Press.

Shin, D.C. (1999). *Mass politics and culture in democratizing Korea.* New York: Cambridge University Press.

Shusterman, R. (1994). Pragmatism and liberalism between Dewey and Rorty. *Political Theory* (22) 391–413.

Simmel, G. (1904) Fashion. In D. Levine & G. Simmel (Edt.). Chicago: Chicago University Press. (Original work published 1972).

Smith, T.W., & Jarrko, L. (1998). National pride: A cross-national analysis. National Opinion Research Center/University of Chicago. General Social Survey Cross-national report No. 19.

SSA (Statistics South Africa). (1999). *South Africa in transition: Selected findings from the October household survey of 1999 and comparisons between 1995 and 1999.* Pretoria: Government Printers.

Statistisches Bundesamt [Statistical Office] (eds.) (2002). *Datenreport 2002. Zahlen und Fakten über die Bundesrepublik Deutschland/Information Report 2002.* [Data and Facts about Germany], Bonn: Bundeszentrale für politische Bildung.

Soneira, A. et al. (1996). *Sociología de la religión.* Buenos Aires, Fundación Universidad a Distancia "Hernandarias": Editorial Docencia.

Sorokin, P. (1957). *Social and cultural dynamics.* Boston: Porter Sargent Publisher, 1957.

*South Africa Survey 2001/02.* Kane-Berman, J. et al. (eds.) Johannesburg: South African Institute of Race Relations.

*South Africa Survey 2003/04.* Kane-Berman, J. et al. (eds.) Johannesburg: South African Institute of Race Relations.

Stacey, J. (1996) *In the name of the family: Rethinking family values in the postmodern age.* Boston: Beacon Press.

Statistics Canada. (2003). *2001 Census Analysis Series: The changing profile of Canada's labour force.*

—— (2003). *2001 Census Analysis Series: Education in Canada: Raising the Standard.*

Steyn, C. (2002). *Work value change in South Africa.* Unpublished MA Thesis, University of Stellenbosch.

Steyn, C., & Kotzé, H.J. (2003). Work value change in South Africa between 1990 and 2001: Race, gender and occupations compared, *South African Journal of Labour Relations Vol. 28* (1), 4–33.

Svallfors, S. (1999). *Mellan risk och tilltro: opinionsstödet för en kollektiv välfärdspolitik.* Umeå universitet: Umeå studies in sociology.

Therborn, G. (1988). Hur det hela började. När och varför det moderna Sverige blev vad det blev. In U. Himmelstrand and G. Svensson (Eds.), *Sverige—vardag och struktur. Sverige—vardag och struktur,* Stockholm: Nordstedts.

Tilton, T. (1990). *The Political theory of Swedish social democracy: Through the welfare state to socialism.* London: Clarendon Press.

Timur, T. (1994). *Osmanlı kimliği.* 2nd ed. Istanbul: Hil Yayin.

Tocqueville, Alexis. (1988). *Democracy in America.* (G. Lawrence, Trans.) edited by J.P. Mayer. NY: HarperCollins.

Traugott, M.W., Groves, R.M., & Kennedy, C. (2002). How American responded: Public opinion after 9/11/01. Paper presented at the 57th Annual AAPOR Conference, St. Pete Beach, FL, May 17.

Ulram, P.A. (1990). *Hegemonie und Erosion. Politische Kultur und Politischer Wandel in Österreich [Hegemony and Erosion. Political Culture and Political Change in Austria].* Wien et al.: Böhlau.

Ultee, W., Arts, W., & Flap, H. (1992). *Sociologie. Vragen, uitspraken, bevindingen.* Groningen: Wolters-Noordhoff.

United Nations Development Programme. (2000). *South Africa: Transformation for Human Development.* Pretoria.

UNDP. (2005). *Human Development Report.* New York: UNDP.

Van Aardt, C. (1994). *The Future South Africa: issues, options and prospects.* Pretoria: Van Schaik.

Van den Akker, P., Halman L., & de Moor, R. (1994). Primary Relations in Western Societies. P. Ester, L. Halman, & R. de Moor (eds.). In *The Individualizing Society* (pp. 97–127). Tilburg: Tilburg University Press.

Van den Broek, A. (1996). Cohort Replacement and Generation Formation in Western Politics. L. Halman & N. Nevitte (eds.). In *Political Value Change in Western Democracies* (pp. 237–260). Tilburg: Tilburg University Press.

Van Deth, J., & Scarbrough, E. (Eds.). (1995). *The impact of values.* Oxford: Oxford University Press.

Van de Kaa, D. (1987). Europe's Second Demographic Transition. *Population Bulletin,* 42, 1–57.

Van Deth, J., & Scarbrough, E. (1995). *The Impact of values.* New York: Oxford University Press.

Verba, S., Nie, N., & Kim, J. (1978). *Participation and Political Equality.* New York: Cambridge University Press.

Vinken, H., Soeters, J., & Ester, P. (2004). Cultures and Dimensions. H. Vinken, J. Soeters, & P. Ester (eds.). In *Comparing Cultures. Dimensions of Culture in a Comparative Perspective, International Studies in Sociology and Social Anthropology.* Leiden: Brill.

Wagner, P. (1994). *A Sociology of Modernity.* London and New York: Routledge.

Waters, M. (1994). *Modern Sociological Theory.* London: Sage.

Webster, E.C. (1999). Race, Labour Process and Transition: The Sociology of Work in South Africa, *Society in Transition.* 30 (1), 28–42.

Welzel, C. (2003). Effective Democracy, Mass Culture, and the Quality of Elites: The Human Development Perspective. International Journal of Comparative Sociology, 43 (3–5), 260–298.

Welzel, C. & Inglehart R. (2001). *Human development and the 'explosion' of democracy: Variations of regime change across 60 societies.* Discussion Paper for Wissenschaftszentrum Berlin für Sozialforschung (WZB). Berlin.

Welzel, C., Inglehart, R. & Klingemann, H.-D. (2003). The theory of human development. A cross-cultural analysis. *European Journal of Political Research,* 42 (3), 341–379.

Widmaier, U. (1988). Tendencies toward the erosion of legitimacy. *Comparing Pluralist Democracies: Strains on Legitimacy.* M. Dogan. (ed.). Boulder, CO: Westview Press.

Wolfe, A. (1998). *One Nation, After All.* NY: Viking.

World Bank. (2005). *World Development Indicators 2005.* Washington, DC: World Bank.

Wright, E., (Edt.). (1975). *Korean Politics in Transition.* Seattle: Univ. of Washington Press.

Wuthnow, R. (1998). *After Heaven: Spirituality in America Since the 1950s.* Berkeley, CA: University of California Press.

# INDEX

Abortion  16–17, 49, 68, 78, 86, 185,
    200–201, 205, 207, 209, 223–25, 227,
    243, 354–55
Abramson, P.  214, 316, 318, 341
Absolutism  9, 11–13, 16, 33, 35, 37,
    40
African National Congress (ANC)  337,
    338, 348, 355, 365
Afrikaner  348
Afrobarometer  84
AIDS  158, 161, 162, 264, 266, 296,
    298–99
Akseptanz Werte  180
Almagor, U.  11
Almond, G.A.  136, 201–202, 293
Altruism  183, 228
America  1, 7, 12–13, 9–21, 23–41, 48,
    75–76, 78–79, 82, 84, 87, 89, 275
American Creed  9, 27
American Exceptionalism  9–10, 15,
    30, 35
American National Election Studies  82
Análisis Sociológicos Económicos y
    Políticos (ASEP)  249, 256, 259, 260
Anderson, B.  28
Andrews, F.  308
Antinomianism  11
Apartheid  335, 337, 347, 349, 351,
    356, 359, 363–64
Argentina  14, 20, 63, 75, 85, 95–119
Aristotle  3, 293
Armed Forces  96, 105–107, 172, 185,
    291–92, 358
Aronsson, P.  125
Arts, W.  ix, 184
Ashford, S.  149
Asia  18, 48, 337, 353
Atheist  12, 27, 33–34, 220, 236
Auh, S.Y.  305–306, 308, 310, 312,
    314, 316, 318, 320–22, 324, 326,
    328
Australia  14, 18, 20–21, 175
Austria  45, 14, 227, 230, 199–215
Authoritarian  77–78, 85, 153, 157,
    164, 169, 184, 243–44, 255, 293,
    305, 320, 325
Avineri, S.  179

Bahrain  277
Baker, W.E.  9–10, 12, 14–18, 20–34,
    36–40, 146, 199, 202
Bangladesh  14, 63, 277
Basáñez, M.  x, 75–76, 80, 84, 88
Basic Conditions of Employment Act
    339
Bauer-Kaase, P.  202
Bauman, Z.  169, 17
Beck, U.  345
Belgium  14, 20, 45, 175, 220, 227,
    235, 241–42
Bell, D.  11, 35, 78, 89, 162, 165, 199
Bellah, R.N.  26
Berg, V.D.  343
Berg-Schlosser, D.  202
Birnbaum, P.  178
Birthright Community  28
Black Economic Empowerment  339,
    349
Block, J.  307
Bowman, C.  27
Bråkenhielm  140
Breath of Perspective  177
Bréchon, P.  219, 231, 239
Bryson, B.  39–40

Camp, R.A.  88
Canada  14, 18, 20–21, 45–49, 53–59,
    60–63, 76, 85, 175, 284, 291
Cape Town  341, 356
Carballo, M.  95
Castells, M.  40, 167, 351
Catholics  24, 26–27, 79, 235
Catterberg, G.  77–78, 82, 84
Central Europe  199
Charter for Effective Equality  339
Chesterton, G.K.  25
Christianity  276
Church  9, 16, 23–27, 31, 33–35, 39,
    49, 51–54, 56–59, 66–67, 79–82, 105,
    107, 113–16, 118–19, 125, 150, 159,
    172, 176–77, 180–81, 185, 204, 206,
    220, 250, 269–70, 344, 349–351,
    364
Citrin, J.  82, 84
Civic Culture  136, 201–202, 293

# EUROPEAN VALUES STUDIES

ISSN 1568-5926

1. P. Ester, L. Halman & R. de Moor (eds.), *The Individualizing Society*. Value Change in Europe and North America. 1994. ISBN 90 361 9993 X
2. R. de Moor (ed.), *Values in Western Societies*. 1995. ISBN 90 361 9636 1
3. L. Halman & N. Nevitte (eds.), *Political Value Change in Western Democracies*. 1996. ISBN 90 361 9717 1
4. P. Ester, L. Halman & V. Rukavishnikov (eds.), *From Cold War to Cold Peace?* A Comparative Empirical Study of Russian and Western Political Cultures. 1997. ISBN 90 361 9737 6
5. L. Halman & O. Riis (eds.), *Religion in Secularizing Society*. The Europeans' Religion at the End of the 20th Century. 1999; 2002. ISBN 90 361 9740 6 (1999), 90 041 2622 8 (2002)
6. W. Arts, J. Hagenaars, J. & L. Halman (eds.), *The Cultural Diversity of European Unity*. Findings, Explanations and Reflections from the European Values Study. 2003. ISBN 90 04 12299 0
7. W. Arts, L. Halman (eds.), *European Values at the Turn of the Millennium*. 2004. ISBN 90 04 13981 8
9. T. Fahey, B.C. Hayes & R. Sinnott, *Conflict and Consensus*. A Study of Values and Attitudes in the Republic of Ireland and Northern Ireland. 2006. ISBN 90 04 14584 2
10. P. Ester, M. Braun & P. Mohler (eds.), *Globalization, Value Change and Generations*. A Cross-National and Intergenerational Perspective. 2006. ISBN-10: 90 04 15127 3, ISBN-13: 978 90 04 15127 7
11. L. Halman, R. Inglehart, J. Díez-Medrano, R. Luijkx, A. Moreno & M. Basáñez, *Changing Values and Beliefs in 85 Countries*. Trends from the Values Surveys from 1981 to 2004. 2007. ISBN 978 90 04 15778 1
12. T. Pettersson & Y. Esmer (eds.), *Changing Values, Persisting Cultures*. Case Studies in Value Change. 2008. ISBN 978 90 04 16234 1